ANNALS OF THE NEW YORK ACADEMY OF SCIENCES

VOLUME 175 ARTICLE 3 PAGES 781-1065

October 30, 1970

THE IMPACT OF FERTILITY LIMITATION ON WOMEN'S LIFE-CAREER AND PERSONALITY *

Editor and Workshop Chairman
ESTHER MILNER

CONTENTS

Workshop Participants 783
Organizer's Introductory Remarks. *By* ESTHER MILNER 787

Part I. Points of Departure

Anatomy and Destiny. *By* NANCY REEVES 793
Needed Research on Current Population Trends. *By* WILLIAM PETERSEN 810
Discussion of Contraceptive Technology: Current and Prospective Methods. RUTH B. KUNDSIN, *Moderator* 823
A Digest of Three Papers by Joseph D. Beasley. *By* CHANA HEFFNER 827
Cultural Factors in Family Planning. *By* LUCILE F. NEWMAN 833
Looking Ahead: Some Social and Individual Consequences of Mass Acceptance of the Two-Child Family in Britain. *By* DEREK G. GILL 847
Probable Social and Psychological Consequences of an American Population Policy Aimed at the Two-Child Family. *By* CATHERINE S. CHILMAN 868
Leads on Old Questions from a New Revolution: Notes on Cuban Women, 1969. *By* VIRGINIA OLESEN 880
Current and Emerging Occupation-Centered Feminine Life-Career Patterns and Trends. *By* CYNTHIA FUCHS EPSTEIN 898
Contraception and Female Job-Choice and Career Prospects. *By* DAVID CHESSLER 915

* This series of papers is the result of a workshop entitled The Impact of Fertility Limitation on Women's Life-Career and Personality, held by The New York Academy of Sciences, on February 19-21, 1970.

Our Species Learns To Be Human: Some Societal and Individual Life-Career Implications. *By* FLORENCE A. RUDERMAN 918
Our Species *Learns* To Be Human. *By* ESTHER MILNER 935
Comments on the "Points of Departure." *By* VIRGINIA OLESEN 948

Part II. Feminine Life-Career and Personality in a Free-Choice Society: What Are the Most Desirable Models?

Position Paper: Models of Sex Equality. *By* ALICE S. ROSSI 950
Position Paper: Out of The Frying Pan—? *By* ESTHER MILNER 953
Discussion. MARGARET MEAD, *Moderator* 956

Part III. Impediments to Women's Development of New Self-Definitions and Life-Styles

Position Paper on Cultural and Psychological Impediments: Are Mental Health Practitioners Contributing to the Problem? *By* WILMA SCOTT HEIDE 976
Position Paper on Structural/Institutional Impediments. *By* ROXANE DUNBAR 977
Discussion. MELVIN TUMIN, *Moderator* 979

Part IV. Directions of, and Strategies toward, Change

Position Paper: On the Formation of RESPA. *By* ESTHER MILNER 990
Discussion. SANDRA S. TANGRI, *Moderator* 992

Part V. Next Steps

Position Paper on Additional Directions and Strategies Requiring Exploration: Some Egalitarian Alternatives to Androcentric Science. *By* WILMA SCOTT HEIDE 1003
Discussion. CATHERINE S. CHILMAN, *Moderator* 1004

Postscript: Analysis and Evaluation. *By* ESTHER MILNER 1016

Resource Bibliography. *By* MIRIAM G. KEIFFER AND PATRICIA A. WARREN 1039

WORKSHOP PARTICIPANTS

BERNARD, JESSIE, Ph.D., Sociologist, Washington, D.C. (Retired, University of Pennsylvania, Philadelphia, Pa.)

BERNARD, VIOLA W., M.D., Columbia University College of Physicians and Surgeons, New York, N.Y.

CALDERWOOD, ANN, Graduate Student, Columbia University, New York, N.Y.

CHESSLER, DAVID, M.A., Department of Economics, Lehman College, Bronx, N.Y.

CHILMAN, CATHERINE S., Ph.D., Dean of Faculty, Hood College, Frederick, Md.

COMBS, JERRY W., JR., Ph.D., Center for Population Research, National Institute of Child Health and Human Development, Bethesda, Md.

DELL'OLIO, ANSELMA, Actress, Founder, New Feminist Repertoire Theater, New York, N.Y.

DUNBAR, ROXANE, Southern Female Rights Union, New Orleans, La.

EAST, CATHERINE, Executive Secretary, Citizens' Advisory Council on the Status of Women, Department of Labor, Washington, D.C.

EPSTEIN, CYNTHIA FUCHS, Ph.D., Department of Sociology, Queen's College, Flushing, N.Y.

FAVA, SYLVIA, Ph.D., Department of Sociology, Brooklyn College, Brooklyn, N. Y.

FISHMAN, ADASSAH, Ph.D., Department of Psychology, Fairleigh Dickinson College, Rutherford, N.J.

GARAI, JOSEF, Ph.D., Department of Psychology, Pratt Institute, Brooklyn, N.Y.

GARDNER, JOANNE E., Ph.D., Learning Research Program, University of Pittsburgh, Pittsburgh, Pa.

GILINSKY, ALBERTA, Ph.D., Department of Psychology, University of Bridgeport, Bridgeport, Conn.

GILL, DEREK G., B.Sc., Medical Sociology Research Unit, Centre for Social Studies, Aberdeen, Scotland.

GOODE, WILLIAM J., Ph.D., Department of Sociology, Columbia University, New York, N.Y.

HEFFNER, CHANA, Student, Brooklyn College, Brooklyn, N.Y.

HEIDE, WILMA SCOTT, M.A., American Institute for Research, Pittsburgh, Pa.

JECH, ALENA, Graduate Student, New School for Social Research, New York, N.Y.

KAMM, FRANCES, Graduate Student, Massachusetts Institute of Technology, Cambridge, Mass.

Keiffer, Miriam G., Ph.D., Educational Testing Service, Princeton, N.J.

Kott, Evelyn, Student, University of Bridgeport, Bridgeport, Conn.

Kundsin, Ruth B., Sc.D., Surgical Bacteriology Laboratory, Peter Bent Brigham Hospital, Boston, Mass.

Lader, Lawrence, Executive Secretary, National Association for Repeal of Abortion Laws, New York, N.Y.

Laws, Judith Long, Ph.D., Graduate School of Business, University of Chicago, Chicago, Ill.

Lewit, Sarah, The Population Council, New York, N.Y.

Lieberman, E. James, M.D., Child Psychiatrist, Washington, D.C.

Major, Sylvia, Public Relations, Santa Monica, Calif.

McGraw, Myrtle B., Ph.D., Department of Psychology, Briarcliff College, Briarcliff Manor, N.Y.

McLaughlin, Loretta, Public Relations, Massachusetts Eye and Ear Infirmary, Boston, Mass.

McMurray, Georgia L., M.S.W., New York City Human Resources Administration, New York, N.Y.

Mead, Margaret, Ph.D., American Museum of Natural History, New York, N.Y.

Mednick, Martha, Ph.D., Department of Psychology, Howard University, Washington, D.C.

Merriam, Eve, Writer, New York, N.Y.

Millett, Kate, Ph.D., Department of English, Barnard College, New York, N.Y.

Milner, Esther, Ph.D., Department of Education, School of General Studies, Brooklyn College, Brooklyn, N.Y.

Moore, Emily, M.A., The Population Council, New York, N.Y.

Nag, Moni, Ph.D., Department of Anthropology, Columbia University, New York, N.Y.

Newman, Lucile F., Ph.D., Department of Sociology, University of California Medical Center, San Francisco, Calif.

Newman, Sidney, Ph.D., Center for Population Research, National Institute of Child Health and Human Development, Bethesda, Md.

North, Augusta, Journalist, Brooklyn, N.Y.

Olesen, Virginia, Ph.D., Graduate Program in Sociology, University of California Medical Center, San Francisco, Calif.

OZER, JOY, Ph.D., Biochemistry Laboratory, National Heart and Lung Institute, Washington, D.C.

POLGAR, STEVEN, Ph.D., Carolina Population Center, Chapel Hill, N.C.

RAINONE, NANETTE, WBAI, New York, N.Y.

REEVES, NANCY, A.B., L.L.B., Lecturer, Writer, and Attorney, Los Angeles, Calif.

ROLLIN, BETTY, *Look Magazine,* New York, N.Y.

RUDERMAN, FLORENCE A., Ph.D., Department of Sociology, Brooklyn College, Brooklyn, N.Y.

SASSOWER, DORIS L., L.L.D., Attorney, New York, N.Y.

SHAINESS, NATALIE, M.D., Psychiatrist, New York, N.Y.

TANGRI, SANDRA S., Ph.D., Carolina Population Center, Chapel Hill, N.C.

THOMPSON, VAIDA, Ph.D., Department of Psychology, University of North Carolina, Chapel Hill, N.C.

TUMIN, MELVIN, Ph.D., Department of Sociology, Princeton University, Princeton, N.J.

WAXENBERG, SHELLEY E., Ph.D., Research Clinical Psychologist, New York, N.Y.

YGLESIAS, HELEN B., Editor and Journalist, New York, N.Y.

ORGANIZER'S INTRODUCTORY REMARKS

Esther Milner, Ph.D.

Department of Education
Brooklyn College
Brooklyn, N.Y.

I see my role in connection with this workshop as that of an enabler, and in my usual task-centered way I would like to enunciate four workshop-related themes: first, the rationale, as Jessie Bernard and I see it, behind the convening of this workshop; second, the additional, underlying motivations that impelled me to initiate this gathering, insofar as I am able to discern them; third, a prospectus of the matters that will engage us here; and, fourth, acknowledgment of my—or rather, of our collective—indebtedness to a number of people who have made major contributions to this undertaking.

In regard to this workshop's rationale, there is by now almost unanimous agreement among social policy-makers in both developed and underdeveloped countries that the two-child family must very soon become the planetary norm if the human race is not to breed itself into extinction. Traditional attempts to deal with the problem of overpopulation on a mass basis have been through the development and dissemination of contraceptive technology. Yet, despite the continuing limited effectiveness of this gadgeteering approach, current and projected efforts to deal with excessive fertility amount to little more than its intensification!

Potentially more efficacious means of effecting mass acceptance of the two-child family continue to be ignored, partly because they do not fit into existing research and programmatic—and attitudinal—niches. Questions such as the following are not being raised, nor attempts to answer them being made: How do various populations of women feel about the virtual elimination of their traditional sources of identity and self-regard which this new social pattern implies? What are women going to do with their life when only a fraction of it is to be invested in maternity? Would they be more willing to accept the two-child—or no-child—norm if pressures to do so were accompanied by explicit societal provision of personally meaningful and socially rewarded alternatives and supplements to the traditionally child-centered feminine life-career? How should preparation for such other possibilities be incorporated into girls' rearing and education? Exploration of such structural and human-factors problems as these are urgent and long overdue.

This workshop has been convened to provide a rather carefully selected group of persons an opportunity to communicate their respective perspectives on problems such as these to one another, and also to formulate a number of related heuristic questions and strategies. By "carefully chosen," I mean I have tried first, to include persons who represent a variety of related disciplines and theoretical orientations, and second, to make it intergenerational. Third, I have tried to anticipate a kind of elitist ethnocentrism that frequently renders gatherings such as these ineffective even before they begin: Articulate, college-educated, career-oriented women have a tendency to assume either that they speak for all women *or* that theirs is the ideal life-style to which all women either do or should aspire—or, typically, both. I have attempted to compensate for this strong-yet-unconscious bias by including first, persons with a broad and deep cross-cultural experience and perspective, and second, persons with an extensive cross-subcultural experience and perspective, i.e., those who are or have been directly and deeply involved with poor and working-class girls and women.

Concerning my additional, underlying motivations for organizing this inquiry, let me be, as usual, blunt: I am both deeply impatient with, and affronted by, the credo of our current *Zeitgeist* (and I am using a German word deliberately) that any problem, no matter how complex and how human in its ramifications, is solvable through the expedient application of technological, including human engineering, means, shoveled out in innundatingly massive amounts (the younger generation has a vivid four-letter word for what I am referring to).

Quite simply, I am, and have been for some time, fed up to my eyebrows with the unabating propensity of the majority of the world's women toward passive acceptance of male estimates of their worth and of male prescriptions for their style of being and living. In a recent interview, Gore Vidal capsulated the current United States version of this vintage puppet show in a few trenchant sentences (*Look*, July 29, 1969):

> Modern American writers are preoccupied by the "castrating U.S. woman." In print, they pay off women for some grudge in their own psyches or treat them as pneumatic mattresses for their lust. That's the *writer's* hang-up. Women simply want to please; they'll act out any role the male wants them to.

Let me repeat that sadly accurate last sentence: "Women simply want to please; they'll act out any role the male wants them to." Present company excepted, of course!

I am even more fed up, right over the topmost layer of my neocortex (yes, women have one, too) with the style of reaction of an ostensibly quite-different sort of woman than the great majority to whom Vidal refers—a kind of woman who really should know better. Some of our best-educated and brightest women of all ages who, having quite properly rejected the male-propounded "feminine mystique," are displaying another propensity every bit as dominated by the immature male's fantasy-life as the one they scorn so vehemently: They have embraced the obsolescent "masculine mystique" which, with its reaction-formation commitment to power over and manipulation of both man *and* nature, has brought us to the historical point of threat to the very survival of our species and of our physical habitat. Since this polemic is the jumping-off point for one of my position papers, I shall not provoke you further at this stage.

The relationship between these two personal points of view and the agenda of this workshop is, as is probably obvious to some of you, analogous to the relationship between the submerged base of an iceberg and its visible tip. Let me provide a quick survey of that visible tip: Our opening sessions constitute a preface to the workshop proper. The various advance papers and supplementary papers were intended to provide a common, point-of-departure survey of a variety of concerns and/or factors that relate to women's heretofore-primary functions as child-bearers and rearers. The topics covered by these papers were originally conceived to be as follows: *

1. The broader social setting.
2. How close are we to mass acceptance of the two-child family, in the United States and abroad?
   a. Current demographic trends in the United States and abroad—needed research.
   b. Current fertility-control techniques and strategies and their effectiveness.
   c. Impediments—cultural, institutional, and individual—to such acceptance.
   d. Looking ahead: Some social and individual consequences of such acceptance.
3. Anthropological and sociological precedents and analogies.
4. Current and emerging feminine occupation-centered life-career patterns and trends in the United States: A status report—needed research.
5. Our species *learns* to be human: Some societal—and individual life-career—implications.

The workshop proper begins with an airing of the diverse points of view concerning this crucial, future-oriented, positively phrased issue: What are the most desirable feminine life-style models in the currently emerging post-compulsion era when women may freely choose or not choose to bear and to rear children? Next, we shall try to analyze in depth the various types of impediments—biological, cultural and psychological, structural or institutional—which have contributed to the current situations and life-styles of women, and to formulate research issues bearing on these factors. We shall then have the opportunity to propose strategies for change within four overlapping-yet-different direction-contexts:

1. What are alternative and supplemental sources of self-regard *and* satisfying alternative and supplementary ways of spending daily time among women of various subcultures and income levels?
2. What structural/institutional changes are needed to facilitate new self-images and life-styles among girls and women?
3. How can resistive/obstructive public/male attitudes *and* girls' and women's self-attitudes be changed?
4. What should be the respective "change" roles of: parent education, public schooling, the mass media, arts and letters, social planning/governmental programs, political pressure/women's groups?

In our concluding discussions, we are charged with constructing the beginning spans of various bridges intended to link this workshop to particular future developments—that is, to address ourselves to four topics:

1. Social-psychologically oriented approaches to fertility control.

* *Note added in proof:* It turned out to be necessary to change the order of the discussion of the advance papers in one instance: The discussion of Professor Petersen's paper followed rather than preceded that of the Segal and Tietze reprint.

2. The *individual* life-career and personality in a machine-serves-people society.
3. Additional related areas requiring exploration not included in the workshop.
4. Initial planning for a "carryover" conference.

I anticipate that many of you will refer to various publications and/or authorities at some point in your comments, and that others will subsequently want to consult one or another of these sources. Unfortunately, it will not be possible, for very practical reasons, for me or for anyone else to prepare a post-factum workshop-discussion bibliography (although a resource bibliography has been prepared). I would therefore suggest that those who wish to track down a source referred to in the discussion address an inquiry, by mail if necessary, directly to the person citing the reference.

This gathering represents a milestone in a fairly lengthy professional and conceptual odyssey. This journey began for me in 1960, at a time when informed concern over the ramifications of over-rapid population-increase was limited to concern for the availability of food and to countries other than the United States. I was interested enough in the psychological implications of increasing population right here in the United States and in the urgent need for social-psychology to adopt this problem-area as a new research-frontier, to become founding-chairperson of an SPSSI (Society for the Psychological Study of Social Issues) study-group on this topic in 1961, and to keep this small but dedicated group going until 1963. My association with Josef Garai and Steven Polgar, two of the participants in this workshop, goes back to that period. Since a major aspect of our group's *raison d'etre* was to try to convince related professionals of the need for research in this complex and important area, we mounted two professional-organization symposia during 1962: one at the annual American Psychological Association conference entitled "Social and Psychological Obstacles to Population Control," and another at the annual American Association for the Advancement of Science conference entitled "Psychological Implications of Increasing Population: Some Questions That Need Answering." A few of the questions included in a paper that I prepared for the latter symposium proved to be the harbinger for the present workshop topic. The SPSSI-sponsored study-group became inactive in 1963, for reasons which provide documentation for some of the neofeminist rhetoric but which I shall not recount here. During the succeeding five years, my earlier interest in the broad area of "psychological implications" distilled into the issue that is the topic of this workshop, and in 1968 I made three different attempts to bring it to my fellow professionals' attention—to no avail. My correspondence-association with Jessie Bernard began in connection with the first of these attempts. My 1969 dues notice from The New York Academy of Sciences was partially responsible, believe it or not, for our being here today. It reminded me of the Academy's dominantly medical-sciences-related conferences and publications, which seemed to me to reflect an overly narrow spectrum of "the sciences." I was seriously contemplating the possibility of not renewing my membership when a way of partially remedying my complaint occurred to me: perhaps The New York Academy of Sciences would be willing to sponsor the inquiry-group I had had in mind for so long. The Academy turned out to have a rational, three-step procedure for the organization of such an effort—and, with the help of Margaret Mead at a crucial point, here we are!

I would like to "read into the record" at this point just how the Workshop's agenda and ground-rules have come about, since they by no means represent a unilateral, organizer-developed and imposed effort. The first letter to the first mailing list of invitees, mailed during April, 1969, included this sentence:

> Rather than asking you to attend a fully planned "fait accompli," I am hoping you will contribute to the planning by giving me your answer to this question: What in this general topic-area are *you* particularly interested in and would like to see included in such a "preliminary" workshop?

Many thoughtful contributions were received in reply—and were used. The first draft of the workshop's agenda was mailed out to a larger mailing list during June, 1969, accompanied by an explanatory letter which, among other items, invited those who did not wish to prepare one of the advance papers but who had definite points of view on any of the workshop topics to prepare brief, one- or two-page position papers, to be distributed on the spot to the workshop's participants. My next mailing, dated September, 1969, included this passage:

> Will those of you who may have a substantive contribution to make to any of the point-of-departure papers to be circulated in advance submit such contributions in a form similar to that suggested previously for the position papers, but longer, if necessary?

And finally, this paragraph was included in the letter sent out during January, 1970, together with the first mailing of advanced papers:

> Since the papers' writers were all given full freedom to select and organize data and present ideas pertinent to her/his topic, and since there is, by design, a rather wide diversity of disciplines and viewpoints represented among the Workshop invitees, I anticipate that some of you will either find yourselves differing sharply with one or more aspects of one or more of these papers *or* conclude that relevant data and/or viewpoints have been overlooked. Rather than holding your disagreement or supplementation and expressing it verbally the first morning or afternoon, I urge you to prepare a statement presenting and documenting your disagreement as soon after your receipt of the papers as possible, and to mail two copies to me, as well as to bring along copies for on-the-spot distribution to Workshop participants.

I have deliberately reviewed these advance-preparation aspects of the workshop to make clear the opportunities for participation in every phase of the workshop that were made available to everyone invited—opportunities that some participants, I am pleased to report, took advantage of. My role *during* this workshop is that of a participant among participants. Any attempts on my part to influence your deliberations have ended, I trust, where they began—with setting up the issues to be focused on and submitting a few papers.

In closing I want to express our collective indebtedness to a number of people, and to do so in chronological order. First, to Dr. Jessie Bernard, who, by giving me the moral support I very much needed initially, by suggesting names of participants and possible contributors of advance papers, and by offering several creative agenda ideas, has served as co-organizer of this workshop. Second, thanks to Dr. Sidney Newman, who, by being not merely supportive at key points, but by being both practically and critically supportive, was of major assistance to me. Third, to the many persons, most of them participating, who responded to my early request for agenda ideas, and with whom I have had stimulating and helpful interchanges by letter and telephone. Fourth, to the members of the Academy's Conference Organization Committee, chaired by Dr. Kenneth Thompson, and to Dr. Margaret Mead of the Academy's Board of Governors, who were good enough "sports" to take a chance in deciding that The New York Academy of Sciences would sponsor so innovative—from the Academy's point of view—a program. Fifth, to those who prepared the advance papers, both basic and supplementary: Mrs. Nancy Reeves, Dr. William Petersen, Mrs. Chana Heffner, Dr. Lucile F. Newman, Mr. Derek G. Gill, Dr. Catherine S. Chilman, Dr. Virginia Olesen, Dr. Cynthia Epstein, and Dr. Florence Ruderman. Sixth, to Dr. Miriam G. Keiffer, who has prepared a resource bibliography for the workshop. I would also like to recognize all the members of the Academy's staff for their strong interest in and support of the workshop. My warm thanks in advance, as well, to those persons chairing or recording the various plenary sessions and concurrent roundtable discussion groups.

PART 1. POINTS OF DEPARTURE

ANATOMY AND DESTINY

Nancy Reeves, A.B., L.L.B.

Member, New York and California Bars
Attorney at Law
Los Angeles, Calif.

It would be an unsound fancy and self contradictory to expect that things which had never yet been done can be done except by means which have never yet been tried.

Francis, Lord Bacon
Novum Organum, 1620

BIOLOGICAL DETERMINISM AND HISTORICAL INVISIBILITY

The tyranny of biology as normative absolute remains an unexamined assumption about the status of women across the centuries. Man was *homo faber,* adapting himself and modifying his environment; woman was *femina genitalis,* eternally gravid, preprogrammed, and static. This assumption is, moveover, woven into all conjecture on the human condition: The condition of man is his relation to the universe; the condition of woman is her relation to the nest. Variation, the fact of process, of dialogue between man and nature, punctuated by a changing ecology, received and devised, are temporal events apart from immemorial woman; mankind and its intricate history plots the course of man.

This history reflects, of course, a certain ethnocentrism. In the familiar social scaffolding, the technosphere is certainly a male monopoly, and, of the crystallized institutions on which it is balanced, only one—that of kinship—is properly woman's place. It also reflects a form of chronocentrism, imposing contemporary patterns on all pasts. Suburban matron is projected as paradigm —divorced from the economy, dependent on the domicile, the symbols of her status become historical imperatives, the benchmarks of feminine gender in all todays and yesterdays. With only a change of costume and conveniences, women are seen in each epoch as extraneous to community endeavor, supported for perpetual confinement in a timeless sexual ghetto.

Rudimentary reasoning lifts the veil. Until the species wrested surplus sustenance from a modified environment, there were no immured individuals. Woman could not, in unstratified societies, be specialized to sex and kindred service; as indispensable unit, she fed the chain of energy in the search and struggle for continuing existence. Later, as stratification occurred, only a minority were privileged; the majority, laborers and the wives of those who labored, were never exempt from common toil. The errors, then, are dual: 1. to suppose that in societies that anteceded surplus and stratification it was possible for women to be a sex apart, released from the rigors of survival; and 2. to suppose that in the layered societies that followed, woman was a single conceptual category.

In one or another guise, the mischief in such a mental set is that it tends to project final designs on all futures. Avoiding complexities, discussion on the social integration of the second sex still goes forward apart from social structure.

Because existential possibilities are bound up in space and time, the scale and speed of today's cultural metamorphosis, including as it does a revolution in the very arena of biological determinism, make this a crippling error. Henry Adams remarked that simplicity is the most deceitful mistress that ever betrayed man. It is an even greater betrayer of woman, for when social critics view man, whatever their historic disorientation, they relate his role, in some degree, to the social rafters from which he is suspended. Woman's role, by contrast, is examined exclusively in terms of sexual and psychological triggers. Even her entry into the labor market is viewed as a purely private decision, made possible by the pill, but still a subjective and independent variable, unrelated to market conditions. In each discipline, the tradition of invisibility promotes disengaged doctrines of exceptionalism.

With this preliminary exhortation, let it be stressed that change certainly widens the perimeter of individual choice, but it concomitantly produces new social limits. In an entirely neoteric sense, feminine self-determination may now be a viable option, but it is not simply a function of feminine militancy. Patterns of integration can neither be considered nor realized apart from process. Today we live in a vast web that, touched at any point, transforms the whole. This is made more critical in its consequence than change in former epochs because of the simultaneity of our revolutions. Uprooting all reference points, they reorder—at both terminals and in quantum leaps—the dynamic relation between people and planet as not only the environment but man himself becomes increasingly man-made. And, still, in the perceptive words of Erik Erikson, ". . . man, not being a natural species any more, is not a mankind as yet. . . ." The underlying idea offers no guidelines, but it does delineate a goal: to incorporate the multiple variables of concurrent change to the measure of the human dimension. We are faced, then, with the following revolutions, first to comprehend, then to control.

Transcending the Given in Environment

The Cybernetic Revolution in Production

This technological leap may mean that toil, as a necessary economic enterprise, can now be eliminated. "Only an extraordinarily elaborate exercise in social camouflage," writes John Kenneth Galbraith, "has kept us from seeing what is happening."[1] Cybernation, like other technical leaps, reflects change in the relationship between man and his matrix. At the same time, such transformations have always triggered change in the structural adjustments of society, in the relationships between man and man.

The choice before us becomes not one between change and non-change, but between change measured by the anarchy of machine and change tailored to the measure of man. All too often today, technology is tendered as the independent variable. It is as though we can recognize the possibility of transcending the given in nature, but are transfixed by the given made by man. The economic and social hazards latent in such inertia are spelled out by Norbert Wiener:[2]

> Let us remember that the automatic machine, whatever we think of any feelings it may have or not have, is the precise economic equivalent of slave labor. Any labor which competes with slave labor must accept the economic conditions of

> slave labor. It is perfectly clear that this will produce an unemployment situation, in comparison with which the present recession and even the depression of the thirties will seem a pleasant joke.

On the other hand, optimistic forecasters insist automation phases out jobs, not work. According to this, what is required is only a shifting of human gears so that men and machines can be creatively synchronized. "Technology is not a vessel into which people are to be poured and to which they must be molded," comments the National Commission on Technology, Automation, and Economic Progress. "It is something to be adapted to the needs of man and to the furtherance of human ends, including the enrichment of personality and environment." [3] Without planning, however, the shift imperative could in itself lead to chaotic conditions and mass suffering. If, without delay, man takes the initiative, recognizing his autonomy, the new technology can, it is argued, be the supreme servant of a rational culture. Here is the analysis of Thomas J. Watson, Jr., Chairman of the Board of IBM:[4]

> Less developed, but becoming feasible, are some new ways of understanding our people resources; and we know that people are not infinitely versatile. A bond trader makes a very fine executive, but so far none has done much in nuclear physics. To what degree can we shift—to what degree can we find people to take on new tasks? That, I believe is our greatest constraint, and it isn't considered very often. As I said earlier, if we're going to get these problems solved in the future, goal setting and goal analysis have to be elevated in government. Presidential commissions aren't enough, and we've got to get started.

This perspective, despite its radical call for central planning, is nonetheless based in the conventional assumption that the new technology will not disemploy humans. There are other views, e.g., those of Dr. Louis Fein,[5] rooted in the same assumption, that there may even be a "net gain—not a net loss—in requirements for human labor to fulfill an ever increasing demand." Contrary conclusions are founded in his counter assumption "that machines are already so numerous, productive, versatile and reliable, that any future demands could be met by largely utilizing such machines together with a relatively small fraction of the labor force." [5] Dr. Fein argues that instead of adopting one or the other assumption, it is imperative that our government develop concrete data on which viable economic policies can be based, for ". . . we shouldn't accept as evidence what amounts to hope that what was valid in the past will be valid in the future." [5] *

And still, even these approaches, while they certainly recognize the need to enter the cybernetic age with more than *laissez faire* attitudes, are still sufficiently traditional to equate unemployment with catastrophe. There is a more radical vantage: to view total unemployment as the ultimate goal. In the framework of this philosophy, unemployment as a problem is an element in bypassed theory, unemployment as a liberation from bonds of necessity is the arc of the future. Such freedom from mandatory labor could accordingly become the prerequisite for "the good life" in the Greek sense, i.e., the life of the citizen.

* "Isn't it plausible that U.S. science and technology is advancing at a sufficiently great rate that at some instant soon we will have just one more person than we need, then two more, then 10 more, then thousands more, then 3.5 million more, then tens of millions more . . . ? . . . There is so much to lose by being unprepared for such an eventuality—and so much to be gained by being ready for it."[5]

Arendt[6] says that such "good life," the term Aristotle employed for the life of the citizen,

> was not merely better, more carefree or nobler than ordinary life, but of an altogether different quality. It was "good" to the extent that by having mastered the necessities of sheer life, by being freed from labor and work, and by overcoming the innate urge of all living creatures for their own survival, it was no longer bound to the biological life process. At the root of Greek political consciousness we find an unequaled clarity and articulateness in drawing this distinction. No activity that served only the purpose of making a living, of sustaining only the life process, was permitted to enter the political realm. . . .

Admittedly, a transformation of basic institutions is implied by this course, which sees human beings as now able to free themselves not only "from the external tyrannies and caprice of toil, famine, and disease, but from internal constraints of our animal inheritance, our physical frailties, our emotional anachronisms, our intellectual limits. . . ."[7] In Robert Sinheimer's formulation, we are moving out of a world "we never made but were biologically more or less adapted to, for better or worse, to a world of our own creation, a world shaped increasingly by the motivations and limitations of man alone; we can and must and will direct the form of that world, and how well we do must depend increasingly upon our ability . . . to anticipate the consequences of our acts."[7]

Anticipation, then, in a world of flux, is the single quality required, in all the projections, to save us from the consequences of after-image lag: anticipation of labor shifts, of economic needs, or of the consequences of human disemployment. Yet, even sophisticated predictions continue to be based in current trends, without intervention. Specialists in various disciplines know, with S. Lee Pogostin, that the world is not changing; it is changed. Yet it is just this that has not been internalized by the generalists, especially by those generalists in the top tiers of the received structure: politicians and their partisans still assume that the future will unfold in an orderly manner from the present. This is, perhaps, the essence of the current crisis, foreseen by Whitehead long ago, a crisis "wherein the people responsible for putting things together . . . would have fallen so relatively far behind the regenerative reaches of the specialists in exquisite knowledge extension as to be practically incapable of comprehending" the significance of their findings.[8]

The paradox is that, given intervention conscious of the dimensions of change and the extent of the variables involved, we are not at all faced with absolutes. It is only in the context of denial and drift that events appear inexorable. Kenneth Boulding, describing mechanisms now available to economists, for example, likened them to a thermostat that can be set according to the desired temperature. Without anticipation and plan, however, even the most sophisticated knowledge remains irrelevant. Instead, hope based in bypassed reality, and improvisation based in exigency, define the trend. Subversion of the institution of work is countered by a patchwork of social inventions such as shorter hours, the illusion of labor, and the production of spurious goods and services made saleable by contrived demand. Most of all, however, the employment gap created by a "society which still insists that man should compete with machine systems in order to earn a living" has been filled by the military establishment.[9] "Above and beyond the call of duty, the war economy has given us affluence."[9]

Perhaps the only way even to consider our situation is to pose possibilities first in the short run, then in the long one. To begin with, it is necessary to anticipate, to gauge the extent of social invention and of thermostatic resetting that will be required if: (a) the war machine is delimited; (b) excluded minorities are to be economically integrated; and (c) the sequestered two-thirds of the female population, currently engaged in "occupation: housewife" continue to question the traditional limits of woman's place. An enlightened course for the immediate future might consist of programmed economic endeavor around critical social needs: health, education, urban transport, housing, the enhancement and conservation of natural resources, public works. "Most of these activities and institutions are now short-changed. With abundance to support the expanding portion of the population engaged in them . . . for some time to come, we can be sure, the real work that remains to be done in the world will stave off the specter of universal leisure." [10]

An enlightened course for the long term might consist of the acceptance of human disemployment in tasks unworthy of human engagement as a positive mutation; man's loss of significance as an automaton as blessing and release. Man's function would then be related to the more subtle tasks of purpose, politics, and priorities. "Man has never really tried to use science in the realm of his value systems . . . never really tried deliberately to create a better society for man qua man. . . ." [11] The social stage seems to be set for the level of civilization in which the full implication of the current technological revolution is politically comprehended and culturally internalized.

The Scientific Revolution in Destruction

This development, often referred to as CBR, includes the chemical, biological, and radiological techniques for waging total war. Historically, war is a social institution based in scarcity, the need to wrest a living from the unmodified environment, to compete and struggle for scarce resources. As life became more complex, additional categories of difference arose between groups. But the conflict, however ideologically packaged and legitimated, has been for survival, or survival at a certain level: to occupy and exploit the same place. The choice, then, that technology offers in destruction parallels that in production; is it intricate machine or perceptive man which is to be the measure, the independent variable? New productive methods make feasible an economy of abundance, provided ideas and configurations rooted in bypassed ecology are scuttled. In the human perspective, the revolution in production can make struggle—because there may be no spoils—irrevelant, the revolution in destruction can make war—because there may be no survivors—inconceivable.

The Revolution in Manipulation

Groups in power, political and economic complexes, achieve their leverage through the consent of the governed. Traditionally, this consent has been obtained by persuasion and by coercion, with argument a hit-or-miss affair, and the "big stick" immediately available for crisis management. Today's technique, on the other hand, makes it possible for people to be programmed. Persuasion has become a precise science; naked coercion is no longer an operative necessity. Once again, the metamorphic age (the term is Zbigniew Brzezinski's) provides an unprecedented arena of choice. "The growing capacity for calculating instantly most complex interactions," writes Brzezinski (REF. 12, p. 8), "and the increasing availability of biochemical means of human control increase the potential scope of self-conscious direction, and thereby also the pressures to direct, to choose and to change." The issue then becomes one of utilizing these mechanisms to diminish the influence of the demonic in man, or of surrendering them to the self-serving purposes of demonic men. Here, the concept, employed by Norbert Wiener, of the automatic machine as the economic equivalent of slave labor, lends itself to a constructive projection. Classical peoples were able to devote their full time to the *res publica* precisely because the mechanics of life were the province of slaves. Technology, by offering a new slave class, can thus remove the disabilities inherent in the received amalgam of democratic ideals and ecological patternings of the first industrial revolution. The number of intermediaries between citizen and participatory decision could conceivably be reduced by such robots of cybernation, and the contemporary populace released to address itself to the general welfare. The material world would be left to the machines; the philosophical and the spiritual worlds would be the province of man. Camus has noted that the Greeks used reason to restrain the will while we have ended by placing the impulse of the will at the heart of reason. In the context of the manipulative revolution, it is the impulse of the will of the powerful that is placed at the heart of reason. Such use of the will, according to Camus, causes reason to become murderous. In our context it implies the surrender of rational forces to demonic ends, converting scholars into "house-ideologues for those in power . . . , organization-oriented, application-minded intellectuals . . ." (REF. 12, p. 18), amoral servants of the political system, instruments of technique.

The Revolution in Concepts of Time and Space: Communications and Transport

Manipulative programming derives from quality-controlled production and consumption of ideas in continuous visual and audial contact. Its immediacy levels old boundaries of lag and latitude. "It is commonly said that with the new modes of transport distance no longer exists; and indeed, man has vanquished space." [13] With instantaneous communication, the same may be said about time. What then does this signify, apart from manipulation, for morality? Jacob Bronowski, scholar and poet, has observed: [14]

> . . . that at the basis of human thought lies the judgment of what is like and what is unlike . . . the human values are bound up with what we judge to be like and unlike; and when science shifts that judgment, it makes as profound a shift in these values. The Greeks built a wonderful civilization, yet it did not outrage their sense of values to hold men in slavery. They did not feel the slave and citizen to be alike men. By the end of the eighteenth century, it was felt in the western world that all white men are alike; but William Wilberforce spent a lifetime in persuading his generation that black slaves and white are alike in human dignity. Science helped to create that sensibility, by widening the view of what is like and what unlike.

Unprecedented communication and transport have not yet created the global village but they have steadily expanded the areas of likeness between peoples, shifting values based on xenophobia. Telstar can transmit trivia. Jumbo jets can carry jingoists. But representatives of the human nation are now within sight and sound of one another, an initial step in the discovery of their common destiny in the cosmic age.

The Biomedical Revolution: Life Prolongation, Life Limitation, Life Transformation

"Man," writes Paul Ehrlich, "has been extremely successful at lowering the human death rate, but has made no significant effort to lower the birth rate."[15] Yet the biomedical revolution has not only provided techniques for controlling the rate of reproduction, it has transformed the life-styles of men, and more particularly of women, in relation to that process. "The great Polish poet, Adam Mickiewicz, proclaimed in a song he wrote for his fellow students, that they should 'measure their strength to match their purposes, not their purposes to match their strength.' "[16] This remains the challenge, not only in human longevity and human multiplication, but also in the newer areas of biological advance, such as genetic engineering, which have profound social, ecological, and ethical implications for the human community as we conceive it.

The Revolution in Rising Expectations

Insulating factors of time and space having disappeared, outsiders have become aware of alternative designs for living. They have also begun to realize that man no longer subsists in a habitat of scarcity, that material and energy resources derived from technological effort are virtually limitless, that abundance is now accessible to all without depriving any. Underprivileged nations, underprivileged minorities, and the underprivileged sex all demand integration, as hunger, deprivation, and second-class status become conditions supererogatory and not to be borne.

Identity: Traditionalized Models

This, then, is backdrop for the identity crisis that besets contemporary men and women. It is complicated by the fact that in received wisdom the human condition has been operational and the individual role functional. And, further, a fixed dichotomy in the basic natures of women and of men is presumed to have bisected the world into unalterable social hemispheres, with production the determinant of his identity, reproduction of hers.

The Male Model

Man is what he does: butcher, baker, candlestick maker. The definition remains prescriptive even though assembly-line techniques have brought alienation first to blue-collar, and more recently, to white-collar workers who have now become ". . . one of hundreds of tiny pink men in white shirts, forever shifting papers and frowning into telephones."[17] One finds, moreover, lurking in the imperative that derives identity from work function, the contemporary irony that most employees operate in situations ideally suited to the new machines, situations so structured that there is virtually no individual challenge and no intrinsic content. In consequence, alienation now extends beyond the assembly line in factory and office, penetrating all the higher echelons of supervision, technology, and management, as power over occupational effort is increasingly stripped from the person. The market determines where he works, the machine dictates how he works, and the boss decides when he works. The result is a life-style which eclipses the individual for the significant segment of his days, with standardization of technique flowing into standardization of thought, as the ego becomes a cog in the labor-saving system. Yet, despite these countervailing forces, identity imperative remains constant. "In America what you do is what you are," reports Daniel P. Moynihan. Thus, he continues, "to do nothing is to be nothing; to do little is to be little. The equations are implacable and blunt, and ruthlessly public." [18]

The Female Model

But, "We don't ask what a woman does—we ask whom she belongs to." [19] Even when, as career woman, she escapes the traditional stereotype, her role continues to be that of supernumerary in significant social drama, segregated from power, and living in what one writer has described as the lingering light of the harem. The only normal woman is still a "little woman" with all her options opening from the bedroom door. Loving for a living—as wife and as mother—remains her proper profession. And there are perquisites: The president's wife participates in the inaugural ceremony, without standing for election; the wives of astronauts ride in triumphal procession, without leaving *terra firma.* The difficulty, however, lies in the unacknowledged stigma of derived status—nobody has been listed in "Who's Who" for being a good wife and mother, and there's the rub! Clearly, in our society, to be visible in the kinship order is "to do nothing [and] to be nothing," declarations to the contrary notwithstanding.

Chafing under cultural depreciation of this, their mandatory milieu, women have taken two courses. Some have sought to elevate the status of the sexual ghetto; others have sought to climb out of it. There are structural reasons for disappointment in both directions.

The First Course: Elevating the Status of the Kinship Order

The kinship order is one which "is made up of institutions which regulate and facilitate legitimate sexual intercourse, procreation, and the early rearing of children." [20] Certainly, looking across the centuries to tribal societies where family and clan organized the total life, and where replenishment through the capacity to be fruitful and multiply was of urgent significance, visibility in the kinship order could connote organic relation to production and power. By contrast, and despite our custom to deny it, the life stream of industrial societies is money not blood, with products, not people, at a premium. Kinship institutions now have only marginal utility; their dividends have been relegated to the vital statistics columns and the woman's page. In fact, according to *The New York Times,* today's overriding question is, "How to persuade the mass of Americans that limitation of family size below existing levels is vital to the welfare of this nation, and not just to that of the underdeveloped countries . . . ."[21]

In watertight compartments, insulated from other ideas, this is recognized reality. Our religion is not based in fertility rites nor our economy in human fructification. Children are additional mouths to feed, not auxiliary hands to labor, and bringing them forth begets public approbation only on Mother's Day. Nevertheless, and for the most part, imperatives of social myth cause symbol to be substituted for inconvenient fact. As in ancient tribes in which the shaman sought to create a phenomenon by naming it, today's conjuring savants try to name the private as pivotal in the postindustrial epoch. Unfortunately for this theory, the received power structure has not yet been exorcised. The private continues inconsequent to the umbilical politico-economy.

It is therefore disappointing to find engaged women, after years of quiescence, advancing proposals that were progressive when feminism was young. Like their forebears, they focus on marketplace activity, full admission to the operative sector of the economic order, as the touchstone of liberation. Although the specific challenges take various forms—e.g., that there is a conspiracy by the manipulators to keep women consuming in the home; that the system keeps women "cabined, cribbed, confined" by failing to provide institutional support (child care and other services); and that the problem is psychological, traditional models binding women to lives without motivation—all these analyses proceed at the secondary level, all are founded on the primary assumption that women have heretofore been excluded from the world of work and that unprecedented participation in that world is the open sesame to cultural inclusion.

But yesterday's slogans may be based in hopes exploded by their realization: Our experience does not thus far confirm the hypothesis that simple earning power is directly related to ultimate power, to actual integration. And yesterday's slogans are not always relevant to today's realities: We are not sure there will continue to be a world of work for women to enter.

The Second Course: Entering the World of Work

Alfred North Whitehead has noted that it requires a very unusual mind to undertake the analysis of a fact. Perhaps this explains why the fact that women have always participated in the world of work continues unexamined. Although full-scale tracing is not suitable in this context, let us at least essay a synoptic review.

Clearly, in rudimentary groups, the labor of all members was indispensable for survival. Later, as tools were devised, differentiation of function became possible; implements replaced hands—first a few hands, then a whole group of hands. This process accelerated with the advance of technology. Step by step, as skill transformed environment, special categories of humans could be withdrawn from primary production. But not to be overlooked is the overarching fact that, irrespective of age or sex, the great majority of social populations remained part of the essential work force, for the economic surplus was, until very recently, always marginal. The level of social ecology was, on balance, the determinant of all these changes, and the phenotypes of men and of women, at each stage and at every stratum, were affected by them.

Certainly the life-styles of wives of slaves or wives of serfs do not verify our cultural preconceptions. But, of course, it is also true that women were once queens and consorts, abbesses and chatelaines, performing tasks and wielding power unregistered by our short historical memories. At the same time, in assuming that women in the past were outsiders, there persists the corollary assumption, as Klein notes,[22] that women were:

> of old, excluded from the economic life of society, and are only now reluctantly and gradually being admitted into the masculine sphere of work. This is a misrepresentation of the facts. Before the agricultural and industrial revolution there was hardly any job which was not also performed by women. No work was too hard, no labour too strenuous to exclude them.

Then came the great divide, the revolution that replaced more hands than ever before in human history, and it affected women whatever their station. Lower-class women, who had previously been essential to the business of life, now became a marginal group competing with children and with men for employment. From the cooperation of family effort and family income came the competition of each individual against all comers and a precarious foothold in the labor market. At the same time, sophisticated machines, releasing hands, made it possible for women of the privileged classes to be withdrawn from all connection with the work of the world. Thus, the wives of the lowly ceased to be a primary work force and found themselves reduced to a reserve energy pool, contingent and vulnerable; and the wives of the powerful lost all economic function and became dependent and dispensable. This, then, was the prelude to woman's exclusion from the principal public institutions of our time and her marginal relation to the market economy.

Subsequent events have tended to reinforce that exclusion, for, as machines continued to evolve, ever fewer hands were required to serve them. In the main, the expendable group has been women. More and more have disappeared into the home, either because they could not find work, or because they could find a good provider. In today's America, with its enormous social surplus, the largest proportion of adult women take no part in formal economic activity. Ironically, the full-time wife and mother, as a style of living, is the contemporary byproduct of technological unemployment.†

Since the exclusion is structural, no biographical resolve can, essentially, counteract it. For, to use an architectural phrase, form follows function. That is to say, in the first instance, the requirements of the social organism establish the broad design of people's lives.‡ The values of the culture then, as Ruth Benedict has shown, reinforce that design; they legitimate it; it becomes the mode. And finally, the individual strand weaves its way in the tapestry, accepting, modifying, rejecting the pattern—but caught up in it. Thus, Rosie the Domestic Relation did not become Rosie the Riveter at the moment when she

† Those who deplore this pattern, viewing it as a continuation of outsider status, legitimated by the feminine mystique, might consider the counsel of C. Wright Mills: rather than explain something as a persistence from the past, we ought to ask why it has persisted. In our context, this means examining contemporary features of society in terms of contemporary function. Because women are not an exotic epiphenomenon, their outside position may have structural relevance; their inside position may require that we clear the ground for new beginnings.

‡ This should not be confused with simple determinism. The economics button does not control humans like automata; it does, however, affect the limits of social range.

wearied of kitchen work, although this may have entered into her decision, but when it became socially necessary and socially approved, because the men had gone to war. The picture that comes to me is that of the old world weather-huts where, if it's going to be fine, the little man is all that is visible, but where, if there's a change in prospect, the little woman swings into view. It is not, then, fortuitous that no mystiques develop in periods of shift.

Surveyed as a whole, what then is the structural significance of the 29 million women currently visible in the labor market—37% of the labor force—three out of five of whom are married and living with their husbands? To extract the meaning from these figures we must realize that the United States is currently in transition between the first and the second industrial revolutions and that phenomena associated with both patterns are both present. This is puzzling unless one recognizes the norm of process and the nature of the revolution that is passing and of the one that is impending.

The First Industrial Revolution

The first industrial revolution multiplied the muscles of men. Here, although the machine extended human energy, the human being attached to the machine still had to feed his energy into it. This combination of puissant man and primary machine was traditionally classified as blue-collar work and traditionally considered a masculine preserve. As machines became more sophisticated, however, less and less physical power was required of the human attendants. In the later stages of this revolution, therefore, blue-collar work tended to be transformed into white-collar work. Women were then recruited. At the same time, efficiency experts created the office assembly line. Again, women were recruited. What made female labor attractive? The answer is simple: its vulnerability. As a marginal group it could not lay claim to the same pay scales or the same social protection as the primary male work force.§

Greater visibility of women in this, the final stage of the first industrial revolution, thus reflects a change at the level of process, not of progress. Woman's place remains constant. She is still peripheral to the economic order, an energy reserve available for marginal occupations and minimum earnings. Glowing predictions respecting integration produced by such inclusion seem, curiously enough, to completely overlook the second industrial revolution, which is already upon us.

The Second Industrial Revolution

This, the cybernetic revolution, not only extends the human being, it releases him; the new robots have an artificial nervous system which disemploys the mortal one.|| For the first time in history, the silver cord between man and

§ "In fact, since women were cheaper to hire in the depression, they got the lioness's share of the jobs that were available. The female labor force grew faster in the thirties than it had done in the previous decades, while men in the millions were forced to stay at home with the children and fret at their wife's role. The depression did much to bring equality in work and homemaking to the sexes, by putting women in the factory and men in the house." [23]

|| "The most revolutionary of all man's prosthetic devices is probably the computer, which may be used as a replacement for, or an extension of, the human mind." [15]

machine has been severed. In certain manufacturing settings, the evidence is strong that these robots already outnumber human workers. Nor does it require much imagination to surmise that women, who are now being sought to tend sophisticated machines, may soon be superseded by more sophisticated machines that need no tending. Women may be cheap labor, but robots may, in time, be cheaper. In the language of Brzezinski, ". . . automation discriminates equally against males and females . . ." (REF. 12, p. 10).

STRUCTURAL CONSIDERATIONS

The outside position of women does not exempt them from economic imperatives. Fewer hands needed means fewer women's hands too. This may be the long-range forecast, despite the current statistical upswing. We can no longer make facile projections from the past, assuming they delineate the future. Social advances are bounded by structural need—and structural need is subject to transformation. It is this that puzzles the students of woman's position. It seems to them paradoxical that an expansion of the feminine work force coexists with a contraction in significant posts and a constriction in proffered designs for living. The idea that labor force participation is the obvious gauge of both structural inclusion and economic function has been an article of faith for so many years that it continues unquestioned.

Yet, examined at a deeper level, such a frame of reference, while it is useful for some purposes, conceals more than it reveals about woman's position relative to prestige and power. For one thing, it tends to consider all women job holders in a single category, perpetuating the notion that all work is essentially the same—Tillie the Toiler betokening breakthrough in the same count as the Dean of Women. It would thus appear the only criterion is a single statistic: out of the home and into the marketplace.

Such a frame of reference, moreover, is misleading in its emphasis on employment as the exclusive measure of labor. Structurally considered, more women working outside the home today may represent mobility in situs rather than in status. No data are needed to postulate that in every technological period, according to the ratio of hands to machines, a certain proportion of women have earned their own livings. It is because history is written about the privileged part of the population that we tend to overlook this sector. Once it was involved in domestic economy, but once all economy was domestic economy. Now it functions in factory, farm, store, and office. Styles have changed, but the imperative for the unprovisioned remains the same: to earn their own bread, married or not. Women who, in the recent past, might have supplemented their husband's earnings or made their own way by taking in washing or sewing or lodgers, now work in a laundry, a factory, or a hotel. The relative number of such women, moreover, is probably not greater today than it was in the past. They may just be more visible, and more countable. In theory, even taking into account the rise in living standards, their total should be smaller, since the rate of productivity of the economy as a whole has increased. To say it another way, the portion of the population released from the obligation to toil for a living has probably grown; most of the women in the labor force today are there because of need,¶ because they have not thus far been released

¶ "Decisions of individual women to seek employment outside the home are usually based on economic reasons. Most women in the labor force work because they or their families need the money they can earn. . . . Relatively few women have the option of working solely for personal fulfillment." [24]

from that obligation; and, finally, their participation in the world of work may constitute not breakthrough, but merely a shift to market employment.

In the main (80%, according to Donald Michael), this female labor force is no more than semi-skilled—which reinforces my hypothesis that contemporary working women are analogues of that original fraction of females whose toil derived not from aspiration, but from need. Work for this group is nothing new and does not in any sense signal social recognition. Even more significantly, it is just this group that labors because it must, which is the first scheduled to be phased out by cybernetic processes. "In terms of social stratification, the human, low-skilled workers are simply eliminated. They are not just placed at the bottom of the status and economic reward ladder; they are removed from it."[25]

Optimists point to the influx of women into clerical fields, the burgeoning need for services and the potential market for skills related to automated machinery, as sectors of labor absorption. But it is undeniable that the computer is already in full operation in the office, as it is in the factory; that services tend more and more to be self-services cum machines; and that computer-related skills continue to be more and more complex.

This seems to underscore the argument for upgrading women's skills, on the theory that there will only be room at the top. Even this approach may not, however, be realistic in long-term perspective. Already many upper-echelon specialties are being eliminated. What is the willing woman to be trained for? How can we be sure that those who head for the top now will not be redundant by the time they are qualified? Moreover, given the scramble for places as work becomes "a privilege reserved for the most talented" (REF. 12, p. 6) and given the traditional cultural values that have frozen even accomplished women into subordinate positions,** why should we imagine that, short of social revolution, there will be a thaw at the pinnacle? The fact is that the route of jobs, even of significant jobs as a way for women to be integrated, is being swiftly bypassed by scientific events. In disregarding the ascendant industrial revolution and its impact on cultural design, neofeminist movements are as far outside the real dilemmas of our time as their subjects are outside the mainstream.

That is one side of the dilemma. The other is the effort of searching women to find a new identity, a new relationship to society, in an old functionalism. Even assuming full employment as a possible alternative to the immediate trend, is this an appropriate strategy for liberation? Today, instrumental housewife deals with instrumental breadwinner. Will two instrumental

** "Despite the increased diversification in women's professional employment, women continue to hold a disproportionately small share of positions in the leading professions. Although women have traditionally made up a large part of the teacher corps, in 1964 only 22 percent of the faculty and other professional staff in institutions of higher education were women. . . . Although women are heavily represented in the health fields, in 1964 only 6 percent of physicians were women. Similarly women had only token representation among scientists (8 percent), lawyers (3 percent), and engineers (1 percent). Moreover, a recent survey by the Harvard Business Review states that 'the barriers (to the employment of women in management positions) are so great that there is scarcely anything to study. . . .' More than one-fifth of employed women with 4 years of college were working as service workers (including private-household), operatives, salesworkers, or clerical workers in March 1965. A startling 7 percent of employed women who had completed 5 years or more of college were working in the same unskilled or semi-skilled occupations."[26]

breadwinners support a more meaningful and mutual life, given present designs for living, and given present designs for earning a living?

From a sociological vantage, neither man's anatomy nor his psyche fix his destiny. According to Gerth and Mills: [20]

> He creates his own destiny as he responds to his experienced situation and both his situation and his experiences of it are complicated products of the historical epoch which he enacts. That is why he does not create his own destiny as an individual but as a member of society. Only within the limits of his place in an historical epoch can man as an individual shape himself.

In received tradition, the hemisphere of the public has been assigned to the male and the hemisphere of the private to the female. Each sex has become a symbol for its territory. The conflict between them can thus be seen as reflection of the longing of each to be part of the other's sphere, to link the public with the private in our schizoid world, to embrace the whole of life. Buckminster Fuller once commented that thinking is the result of removing irrelevancies, a few at a time, selectively, until only the relevant remains. In our struggle to encompass the future, we may discover the ultimate relevance in the words of Rilke, as he foreshadows the dream: [27]

> And perhaps the sexes are more related than we think, and the great renewal of the world will perhaps consist in this, that man and maid, freed of all false feeling and aversion, will seek each other not as opposites, but as brother and sister, as neighbors, and will come together as *human beings,* in order simply, seriously and patiently to bear in common the difficult generation that is their burden.

References

1. Galbraith, J. K. 1966. Labor, leisure and the new class. *In* The New Technology and Human Values. J. G. Burke, Ed. : 183. Wadsworth. Belmont, Calif.
2. Wiener, N. 1950. The Human Use of Human Beings. : 162. Houghton Mifflin Co. Boston, Mass.
3. National Commission on Technology, Automation, and Economic Progress. 1966. Technology and the American Dream. **1:** xiii.
4. Watson, Jr., T. J. 1970. Speech delivered to the Bond Club of New York; quoted in I. F. Stone's Bi-Weekly. January 26.
5. Fein, L. 1965. Datamation Magazine. Jan.
6. Arendt, H. 1958. The Human Condition. : 36–37. University of Chicago Press, Chicago, Ill.
7. Sinheimer, R. 1967. End of the beginning. Bull. Atomic Scientists. Feb.
8. Fuller, B. 1963. Ideas and Integrities. : 72. Prentice-Hall, Englewood Cliffs, N.J.
9. Piel, G. 1963. The advent of abundance. Bull. Atomic Scientists. June.
10. Piel, G. 1961. Consumers of Abundance. Center for the Study of Democratic Institutions. Santa Barbara, Calif.
11. Hoagland, H. 1967. Biology, brains and insight. Columbia Univ. Forum, Summer : 29.
12. Brzezinski, Z. 1967. America in the Technetronic Age. School of International Affairs, Columbia University. New York, N.Y.
13. Ellul, J. 1967. The technological Society. : 328. Alfred A. Knopf. New York, N.Y.

14. BRONOWSKI, J. 1951. The Common Sense of Science. : 134. Harvard University Press. Cambridge, Mass.
15. EHRLICH, P. 1969. The Center Magazine (Nov.). Center for the Study of Democratic Institutions. Santa Barbara, Calif.
16. RABINOWITCH, E. 1969. Responsibility of scientists in our age. Bull. Atomic Scientists. Nov.
17. YATES, R. 1961. Revolutionary Road. : 120. Little, Brown & Co. Boston, Mass.
18. MOYNIHAN, D. P. 1965. Employment, income, and the Negro family. Daedalus. Fall: 746.
19. ELIOT, G. 1860. Mill on the Floss. (1960. : 415. Dodd, Mead & Co. New York, N.Y.)
20. GERTH, H. & C. W. MILLS. 1953. Character and Social Structure. Harcourt, Brace & World. New York, N.Y.
21. THE NEW YORK TIMES. 1967. Two Hundred Million (Editorial). November 21:46.
22. KLEIN, V. 1949. The Feminine Character. : 9. International Universities Press. New York, N.Y.
23. SINCLAIR, A. 1965. The Better Half. : 347. Harper & Row. New York, N.Y.
24. WOMEN'S BUREAU. 1970. Why Women Work. GPO 886-801.
25. BOGUSLAW, R. 1968. The power of systems and the systems of power. *In* The Triple Revolution. R. Perrucci & M. Pilisuk, Eds. : 359. Little, Brown & Co. Boston, Mass.
26. WOMEN'S BUREAU. 1966. Fact Sheet on Women in Professional and Technical Positions. WB 67-164.
27. RILKE, R. M. 1934. Letters to a Young Poet. : 38. W. W. Norton. New York, N.Y.

DISCUSSION

Ruth B. Kundsin, Sc.D., *Moderator*

REEVES: The backdrop for my paper is, essentially, the series of revolutions that are simultaneously taking place, that we are trying to understand and adjust to. I have termed them "transcending the given in the environment," and "transcending the given in the species." I have listed the revolutions, but my chief concern, of course, was the historical invisibility of women in relation to social change. It is always assumed that the history of the species is the history of man, and women somehow also came along. And so, when there is a discussion of woman's role, it is usually in terms of first person singular, and the external vectors that bear on her personal situation are more or less forgotten.

I wanted particularly to relate some of these vectors to the woman, so I have listed the major changes and then developed a male model, and then a female model, and finally tried to relate the changes to the models. I also wanted to point up the relationship of the backdrop and the models—the male model and the female model —and to recognize Turner's point, that even in this apparent freedom of the male to do what he wishes in this society, to play the role he wishes, he, too, is bound up by the new *Gesellschaft* which has taken the place of *Gemeinschaft,* so that alienation and lack of function beset him, too.

CHESSLER: I agree with your final point that women have always worked, and that production takes place even in a primitive economy, and it takes place in the household. As economies get more complex, of course, some production begins to take place in the market. Through specialization, households provide services that cause production to take place in the market, and then households obtain in the market things they had formerly produced at home. This is most obvious with food production, some of which no longer takes place in the home, although the final cooking does.

It happens that much of the female part of production has remained in the household. It is not clear that this will be true in the future, and I think the statistics indicate that women are participating more and more in the labor force. They also indicate that more and more women are choosing to go into the market to provide services, and then with the earnings from these services to buy in the market things that they had formerly produced at home. Thus, a restaurant meal is a substitute for a home-cooked meal, and a vacuum cleaner is a substitute for spending more time sweeping.

You have also raised the question of automation and cybernation. On that point, I am afraid that, as an economist, I must disagree with you rather strenuously. In economic theory there is no reason, no matter how much we improve machinery and the ability of machinery to do man's work, why this will cause any reduction in this demand for some kind of labor, although particular jobs may be phased out. For example, I don't notice any great demand for blacksmiths now, but on the other hand more people than ever are engaged in the production of vehicles for transportation. As long as people are required to direct the machines, there is no particular reason why there will be any reduction in the demand for labor in the market.

Of course, as Mrs. Reeves has pointed out, even if production by human beings ceases completely, the only reason for the production is consumption, and, therefore, there will have to be payments to human beings in order for them to consume what the machine has produced. People will continue to consume, and some different mechanism will have to be made for payments to households in order for them to consume.

In point of fact, if cybernation were causing machines to replace human beings, this would have had certain noticeable and detectible effects, particularly in productivity statistics. Workers who are employed would have become more productive. No such change has taken place. The annual increase in productivity has remained remarkably constant, dating back as far as we have records, which would be to the mid-19th century, or perhaps the last third of the 19th century. Thus, there is a strong factual argument for saying that cybernation is not a threat to the labor force. Whatever happens, however, there is no particular reason to believe that women who want to participate in production outside of the home, or men who want to participate in production outside of the home, will have any difficulty finding an opportunity to do so.

MERRIAM: This last point on the freedom and mobility to go out to work reminds me of the old wheeze about how the rich and the poor are equally free to sleep in the beautiful outdoors under the bridge: the rich may, but the poor must. In the past, women have had the disability of being responsible for the family unit and therefore have not had the freedom and mobility to go out to work, primarily because of child care and the household.

I find myself in strong disagreement with some of the comments that have been made about economics, about the possibility that our present economic system is going to be able to provide jobs for all, and that automation and cybernation represent no threat. Where have I been? Have I been living on a different planet these past few years when I have heard cries of alarm from economists other than Mr. Chessler, and from labor leaders and from all sorts of authorities who have been upset about this? I am not an economist so I can't furnish the statistics about this, but it seems logical to me that, from the theoretical point of view, if you have one person operating machines rather than the 20 or the 2,000 who formerly operated them, something is awry!

REEVES: I did not mean to imply that it has been clearly enunciated by either one school of thought or another that this will be our path. Nobody really knows yet what is going to happen, because there are so many variables. Our plea is, then, for a large-scale study, which has not been attempted thus far; if we are wrong in our optimism, the hazards are enormous. Furthermore, if, in fact, there will be sufficient jobs, and one can arrange the necessary shifts, then even these shifts have to be planned. We have to know whether people are needed. We are teaching the poor to punch cards, but we don't need punched cards any more. We are teaching certain skills that are no longer marketable, and nobody is very clear on what the marketable skills are. My plea was not meant to discuss the pros and cons of the future; my plea was that we address ourselves to the need to know what we are about.

NEEDED RESEARCH ON CURRENT POPULATION TRENDS

William Petersen, Ph.D.

Robert Lazarus Professor of Social Demography
The Ohio State University
Columbus, Ohio

When Robert Lynd asked the question, "Knowledge for what?" he himself answered: to bring about desired changes in our institutions. "The responsibility of social science," he wrote, "is to keep everlastingly challenging the present with the questions: but what is it that we human beings want, and what things would have to be done, in what ways and in what sequence, in order to change the present so as to achieve this?"[16] A generation ago, when Lynd published this deviant manifesto, it was a socialist's response to a culture dominated (as he saw it) by false, conservative, and antihumanist values. Like so many other originally radical proposals, this one has become a cliché. The "establishment" that now governs the distribution of research funds in the social disciplines, whether government agencies or the major private foundations, typically sets "relevance" as a principled criterion of a proposal's worth. A scientist who would like to study a matter of basic importance to his discipline, thus, is often constrained to disguise his absorption in fundamentals with a professed interest in the instant solution of pressing social problems.

For a time, the differentiation between "basic" and "applied" research seriously hampered the development of the physical sciences, but today this distinction is sharply drawn only by those who know little of the subject. In the social disciplines, where our ignorance of basic processes is thorough and all-encompassing, we have taken over this philistine dichotomy and applied it with a sometimes ruthless fervor. Paradoxically, my main argument against so-called "relevant" research is that it so often lacks pertinence. Unless we learn some of the underlying facts as yet unknown, and unless we can study more proximate data in an environment that is not supercharged with emotion, the expenditure of time and money—no matter how much—is hardly likely to effect either increased knowledge *or* social reform.

The transformation of the quest for knowledge has affected research in all social disciplines, but in none possibly so much as in demography. A quarter of a century ago, a demographer was a relative isolate, cut off even from fellow sociologists or economists by the technical skills of which he was master, and with hardly any contacts with a public generally uninterested in his work. In the United States, demographers of that day were, in extraordinarily high proportion, Southerners; the reason, one presumes, is that it was feasible to study the relation of face to social structure only within a discipline perceived as completely removed from everyday politics. Today, the demographer is becoming a kind of social worker, fully involved in political disputes peripheral to the discipline as it was once defined. The skills that used to mark a member of the profession are now of less importance.* More and more, competence is defined by social concern.

The general lack in population research today is a concern with the discipline itself, with a sharpening of its tools and thus a refinement of its insights.† But it will save space and improve the debate if we accept the main premise of the Lyndites—that research in population should be focused on how to limit family size—and enquire how successfully this orientation has been in realizing the desired goal.

THE DETERMINANTS OF FAMILY SIZE

In the classical analysis of why fertility declined in Western countries, this process was taken to be the effect of a basic social-economic transformation.[1, 29] Industrialization opened up new posts in the top and middle ranks of developing economies, and those with the lightest family responsibilities could compete most successfully for these better positions. The traditional family system was fundamentally altered, also, when the females who had been restricted to the single social role of wife-mother could find jobs and sometimes meaningful careers outside the home. Once the new middle class led the way, strata lower on the social scale emulated its life-style and adopted the small family as their own norm. In short, the independent variables—occupation, education, income—were typically indicators of one's place in the class structure. Other indicators—religion, rural residence, national minority—marked various types of insulation from the dynamic influences of modernization. The analysts' intent, thus, was to demonstrate both positively and negatively how certain structural and institutional changes resulted in a general decline in fertility.

In this classical analysis, writers generally pointed out the effect on fertility of inefficient contraceptives, or of the ignorance of those that were available, or of moral inhibitions against using them. But in every account with historical depth, the author could hardly escape the facts that fertility declines began long before modern contraceptives were invented, that the average family size fell most in some of the countries (such as France and the United States) with the strongest religious and legal bars to birth control, that when the will to cut fertility was strong enough some means of achieving this end was always found. In a biological context, the present emphasis on the physiology of reproduction, and thus on improved means of controlling conception, is praiseworthy; but for sociologists the determinants of fertility cannot be reduced to this

* The president of the principal organization to fund research in population is a specialist in communication; the head of the population institute at America's most prestigious university is an oceanographer; and dozens of others who lack even elementary training in the field guide research on population issues.

† At the 1968 meeting of the Population Association of America, to cite a striking example, there was not a single paper on mortality. Whether this omission reflected the predilections of those who organized the sessions or the interests of the participants—influenced by the trend in the discipline and, more specifically, by the sources of research funds—is of no consequence. The point is that, in several respects, the analysis of mortality is the most advanced branch of demography, and that at least some of the attempts to develop professional competence further might well have been concentrated there.

single factor. As long as family size depends on the will of the two parents, the most efficient, cheapest, and esthetically least objectionable contraceptive means is no more than an instrument by which their purpose can be realized.

In the classical model, finally, the number of children that parents desired or expected constituted an unanalyzed variable, intermediate between the institutional constraints that shaped such attitudes and the consequent behavior patterns. Today, on the contrary, most fertility research relates more to attitudes than to institutions, more to psychological than to sociological theories. This new mode of analysis has added immeasurably to our knowledge, particularly concerning non-Western countries, of whose populations the larger part ("the peasantry") had usually been beyond the reach of earlier probes. But in Western countries, with data on fertility far superior to those on attitudes, the shift to the latter has incurred an inevitable cost in the quality of analysis.[28]

No knowledgeable person doubts that what I have termed the classical model fundamentally explains the historical trend in advanced countries; but how to apply this explanation to present population policy, particularly in underdeveloped areas, is something of a puzzle. The prime mover in the model is industrialization, which affords new opportunities for social mobility, which, in turn, motivate the more ambitious to reduce their family responsibilities. But if industrialization is significantly blocked by, among other things, a population growth far more rapid than in the past Western experience, then what other factors can governments bring into play to strengthen (or, in the worst cases, generate) an antinatalist trend?

The Family-Planning Tactic

Current antinatalist policy typically ignores the underlying institutional structure and concentrates on two intermediate variables, the availability of contraceptives and the attitude toward family size. This orientation is based in part on the methods of market research applied to a new type of consumer demand. Advertising methods effective in inducing persons to buy a certain brand of a commodity, it is assumed, will also bring about changes in attitudes embedded in family norms, religious beliefs, and other solidly based values. In part, the policy derives also from the beliefs that most demographers held in the 1930s—that the general pressure of modern society was entirely antinatalist; that remaining pockets of high fertility, consequently, were the result of ignorance of contraceptives or of a moral or monetary reluctance to use them; and that, because these anomalous sectors were disappearing with continued education and secularization, Western populations were in "incipient decline."[18, 19] That the postwar "baby boom" forced demographers to revise this overall analysis should have raised questions about policy recommendations based in part on the earlier prognosis.

A third reason for adopting the family-planning tactic is that it is perhaps the easiest among possible alternatives. Whether the criterion is "political viability," "administrative feasibility," "economic capability," or "ethical acceptability," an antinatalist program that combines voluntary control of family-size ("maternal care") with education for family planning ranks relatively high.[2] The convenience, however, is irrelevant once the method has proved itself to be ineffective. A cheap but ineffective nostrum that affronts no one and is easy to administer cures no disease.

The advocacy of planned parenthood has been effective in cutting fertility only where the social-economic environment itself generated antinatalist attitudes—e.g., in the general populations of Western countries, a few atypical small countries transitional to economic development (Taiwan, South Korea, Puerto Rico, etc.), and the minuscule westernized elites of the major underdeveloped countries. Among the vast masses of India, Pakistan, Indonesia, the Middle East, Negro Africa, and most of Latin America, the family planning tactic can claim no victories. In many cases, it is true, the programs are barely under way. The crucial test is India, where a 20-year program that included several contraceptive means in a variety of social settings has failed completely to reduce the country's fertility.[21] Another test, with less conclusive results, relates to such subpopulations as lower-class Negroes in the United States, whose response to antinatalist propaganda and free birth-control clinics has generally been disappointing.

The family-planning tactic, typically ineffective in realizing its goal, has had a number of ancillary consequences, most of them quite unfortunate for both the discipline of demography and the efforts to reduce the world's birth rate:

1. The process of bringing another generation into being is of legitimate concern both to the two potential parents and to the state, which acts as the guardian of the society's general interest. As a democrat, I believe that parents should be free to choose whether or not to have a child; but as a sociologist, I know that this freedom of choice is exercised in a social context, generally pronatalist, of laws, norms, accepted practices, and so on, any of which might be altered without restricting the parents' freedom. The family-planning tactic, by its implicit assumption that the sum of parents' desires will always constitute good social policy, has seriously obscured the main dilemma to be resolved, which is how to effect a population policy when each family has precisely the number of children the parents desire and this level of fertility effects too great an increase in numbers.[7] In underdeveloped countries generally, according to the results of a large number of attitude surveys, the ideal family of more than half the respondents had four or more children.[3] Given the low or falling death rates in underdeveloped countries and their population structures favoring high fertility, such attitudes spell demographic disaster even if every woman were enabled to plan her family completely.

2. The effort to change attitudes by mass propaganda has not usually succeeded, and in many places a frontal attack has been politically impermissible. Thus, so-called attitude surveys have often constituted "a relatively noncontroversial way of initiating activity in population control in countries where direct efforts are not possible."[24] The reason that the first canon of scientific research prohibits such a combination of objective investigation with purposeful social policy is that the results are entirely ambiguous. From a survey of this kind, the "action researcher" can know neither what the attitudes of the population are nor how effective his efforts to change them have been.

3. A family-planning project designed both to reduce fertility and to test certain means of achieving this goal tempts every researcher to exaggerate his success. Overall appraisals by responsible demographers have sometimes been wildly optimistic:[4] "The world population crisis is a phenomenon of the 20th century, and will be largely if not entirely a matter of history when humanity moves into the 21st century."[5] At a time when all the professionals interested

in population policy ought to be thinking of how to improve the present inadequate means of controlling fertility, some have been diverted into rehashing anti-Malthusian arguments.

In sum: Because research in fertility is dominated by policy considerations, and since "policy" generally means an orientation toward family-planning programs of the current type, in fact the research as a whole has been less "relevant" than would have been a continuation of the objective search for understanding of how social determinants of all types affect family size. It is manifestly not desirable to wait for economic development to stimulate a reduction in the rate of population growth. The question is whether one can more effectively hurry this process not by attempting to change attitudes, as at present, but by making appropriate alterations in social factors underlying the attitudes. Obviously, an attempt to change institutions is politically and socially more complex than any effort merely to propagandize for a goal that increasingly various governments have had to accept. But if the methods that worked in Taiwan do not work in India, for example, we should know what other means are feasible to reduce the rate of population growth.

Areas of Proposed Research

If the rationale outlined here is correct, present family-planning programs are in a blind alley; thus, all the research tied to such programs, however successful in its own terms, cannot lead us out of that blind alley. The analytical framework that Davis and Blake [8] used in their well known paper on social structure and fertility is useful in organizing the discussion of possible research efforts. It follows the order of the physiological steps from coitus to viable birth, analyzing for various types of society the institutional constraints to fertility at each stage. The purpose here, of course, is to go beyond such a typology and suggest what modifications in institutions, feasible on other grounds, might result in greater constraints.[27] The following topics are not intended to cover the full range of research that might be fostered, but only to indicate some of the important and interesting subjects on which our knowledge is still too slight to lay a sound foundation for population policy.

Illegitimate Births. These constitute a sizable percentage of the fertility in some portions of Latin America and among lower-class Negroes in the United States, among other groups. The literature on the subject is often emotional,[22] partly because conclusions must often be based on partial and inaccurate data. It would seem that in Latin America consensual unions have fewer children than married couples; in the United States, more. The first task is to gather data from the existent literature, perhaps to distinguish several types of illegitimacy, and to indicate researchable propositions that would clarify the issues.

Socialization in Family Norms. Little systematic work has been done to analyze how persons in a modern secular society acquire ideas about the appropriate age for marriage, the correct number of children, and similar key variables in the analysis of fertility; even preliminary research on several such questions would bring enlightenment. Antinatalist sentiments, I have argued, cannot be effectively disseminated through advertising media, but is a more intensive inculcation in modernist ideas not likely to be more effective? What might be the effect of a period in the army, or such a counterpart as the CCC (Civilian

Conservation Corps), on the family norms, particularly of persons from high-fertility sectors of the population? Perhaps the best place to analyze this relation would be Israel, where military service is in principle required of all young persons, both male and female; the army is used not only for narrowly military purposes but also to help the recruits' acculturation to the country's modernist aspirations. Because Israel's general policy is pronatalist, it can be assumed that this is followed in the army's socialization; but even so, according to a reasonable hypothesis, oriental Jews who are drawn somewhat away from their traditional families have fewer children subsequently than those of the same background who, for one reason or another, do not undergo this training.

Family Structure. Family sociology, in spite of its usual heavy emphasis on dating practices and marital happiness, could manifestly lead to a fuller understanding of fertility.[23] In particular, some of the more recent work in comparative perspective (for example, an as yet unpublished monograph by Aaron Cicourel on the relation between structure and size in the Argentine family) can offer many new clues to policy-makers seeking to control fertility. One especially difficult point is the contrast between joint and nuclear families in their effect on the typical number of children. *A priori,* an institution that assigns the responsibility for child-rearing to a group larger than the two-parent unit facilitates reproduction as soon as it is physiologically possible,[8] but the evidence from Indian studies is contradictory,[17] partly because it is not always clear whether "joint family" means joint residence or shared responsibility. The relevance of this dilemma to the American scene relates to what Sussman called "the help pattern"[25, 26] through which socially immature persons are able to marry and have children. What is needed is to gather whatever data exist on student marriages, for instance, to suggest further research that would be useful, and to make tentative policy recommendations concerning institutional arrangements that facilitate breeding by adolescents.

Nonmarriage. One of the main means of restricting fertility in the Western world used to be the stem family, which ideally restricted marriage to one male out of any set of brothers.[13] Among cohorts of white American females whose fecund periods fell between 1888 and 1917, one in ten never married.[12] In recent decades, however, this proportion has fallen off sharply. Three kinds of research related to this topic would be useful: (*1*) the nonmarried as a population, their personal and social characteristics, and what institutional arrangements facilitate their adjustment to their statistically abnormal situation; (*2*) the social pressures in American society to marry, at what age the norm of inevitable marriage is absorbed, and differential resistance among various social groups; and (*3*) legal discrimination against the unmarried in taxes, conscription, etc., on a cross-cultural basis.

Childless Marriages. During the depression of the 1930s, one out of every five ever-married women had no children at all, in many instances obviously by choice.[21] This extraordinarily high proportion was due partly, but only partly, to economic privation, and the subsequent decline in childless marriage, thus, to present affluence. But the more general incentives to reduce the size of the family always apply most strongly to the first child, which costs parents the most in money, effort, and loss of freedom; thus, the proportion of childless marriages had risen steadily from the last quarter of the 19th century to this high point in the 1930s. Three lines of research, parallel to those noted in previously noted, would be useful: (*1*) childless couples as a population, the personal and social characteristics of those who choose to have no children, and what institutional arrangements facilitate their adjustment to their statistically abnormal situation; (*2*) the social pressures in American society that set two children as the minimum permissible per family, the age at which this norm is absorbed, and the differential resistance to this pressure among various social groups; and (*3*) legal discrimination against childless couples in taxes, conscription, etc. on a cross-cultural basis.

Age at Marriage. The nonmarriage of a portion of the adult population was associated in the Western tradition with a relatively late age at marriage of the others.[13] In the modern world, the pattern is clearest in Ireland, where marital fertility has already been very high; delayed marriage and nonmarriage respectively represent, in the absence of acceptable substitutes, Ireland's relatively less and more stringent means of birth control. In the United States, however, the meaning of the age at marriage is far from clear. The long-term decline during the 20th century may have been due partly to the fact that, with better contraceptives, one could enjoy marital life without the risk of immediate conceptions. But since many early marriages are followed by planned early first and second births, the decline in age at marriage may be partly the consequence of the trend, noted previously, toward the acceptance of family responsibilities by various types of broader kin. It would be useful to compile the data on age at marriage, which are often confusing and generally relate to far-too-heterogeneous populations, and to interpret the upward or downward shifts in various subgroups.

Family Subsidies. David Glass's book,[11] which concluded that the pronatalist effect of payments for children was generally nil, may still be close to definitive for the cases he examined, but its conclusions should not be extended indiscriminately. In the European countries he analyzed, payments were generally instituted only after a considerable decline in fertility had taken place, and they were expected to compensate fully for the continuing antinatalist pressure in those societies. Where fertility is still relatively high, reflecting the overall pronatalist effect of legal and institutional norms, family subsidies may strongly reinforce these other incentives.[20] It would be a valuable addition to Glass's analysis to review the literature that supplements it, particularly on the more recent period and on countries (such as the Netherlands and Canada) that he passed over. More directly pertinent would be an analysis of welfare payments in the United States (as well as the guaranteed annual income that Moynihan and others have advocated) as half-disguised functional substitutes for family subsidies, in order to determine what effect they probably have on the fertility of the recipients.

Antinatalist Payments. In various publications, Enke[9] has suggested that the benefit that accrues to the Indian economy from each nonbirth should be shared with the individual responsible. Contributors to several economic journals have both discussed this idea and offered cost-benefit analyses of population controls of other types. It would be useful especially for sociologists to compile a bibliography of these analyses and to compare the premises and conclusions of the various authors. Research is also needed to link antinatalist subsidies to the theory relating social mobility and fertility, which for Western nations in the 19th century has been firmly established as the most plausible explanation of the inverse correlation between income and family size.

Working Wives. The most direct mode of analyzing the effect of alternatives to child-bearing, it would seem, is to compare the number of children of otherwise comparable women who work away from home with those who do not. In fact, the comparison is not so clear-cut, and the conclusions from various studies are contradictory. One reason for the confusion, it would seem, is that pioneer feminists in any country are forced to make a hard choice, either family *or* job; typically, however, with a change of laws and social norms, adaptive institutions in both areas (creches to permit mothers to take jobs, for example, and part-time positions to accommodate mothers) make it possible, and even increasingly easy, to combine both roles. It would be useful to review the literature in order to test this hypothesis, and, if it seems to be substantiated, to criticize policy suggestions in terms of their probable antinatalist effect. Second, one needs to review laws and studies on the social norms that in the United States and comparable nations discriminate against females, or against married women in particular, and reinforce their reluctance to forego parenthood for an alternative career.

Summary

According to most analyses of the long-term trend in fertility, birth rates declined mainly in response to the broad structural changes in each society. Attitudes favoring smaller families derived from such overall transformations; and, once the will to reduce fertility existed, any contraceptive means, even if not efficient by present standards, sufficed to bring about sizable declines. Even so, present efforts to reduce fertility and the research to back them up have both concentrated, paradoxically, on attitudes and contraceptive means. According to Blake: [3]

> Population growth is clearly impeding economic development in many poor countries, rather than itself being reduced through the modernization process. Family-planning programs are not lowering birth-rates among the mass of the people in such countries, and their failure is understandable in view of their superficiality. We are thus led to ask whether additional types of direct action for reducing family-size cannot be incorporated into population policy. In answer, we have taken the position that the limitation of alternatives is more a function of insufficient thought and analysis than actual circumscription of choice.

There is need for a stronger program of research in how to facilitate changes in the institutional structure that would be antinatalist in their effect.

A number of topics on which such research would be feasible and useful has been listed. On some of these topics there has been a certain amount of prior research (e.g., age at marriage and the effect of family subsidies on fertility); but it would be useful to review the literature, to list those propositions on which there is consensus, to suggest what research is required to resolve disagreements, and to apply the findings to related problems. On other topics there has been little or no research specifically relating the factor to fertility (e.g., the characteristics of persons who do not marry and of couples who choose not to have children); here research would have to begin with gathering data from whatever sources there may be and designing research from which firmer conclusions might be drawn.

Abstract theory on the social determinants of family-size underlies, at least implicitly, both policy decisions and the research to bolster them. In the past several decades, many demographers have criticized the premises of the transition theory or in other ways have sought a basis for a fresh start.[3, 6, 8, 10, 14, 15, 27, 30]

In the considerable rethinking stimulated by the postwar revival of Western fertility and the failure to reduce the fertility of many nonWestern countries, it is reasonable to assume, lie many researchable propositions that must be brought to the surface if they are to lead to new policy suggestions.

References

1. Banks, J. A. 1954. Prosperity and Parenthood: A Study of Family Planning among the Victorian Middle Classes. Routledge and Kagan Paul. London, England.
2. Berelson, B. 1969. Beyond family planning. Studies in Family Planning **38.**
3. Blake, J. 1965. Demographic science and the redirection of population policy. J. Chronic Dis. **18:** 1181–1200.
4. Bogue, D. J. 1964. The demographic breakthrough: From projection to control. Population Index **30:** 449–454.
5. Bogue, D. J. 1967. The end of the population explosion. Public Interest **7.**
6. Carlsson, G. 1966. The decline of fertility: Innovation or adjustment process. Population Studies **20:** 149–174.
7. Davis, K. 1967. Population policy: Will current programs succeed? Science **158:** 730–739.
8. Davis, K. & J. Blake. 1956. Social structure and fertility: An analytical framework. Econ. Devel. Cultural Change **4:** 211–235.
9. Enke, S. 1960. Government bonuses for smaller families. Population Rev. **4:** 47–50.
10. Freedman, R. 1961–1962. The sociology of human fertility: A trend report and bibliography. Current Sociol. **10–11**(2).
11. Glass, D. V. 1940. Population Policies and Movements in Europe. Clarendon. Oxford, England.
12. Grabill, W. H., C. W. Kiser & P. K. Whelpton. 1958. The Fertility of American Women. John Wiley Sons. New York, N.Y.
13. Hajnal, J. 1965. European marriage patterns in perspective. *In* Population in History. D. V. Glass & D. E. C. Eversley, Eds.: 101–143. Aldine Press. Chicago, Ill.
14. Heer, D. M. 1966. Economic development and fertility. Demography **3:** 423–444.
15. Hill, R. 1968. Research on human fertility: Range in methodological stance by participating disciplines. Int. Soc. Sci. J. **20:** 226–262.
16. Lynd, R. S. 1964. Knowledge for What? The Place of Social Science in American Culture. : 250. Grove Press—Evergreen. New York, N.Y.
17. Nag, M. 1962. Factors Affecting Human Fertility in Nonindustrial Societies: A Cross-cultural Study. Yale University Press. New Haven, Conn.
18. Notestein, F. 1945. Population—The long view. *In* Food for the World, T. W. Schultz, Ed. : 35–37. University of Chicago Press. Chicago, Ill.
19. Notestein, F. W. The population of the world in the year 2000. J. Amer. Stat. Ass. **45:** 335–349.
20. Petersen, W. 1964. The Politics of Population: : 152–165. Doubleday. Garden City, N.Y.
21. Petersen, W. 1969. Population. 2nd edit. : 500 & 613–619. Macmillan & Co. New York, N.Y.
22. Rainwater, L. & W. L. Yancey. 1967. The Moynihan Report and the Politics of Controversy. Massachusetts Institute of Technology Press. Cambridge, Mass.
23. Rossi, A. S. 1968. Transition to parenthood. J. Marriage and Family **30:** 26–39.
24. Stycos, J. M. 1965. Opinions of Latin American intellectuals on population problems and birth control. Ann. Amer. Acad. Pol. Soc. Sci. **360:** 11–26.

25. Sussman, M. B. 1953. The help pattern in the middle-class family. Amer. Sociol. Rev. **18:** 22–28.
26. Sussman, M. B. 1959. The isolated nuclear family: Fact or fiction? Social Problems **6:** 333–340.
27. Tien, H. Y. 1968. The intermediate variables, social structure, and fertility change: A critique. Demography **5:** 138–157.
28. Westoff, C. F., E. G. Mishler & E. I. Kelly. 1957. Preferences in size of family and eventual fertility twenty years after. Amer. J. Sociol. **62:** 491–497.
29. Wrong, D. H. 1958. Trends in class fertility in western nations. Canad. J. Econ. Pol. Sci. **24:** 216–229.
30. Yaukey, D. 1969. On theorizing about fertility. Amer. Sociologist **4:** 100–104.

Discussion *

Ruth B. Kundsin, Sc. D., *Moderator*

Polgar: First of all, the New Orleans experience is by no means the only one in which it has been shown that poor black people do take advantage of family-planning services.† Misra, a student of Bogue's, studied attitudes of black men and, contrary to some suggestions, found that black men are, on the whole, as interested in family-planning services as black women. They do have certain objections, as do most men, or some men more than others (we don't really know), to withdrawal as a contraceptive technique. There may be cross-Atlantic, Muslim-Christian, and other cultural differences on this subject. I am bringing up these studies because of Petersen's statement to the effect that another test of family-planning "with less conclusive results, relates to such subpopulations as lower-class Negroes in the United States, whose response to antinatalist propaganda and free birth-control clinics has generally been disappointing." I reject that particular statement.

Milner: I think it is out of date.

Polgar: More dramatically, it shows him to be ignorant. This ignorance is extremely fascinating in view of his earlier remark that anybody who has not been trained in demography doesn't know anything about this field and can only be a social worker, or words to that effect. This attitude leads to a kind of "demographic imperialism" between the United States and other countries, and further, an internal imperialism of man against woman, and of white against black. I think that the demographer's mythology includes a certain number of fundamental errors, one of which is the assumption that mortality has been very high throughout human history, and that fertility has been pushed by various kinds of social institutions to be equally high or higher, because otherwise man was at risk of dying out. This assumption is, according to anthropological evidence, completely erroneous.

The second thing demographers say that leads to some of these erroneous conclusions is that the crucial thing about which we should be concerned is family-size norms. Professor Newman's paper points out that there are "spacing" practices in practically all cultures, but there are very few practices concerned with family-size norms. I put it to you that the advent of a family-size norm is a cultural development that occurs only after reasonably effective contraceptive methods become available. It does not happen before. Here I disagree somewhat with those people who are in a big hurry to downgrade technology. I think that technology has to be kept in its place, but it cannot be completely dismissed.

The third point of the demographers that ties in with this issue is the matter of motivation. This particular error is very prominent in the Petersen paper. They say, in effect: Here is this large-size family norm, and people are motivated to try to achieve it. So in order for us to do anything about the population problem, we have

* Dr. Petersen was not present during this discussion.

† See the Beasley digest, pp. 827–830.

to counteract these large-family motivations. People do not have large-family motivations; people have specific motivations to have children for particular kinds of social functions. Again, as others have repeatedly pointed out, the matter of decreasing mortality is of extreme importance in this connection.

Just as a footnote here to the question whether family planning should be made part of comprehensive health care or should be offered separately, my view is this: When there are health facilities available in a country, family-planning services should certainly be made part of them. Perhaps there should also be some other channels, such as, for example, through the mails. But when, in many countries, there are no adequate health facilities in rural areas, one should not wait just because this principle of comprehensive care is a good one. One should not wait until all doctors are fully trained before starting family-planning services. These services should be made available to help people achieve existing social norms for wider spacing, for preserving the woman's self, and even to obtain children through fertility drugs.

I simply cannot let such statements in Petersen's paper as the following stand without comment: "A cheap but ineffective nostrum that affronts no one and is easy to administer cures no disease." I think that the difference between abortion as obtained in Chile—some of you may have seen the movie "Abort," and if you haven't, you should—and an abortion as obtained, for example, in Yugoslavia or Japan, is very great. He continues: "The crucial test is India, where a 20-year program that included several contraceptive means in a variety of social settings, etc." They have had a positive *policy* in India for 20 years, but to call what they have had until recently a "program" is a travesty on words. What they have now, as I have previously indicated, is dominated by demographic thinking that one should change people's family-size norms. Thus, they are having physicians meet targets and providing payment incentives for sterilization, and so on. This approach leads to very bad programs, quite contrary to this comprehensive health concept, even though they do have, at least in some areas, quite adequate health facilities. This is an important point, because it shows a general attitude which can be tied up in this context with male chauvinism. In other contexts, one might call it racism or some other term.

At another point, Petersen talks about family subsidies, and like some other demographers, he is much opposed to a negative income tax and to family subsidies, because he thinks that will influence irresponsible sectors of society to have more children. On this point, he knows his literature up to about 30 years ago; he doesn't know the more recent literature. Vincent Whitney, a demographer at the University of Pennsylvania who has analyzed the Netherlands, Canada, United States, and has evaluated other recent data, has found that subsidies for children do not increase the birth rate. Alvin Shore also found exactly the same thing.

FAVA: I am not speaking as a demographer, but as a sociologist. I think Dr. Polgar missed the point of what Will Petersen was trying to say. We have been talking very much in medical terms. But we are, after all, supposed to be dealing with the two-child family in terms of the role of women in society. It seems to me that this interest takes us away from medicine, and makes medicine a peripheral aspect. All the technology involved in it leads us back into the social sciences. I would like to quote one of Petersen's summary paragraphs, in which he begins to indicate why demography is part of the social sciences and why it is not a part of medicine per se.

> According to most analyses of the long-term trend in fertility, birth rates declined mainly in response to the broad structural changes in each society. Attitudes favoring smaller families derived from such overall transformations; and, once the will to reduce fertility existed, any contraceptive means, even if not efficient by present standards, sufficed to bring about sizable declines.

I might add, parenthetically, that even as a nondemographer, it is well known that the birth rates declined beginning about the middle of the 19th century in the industrialized countries, and this was long before we had modern, efficient means of contraception. Petersen continues: "Even so, present efforts to reduce fertility and research to back them up have both concentrated paradoxically on attitudes and contraceptive means."

Perhaps our reaction is a very American one. We are very involved in gimmicks and technology, and it is very easy for us, I think, to reduce the kind of issue we are dealing with to technology. I don't think this will work. We have had efficient contraception for a long time. It is not something that has necessarily gone hand in hand with smaller family sizes in the United States. We are all acquainted with the swings up and down in the birthrates in the United States, and they have been very sharp. The fact is that changes in birthrates in the United States have not necessarily been on the part of women who are unacquainted with contraception. On the contrary, after World War II, the baby boom was concentrated mostly in that category of women who were highly educated and highly motivated to control their families. It turned out they were the ones having more of the babies. There was also an increase among less-educated and lower-income women, which has, fortunately, declined. I think our discussion should come back to some of the sociological, and to some extent psychological, aspects of the topics we are dealing with.

I would like to quote several other sentences from Petersen's paper to indicate something along these lines that we might consider. In his section on socialization in family norms, he says: "Little systematic work has been done to analyze how persons in a modern secular society acquire ideas about the appropriate age for marriage,"—there is a birth-control device for you!—"the correct number of children, and similar key variables in the analysis of fertility; even preliminary research on several such questions would bring enlightenment." Some of us should be concerned with such questions as: what are the kind of supports in society that influence women to decide not to marry, or to have fewer children, and that make it structurally possible for them to work outside the home even if they are married or have children? These are the kinds of things I think Will Petersen's paper is all about, rather than the kind of out-of-context comments that Dr. Polgar made.

LIEBERMAN: I can't pretend to defend Dr. Petersen's paper on demographic grounds. I will say, as a psychiatrist, that I find myself stimulated by many points, particularly one on childless marriages. I am not as interested in childless marriages throughout life as I am in childless marriages for the first two years or more of the marriage. What I am concerned about is the lack of intention to delay the first child. From the mental-health standpoint, the postponement of the first child is most critical in terms of the psychological transition from nonparenthood to parenthood status.

I would like to link this with another point Petersen makes, which is simply the interaction between the state and the individual couple, and the recognition (which I think psychologists have and which other behavioral scientists need to acquire) that there are certain social reinforcers operating, but we don't know how strongly. My modest proposal is that because the state already has an interest, not perhaps in number of children but in age at marriage, we focus on this aspect of the reinforcement. Because all states have laws stating when a woman and a man may legitimately marry, let us consider changing these laws so that 21 years is the minimum age at which men and women may marry, and let us reflect on the probable consequences. Many states already have 21 years as the marriage age for men. Most will excuse men and women for younger marriage if the parents consent. Women's prescribed marriage age is usually younger than men's but it is not because women are smarter and more mature so they can make a decision sooner; rather, it is a slight, implying that women's education and women's status is not as important.

One could predict that if a law to push the age at marriage up to 21 years were passed tomorrow, one would very obviously have a rise in fornication and a rise in out-of-wedlock babies and a rise in abortions and a rise in the use of contraceptives; we would also have a dramatic decline in the divorce rate. I suspect that after the initial rise in the first four categories, one would observe a decline in out-of-wedlock babies and the abortion rate. I don't know what would happen to fornication, but one would probably see a commensurate rise in the use of contraceptives.

EAST: My background is more in the economic status of women and their labor-force participation than in any other area. That perspective is important here. The data on women in the labor force include all women who are working in any given year. It is not limited to women in careers. But, even those data show a smaller number of children per career woman than among the women who are home. It is almost one child per family among women who are in the labor force.

MILNER: Are you suggesting that working outside the home is the best contraceptive?

EAST: I would make the suggestion that there should be a study of family size where the wife has a career. I have had a career, and my friends have had, and none of us has more than two children. It is almost impossible both to work and to take care of a large family.

MILNER: But there is a social-class factor here.

MERRIAM: As a matter of curiosity, I wonder how many children each of our workshop participants has.

KUNDSIN: It would be very interesting to circulate a questionnaire and find out! I, for one, have been seriously thinking of putting forth the proposal not to vote for any political figure who has more than two children. Many of our leaders don't set an example for the rest of us. But I think it would be very difficult to get this idea across to the constituency.

MOORE: A pamphlet, "Beyond Family-Planning," is available from the Population Council, and it discusses this issue "Is family-planning enough?" It was written by Bernard Berelson, the president of the Population Council, and he examines such questions as: What are the political possibilities and acceptable economic and administrative feasibility of taxation to reduce family size and incentives?

DISCUSSION OF CONTRACEPTIVE TECHNOLOGY: CURRENT AND PROSPECTIVE METHODS *

Ruth B. Kundsin, Sc.D., *Moderator*

MILNER: Miss Sarah Lewit, who is Christopher Tietze's wife and has collaborated extensively with her husband in his work, will comment on the Segal and Tietze paper, since the authors were unable to participate in this workshop. Their work is extremely encyclopedic, and very up to date. Indeed, had I known last June that it was in press and that a reprint would be available to us, I would, as workshop organizer, have handled their subject area somewhat differently.

JECH: In their description of the contraceptive pill, the authors cite all side effects; in the end, however, their conclusion is, "but psychologically and because of personality it has been found to be the best method." I would like to know how the authors can arrive at that conclusion on the basis of the data provided.

LEWIT: The oral contraceptive has thus far proved to be the most effective method of preventing pregnancies; the rate of accidental pregnancy—which occurs with even the best contraceptives—is lower with the pill than with any method that has been reported.

JECH: If they had said "effective method," I would agree wholeheartedly, but their language emphasized "psychologically." It is almost as though they had made a psychological test of all the women.

LEWIT: The intent of the psychological point is not that there have been psychological tests. Our society is used to taking pills. We take vitamin pills and we take pills for various ailments. We know that the consumption of pills in the United States in particular is enormous. This is just another pill that you take; thus, women are psychologically prepared to take "the pill." Another aspect is that it is not a coitus-related method. Some of the psychological problems connected with other methods of contraception are due to the necessity of interrupting the sexual performance in order to put in a diaphragm, or to douche, or whatever the particular method is. Taking the pill is just something the woman does in the morning, like brushing her teeth, or taking an aspirin, or whatever it is that she ordinarily does in the morning.

TANGRI: Would you comment on the psychological repercussions of the more recently publicized data on the side effects of the pill, and the effect that this will have psychologically on women? Will the general receptivity to pills be counteracted by such more specific information? I would also like to point out the relative absence of research on a male method in general, such as male sterilization. I believe this is related to the fact that the people doing the research are mostly men, and I would be interested in hearing reactions on this point.

LEWIT: In regard to your first question, I think the publicity given to the adverse effects of oral contraceptives during the recent Congressional hearings has already had an effect on American women. I base my statement on the reports of a Gallup poll that was taken very recently, in which 18% of the women who had been taking oral contraceptives said that they had discontinued them. Most of them said it was because of the publicity given to the adverse effects in the newspapers. That is a very large percentage—one-fifth, approximately.

It is true, however, that discontinuation rates for all contraceptives—the pill, the

* The paper on which this discussion is based, "Contraceptive Technology: Current and Prospective Methods," by Sheldon J. Segal, Ph.D., and Christopher Tietze, M.D., was previously published in *Reports on Population/Family Planning* (October, 1969), issued by the Population Council and International Institute for the Study of Human Reproduction at Columbia University, New York, N.Y., and is therefore not reproduced in this volume. The authors were not present during the discussion.

intrauterine device (IUD) and all the rest—have been very high in most populations. Even before these hearings, it was found that the discontinuation rates for any particular contraceptive are very high. It is not clearly understood why. This is something that should be investigated.

TANGRI: My understanding was that the continuation rate for the pill was better than for other methods.

LEWIT: I don't think the difference is very great. I know that in Taiwan and Korea, where oral contraceptives have been introduced fairly recently, there is an extremely high discontinuation rate. Studies made some years ago by Dr. Satterthwaite and others have also shown very high discontinuation rates for the oral method as well as for others. I think that in certain population groups there is a greater general tendency to continue with contraception, although there are more highly motivated women who will have a firmer attitude toward contraception. But we are talking here about mass populations and large groups and clinic populations, in all of which the discontinuation rates are high.

CHESSLER: I have been involved in some research on discontinuation rates of the various methods in a clinic population. One of the problems of such studies is in defining discontinuance. If a woman ceases to come to the clinic, she is considered to have discontinued using the pill. If a woman ceases to come to the clinic she is considered to have discontinued using the IUD. However, if the IUD has not been removed, she is really continuing to use it. This is one reason, I think, that the continuance-rates for the IUD are actually a great deal higher than stated.

It may be that women find the side effects of the pill, although they are much more serious than those of the IUD, to be less noticeable in most cases, and therefore they continue to take it. It may even be that they continue using the IUD or the diaphragm even more than they use the pill. We have not measured attrition properly.

LAWS: I would like to expand on Dr. Tangri's second question, and I would like to discuss it not only with respect to the use of contraception as narrowly conceived, but also with respect to other questions that have been raised in the various advance papers about persuasion and problems of acceptance of family limitation. There is a regrettable emphasis and an unspoken assumption that only women use contraceptives. Thus, we are talking about persuading women, and we should be talking about persuading men and women, families and couples, married and unmarried. I would like to make sure that we come back to that.

LEWIT: The earliest known contraceptive methods were male methods; male methods preceded the female methods. Coitus interruptus is one of the oldest methods known, and there have also been various types of condoms. Some of these were very inadequate, but at least there were attempts made by the male to control procreation. It is only fairly recently that almost the entire control of contraception has been placed in the hands of women. One of the reasons for this, probably, is that the family-planning organizations in the various countries have always been in the hands of women.

EPSTEIN: You say there has been an enormous switch to the use of contraceptive devices on the part of women and not men. Is there really a large body of evidence to indicate that the use of the condom is out, or has been reduced to something like 5%?

LEWIT: No, the condom is still a very much used method of contraception, but it is only fairly recently that the manufacture of the condom has been subject to inspection. There were all sorts of problems, accidents, in which it was torn during intercourse, or was defectively made and had holes, even very minute holes, which made conception possible. Thus, it was not a very safe method until about 1938, when the Food and Drug Administration adopted a product-sampling technique to test the quality of condoms. Condoms remain a very popular method both in the United States and abroad.

V. BERNARD: I'd like to return to the issue of the differing contraceptive methods.

The measures that are suitable to mass approaches need to be supplemented, and are in some areas, by more detailed clinical studies of the meaning of the different methods to different women and couples. For certain couples, the pill is preferred because it doesn't interrupt the actual act, and this point is important to some. For others, the pill is, apparently, on the basis of the more detailed studies, feared by some women as a kind of change of self. They don't want to be chemically changed, quite apart from the realities that were raised at the Congressional hearings. As a psychiatrist, I know we must be concerned sometimes with the unrealities that are at work on fears and preferences. Methodologically, in research, we need to supplement the findings from mass-directed approaches, which are essential with this kind of measure, with more refined methods of study, i.e., studies done on an individual level.

KAMM: A recent report published by the Population Council, also by Dr. Tietze, indicated that a combination of some kind of IUD, plus availability of abortion, if one could be sure of having an abortion when needed, resulted in a still lower mortality rate than that associated with the pill. I don't know how great the differences are or how many people would live if they did have abortions on demand plus the use of devices other than the pill, but, given the increasing concern about the effects of the pill and the often quoted statements that the carcinogenic effects are latent for a period of ten years, wouldn't you say this would be an argument for pushing the abortion method? I haven't seen this particular point ever mentioned as a reason for repealing abortion laws. Would you consider it a valid point?

LEWIT: I would, very much so, but let me give you the relative magnitude of the various mortality risks that are involved. The mortality risk from complications of pregnancy and parturition in the United States, which has a very high level of medical care, is 24 per 100,000 live births, and the mortality risk with thromboembolic diseases that has been established thus far for the oral contraceptive is 3 per 100,000 users. The mortality risk from abortions in those countries where abortions are permitted early in pregnancy and where they are performed in hospitals is about 4 per 100,000 legal abortions.

It is perfectly true that the latency period of cancer is about ten years, or perhaps longer, and therefore the carcinogenic effect of the oral contraceptive is something we may all come to regret. (Or perhaps be very happy about, since we may find there is no association at all.) It is, however, something that requires long-term use to study. Furthermore, many of the other side effects that have been attributed to the pill are very rare and therefore require large numbers of users in order to study them.

All these factors make it very difficult to come to concrete decisions. However, if you are referring to the suggestion in this paper that it would be far better to settle on a method of contraception that is perfectly safe, some mechanical method which carries no mortality risk whatsoever but which is not 100% effective, then it would be sound to permit the woman to have a legal abortion performed by a doctor in a hospital. Together, the risk is minimal.

POLGAR: On the matter of discontinuation, I think that the data on the study in Chicago by Planned Parenthood cited in the reprint (which I am also fond of citing) showed that a tremendous variability in discontinuation can be accounted for not by the cultural-psychological characteristics of the population that receives the method, nor by the method itself, but by the way in which it is taught. I think that the stories of India are pertinent here, about women having IUDs inserted and not even being told there was a foreign object in the uterus, and the IUD might come out; the women didn't know *what* was going on. Then there were epidemics of removal throughout entire villages, and the method's usefulness was ruined from then on. Thus, I think we have to pay a great deal of attention to the ways in which the various methods are provided.

OZER: I would like to go back, perhaps ten years or so, and look at what the situation was then. About ten years ago, this country had not yet reached the point where we could even give contraceptive information in public hospitals to indigent citizens. Therefore, clinics were providing contraceptive information almost entirely to highly educated and highly motivated people. At that time, the diaphragm was the method of choice. The diaphragm is a genitalia-related method; it is not a coitus-related method. It can be used at 6:00 P.M. every night of the year, whether there will be a male around or not, and it will work!

When the statistics on a voluntary population were made available, they showed it to be a 99% + effective means—at least the way the marriage manuals published in the early 1950s were reporting effectiveness, because as soon as the Planned Parenthood data-compilers could identify someone who admitted having intercourse without the diaphragm, she was out of the statistics. When the pill came in, in the early 1960s, the nonusers as well as the users of all other methods were put together, and suddenly the effectiveness of the diaphragm plummeted to 60%. The medical advantage of not saying that this method is 60% effective, but saying that there is a group of people for whom it can be as effective as any other means, and to identify this group of people, is great. For another group of people, this means of contraception is not as reliable, and there might be a risk for *them*. Also, there are some personality factors that might enter into the choice of method, such as sexual aggressiveness, which possibly can be identified in history-taking about sexual attitudes. Also, a woman's familiarity with her own genitalia might be of importance. And telling her that the diaphragm is something that should be used every night and has nothing to do with intercourse, just as with the pill, might make it more effective.

The reason for my affectionate feeling for the diaphragm is that this is a method that has been used for 50 years, and the only statistics about its safety—in terms of health—show that women who are married to uncircumcised husbands have a significantly lower rate of cervical carcinoma if they use a diaphragm than those who do not. We have two generations of information. Women for the last ten years have been going to physicians who have not even tried to determine if they would be good diaphragm-users or poor diaphragm-users before dispensing a drug, a chemical. This practice has been completely irresponsible in my opinion.

As far as the male methods go, I recently had a long conversation with Dr. Aguiles Sobrero, Director of the Margaret Sanger Research Institute. It appears that we are trying to use chemical methods for men also, which may have, in fact, as great or greater side effects as the pill for women. Thus, far, the side effects have been loss of libido and impotence. Impotence may be the ultimate contraceptive. I suspect, however, that it will have a high rate of discontinuance!

A DIGEST OF THREE PAPERS BY JOSEPH D. BEASLEY *

Chana Heffner

Brooklyn College
Brooklyn, N.Y.

Background

"There is a popular feeling that poor women and those who have experienced out-of-wedlock pregnancies are not interested in family-planning." [1] The data on, and client's continued participation in, the New Orleans and Lincoln Parish programs, to be described, refute this widespread conception. Studies before the inception of these programs found that there was a marked lack of knowledge about reproduction and fertility control on the part of lower socioeconomic men and women. But all expressed a belief that they had a right to decide on the number and the timing of their children, indicating that no motivational factors were blocking the acceptance and use of family-planning services.

"There is a relationship between the denial of family-planning services to the poor and the level of social and health problems associated with poverty." [2] In New Orleans, the lower socioeconomic group contributes 56% of the total number of births, 88% of out-of-wedlock births, 80% of maternal deaths, and 68% of births to women under 19 years of age. Figures also indicate that pregnancy is one of the highest causes for young girls to drop out of school. Adequate family-life and sex-education courses are needed to prevent this, in addition to provisions for education for these girls when they are pregnant. Of the women contacted for the New Orleans program (all of whom had had a birth experience), 22% were never married and only 56% of those married were living with their husbands. Without adequate family-planning facilities, it will be impossible to maintain family stability within this population. The data make it clear that this pattern constitutes a social and health problem not only to the individuals involved but to the community and nation as a whole.

Lincoln Parish, Louisiana, was the setting of the first project in the state. It is a rural county with a population approximately 41.8% Negro; the median family income is between $2,000–$3,000 per year. The median age of the women in the project was 23.6 years; more than half had had an out-of-wedlock birth, and the majority had low parity. Hence, these women were being reached at a time when such services were vital to them; 57% of the identifiable available patients were accepted. The four surrounding parishes had similar sociodemographic characteristics and were used as a loose "control." Family-planning services were available in the other parishes, but were not organized or conducted in the same way. In the New Orleans-based program, 95.7% of the patient population was black, primarily because poor whites were/are not willing to attend integrated clinics. Family incomes were under $4,500 per year; the occupations of the family heads were in the service or laborer categories.

* Based on three papers by Joseph D. Beasley, M.D., Director of the Center for Population and Family Studies, Tulane University School of Medicine, New Orleans, La. Complete citations of these papers are given in the References.

The Programs

In Louisiana, there had been no comprehensive family-planning programs previously, so the programs could be organized with no concern for fitting into an existing structure. The purpose of the two pilot programs was to develop and organize a system to identify, contact, educate, and provide services in family planning for all indigent families. Both projects included only women who had been married or pregnant. The emphasis in the programs was on highly individualized contact based on total maternal health and postpartum care; family planning was one related component.

Women were identified by birth records from charity hospitals and tax-supported facilities. The priority basis for contact was as follows: first, current postpartum patients; next, "high-risk" mothers who had had a birth experience within the past two years. Women were classified as high risk when they had given birth to six or more children, or were under 16 or over 40, or had had one or more stillbirths, or whose last birth was out of wedlock, or who had a history of infant or child death. Last to be contacted were the "low-risk" women. Attempts were made to identify and contact the as yet nonidentifiable group.

"The success of a program is to a large degree dependent upon total patient contact; therefore a program must provide dynamic and effective outreach systems."[3] A program nurse made contact with a postpartum woman one or two days after the birth. This contact included an individual education session and the offer of an appointment for postpartum care between four and six weeks after the birth. The woman was also given literature emphasizing the value of family planning and the importance of a postpartum examination to be studied and discussed at home with her husband. Identifiable high- and low-risk women were contacted on an individual basis by a family-planning auxiliary worker, who explained the program and offered them an opportunity to participate. If they showed interest, they were given an appointment.

These auxiliary workers were a vital factor in the operation of the programs. They were women chiefly from the indigent group, who had shown high levels of intelligence despite low levels of education. They were educated in reproductive physiology and in contraceptive techniques, in addition to being oriented to the goals and the operation of the program. Their core function was to act as liaison between the patient and the program, contacting the high- and low-risk women and doing follow-up work in the case of a missed appointment.

If a patient failed to keep her first appointment, she was contacted by mail or phone; if she failed to keep the second appointment, made in response to the call or letter, she received a home visit. The New Orleans program indicated that the total number of women who kept an appointment was increased by 22% as a result of this follow-up system. Figures also showed that the sooner a woman was contacted, the more likely she was to keep an appointment. It was also found that if the programs had had to depend upon the usual referral methods from poverty-oriented agencies, very few of the indigent population would have been reached.

Initial Results

The Lincoln Parish program was begun in 1965; related figures are available through 1967. In the first year for which figures are available, indigent births decreased 32% in this parish, whereas the decrease was only 6% in the control parishes. In 1967, indigent out-of-wedlock births decreased 47% in Lincoln Parish; in the control parishes there was an increase. Indices showing a significant decrease in Lincoln Parish during 1967 included:

1. total number of medically indigent births;
2. total number of out-of-wedlock live births;
3. total number of medically indigent out-of-wedlock live births;
4. the ratio of indigent out-of-wedlock live births per thousand live births; and
5. the ratio of illegitimate live births per thousand live births.

In New Orleans, each fertility-control method offered was explained together with its advantages and disadvantages. Each patient was then given an individual nursing conference to help her decide which method was best for her. Of the first admissions, 96% selected some method of family-planning as a result of this clinic experience. After completion of the clinic program visit, only 3% had not picked a method of fertility control as opposed to 41% who had not done so before the clinic visit. Oral contraceptives were chosen by 62% of the women, as opposed to 24% who had previously used it. The IUD was chosen by 20% as opposed to a previous 0.2%.

Second appointments were scheduled for six to eight weeks after the original visits. Additional visits were scheduled once a year thereafter, unless a woman was on the pill, in which case she came to the clinic for her supply every three months. Of the women who originally came to the clinic, 88% remained with the program over an 18-month period, essentially realizing the program's goal of reaching the identifiable women in all categories within two years of the program's inception.

The New Orleans facilities have since been expanded to include three outlying centers. The original central facility has continued to be the one used most often, however, partly because it is at the hub of public transportation, and partly because the patient prefers to keep her use of the clinic's services private.

Evaluation

Previous family-planning programs for the indigent have failed because of the manner in which these services were provided: there was/is a strong tendency toward general denial of privacy, dignity, and patient-centered freedom of choice. The two programs here described have established that the problem is primarily one of the proper design and provision of adequate maternal health service and family-planning to the indigent, not one of "persuading" the indigent to accept such services. If the services offered provide privacy, dignity and freedom of choice, together with a strong and sustained program of personal contact, they will be utilized because most indigent women are highly motivated to use such services.

References

1. Beasley, J. D. & V. Parrish. 1968. Family Planning and the Reduction of Fertility and Illegitimacy. Unpublished.
2. Beasley, J. D. 1969. View from Louisiana. Family Planning Perspectives, **1**(1).

3. BEASLEY, J. D., R. FRANKOWSKI & C. HAWKINS. 1969. The Orleans Parish family planning demonstration program," Milbank Quart. **47**(3).

DISCUSSION *

Ruth B. Kundsin, Sc.D., *Moderator*

MILNER: I think we should avoid the technical aspects of contraception because this is an emotionally laden area, and we could easily spend the rest of the workshop on this topic. Indeed, conference after conference has been held on the technical and biological aspects of contraception. What we don't have are analyses of the personal and social implications of these things, such as Beasley has provided. The literature indicates that New Orleans has a population that can't be reached, and can't be convinced that it is in its own interest to seek and to use a contraceptive. Beasley's work shows that this conclusion is superficial, and that the research done has not been adequate. Previous research has been much too middle-class oriented; there has been too much unconscious bias on the part of the researcher. Even though Dr. Beasley could not participate in this workshop, I would like to compliment him. Somebody has to make these breakthroughs, and I think he has made a big one.

OLESEN: The Hawthorne effect sprang immediately to my mind when I read Beasley's conclusions. Whether or not it *is* the Hawthorne effect is secondary. If the results were desirable in terms of research, then this is the most important thing. What is it that seems to have produced the result with this type of response?

MILNER: Of course, one must read Beasley's original reports; Mrs. Heffner's paper is merely a digest. Beasley took advantage of the circumstance that there was a total program of public health care with which people in that population group in New Orleans had been provided. They had gotten used to going to these clinics for certain kinds of preventive care. He believes his approach worked because it was incorporated into a comprehensive public-health program. Contraceptive information and advice shouldn't be dispensed in a dirty room underneath the stairs, as is still done for venereal disease testing in many places. He found that if you incorporate it with positive physical care, the people will take advantage of it, first, because they are already used to coming to this facility, and second, because that setting puts the whole thing in a completely different, and positive, light.

MCLAUGHLIN: The conclusion that the approach was effective when the people were afforded privacy, dignity, and personal attention seems not to relate just to this field but to all fields of medicine in general. You can look at the experience of a number of municipal hospital clinics with some of the new prototypes that have been moving into housing projects; when you deal with people on a highly personalized basis, you get the same kind of response. The same kind of thing was said about the fact that "they" didn't want medical care.

MILNER: "They" do not like to sit and wait for hours in a clinic any more than the rest of us do. I would call on our British participant at this point because he has had a lot of contact with another type of low-income population. Would you comment, Mr. Gill, about your group's experience with this kind of population in Aberdeen?

GILL: I think Beasley's findings are very exciting, and they confirm something that we have begun to believe in Aberdeen, namely, a complete and integrated approach to the whole range of reproductive behavior, from prenatal care, through confinement, postnatal care, well-baby clinics—all integrated. This is unique in Britain because of the tripartite structure of the National Health Service. In Aberdeen, positive attempts have been made to provide a completely integrated maternity service, which includes family-planning clinics attached to all areas, including pre-

* Mrs. Heffner was not present during the discussion.

and antenatal care, encouragement at the primary physician level, and so forth. Under the system of general practitioners of the British service, through unification of the three arms of the structure—the public-health side and primary and secondary patient care—every aspect of maternity care is included in this one coherent program in Aberdeen.

In this program, we find it very easy to establish contact and rapport with the fish-workers in Aberdeen, who represent our sort of indigent poor folk. They are responsive. Also, in the clinics in Aberdeen, the pill has been far and away the most popular contraceptive technique utilized. Since the introduction of the pill in 1964, the increase in its use is dramatic.

TANGRI: I would like to mention the work that Jay Palmore did in Chicago, with reference, at least, to the responsiveness of a very poor and largely black section of the female population in Chicago. He found a tremendous response to just the opposite of what you have described—not to this comprehensive kind of offering, but to a kind of postcard which said something to this effect: "Are you interested in family-planning and any means of limiting births? If you are, please send this card back and tell some friends about it." He found the poorest women with the largest number of children to be the most active in spreading the word about the availability of a place to go for contraceptive information. In addition to keeping in mind the attractiveness of a comprehensive program of care, we should also keep in mind that there is a felt need for a specific kind of information and that we shouldn't necessarily drop that kind of specific approach.

MILNER: Are you saying that a multipronged approach, utilizing whatever means may work, should be used?

TANGRI: Yes! It can be very efficient to concentrate on a single problem, such as birth control for the population which has a high felt need for it.

MOORE: I am with the Population Council, and I would like to comment on this point. Running a family-planning clinic in isolation can be effective and efficient, but an argument against it, very often verbalized by members of the black community in particular, is the issue of genocide. Their reaction might be paraphrased as follows: "The church has arranged for *your* style of birth-control. If you were to offer comprehensive health services to us, which we very much need, we wouldn't object to your inclusion of family planning among the array of those services. But when you come in to our area, and the very first thing you offer us as a panacea for the ills of poverty in the ghetto is family planning, and you offer it in isolation, then don't be surprised if we are suspicious."

TANGRI: I would like to comment on that because I have heard this rhetoric many times. Again, as with so much of the rhetoric that goes on in emotionally laden issues, let us distinguish between a politically necessary rhetoric, which a population feels is useful for their political purposes—and which I personally feel is valid for those purposes—and the actual felt needs of the women who want to stop having ten children, for whom that rhetoric may or may not be viable.

V. BERNARD: We all have to recognize that there are differentiated groups within these rather large segments that have just been referred to, and certainly there are some findings that are not in the domain of political rhetoric that would support, for some groups at least, the greater value and acceptability of family planning in conjunction with other health services. I would like to mention a study, which some of you may be acquainted with, reported by Sarrell, an obstetrician at Yale, in which there was a comparison between two groups of young, black, teenage, unmarried mothers. In one group of 100 cases, there was practically 97% resistance among those served at the Yale clinic. In the second group, with the institution of a real comprehensive set of services along with the obstetrical—that is, of public health, educational, social, and psychological services—these girls, after their first baby was delivered under those conditions, and with consideration for the putative father and so forth, later made a very dramatic use of contraception, along with a good social adjustment.

DUNBAR: Since birth-control programs have had a lot to do with black and brown people in the world, I would like to know why there are no black people represented at this workshop to speak from the point of view of black people.

MILNER: At least a few will participate in our subsequent discussions.

CHESSLER: I have had some experience in the family-planning field, and I know of at least two situations related to Miss Moore's comments. One occurred to Joseph Beasley in New Orleans and one of them occurred to Planned Parenthood in Pittsburgh, about a year ago. In the case of Pittsburgh, a Planned Parenthood clinic was actually closed. It turned out that the genocide argument was being raised by black male militants. As soon as the clinic was closed, the black militants who were women made them reopen the clinic! It may suit the needs of the black men to have more black babies to increase the black population, but the black women didn't seem to think that their function was just to have babies, and they insisted on having birth-control services available.

I am inclined to think that this genocide argument, as an argument for influencing people not to use family-planning services, is a bit of a red herring. I think it is raised by people who would not use the services anyhow, and that most of the people, even in the lowest-income, most uneducated groups, do want to use such services and will use them when they are available.

OZER: The genocide issue has caused at least some ambivalence on the part of black women who come even to comprehensive-care clinics. One experience was reported to me by the staff of a Washington, D.C., community clinic. They have decided that birth control or any curtailment of pregnancy that affects a future pregnancy, should, whenever possible, be handled by a black physician in preference to a white physician. The response has been far better than before this approach was attempted.

KAMM: I would like to know about the distribution of unmarried mothers and the so-called question of illegitimacy in a matriarchal society. Children are termed bastards when they do not have a father but have a mother. In Massachusetts and in many other states, pills are available, but only to married people, and not to people below a certain age. In community-funded programs, what is the Planned Parenthood policy of pill-distribution to girls below the age of 16? There are all sorts of legal issues involved here which we have not touched upon. We seem to be assuming that there are no barriers to distribution from the legal standpoint. I think *this* problem should be recognized and discussed.

CULTURAL FACTORS IN FAMILY PLANNING

Lucile F. Newman, Ph.D.

Department of Sociology
University of California Medical Center
San Francisco, Calif.

Population growth has been defined as the most important problem of our time. If this is indeed so, the greatest step toward solving that problem has taken place already. Separation of sex and reproduction through contraception has made a dramatic change in our lives. It means childbearing by choice, by rational choice. The implications of this revolutionary change are broad. It is a dramatic precursor of the possibility of choice overtaking the Fates in other areas of life as well. It also suggests a reassessment of women's roles, which have traditionally been tied to their reproductive capacity.

The concept of "family planning" is a response to birth control that affords the possibility of choice replacing chance in reproduction. The discussion of alternative life-styles for women is a response to the possibility of redefinition of women's roles. For the separation of sex and reproduction to be effective in helping to solve the problem of overpopulation, however, it must move from a suggestion to a mandate, and it must apply to all the peoples of the world.

This workshop focuses on two phenomena also of our time: (*1*) the advent of the technology of birth control, and (*2*) the question of the "liberation" of women as a result of this technology. I have been asked to identify structural, cultural, and interpersonal obstacles to acceptance of family planning, and to relate this cultural view to the general area of women's self definition. The perspective of anthropology is the comparative study of man and his behavior. The method, in this case, is to measure efforts at directed culture change against cultural traditions and social organizations in order to estimate their probable success or failure and account for that success or failure.

My sources, besides standard international literature on population control, are my own field research studying the culture of birth and family planning in Sweden, Japan, India, and the United States. These researches have dwelt on policies as well as behavior, and in each case have been made up of interviews with officials of health departments as well as with nurses, midwives, and the women they serve. Emphasis in this paper is on problems relating to birth control and women's roles in India and the United States.

Because the effectiveness of a family-planning program rests in its universal acceptance, and because a small-family norm is counter to the traditions of the citizens of many nations today, adoption of family planning falls into the category of culture change, and is governed by some of the principles of culture change. The problem has been widely identified as one of motivation from within the society to secure change, incentives to make change profitable (or at least not costly) to the individual, widespread "education" to change the moral framework for behavior. All these things have been attempted in India on a grand scale, but acceptance of family planning is still an uphill struggle. I would like to describe my views of obstacles to this governmental scheme in achieving widespread acceptance and also, to indicate some implications of these obstacles for the United States.

The concept of social structure—the relatively permanently ordered arrangement of parts of a society—allows us to view persons as members of groups, and accordingly sharing behavior and motivations sanctioned by those groups. I shall speak first about *structural* obstacles to acceptance of family planning, the most abstract level at which impediments exist. In the second section I shall define cultural obstacles, and in the third, those obstacles acting on an interpersonal level.

Structural Obstacles

On the most abstract level is the structural problem of cultural and social pluralism—in India called "communalism"—the existence of diverse and competing subcultures in the same area. Domination and subordination are implicit in most instances of pluralism. On a worldwide scale, developed versus underdeveloped nations may provide common, hence in a sense communal, identities; within India, such identities adhere to villagers as distinguished from urban dwellers, Hindus as contrasted to Muslims, and among regional and caste groupings. In the United States they are found in black, white, Chicano, American Indian, and other ethnic distinctions, in religious differentiations such as Protestant and Catholic, and many other groupings.

One example of a communalistic approach occurs in Bernard Berelson's review article, "Beyond Family Planning." The second of his assumptions about family planning is that the (population) problem is most urgent in the developing countries, where rapid population growth retards social and economic development.[1] Stated less formally by one of my informants, it is expressed from the other side of the social scale as, "Why is it that *they* want *us* to have fewer children?"

Whether it is villagers in India questioning city-based population policy, or blacks in America questioning policies constructed for them by whites, or members of any minority political party or group questioning rules or expectations set up for them by the dominant society, there is still the same very valid response. Why are *they* doing that to *us*? What is in it for them? How will we lose from it? Why should we do it for them? Emphasis in the United States on birth control for welfare recipients has little to do with population control. It has to do with saving money, and at times with repression of an unruly subordinate group.

G. N. Ramu, a sociologist in Mysore State writing in the Indian publication *Family Planning News,* notes: "The dominant caste in power never propagates the philosophy of family planning except at policy levels. At the level of implementation, such a caste is not serious regarding the application of the principles to its own members."[2] The President who first proposed a population policy for the United States came from a family noted throughout the world for its large numbers of children. Underdeveloped nations, welfare recipients, and minority groups are all notably unresponsive to policies couched in terms of a worldwide crisis which apply to *them* and not to their dominant brothers who usually compose and advocate those policies. Jean Mayer, in a *Columbia Forum* article, "Toward a Non-Malthusian Population Policy," recognizes that wealthy nations use up resources at a much faster rate than poor ones, and are for this reason much more of a threat to the world's resources.[3] Therefore, population growth in such nations is a greater threat in the long run than in poor nations. Communal differences on a grand scale appear as: "Let's *you* practice birth control." Communal differences on a smaller scale have even more direct and immediate political implications. While changes in numbers in major political parties, in ethnic groups or national identities in the society at large may be inconsequential except in the long run, on the local level they can mean disaster for the group or party that decreases its numbers if the competitors do not do likewise.

Newspaper accounts of the success of birth control among Indians resident in Fiji and among Fijians point out that the Indian birth rate has diminished from 47 per 1,000 to 32 per 1,000, while the Fijian birth rate has stayed at about 36 per 1,000. The population ratio is approximately 200,000 Fijians to 250,000 Indians. "The Fiji Bureau of Statistics says if the trend continues, the gap between Fijians and Indians could begin to close in favor of the Fijians toward the end of the 1970's. Should Fijians become Fiji's biggest racial bloc—a position they lost 25 years ago—the biggest obstacle in Fiji's path to independence would be removed." [4]

When one has been convinced that voter registration is important, it is not a long step to the idea that the more voters to register, the better. The largest structural obstacle to acceptance of family planning, then, is distrust of policies carried out for subordinate groups by dominant groups, no matter how eloquently they are couched in terms of the subordinate group's self interest.

Cultural Obstacles

Cultural obstacles to change refer to those discontinuities between proposed change and traditional values, customs, or social organization of a society. The Family Planning Program in India encounters impediments in many of these areas. In India, there is well-founded lack of faith that two or three children in a family will survive. There would have to be much more evidence of childhood survival and greater life expectancy than there now is for most people to accept as safe the small-family norm. Thomas Poffenberger has shown that in order to assure two surviving sons, a family using the most sophisticated laws of probability should try for five children. Between three and five is in fact the preferred number for families in his collection of studies.[5] Making family planning a part of an effective health program, thereby inspiring faith in survival, would be more rational and humane than the present focus on limiting family numbers alone.

A second major cultural obstacle in India is that the Family Planning Program is tied to both concepts and practice of Western medicine, an alien system of British origin which stands in opposition to two indigenous systems of medicine, Ayurvedic and Unani. For those who have already accepted the idea of Western medicine, this is no drawback. However, for most rural populations and large numbers of city dwellers, these ideas and practices are looked on with great suspicion as remnants of a colonial era. It would be necessary to instill acceptance of both the underlying philosophy of Western medicine *and* the small-family norm (which appear to derive from the same source) before they would consider seriously adopting the methods of birth control offered by the government. It is Western-trained doctors, complete with their paraphernalia of rubber gloves and face masks and their different ideas of "clean" and "unclean," who are at present the only practitioners allowed to insert the intrauterine contraceptive device (IUCD) or to perform the sterilization procedure. Among the target populations of the Family Planning Program—rural and lower class urban Indians—there is little utilization of Western medicine and more reliance on indigenous systems of medicine and, therefore, indigenous medical practitioners. Suspicion of "outside" systems is strong. It would seem that if some of the government effort were turned toward making available and demonstrating the success of Western techniques, it would first inspire faith that such medical practice "works" and therefore that most children can survive, and *then* prepare people to accept birth control as another aspect of that system.

A third cultural obstacle to family planning in India is traditional family organization. In this predominantly patrilineal, patrilocal society, in which the new bride moves to the village of her husband's family and lives in a subservient position, the emphasis in marriage is on her reproductive capacity. Her function is to enable continuation of her husband's lineage. If she is unable to produce heirs she will be disparaged and may be replaced by another wife. An informant who already had two girls and two boys pointed out that if she were sterilized and anything happened to the boys she would be useless to her husband's family and might even have to leave. More directly, another informant when told of the possibility of sterilization, said, "Why would a woman do that? She would lose her value."

Besides family organization, traditional economic practices provide obstacles to acceptance of the small-family norm. According to G. N. Ramu, relatives provide "dependable manpower" not only in the agricultural countryside but also in urban employment.[2] A large family is a large workforce, and hence an economic asset.

Finally, in a society in which most women marry, even those who go out to work expect to have a family also. In a study carried out among middle-class working women living in Bombay, Chandrakala A. Haté discovered a lower fertility rate than is usual for India. It must be noted, however, that employment is not seen as an alternative to reproduction, but as an adjunct to it. The joint family makes both education and employment possible for women, with plenty of surrogate mothers at home. The indication is clear that they have fewer children than their nonemployed counterparts.[6] The combination of double income and fewer children serves to secure their position in the middle class and to assure continuation for the family. Working women make up a very small part of the population of India, but their position is not anomalous. For village women, the picture is quite different. Decisions about reproduction are not theirs to make. Education is not encouraged. Outsiders are suspect. A precarious existence is maintained in which the family represents one of the few stable elements.

The cultural impediments, then, are not necessarily based on tradition, outmoded motives, and a nonprogressive nature, but on real custom and known advantage. Thus, reluctance to accept an outsider's ideas and methods is not simply backwardness, but the distrust and conservativeness described in an article on peasants by May N. Diaz. "One . . . is made conscious of (the peasant's) view when one encounters his often stubborn resistance to new agricultural and other productive techniques, for he fears that any change in procedure is likely to increase the risks of an already risky enterprise."[7] For the common man in India, emotional fulfillment, stability in the family system, and economic benefit from family solidarity are strong adversaries when arrayed against an abstraction like "overpopulation" or the unproven advantage of a small family.

A family-planning program is a Western artifact. Its technology, its implementors, its ideologues are Western-trained. It encounters difficulty when exported, but the particular program in India enjoys full support of the government, and was one of the first such programs in the world. In the United States, on the contrary, except for some religious groups, it is not the problem of acceptance of medical care nor cultural obstacles which impede, so much as it is inadequate *access* to medical care and differences in communal values and objectives, aggravated by governmental reluctance to launch a full-scale program.

INTERPERSONAL OBSTACLES

Wherever it occurs, family planning requires rational thinking about the future; birth control requires choice-making in the present. These are inevitably interpersonal decisions. Impediments to family planning at this level show fewer differences between India and the United States than is the case for structural and cultural impediments.

An extensive literature exists on interpersonal obstacles to family planning. These sources range from discussions of sex as recreation not to be tampered with easily, to evaluations of problems associated with alternative methods of birth control, i.e., some methods have difficult physiological side effects, some interfere with spontaneity, and some interfere with sexual pleasure. There is as yet no perfect method. I shall not expand on that literature, but refer you to some of the excellent sources available, such as Berelson and his colleagues,[8] Chandrasekhar,[9] Nag,[10] and Polgar.[11]

One of the most subtle problems introduced by family planning is above all an interpersonal matter: a shift in the balance of power in the family. In the Indian extended family, the influence of the husband's parents or elder brother extends even to the personal relations between himself and his wife. There is overt pressure for him to have children—especially sons. Birth control provides increased autonomy for the individual couple in the joint family by enabling them to limit the number of offspring. It thus encourages decision-making on a nuclear family basis, because the elder members of the family may not be consulted. The couple may contravene their wishes without their permission and perhaps without their knowledge. For sterilization a woman must have her husband's signature, but she can acquire an IUCD without his consent. The comparative popularity of vasectomy in India is an indication of the male sense of prerogative as well as responsibility in making decisions about reproduction. The continuing influence of joint family members on the individual woman is shown in the following statement from a family-planning administrator: "We encourage women to give birth in hospital because we know the mother-in-law will come to visit. We make a point of contacting her and convincing her to influence her daughter-in-law to take a loop (IUCD)."

Individual differences occur in the balance of power in particular families, but the advent of family planning concentrated on numbers upsets this balance, because it makes available alternatives for the husband and wife and has a corrosive effect on the decision-making function of the joint family to the advantage of the Western nuclear type of family. While a change in family structure is not the goal of a family-planning program, it in effect can function as an agent of such change without any element of anticipatory planning.

Conclusion: A Note On Development

It has been noted, in a recent article in the *New York Review of Books* by Ivan Illich, that the developed nations tend to package their culture and their products together with their problems, and export them under the name of aid.[12] One of Illich's examples is the sending of cars and trucks which inspire in the receivers a need for more cars and trucks and provide them also with traffic jams and smog. Progress has become a worldwide value, and as long as it is defined in terms of Western products, this problem will persist.

Prior to the advent of family-planning programs in India, people planned their families to assure that there would be at least two sons. Religion required a surviving son to perform his parents' funeral rites; economics required one or more sons to do the family work and to inherit property or clientele. Survival rates were such that it was risky to rely on a single male birth to achieve these ends, while the sex ratio, needless to say, necessitated two births for every male birth. A large family was thus a practical necessity.

Limiting of births was not unknown in India. Trips home and taboos on intercourse have been mentioned as spacing mechanisms. The combination of an extended period of lactation with a taboo on intercourse during lactation provides birth control which is still in evidence in much of India. In my own research, it became clear that in mountain villages remote from urban influence, this method is still in use. Breast feeding is continued for three to four and a half years. Few families have children closer than four years apart. In the plains villages I visited, this practice has been modified as being too "jungly" or uncivilized. Lactation there continues for two years, and spacing occurs accordingly. In a small city I studied, Western influence has penetrated far enough to suggest that for sophisticated families even breast feeding is too jungly. Canned milk is available for infant feeding, thereby eliminating lactation except for a few months, and removing postpartum taboos on sexual intercourse at the same time. For these people, then, there is a need for birth control to replace that accomplished through traditional practices now abandoned. For those with funds and understanding, this presents a minimal problem. They are able to acquire birth-control materials at the bazaar or at the Family Planning Office. For those who are poor and do not recognize the need for birth control, the result is the birth of a baby every year.

My point here is that along with the technology of tinned milk itself is brought an idea—the questioning of the desirability of breast feeding. This creates a need for yet another Western product—birth control. In this case, Western ideas about the human body and its functions—about breast feeding in particular—as well as Western answers to the problems introduced by those ideas provide an impediment to practice of an indigenous method of family planning in India.

The point is that Western nations, from a position characterized by Senator Fulbright as "the arrogance of power," seem to assume stupidity and conservatism on the part of people in the underdeveloped nations. Obstacles to family planning are not figments of imagination of those for whom it is advocated. They are real problems of social structure, of politics, of economics, of health and survival. The greatest obstacle to family planning is perhaps this arrogance on the part of the educated and the advantaged. A worldwide crisis requires a worldwide response, not a response aimed at poor people and underdeveloped nations.

In the same sense, while deploring the state of subjection of Indian women in the joint family, it is also necessary for us to recognize that not only is the Prime Minister of India a woman, but there are more women in every level of government than has ever been the case in the United States. Gerald Berreman's article, "Women's Roles and Politics in India and the United States," suggests that the political prominence of women in India can co-occur with their subordination in domestic roles because they are taken seriously as persons in any role which they achieve.[13] This does not diminish the hardships of subordination, but it makes possible mobility into viable participation in political and other roles. Thus, despite discrimination, Indian women can achieve acceptance and even distinction in other than familial roles.

In the United States, by contrast, sexual equality is given lip service, but seriousness of purpose for women is recognized only in their domestic or traditionally feminine roles. Disparagement and ridicule greet deviations from this model. For this reason, the technology of birth control is not relevant to a reassessment of women's roles on a philosophical level. Women's liberation does not refer to liberation from domesticity. Rather it means liberation from repression, from self-doubt, from self-hate. It means freedom of aspiration. It means acceptance, by self as well as by others, of one's personhood rather than simply one's sexuality.

On the practical level, however, birth control becomes very relevant—an efficient if not sufficient cause for realizing aspirations. Relaxation of domestic obligations as well as acceptable alternatives to domestic life are prerequisites for change. In addition, our fear of overpopulation serves a positive function. It fosters a concern for the quality of life and marks this as a time when self-realization for all people can be a serious goal.

References

1. Berelson, B. 1969. Beyond family planning. Science **163:** 533.
2. Ramu, G. N. 1968. Factors that retard family planning movement. Family Planning News **IX**(6): 15. Ministry of Health. New Delhi, India.
3. Mayer, J. 1969. Toward a non-Malthusian population policy. Columbia Forum **XII**(2): 6.
4. Williams, G. 1969. Babies and votes. San Francisco Chronicle. June **20:** 6.
5. Poffenberger, T. 1968. Motivational aspects of resistance to family planning in an Indian village. Demography. : 764.
6. Haté, C. A. 1969. Changing Status of Woman in Post-Independence India. Chap. IV: 101–128. Allied Publishers Private, Ltd. Bombay, India.
7. Diaz, M. N. 1969. Part II: Economic Relations. *In* Peasant Society. (J. Potter, M. N. Diaz & G. Foster.) Little Brown & Co. Boston, Mass.
8. Berelson, B. *et al.*, Eds. 1966. Family Planning and Population Programs. University of Chicago Press. Chicago, Ill.
9. Chandrasekhar, S. 1967. India's Population: Facts, Problems and Policy. Meenkshi Prakashan. New Delhi, India.
10. Nag, M. 1966. Family type and fertility. United Nations, World Population Conf. 1965. **II:** 160–163. United Nations. New York, N.Y.

11. Polgar, S. 1969. Culture and family planning. Paper presented at the Annual Meeting of the Society for Applied Anthropology, Mexico City, April 10.
12. Illich, I. 1969. Article. N. Y. Review of Books.
13. Berreman, G. D. 1969. Women's roles and politics: India and the United States. *In* Readings in General Sociology. 4th edit.: 68–71. Houghton Mifflin Co. Boston, Mass.

Discussion

Ruth B. Kundsin, Sc.D., *Moderator*

L. Newman: I was very intrigued to have heard recently the statement from our Secretary of Health, Education, and Welfare apropos of family planning. I heard a review on the radio and he was quoted as saying, "There are a lot of women who haven't gotten the word yet." It is very interesting that on a governmental level we consider family planning to be women's work!

I would like to raise a point that has come out of my participation in a fair number of women's liberation meetings and other sorts of communication and conferences. This has to do with the possibility of basic changes not only in women's self-definition, but also in men's self-definition. The theme comes through that the redefinition of women's personality and self is only a door to open people's minds to the possibility of *human* redefinition of self, and that such a redefinition is seen as effecting men's release as well as women's liberation. The idea here is that women as women have been storming the wrong bastions, and that men as men have been protecting these same wrong defenses. I find this very interesting. It separates us, is a kind of divergence from, the feminism of the past. It is a more democratic approach.

I would like to reopen the question of genocide because I referred to it in my paper. The genocide issue is not so much related to whether people accept or don't accept family-planning offerings, clinics, or whatever they happen to be, but is a function of their perception that those who are offering these things are offering them from motives which may be defined as genocide. In other words, I perfectly well understand the situation that was referred to previously, where militant black men would say, "Down with family planning," and militant black women would require that the clinics be reopened. This makes sense to me, because what the men were complaining about, I believe, was the motive. Again, this comes back to Steve Polgar's view, that if we offer health care, that is fine, but if we offer only family planning, there is something in it for us and not necessarily for the recipients. To review my paper's key points:

The comparison in my paper is between India and the United States. Professor Moni Nag is present, so I trust I shall be corrected on any errors. My own experience has been in the study of birth practices in India and the United States, as well as in Japan and Sweden, so the subject of family planning is somewhat ancillary. My interests have to do with all aspects of birth, structural obstacles, and, on the most abstract level, the problem of cultural and social pluralism. We have been discussing this all along in this question of genocide. The largest structural obstacle to acceptance of family planning, then, is distrust of policies carried out for subordinate groups by dominant groups, no matter how eloquently they are stated in terms of the subordinate groups' self-interest.

In the United States, it seems to me, we don't have too much in the way of cultural obstacles to acceptance of family planning. We tend to like the idea of controlling our own destinies. We tend to think of this in many different ways, and to transfer it to the question of family planning is simply another way. Many will disagree with me on that point, I know. In India specifically, there is great dissonance in subcultural background between those who are offering family planning and those who are supposed to be accepting it. Part of this has to do with the fact that both the concept and the practice of Western medicine is the basis for family-planning programs in India. This is one of its greatest difficulties in India.

Let me express several thoughts I have not mentioned previously, but which I have discussed with other people at other times. For example, to what extent are family-planning programs another instance of sex racism? To what extent is the idea of family planning imposed by males on females? If this *is* the case, to what extent is this another form of taking control?

Part of the final section of my paper, on interpersonal obstacles, has to do with the balance of power in the family. This is a very interesting question, and nobody talks about it very much. Individual differences are great, of course, so when one speaks of interpersonal impediments to the acceptance of family planning, it is important to remember that we are already in an area which has huge variations, no matter what culture is under discussion. However, cultural factors are part of the definition of expectations within the family, of who is going to do what, and who is going to make decisions about what. This aspect introduces many problems that are rather unidentifiable in many situations. Individual differences occur in the balance of power in particular Indian families, but the advent of family planning concentrated on numbers upsets this balance, because it makes available alternatives for the husband and wife and has a corrosive effect on the decision-making function of the joint family, to the advantage of the Western nuclear type of family. While a change in family structure is not the goal of a family-planning program, it, in effect, can function as an agent of such change without any element of anticipatory planning. Perhaps there should be some research along this line.

Finally, my ultimate point is that Western nations, from imposition characterized by Senator Fulbright as "the arrogance of power," seem to assume stupidity and conservatism on the part of people of the underdeveloped nations. Obstacles to family planning are not figments of the imagination of those for whom it is advocated. They are real problems of social structure, of politics, of economics, of health and survival. The greatest obstacle to family planning in many countries is perhaps this arrogance on the part of the educated and the advantaged. A worldwide crisis requires a worldwide response, not a response aimed at poor people and underdeveloped nations.

There was a political issue here, too, in that the President who enunciated the first family-planning program to the United States came from a family that is noted all over the world for having large numbers of children. So that when some well-meaning professional says to persons in other countries, "Well, you should practice family planning," the response may be, "Who says so?" and the answer is, "The President of the United States does," it seems unlikely to work. But people, I suggest, are not so stupid not to go to clinics because they don't know enough, as was pointed out by the Beasley example already cited. Rather, people see only too clearly what are the motives behind these suggestions. Of course, I am not going to suggest that we stop using family planning. I am simply trying to suggest that it be recommended as a worldwide idea to be used by everyone.

I have one other point. I would like to note some of the ideas of Jean Mayer, who suggests from the ecological point of view, that wealthy nations despoil the earth faster than anybody else, and that perhaps family planning should, among other things, be recommended *first* to these nations.

LIEBERMAN: I am glad you mentioned the last point, which was taken up in a recent article in the *New Republic;* I have forgotten the name of the author. The point he raised is that each middle-class American birth has the ecological equivalent of 80 Indian peasants. We have to begin thinking in terms of such equivalents, and when we talk about population increase we should consider this.

Will you comment on one other point in your paper? You say that canned milk may decrease breast feeding, which may then increase the frequency of pregnancy in the Third World. What happens when Western technology goes even further and introduces sex choice? What will happen when people can relatively simply determine whether they will have a boy or a girl child?

L. NEWMAN: Do you mean in India? That would be the ultimate birth control, because they will choose all males, and we won't have to worry about overpopulation in India anymore.

NAG: You have raised an important point. When we can really find out the sort of sex determination and sex control which occurs in countries like India, it will have a considerable effect upon the whole demographic picture. But that is one thing we may have to wait for 120 or so years to find out.

As an anthropologist, I am interested not only in cultural obstacles but also in the cultural aspects which *favor* family planning. My assumption here is that every society in the world has something in it—social institutions or cultural institutions—that favors spacing of children. Why do people in societes all over the world not invariably have 11 or 12 children or pregnancies? Every society has something, and always had something, which spaced children. For example, why is it in India, without any modern family planning, that the average number of children per family is much less than in Ireland and in other places? In India, family planning is not something which has just been imported from abroad. It was always there, and this is something for investigation. Without formal family planning in many families in India, why are there no more than four children? Things like sexual abstinence and sexual attitudes in general have a lot to do with it.

In reference to cultural impediments, I think the impediments which come from a subculture of physicians are perhaps greater than those of the culture of the people. Their original reactions to male sterilization is an example. Mass sterilization in India by now numbers more than five million people over the last seven or eight years. Ten years ago, the officials were all skeptical about it. They questioned whether the people would accept sterilization. A survey was made in West Bengal in 1962 about vasectomy; women and men were questioned. More than 95% of those surveyed opposed it. The reasons they gave were the sort of false reasons that, it seemed to me, could be easily removed by some sort of public education. At that time, nobody could believe it was possible, and the doctors and family-planning people in West Bengal thought it would fail because people were against it. The doctors especially were opposed to it because of their own reasons.

Subsequently, when the family-planning people really became serious and started educating the people about the technique and promulgating it, the result was that by 1966 there were about 300,000 vasectomies done on men in one year. Even against cultural obstacles that were previously thought impossible to overcome, where the women said they were against operations because the men would become impotent, once the facts were made clear, a large number, now five million—unbelievable for any part of the world—was reached.

With the IUCD, of course, there are the problems of bleeding and pain. Consider the village woman who may have had to walk 10 miles to come to the clinic. The doctor is there only once a week. She has the IUCD inserted and goes back to her own village. Once at home, she complains, and someone brings her back to the clinic. But the doctor is not there; there is a lack of facilities for her. I know of a woman who had such an experience who must have dissuaded at least 200 other women from using the IUCD. That is the reason for the drop in the use of the IUCD. Such situations can't be called cultural.

I agree that there is a limitation-of-motivation problem that we also need to consider. I think most families in India would like to have a number of children, to the extent of four or five or more. But that problem applies not only in India, but also in the United States. We have to motivate people everywhere to have fewer children. And research is needed, as Petersen has said, not only on family planning and attitudes, but also on age at marriage and on employment of women.

But, although I agree with Petersen on this point, I think that his statement about India's lack of success in family planning is completely wrong. To say he was in haste is the best way of defending him. The cultural factors are there, but we should also consider research on cultural factors which have kept fertility lower than what it should have been otherwise, if all people really wanted to have as many children as possible. For example, there are many people raised in India who do not want to have as many children as possible and who practice some method not to. It may be abstinence or other related methods. We should not overemphasize the cultural impediments that are supposedly confined to India; they also exist in Latin America. There is the matter of inadequate facilities and administrative problems. Management of family planning, of modern inventions like one pill a month, is in a terrible mess. Such shortcomings could have a tremendous effect in India.

KUNDSIN: Are these vasectomies you referred to done by Western physicians or Indian physicians?

NAG: These are all Indian physicians. I met some in Bombay who were doing it in a very businesslike way, giving incentives to the middleman. India is the only country that has taken steps of that kind, of paying money to a middleman for collecting people for vasectomies. This approach was unthinkable 20 years ago in India and in other modern countries. It has been done without much political opposition and in spite of the fears of Muslims that the Hindus are growing in numbers and so they, the Muslims, should oppose operations. Although we consider ourselves developed, apparently we are not keeping up with the developing countries.

L. NEWMAN: Would Professor Nag clarify one point? Are the people who perform vasectomies in India Western-trained doctors who are Indians?

NAG: They are Western-trained. There are Western-oriented, modern medical schools in India. Much stress has also been placed on the indigenous medical services, such as those of the Ayurvedic and other people. In most cases, this was because modern medical facilities weren't available in all areas. All the surveys that have been done indicate that if modern devices were available, they would be accepted. For example, when malaria-control programs were started, medical personnel found that the people took the medicine very well. So malaria has been eradicated, even while perhaps 50% of the people are still taking indigenous medicine. They do not necessarily prefer it to modern medicine.

TANGRI: Dr. Newman, will you talk about the usefulness of the family structure, or variants, where it is possible, and its relevance to expanded roles?

L. NEWMAN: You mean in India?

TANGRI: Or the communes of hippies and so on—rearrangements of the marriage situation.

L. NEWMAN: You refer to variations in family structure. Some of this has occurred. In California, there is a fair amount of experimentation with family structure, some of which occurs for the purpose of making possible education or work for mothers of young children. These situations appear to be occurring elsewhere, as well. I have received a communication from Washington University in St. Louis describing a *kibbutz* setup, essentially for mothers of small children. Presumably this includes fathers too, and everybody lives there together. There seems to be a lot of experimentation going on in family arrangements or at least in housing arrangements, in communal living, and in attempts to work out other kinds of systems.

In India, of course, the joint family is a beautiful place for a girl to continue her education; she is considered immature when she comes into the joint family, and there is certainly the expectation that if she is interested in education, she can go on. She has her family. The babies are taken care of by surrogate mothers—grandmothers, aunts, other women who are around. I have heard many Indian women say, "You Westerners don't know what you are missing by not having the joint family, because it makes it so easy to go to school and to work." A study done by Chandrakala A. Haté, to which I refer in my paper, on the working women in

Bombay, found that family numbers among this group were smaller, and that working was a possible alternative for these women. The findings agreed with my other sources on Indian women, that is, even though women are subjugated in India more than almost anywhere else, when they do have aspirations outside the home, these aspirations are taken seriously. Consequently, when they decide that they want to go to work, they are treated as people rather than as subjects.

KAMM: You say that women are freer to go outside the home, but what about men coming into it? You say there are mother-surrogates. Are these only women, or also men, taking care of the children?

L. NEWMAN: Are you talking about India?

KAMM: The question was somewhat general—on the general nature of altering family structure, or redoing the family altogether. The emphasis thus far has been that once women have one or two children, once they have taken care of the home's responsibility, then they can fly the coop. But it seems to me that even if I choose to have ten children, the essential point is that it is not I alone who bear the responsibility for taking care of them. In other words, women will not be free until not only can they go outside the home, but men can come into it. I wonder if there is any evidence that this is taking place?

L. NEWMAN: It is taking place to a large extent. I had a rude, but pleasant, awakening not long ago while teaching a course at San Francisco State College, where I had mainly undergraduate men in the class. I was talking about early socialization and about mother-infant interaction. Soon I could see that things were seething in the room. I attempted to find out why. It finally boiled over into a large number of boys saying, "All you talk about is mother-child interaction. Don't you know there are fathers, too?"

I found an underlying vein of real resentment among them at the emphasis in the psychological and sociological literature that seems to eliminate the male from parenthood. People who have this kind of feeling—and I noticed it among these boys—were those who, in their spare time, were making extra money teaching nursery school and kindergarten and working in day-care centers. Even though they didn't have children themselves, they put themselves in contact with children. Some of the values of the present college generation have to do with this attitude. I think the changes will take place. I think that some of them are already taking place, for example, some of the communal housing arrangements in Sweden *and* in the United States.

KAMM: I think you'll find that the motivations for this switch are not always good. For example, there is a current notion that there is a feminine principle in society, and that this has a bad influence, especially on male children. A recent book stressed this feminization of the male, saying that the reason women should not spend so much time in the home and teaching children in the lower grades is that there is a kind of infection of passivity carried by females that spreads to the male. It is all right for women to be passive, but they must not spread it to the men and that it is in the men's own interest that they take care of their children. This way of thinking is essentially an extension of the Victorian principle that women can take care of women, but men have to take care of men, or else they won't be men when they grow up.

Very often, the motivation in regard to the father-figure in the black family is that he is needed as an authority-figure; that is, with the absence of the male there is an absence of an authority-figure. The notion of the woman as only a mothering or passive figure is not attacked. Rather, the idea is put forth that one has to have an authority-figure around the house, and that it can only be the male. Very often, these moves we are now seeing to bring the man into the home are really deceptive extensions of the superior male in Western dogma.

L. NEWMAN: I did not feel that the students were male supremacists. I did have the impression that they were feeling very much put down by the literature they were forced to read, that they were resentful of the exclusive emphasis on the maternal role because they felt that their role as parents was being denigrated. They placed a very strong value on relationships with children. I didn't sense it to be other than that.

EPSTEIN: I have been conducting interviews with women who were graduated from college in the last three years. In response to the question whether they would like to see more men or more women on the same jobs that they themselves were doing, I find that many of the girls teaching school felt there should be more men in the classrooms. Why? Because there has to be a male model and authority-figure, and without this, the poor children are being feminized and that, of course, is a disease which we should keep them from getting! In other words, the women themselves, the schoolteachers, are very much convinced that the chief problem in the school system has to do with the fact that almost all of the teachers are women, and that this isn't good for the students.

REEVES: The traditionalized division of labor is an assumption that is scarcely questioned in much of the professional literature. It isn't questioned very much in sociology; it isn't questioned very much in psychology. There is a kind of discriminatory sense even among anthropologists, so that they conceive of early women as if they were their own wives, only camping out and with shaggy brows. There isn't the same rigor and critical faculty brought to bear on this traditionalization that is brought to other assumptions. It is familiar, and therefore it must have been eternal. And so, when these young people try to cope with it, they start reversing. The real question is one of stereotype and traditionalization. Perhaps as an anthropologist, Dr. Newman would like to speak to that.

L. NEWMAN: I would be happy to! What you are saying is exactly what came out of that particular set of questions in my class. We thereupon discarded the syllabus and went on to look at this very question as an attempt, on my part, to forestall the opposite overreaction. We found that the lierature is full of this kind of stereotypical thinking. I have known this myself, because I work in the area of birth, pregnancy, and family planning. You begin asking anybody in any culture about pregnancy and birth, and you will hear all sorts of mythology, both from people in administrative positions and the people who have ostensibly lived through it.

In anthropology, I find two mainstreams of thought at present. One, the ethological theme, is one of the more horrifying things going on today, as far as I am concerned. For example, Lionel Tiger's "Men in Groups" is enough to shrivel your soul. This kind of thinking is, unfortunately, being perpetuated by people with great credentials in psychology, as well as by some without much at all in the way of credentials. One has to deal with this kind of approach in introductory courses in anthropology because of the publicity it has been receiving. Then one becomes a propagandist, and it is very difficult to handle the situation unless you devote enough time to it to make students come to their own decisions about these issues. The second view is really the opposite of the ethological school, and the one to which I subscribe. It is a reevaluation of any kind of behavior, looking at that behavior from the point of view of modern knowledge, not from analytic categories developed in the 19th century, which I think the current ethological argument represents.

CHESSLER: The argument that men should perhaps have more of a role in raising children becomes rather obvious when you consider the family as a producing unit. As the woman goes outside the home and starts doing more production in the market, the production in the household still has to occur, and part of that production is the raising of children and other forms of housework. If the woman is not available to do it, the man may do it. I find it just as abhorrent to say, as some female chauvinists do, that men cannot raise children as well as women, as to say that women can't go out into the world and work in offices and factories as well as men.

LIEBERMAN: My own reading of this discussion is that girls need the men in their early years of development almost as much as the boys do, if for no other reason that if they don't have the expectation that men can be parental, then they won't expect it of their own men when they grow up and marry. The answer to the argument of the male chauvinists that women are really bad for children, but we let them do it anyway by default, can be met by such other arguments as: The reason women are the only ones engaged in the rearing of children is that we regard the rearing of children as second-class work. Unless we regard it as first-class work and involvement, only women will be doing it, and not only will women be second class, young children will also be second class.

L. NEWMAN: There are other societies in which neither fathers nor mothers rear their children, but in which children are reared by other women. This perhaps makes them third-class citizens, but I think there are as many different answers to these problems as there are cultures. I tend to mistrust other people's theories and tend to think it is necessary to evolve one's own, because times change, things change, people change, and cultures change. All these things mean that theories have to change too! If we are using 19th century theory on current behavior, we are not going to get anywhere.

COMBS: I am with the Center for Population Research at the National Institutes of Health. What role *should* men play in the rearing of children? The discussion I have heard has not dealt with this "should" or "ought." It seems to me that the problem relates to the role men play in society traditionally, and to the role they play in the education of children. Men are primarily the professional or the occupational performers. Then their role is to train children in occupational roles that are relatively related to men. Where there are changes in these roles, so that there is an equivalence between male and female roles, then you may get a division here. But in the discussion of the role man plays in the school, for example, what role *should* he play? What *can* he contribute?

L. NEWMAN: Are you asking me? I am not going to answer you, because that is a question which has to do with the expectations of a particular society. I am not here to suggest how society ought to run. I view my role merely as describing how society *does* run in various places at various times. This is always the role of the social scientist, I suppose. As far as I am concerned, human beings are human beings, and it runs against my grain to talk about men and women in this way.

I think men should be involved in school. I was impressed with the students who felt this way. I have run into many others since then who felt this way. I did not and do not encourage them or discourage them. I get them to talk about it so they can figure out *what* they are thinking, so that they *are* thinking, rather than overreacting. I want their ideas to be based on real analyses of their own feelings and behavior.

LOOKING AHEAD: SOME SOCIAL AND INDIVIDUAL CONSEQUENCES OF MASS ACCEPTANCE OF THE TWO-CHILD FAMILY IN BRITAIN

Derek G. Gill, B.Sc. (Soc.)

Medical Sociology Research Unit
Centre for Social Studies
Aberdeen, Scotland

Trends in Family Size

The mean ultimate family size in England and Wales in 1861–1869 was 6.16 children; by 1952, it had fallen to 2.21. The figure of 6.16 is for cohorts married between 1861–1869 at all ages under 45 years and is, therefore, an actual mean ultimate family size. The cohort married in 1952 could still be producing children, and the mean of 2.21 children is an estimated mean ultimate family size using fertility rates for 1956–1957.[1] In the same period, rates of infant mortality also declined. This fall in infant mortality in the second half of the 19th century is attributable to a rise in the material standard of living occasioned by the introduction of public-health measures which, through the provision of clean water and efficient sewage disposal, helped to create an environment less favorable for the spread of infectious disease. Research into the reasons for the fall in family size is incomplete and still poses great problems, but it is reasonable to postulate a similar relationship between a rising standard of living and education and a gradual reduction in family size, at least in a British setting. As the 20th century progressed, the growth of knowledge and sophistication in obstetric techniques, improvements in general medicine, and the establishment of a National Health Service have made it possible to reduce reproductive losses at confinement to a minimum. Today, in Aberdeen, the majority of deaths preventable by technical skill have been eliminated.[2] Thus, while actual family size has fallen, parents can be almost certain that each pregnancy that continues to term will result in a live-born child whose subsequent morbidity experience leads to the prediction of an average life expectancy of 70 and 75 years for males and females, respectively. This situation contrasts sharply with the number of pregnancies necessary to achieve a particular family size in mid-19th century Britain. With rates of infant mortality reaching as high as 40–50% over the first five years of life, to reach an ultimate family size of six children, the average mother would have had to produce at least twelve children.

In Aberdeen, the reduction of reproductive loss to an irreducible minimum, given the present standard of biological efficiency in the contemporary reproductive cohorts, has been achieved by creating an integrated maternity service that cares for almost the total population of pregnant women. Hospital confinements under the care of specialist obstetric and pediatric staffs account for virtually all deliveries to women resident in the city.[3] Women who are poor obstetric risks, [e.g., short women (below 5′1″) whose husbands are unskilled manual workers, the "grand" multipara, diabetics, etc.] can be accorded the maximum of care and attention which a modern well-equipped and adequately staffed hospital can provide.

But a maternity service organized as outlined can also operate in the sphere of what might be described as positive obstetrics by the introduction of ameliorative and preventive measures. While average family size has declined, there is still a social-class gradient in fertility, with the largest number of children born to families in social class V (unskilled manual workers). In these families, pregnancies may succeed one another with monotonous regularity until the mother is worn out by excessive childbearing and the struggle to nurture and rear an overlarge family. Alternatively, an unwanted pregnancy may occur when efforts to prevent conception have failed, leading to excessive strain and anxiety in an already debilitated woman sufficient to persuade the family doctor and obstetrician that continuance of the pregnancy would involve a risk to the mother's physical and/or mental health. When such unfavorable environmental circumstances exist, the pregnant woman may be offered postpartum sterilization, termination of pregnancy, or, possibly, both.

Abortion is, however, an inappropriate measure for routine fertility control. Contraceptive advice has been available as part of postnatal care in Aberdeen since 1946, but attendances were poor, especially among the lower social classes, where a lack of expertise and feelings of estrangement in a bureaucratic setting among some sections of the working class may discourage attendance at clinics.[4] In 1948, the voluntary family-planning clinic established in 1936 under the instigation of Dr. Marie Stopes was taken over by the local authority, and its services were provided free of charge after October, 1966. Again, attendances were poor, with only 48 new attenders registering at the clinic in the first quarter of 1964. The introduction of the oral contraceptive in May of 1964 led to a dramatic increase in new registrations—from 388 new attenders in 1964 to 1,280 in 1968, with nine out of every ten new attenders being prescribed and accepting the pill in that year. Similar conclusions were drawn from an examination of the records of family doctors: the increase in use of the pill, particularly for younger women, was quite marked. Clearly, general practitioners can no longer stand aloof from the question of family planning. Previously, contraceptive techniques requiring professional medical advice—the intrauterine contraceptive device and the vaginal diaphragm—were fitted, in the majority of cases, by the staffs of family-planning clinics. The advent of the pill has forced the general practitioner to take on a more positive role in fertility control. However, it may be necessary to go even further, to introduce a domiciliary-based family-planning service if the "hard core" of women unable to control their own fertility are to be reached.

Some indication of the change that has occurred in contraceptive habits resulting from the introduction of the pill can be derived from two surveys of married women, drawn in 1955–1958 and 1967, associated with other studies, of women who had been married between five and nine years. The use of both coitus interruptus and the diaphragm had declined, suggesting that couples (mainly the upper socioeconomic group) now reject the diaphragm in favor of the pill and that others (mainly the lower socioeconomic group) who previously would have risked the uncertainties of coitus interruptus now prefer to use oral contraceptives.[5]

This combination of trends—the advent of the pill, the ready availability of contraceptive advice and services, and, to a lesser extent, the continuation of the program of sterilization and/or abortion for the grand multipara established well before 1964—has resulted in a fall in the number of legitimate births to Aberdonians in the last five years. By 1968, the total annual number of births had fallen from 3,073 in 1963 to 2,580, a reduction of almost one-sixth. The Scottish Registrar-General's annual Statistical Reviews show that the estimated population of Aberdeen between 1964 and 1967 has not changed appreciably; hence, the fall in the number of births cannot be attributed to a sudden increase in outmigration. If this tendency for women to make effective use of the facilities and services available to control their fertility continues, then an average, completed family size in Aberdeen of approximately two children is likely to ensue in the near future. Certainly, some women are beginning to demand a complete and final cessation of their reproductive careers. By the end of 1967, a few women, after three or four years of oral contraception, were requesting tubal ligation.

While legitimate births have fallen quite sharply, illegitimate maternities,

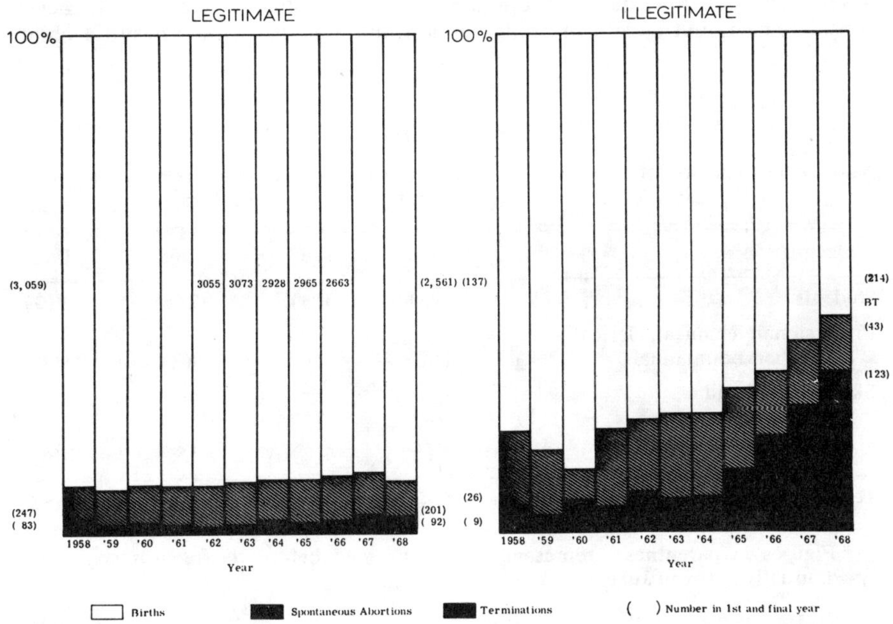

FIGURE 1. Outcome of pregnancies for Aberdeen city women, during the ten-year period 1958–1968.

despite an increase in the number of such pregnancies terminated, have continued to increase throughout the same period, as illustrated in FIGURE 1. Moreover, this increase in illegitimacy has not arisen because fewer pregnant women are prepared to enter a hasty and ill-prepared marriage, since the number of prenuptial conceptions has also increased over this period.[6] Clearly, the advent of oral contraception has had little influence on the illegitimacy ratio. This is hardly surprising because it is a form of contraception that demands a high degree of preparation. Sanctions against premarital intercourse have probably weakened in British society in recent years, but societal attitudes toward contraception for the unmarried, particularly young people, are, to say the least, confused. In consequence, adequate sex education and instruction in contraceptive technique is usually not available to adolescents either from their parents or from the schools. But even if contraceptives were freely available to all ages and without reference to marital status, Schofield's study suggests that some people would not use them because they do not like contraceptives or could not be bothered with them.[7] However, evidence from Aberdeen again suggests a trend that may become increasingly common in the future.

TABLE 1 shows that among students and women in nonmanual occupations, there has been a sharp increase in the number of unmarried women attending the family-planning clinic for the first time and who remain single for three months or more thereafter. The provision of an integrated and continuous program of sex education geared appropriately to each age group, and introducing contraceptive information as maturation proceeds, would perhaps assist the development of a climate of opinion in which sexual intercourse is never considered without benefit of contraception unless both partners desire a child.

TABLE 1

NEW ATTENDERS TO THE FAMILY-PLANNING CLINIC DURING THE FIRST QUARTER OF EACH YEAR WHO ARE UNMARRIED AT FIRST VISIT *

Occupation	1965	1966	1967	1968	1969
Students	1	3(3)	3(3)	12(5)	39(9)
Professional, technical, clerical and other nonmanual	2(2)	1(1)	4(4)	6(3)	23(17)
Skilled, semi- and unskilled manual	1(1)	—	3(3)	7(5)	4(2)
Not stated	—	1	4(2)	5	8(5)
Totals	4(3)	5(4)	14(12)	30(13)	74(33)

* Figures in parentheses represent women married before the records were analyzed, usually between June and August each year.

Perhaps such a program should also emphasize that the condom provides a degree of protection against venereal infection. This, together with the development of a contraceptive that prevents implantation of a fertilized ovum when a woman has been exposed to the risk of conception (the "morning after" pill), may combine to initiate a reduction in the illegitimate birth rate.

Where the rates of illegitimacy and prenuptial conception are over 50%, as among Aberdeen fish workers[8] (a numerically important and socially distinct local occupational group), and to a lesser degree in other unskilled manual occupations, a different approach to sex education might be necessary. These groups are certainly exhibiting a "behavior stretch" in that their patterns of sexual behavior are clearly far removed from the norm prescribed by the middle-class-dominated value system of British society. In this sense, Rodman's[9–11] formulation of a "lower-class value stretch" might be an appropriate model for analyzing the process whereby fish workers and others have developed a different set of attitudes and behavior in the sphere of sexuality. Such a study would attempt to understand and explain this particular pattern of sexual behavior and to incorporate the findings into a specially designed program of sex education in schools where children from these backgrounds predominated.

The Future Situation of Women

The account of child-bearing outlined in the previous section suggests that the trend from five or six toward a one or two child family is already firmly established in Aberdeen, and Titmuss has described the impact that the fall in family size has had on feminine life chances.[12] At the turn of the century, the expectation of life of a woman aged 20 was 46 years (i.e., age at death would be 66 years). Approximately one-third of this life sphere was likely to be spent in a state of pregnancy and in nursing a child for the first year of its life. By midcentury, the expectation of life of a woman aged 20 had risen to 55 years (i.e., age at death would be 75 years) and only about 7% of the adult life cycle would be concerned with childbearing and maternal care.

Not only are marriages lasting longer, but the institution itself is becoming more popular. By 1965, it was estimated that in the age range 35 to 44 years, 863 males and 882 females were married per 1,000, against 1931 ratios of 855 males and 752 females per 1,000. This increase in the proportion of women married in each age group and in the total number of marriages contracted has also been accompanied by a falling age at marriage. The mean age of spinsters marrying bachelors in 1951 was 23.50 years; by 1965, this had fallen to 21.95 years, as is illustrated by the increase in the proportion of spinsters who marry in their teens—from an annual average of 186 per 1,000 for the period 1951–1955 to 306 per 1,000 in 1964. Part of the reason for the increase in the marriage rate may be related to demographic factors. The sex ratio at birth in Britain today is about 106 males to every 100 females, and in the age range 15 to 45 years men outnumber women until the age of 43 years, when parity is achieved.[13] At present, the discrepancy in numbers is small, but there is no reason to suppose that the declining level of infant mortality, which has had a differential effect on the comparatively high rate of infant deaths among boys, will be halted. Moreover, the last two decades have not involved the British in a major international conflict of the kind which, at least in the recent past, has entailed the loss of considerable proportions of young adult males. In these circumstances, presumably, most females who wish to marry are able to do so.

The Family Life Cycle

We generally think of the family life cycle as divided in seven stages, as given in Table 2. The fall in average family size and the decline in the average age at marriage have combined to truncate stages I–III. Stages IV and V are now completed at an earlier point in the life cycle, and stages VI and VII have lengthened considerably as a result of the increase in longevity.

TABLE 2

THE FAMILY LIFE-CYCLE

Stages	Characteristics
I	Development phase; young married couple euphoria and gradual adjustment
II	Child bearing and infant care; families with preschool children
III	Families with young children at school
IV	Families with teenagers
V	Families as launching centers; new family units being created
VI	Middle Years; "empty nest" to retirement
VII	Aging families; retirement to death of one or both spouses

PATTERNS OF FEMININE EMPLOYMENT

The change in the life-style of women in the second half of the present century is best demonstrated by the phenomenal increase in the number of married women working (both full- and part-time), from approximately 1 million in 1946 to 3.75 million in May, 1955. This latter figure represented 48% of women gainfully employed. By 1966, there were nearly 5 million working wives, representing more than one-third of all married women, out of a total female labor force of nearly 9 million, and it is clearly evident that the biggest source of recruitment has been married women over 30 years of age.[14] But, as Nancy Seear has so ably demonstrated, women are underrepresented in the higher echelons of the civil service, in the professions, and in higher grades in industry. In general, with the exception of nursing, and to a lesser extent teaching, social work, and clerical work, women tend to be employed in the less-skilled occupations.

This concentration of female employment on the bottom rungs of the occupational ladder is highlighted by the low earnings of women workers. Frank Cousins, addressing a recent meeting of the Trades Union Congress, stated that British women workers average only about 57% of the male rates. Average earnings in 1966 of administrative, technical, and clerical employees in a sample of industries including manufacture, services, and extraction were £26. 14.1 per week for males and £11.2.7 per week for females.[15] This difference in average earnings by sex must be due in part to the much smaller proportion of women in the higher-status and better-paid administrative positions. Thus, while the average weekly rates of pay of women in manufacturing industry in the administrative, technical, and clerical group of occupations were 49% of the average male rate, for the monthly salaried female employees (a crude but reasonable indicator of higher-status positions) their pay was only 43% of their male equivalents. This difference suggests a stronger association between sex and status among monthly paid workers. The lower rates of pay for women also reflect a degree of financial discrimination in favor of the male sex when both sexes are employed in the same occupational role. The Institute of Personnel Management has estimated that among clerical workers in the engineering industry, the average basic pay for a job of "routine responsibility" was £15.19.1 for men and £10.9.8 for women. Such clear evidence of discrimination against women on the grounds of sex alone has raised the tempo of the campaign for equal pay for women. Not long ago, the strength of feeling among female employees was demonstrated by women workers at the Ford factory in Dagenham when they struck, demanding parity in rates of pay. Recently, the British government has accepted the justice of the campaign for equal pay and has stated that this form of discrimination should be gradually phased out by 1975. This is a decision to be applauded, but it creates a range of problems requiring urgent attention before the issue may be considered closed. Perhaps the most intractable problem stems from attempts to define exactly what is equal work. In the Ford Motor Co. dispute, it was pointed out that the men doing the same work as the female strikers were required to work a shift system and accept periods of night work. Presumably, a claim for extra financial reward is valid when the occupational role necessitates periodic absences from home outside what are viewed as "normal" working hours. Other difficulties arise when the question of evaluative and enforcement mechanisms is considered. Who shall judge what is and what is not equal work? What criteria are appropriate for such a task? For occupations in which women predominate or make up the whole labor force, it will be extremely difficult to say what the rate of pay "ought" to be. The latter point might be related to the arguments in favor of a national minimum wage, but this suggestion is usually related to attempts to define a rate of pay which takes into account the average (male?) wage earner's "family responsibilities." But, even assuming that these problems of comparability could be resolved and a decision-making body established, what agency would be capable of enforcing equal pay? A consistent and militant policy on the part of the trade unions in favor of equal pay probably offers the highest chance of success, but in 1965 only about 25% of the female labor force were members of trade unions, as against almost 66% of male workers. If a militant trade union policy in favor of equal pay were to be successful, it would require considerable male support and, presumably, a high degree of altruism on their part.

Given such relatively low rates of pay for women it is surprising that such large numbers have rejoined the labor force in the last two decades. Several studies of women and women workers carried out in Britain[16, 17] have shown that while financial considerations do play a large part in recruiting married women, other factors are also of considerable importance. These include a range of motivations which appear to be associated with the fall in family size, early age at marriage, and increased longevity. When the "empty nest" looms large on the horizon, the reaction seems to be a desire to fill the empty years with something in addition to less-demanding domestic duties. Women state that they return to work "for companionship," to "escape the drudgery and social isolation of housework," when "the children have grown up" or "no longer require constant attention," or even "just to fill in time." But for many, the major incentive is financial, whether it be to enable the family to afford a wider range of luxury goods or simply to supplement the husband's inadequate wage. In the mid-1950's, it was fashionable to condemn women with young children for returning to work. In the House of Lords, the phrase "latch-key children" was common currency to represent a whole range of pejorative attitudes toward women workers with young children.[1] These sentiments were almost certainly associated with the age-old propensity to argue that "the country is going to the dogs" and that "the family is not what it used to be" suddenly becoming quasirespectable as a result of an over-enthusiastic emphasis and interpretation of the Bowlby thesis on maternal deprivation. More recently, theories of socialization and learning in childhood have stressed the need for preschool children to interact with children of their own age in semistructured play group/learning situations. Middle-class mothers, the women best equipped to respond to these new demands and thwarted by the lack of state provision of nursery schools and play groups, have started to take the initiative by combining together to provide such activities either in their own homes or in other available accommodations.

Women who *want* to work may be less incensed by low wages and the totally inadequate provision of child-care facilities by the state, but women who *have* to work are in a more difficult situation. Unsupported mothers (the widowed, deserted, separated, divorced, and the unmarried), if they have to work, must meet any costs involved in the provision of substitute care for their children out of a wage well below the average for complete family units. Moreover, officials of the Supplementary Benefits Commission (formerly the National Assistance Board Officers) may sometimes try to persuade women to return to full-time work, although assistance for unsupported mothers is a right, and despite the fact that part-time work plus supplementary benefit [providing she does not earn more than £2 per week (1966 values)] provides a higher income than the national average for women workers.[18]

Women's Roles and Feminine Socialization

Although equal pay and a greater proportion of men entering traditionally women's occupations (e.g., teaching and social work) may combine to force women's wages upward, it is unlikely that these factors will alter the overall low status of female work; attention must be directed toward the more subtle aspects of sex-role discrimination. In the 19th century, a woman's place was unequivocally seen to be the home, and Hoggart[19] has suggested that in the 1950s late adolescence for girls was viewed among working-class groups as a brief butterfly-like existence between leaving school and settling down to the dreary but dominant job of marriage and child rearing. Today, the force of events—sociodemographic changes and the growing demand for social emancipation—calls for a new approach to feminine roles, but patterns of child rearing and socialization still reflect a more traditional attitude to male and female roles.

Parsons and Bales have likened the patterns of instrumental and expressive leadership observable in small-group situations to the differentiation of husband and wife roles present in the nuclear family:[20]

> . . . The area of instrumental function concerns relations of the system (the family) to its situation outside the system, to meeting the adaptive conditions of its maintenance of equilibrium, and "instrumentally" establishing the desired relations to *external* objects. The expressive area concerns the "internal" affairs of the system, the maintenance of integrative relations between the members, and regulation of the patterns and tension levels of its component units.

Zelditch provided support for the Parsons-Bales hypothesis by analyzing ethnographic materials defining the instrumental and expressive leader of the nuclear family in the following terms: [21]

Instrumental: "Ego is boss—manager of the farm; leader of the hunt etc. Ego is the final court of appeals, final judge and executor of punishment, discipline, and control over the children of the family.

Expressive: "Ego is the mediator, conciliator, of the family; ego soothes over disputes, resolves hostilities in the family. Ego is affectionate, solicitous, warm, emotional to the children of the family; ego is the 'comforter', the 'consoler', is relatively indulgent, relatively unpunishing."

While the above hypothesis and Zelditch's findings suggest that the major orientation of feminine roles is toward expressive-integrative tasks in stages II and III of the family life cycle, it is less certain that women's complete career is similarly oriented, especially in the one- or two-child family. Were the dominant family organization in Western society of the traditional extended pattern, then expressive-integrative roles could persist through the familial and feminine life cycles. But with the (relatively?) isolated nuclear family predominating, women are increasingly turning to paid employment for a second career. It could be argued that women with professional training and qualifications are beginning to view reproduction and child rearing as temporary but unavoidable breaks from an otherwise dominant interest in an occupation. A process of socialization which prepares girls for a predominantly expressive-integrative role in adult life is inappropriate for the type of life-styles and life-chances which will become available to more and more women if the sociodemographic and societal changes discussed previously ensue. Indeed, if sex-role socialization is considered from another point of view, the distinctions between male and female roles smack of another dichotomy, that between achievement and ascription. Women in Western society may not take the initiative in seeking a mate, but the "right" distribution of adipose and glandular tissue enables some women to "date the field" before accepting or selecting a permanent partner. But success here is only marginally under the control of the individual woman; nature's handiwork can be improved but not, as yet, completely recast. In the "rating and dating complex," women tend to play down their intellectual abilities, subdue their own interests, and feign concern for those of the current male escort. Zelditch's list of characteristics that fit the role of the expressive leader in the family suggest that the incumbent may have to suppress his or her own feelings and own self-interest if he or she is to perform successfully. To be the "comforter," the "consoler," to be affectionate, solicitous, and warm, the expressive leader must be adaptable, even malleable, to the forces operating in the nuclear family. Parsons and Bales [20] argue that in Western society the male is the instrumental head and therefore the power figure in the nuclear family, and the wife must respond to the husband's definitions of situations and prescriptions for behavior. The type of conjugal-role relationships—joint or segregated—clearly affect the degree and the spheres of influence of male dominance, but when the balance of power shifts, as it is said to do if the wife/mother is earning, then it is possible that the rigid distinction by sex between expressive and instrumental roles also declines.

Angrist has shown that female graduates and undergraduates often prepare for a multiplicity or roles, if often only implicitly, and that "to some degree women perceive themselves and are seen as having options in their adult roles.

These options are considered as contingencies around which women's sex-role learning occurs." [22] While childhood socialization continues to stress initiative, encourage enterprise, and even condone aggression for boys, and emphasize supportive, nurturative, and, in a sense, subsidiary, roles for girls, subsequent adult generations will not be equipped to deal with the new patterns of marital interaction, patterns that are consequent upon the emergence of newer life-styles and life-chances for women.

Society has yet to comprehend fully the impact of advances in contraceptive technology. Modern contraceptive techniques make it possible to separate sexual intercourse and procreation so that love-making need no longer be associated with a fear of its consequences. In the past, women have been sanctioned more severely than men for sexual transgressions (the double standard of sexual morality), and the fear of illegitimate pregnancy has undoubtedly contributed to the preservation of the norm that sexuality should be restricted to the marital bed. Oral contraception, virtually 100% effective, creates new possibilities in the sphere of sexual behavior. Women may now exercise the same freedom of choice with respect to pre- and extramarital intercourse formerly reserved for men under the double standard of sexual morality. As Sprey has argued, "sexuality is becoming institutionalized autonomously, that is, in its own right rather than primarily within the institutional contexts of reproduction and child-rearing." [23] Rather than "The Sex Game," sex as a game may become a part of future attitudes to sexuality.[24] Sexual interaction constitutes a reciprocal person-to-person relationship affording rewards and satisfactions to the participants. The nature of the rewards and the degree of satisfaction reflect the bargaining positions taken by the actors in the game. It is therefore appropriate to analyze sexual behavior "within a sociological framework of reciprocity and exchange." [23] It would be surprising if the trends analyzed previously, suggesting the likelihood of improvements in the status and position of women, were not also reflected in the sphere of sexuality, with women taking a stronger position in sexual exchange.

This view of sex as a game also receives support from another theoretical perspective, that of symbolic interactionism. Because overt discussion and expression of sexual behavior is taboo in our society, the normal procedure in sexual interaction is often via highly indirect cues and symbols.[25] Young men and women gradually build up experience in determining what areas and symbols are effective at particular stages of the game until, presumably, as the degree of intimacy increases, the verbalization of feelings and attitudes becomes possible. If, as Sprey suggests, sexuality is institutionalized autonomously, and the cues and symbols appropriate to a generally restrictive and restricted attitude to sexual behavior are changes, then the rules of the game may change, permitting freer and easier communication between potential sexual partners.

Discussion

Thus far, this analysis has been mainly restricted to interpretation and extrapolation of trends already extant in British society, and to an examination of certain aspects of sexual and sex-role socialization theory. These trends and theoretical perspectives have clear implications for the future provision of educational and medical services under the British system of overall state responsibility in these areas. Although the implications of these changes may be clear, the extent to which British society will adapt to changing female roles and role sets is more problematic. An attempt will thus be made to assess the nature and extent of the changes consequent on or in preparation for the mass acceptance of the one- or two-child family in the spheres of sex education, women's occupations, and family-planning services:

Sex Education in Schools

Slowly, the need for the provision of sex education in the schools is becoming accepted. The British Broadcasting Corporation has recently introduced a series of such programs into its television service for schools, and public response has been generally favorable. This is perhaps indicative of a changing attitude to sexuality in general: [6]

> Today sexual relations in marriage are less concerned with procreation than with providing mutual satisfaction and support within the marital relationship, a change made possible by the development of simple and effective methods of contraception. Confirmation that sex does play a more overt, probably a more crucial, role in marriage is provided by the frank discussion of such matters in modern mass media and by the appearance of and great demand for "marriage manuals"—a euphemism for texts providing instruction in sexual techniques and the psychology of sexual adjustment.

The gradual withering away of the double standard of sexual morality, a heightened public concern with rising rates of illegitimacy and prenuptial conception, and a growing awareness that an older, stricter, more dogmatic code of sexual behavior is no longer appropriate have combined to create a climate of opinion in favor of sex education. It is often argued that sex education should be the responsibility of the parents, but this view now receives less support. Illegitimacy and prenuptial conception occur most frequently in the lower socioeconomic groups, but recent work has shown that both these pregnancy categories have increased fastest in recent years among women from the upper end of the social-class continuum. Assuming that the existing provision of sex education in the schools has not deteriorated in recent years, then it would seem that the control that even the middle-class parents exercise over their children's sexuality has become less effective.

While the need for sex education in schools is generally accepted, considerable confusion still exists concerning what should be taught, who should teach it, in what context, and at what age instruction should commence. Ideally, instruction in human sexual behavior would proceed throughout the educational experience. Children's initial half-formulated questions would be answered fully and frankly but at a level commensurate with the child's level of understanding. As maturation proceeds, the complexity and social context of human sexual response can slowly be revealed. Most certainly a program of sex education would have to deal with the consequences of teenage sexuality. Teenagers do have sexual intercourse, and, as a result, an increasingly large number of unwanted babies are conceived. A course that sets out to describe the anatomy and physiology of human reproduction, emphasizing the part played by contraception, would provide a basis from which the individual could control his or her future sexual life and choose the circumstances under which the responsibilities of parenthood will be accepted. Put more briefly, the concept of family planning is now an integral part of a civilized existence, and like any other basic skill, needs to be taught.

Larger issues are introduced when discussion turns to the social and moral problems associated with teenage and adult sexuality. The debate on curriculum reform now attracts the attention of more and more educationalists and often centers on the need to equip young people for their eventual roles in an increasingly complex social system. Most schools now provide some instruction, variously described as "civics," "modern studies," and so on, the aim of which is to enable school children to acquire some of the skills they will need to become full members of the adult society. In adolescence and adulthood, sexual behavior and relationships play an important part in the process of living, and, clearly, courses aimed at preparing the school child for his or her future adult role cannot afford to ignore the problem posed by human sexuality.

The dichotomy proposed here, between sex instruction per se and the incorporation into a modern studies course of a discussion of the social and moral problems connected with sexual behavior, has certain advantages. Sex is an emotional topic, and the first part of the program, aimed at providing information on the "mechanics" of sex, is probably best dealt with in a morally and emotionally neutral atmosphere. Moreover, school teachers, even when they are specially trained, may find it difficult to handle the problems posed by placing such a course alongside their normal teaching responsibilities. Some schools are utilizing health visitors to undertake this responsibility, but within the context of a health-education program in general, so that sex instruction is provided in a relevant framework, eliminating to some extent the children's tendency to perceive the subject as a salacious interlude.

On the other hand, a course in modern studies has to incorporate material on controversial subjects and, in any case, is an attempt to prepare the schoolchild for adolescence and adulthood. What more appropriate context could be provided for examining the problems associated with human sexuality and family living? Ascriptive versus achievement elements in sex-role socialization could be discussed and related to the view that the distinction between the sexes stems from the expressive role of the wife and the instrumental role of the husband in the institution of marriage. The inadequacy of the latter viewpoint would be exposed as, through discussion, the multidimensional nature of feminine roles became apparent. Young men and women could be encouraged to face realistically the problem of choice, of decision-making, which the revolution in contraceptive technology has presented. What factors will determine the selection of a desired family size within the matrimonial diad? The mass acceptance of the one- or two-child family is *not* a foregone conclusion, as Betty Freidan's provocative comments—albeit cast in racy journalese—in "The Feminine Mystique" have indicated.

But, above all, the second part of the proposed course provides a vehicle for discussing the bargaining element in heterosexual activity. Sprey's approach to human sexuality in terms of reciprocity and exchange requires extension, with particular reference to Blau's formulation in "Exchange and Power in Social Life." The rules of the game are changing; Ira Reiss has suggested that the new standard may become sex with affection. In this context it can be argued that more emphasis should be placed on the part that the condom could play. Apart from providing a high degree of protection from venereal infection, it is a contraceptive technique that demands a lesser degree of preparation. Such female-specific contraceptive techniques as the pill and the diaphragm require the individual to acknowledge that intercourse is *likely* to occur, but possession of a sheath only requires one to acknowledge that intercourse *may* occur. Thus, when bargaining proceeds, culminating in sexual exchange, the dictates of prophylaxis and prevention of conception can be observed, however unanticipated the encounter, as long as the male partner is carrying a sheath.

Finally one must pose the question: are parental attitudes and public opinion sufficiently "advanced" to accept the principles underlying the course as outlined? Data from interviews with parents (part of a larger study of mass-media influences) focusing on attitudes toward sex education in schools and on what should be included are still being analyzed, but some general impressions have already emerged. It appears that a majority of the mothers interviewed favored the inclusion of topics such as "pregnancy before marriage," "marriage and the family," "biological and physical aspects of sex," "sexual morality," and "birth control and family planning" in a course of sex education for children.

Women's Occupation: Biological and Social Forces

Recent experience in Britain has suggested that the fall in family size is, in part, responsible for the increase in the proportion of married women remaining in or returning to the work force. This itself represents a considerable change in women's life-styles and life-chances, but it does nothing to dispose of the problems posed by the episodic nature of women's working lives when they attempt to combine child bearing and rearing with a career. The interval between confinement and return to the work force will depend upon societal and individual attitudes toward the degree of intimacy appropriate to, and the necessary extent of, a close and continuing relationship between mother and child during the infant's early development. A few factories in Britain, through the provision of creches and a kindergarten at the work location, are helping young mothers to return to work earlier than would otherwise be possible. Bernstein's work on restricted and extended language codes further emphasizes the need for an extension of the nursery school movement. Formal schooling uses largely an extended form of language code, but working-class families tend to communicate via more simple and direct modes of speech. Children in nursery schools could be provided with the opportunity to learn the extended language code as soon as verbal interaction becomes possible.

Allocation of resources to extend the nursery school sector in public education is dependent upon political processes aimed at persuading governments of the need for and advantages of this kind of innovation in education. Force of circumstances may persuade more private firms to provide facilities for infant care where scarcity of labor predominates. Britain's restrictive attitude toward immigration has eliminated one source of recruitment to the labor force, and manufacturers may attempt to persuade women to return to or remain in the work force (after a period of extended leave covering confinement and the immediate postnatal period) by the provision of such facilities.

Nevertheless, the majority of women's careers will still be subject to disruption. This fact is sometimes used to justify the view that training women for other than routine operations or minor clerical roles is a waste of scarce resources. When women were likely to enter the labor force only during the interval between leaving school and getting married, and subsequently devoting their energies to rearing four or more children, the above statement was justified, but with the general acceptance of the one- or two-child family, that objection is no longer valid. Moreover, employers are increasingly required to acknowledge the spasmodic nature of a whole range of occupations dictated by changing economic and technological circumstances. In the second phase of the industrial revolution, technological change may be so rapid that skills painstakingly acquired through long periods of training and apprenticeship may become redundant almost overnight. A whole range of workers, from miners to aircraft workers, are being forced to acquire new skills, and government retraining centers are being established to deal with these problems. In the professions, too, the need for periods of retraining is increasingly being recognized. Academics are provided wth sabbatical years; under the National Health Service, general practitioners are given paid leave (six months) to attend refresher courses at medical schools; businessmen may be required to undergo training in new management techniques; and social workers are beginning to recognize that training acquired in the late 1940s is no longer appropriate to the conditions affecting social-work practice in the 1970s. What now of the argument that women are inevitably disadvantaged in the work situation because of their biological role as mothers? Mothers could combine an enforced absence from the work situation, occasioned by the requirements of child bearing and rearing, with part-time attendance at refresher, retraining, or further education courses designed to facilitate their return to the work force.

One final point: As material standards of living continue to improve, society may choose to utilize excess capacity to reduce the length of the working week. Accompanied by a rearrangement of working shifts, such a choice could further improve women's capacity to combine the roles of mother and worker.

Family-Planning Services

The possible changes in women's life-styles and life-chances outlined in the foregoing paragraphs are dependent not only on mass acceptance of the one- or two-child family, but also on the provision of adequate family-planning services to make the choice a realistic one. When family-planning services are provided free, when primary and secondary physicians, public health doctors, and paramedical workers all combine to create an integrated maternity- and child-care service, then couples seem to be prepared to choose to control their own fertility. Aberdeen is one of the few areas in Great Britain where an attempt has been made to provide an integrated maternity- and child-care service, and is the only local authority to provide family-planning services without cost to the patient. In other areas, where family-planning clinics are provided at all, they are often run by the Family-Planning Association—a voluntary body—but with assistance from the local authority, usually in the form of premises, and contraception advice, information, and sometimes appliances are provided on a fee-for-service basis. The organization of the National Health Service is at present under review, and, among other things, attention is being directed toward the way in which family planning might become the complete responsibility of the state. Given that adequate resources are provided, and that "the services offered provide privacy, dignity, and freedom of choice" (as described in Chana Heffner's review for this workshop) then "the fifth freedom"—Sir Dugald Baird's phrase to describe the capacity to control one's own fertility—will become part and parcel of the British way of life.

Some Conclusions and Some Questions: Male and Female Roles in a New Situation

In the past, a woman's status and position in society was determined by that of her husband.[26] Indeed, the single woman—the spinster, the maiden aunt—was the butt of humorists because she did not fit society's prescription of what a woman's role should be: materfamilia. When sociodemographic conditions required women to maximize their fertility, or when national and political ambitions emphasized the need for population growth, such an attitude might have been appropriate, but today, and increasingly in the future, a different approach to women's roles is called for. Class, status, and power combine to define the individual's position in a hierarchically organized social system. Power is perhaps the key factor in this equation with respect to women's roles, and the power to control their own fertility is a basic requirement. We need to know if programs of sex education in the schools do, indeed, provide the information necessary for women to control their own fertility. Do such programs provide the opportunity for both sexes to consider the problems posed by human sexuality and to discuss the relative merits and demerits of various contraceptive techniques? For the contemporary cohorts of adolescents and young adults, contraceptive education should become part and parcel of the whole area of maternity services, at antenatal clinics, postnatal examinations, and during home visits by health visitors and other paramedical personnel, even when the purpose of such visits is primarily centered on the processes of child rearing. In the interim, the backstop of abortion is a necessary and humane measure, and we need to know how these procedures can be routinely incorporated into obstetric practice. Who should control, and what factors should influence, the process of decision-making *vis à vis* abortion and sterilization?

In the spheres of sex-role and sexual socialization, how can we ensure that the new factors affecting women's life-styles and life-chances are adequately discussed? How can we raise women's own aspirations in relation to employment? A cursory glance at children's fairy stories, primary readers, and comics reveals a strong tendency for success in male roles to be associated with achievement criteria. Successful performance of feminine roles is, however, often dependent on the presence of such characteristics as charm, grace, and a pleasant appearance where ascriptive criteria tend to predominate. Clearly, studies are required of the processes of child rearing and socialization in relation to sex-role identification. Patterns of socialization which train women only for the roles of wife, housewife, and mother cannot be considered as appropriate preparation for adult roles in the last quarter of the 20th century.

Acknowledgments

I wish to express particular thanks to Dr. I. A. G. McQueen, M.O.H., Aberdeen, and to Dr. M. McGregor, of the Family Planning Clinic, for providing access to their records, and to Dr. B. Thompson, who was responsible for the analyses of the data presented in TABLE 1. I am also indebted to Jean Aitken-Swan for providing the data upon which FIGURE 1 is based, and to other colleagues, in particular, Sir Dugald Baird, Professor I. MacGillivray, Professor R. Illsley, Mr. G. Horobin, and Mr. J. McKinlay, who provided invaluable encouragement and advice.

REFERENCES

1. FLETCHER, R. 1962. Britain in the Sixties: The Family and Marriage. : 113–114. Penguin. London, England.
2. BAIRD, D. 1969. Fertility control. Brit. J. Hosp. Med. **2:** 597.
3. BAIRD, D. 1969. An area maternity service. Lancet **i:** 515.
4. MCKINLAY, J. B. 1968. Better maternity and child care for whom . . .? Med. Officer **120**(20)**:** 275.
5. THOMPSON, B., D. DURNO, J. E. MACGREGOR & M. S. M. MCGREGOR. 1969. Med. Officer **121**(8)**:** 93.
6. ILLSLEY, R & D. G. GILL. 1968. Changing trends in illegitimacy. Soc. Sci. Med. **2:** 415.
7. SCHOFIELD, M. 1965. The Sexual Behaviour of Young People. Longmans, Green & Co., Ltd. London, England.
8. GILL, D. G. 1969. Changing trends in illegitimacy and changing modes of explanation. Proc. Roy. Soc. Health.
9. RODMAN, H. 1967. The lower class value-stretch. Social Forces **42:** 205.
10. RODMAN, H. 1966. Illegitimacy in the Caribbean social structure. Amer. Soc. Rev. **31:** 673.
11. RODMAN, H., F. R. NICHOLD & P. VOGDANOFF. 1969. Lower-class attitudes towards "deviant" family patterns: a cross-cultural study. J. Marr. Fam. **31**(2)**:** 315.
12. TITMUSS, R. M. 1963. Essays on the Welfare State. Allen & Unwin. London, England.
13. REGISTRAR-GENERAL. 1967. Statistical review of England and Wales for the year 1964. Part III, Commentary. Her Majesty's Stationery Office. London, England.
14. SEEAR, N. 1968. The world of work. *In* In Her Own Right. Harrap & Co. London, England.
15. CENTRAL STATISTICAL OFFICE. 1967. Annual Abstract of Statistics. Her Majesty's Stationery Office. London, England.
16. JEPHCOTT, P., N. SEEAR & J. H. SMITH. 1962. Married Women Working. Allen & Unwin. London, England.
17. GAVRON, H. 1966. The Captive Wife. Routledge & Kegan Paul. London, England.
18. MARSDEN, D. 1969. Mothers Alone. Allen Lane. London, England.
19. HOGGART, R. 1958. The Uses of Literacy. Penguin. London, England.
20. PARSONS, T. & R. F. BALES. 1956. Family Socialization and Interaction Process. Routledge & Kegan Paul. London, England.
21. ZELDITCH, JR., M. 1956. Role differentiation in the nuclear family: A comparative study. *In* Family Socialization and Interaction Process. Routledge & Kegan Paul. London, England.
22. AGRIST, S. S. 1969. The study of sex roles. J. Soc. Issues **25**(1)**:** 215.
23. SPREY, J. 1969. On the institutionalization of sexuality. J. Marr. Fam. **31**(3)**:** 432.
24. BERNARD, J. 1969. The Sex Game. Leslie Frewin. London, England.
25. STRONG, P. 1969. Some problems of sexual interaction. Paper presented to the Third National Deviancy Conference, York, July (unpublished).

26. LENSKI, G. E. 1966. Power and Privilege. McGraw-Hill Book Co. New York, N.Y.

DISCUSSION

E. James Lieberman, M.D., *Moderator*

GILL: The purpose of my extended discussion was to provide a further set of extrapolations and more speculation on certain trends discussed in the basic paper, with specific reference to the problems of sex education in schools. First, I hypothesized that sex education might be dealt with in a dichotomous situation, creating the opportunity to teach sex education in schools in accordance with two distinct and different processes: the first dealing with the mechanics of sex in an emotionally and morally neutral atmosphere, and the second covering discussion of the values and attitudes taken toward sexuality in different social systems.

Second, I discussed some of the implications of the acceptance of the one- or two-child family on the British scene for women's occupational roles, speculating again upon changes that may or indeed are likely to occur, and some of which one can see as tendencies already extant on the British scene. Then, finally, I discussed the problem of providing family-planning services, arguing very briefly from the Aberdeen experience that utilizing family planning as part of an integrated system of maternity care seems to be the most effective way of getting this sort of information over. Indeed, as the paper itself shows, this has been successful in Aberdeen in reducing the average family size without the pushing of any particular family-planning program on the part of the maternity-service organization in that part of the city.

WAXENBERG: Who decided on the program?

GILL: It grew out of the interest of two people, really. First, the Professor of Obstetrics and Gynecology, Sir Dugald Baird, who became convinced that efficacy in reproductive performance was based on environmental factors, and that obstetric intervention could do only a certain amount. He then cooperated, second, with the local-authority medical officer to provide a system of integrated maternity care. This system reached all women confined in hospitals, and it provided antenatal services both at a centrally located premises and at peripheral stations. As a result, it insured a situation in which the maximum amount of prenatal care was not only available, but was, indeed, utilized by the population. It further insured that in this comprehensive treatment of pregnant women, adequate opportunity for family-planning services was available. Slowly, this integrated approach was extended into general practitioner work as well, and into the family-planning clinics, including services for single women.

WAXENBERG: That brings up the question whether and where women came into the planning of any of this ongoing, apparently long-term, program.

GILL: Insofar as there were women on the staff of Professor Baird's department, they did participate. But this was a program that was instituted in terms of logic and rationale, really, rather than with any specific concern for ameliorating the station and position of women, as it were.

OLESEN: Would you comment more fully on what I think is one of the most tantalizing points in your paper, that is, the socialization of girls to the notion of a life ahead in which work and family life are balanced out equally, that bearing the family becomes a time away from work, and vice versa. This idea is a distinct departure, at least from the American girl-child's socialization picture, which at present shows her being socialized exclusively in rearing the family.

GILL: It seems to me that this point encompasses two problems. First of all, there are the trends demonstrating the reduction in family size, and the increased numbers of married women returning to or remaining in the work force in the United Kingdom. There is, then, a requirement to understand this from a theoretical perspective. One is confronted with that dreadful work of Parsons and Bales, defining male and female roles as instrumental and expressive, respectively. The situation needs to be reevaluated, in my opinion, in terms of ascription and achievement. One is driven back to the consideration of the family life cycle, the implications of the fall in family size, the dramatic extension of stages IV, V, and VI of the life cycle, and the truncation of stages II and III particularly, creating these vast empty years. This, in turn, requires another step in our analysis, to look at the way in which people are socialized for what, in effect, will be a new situation if the trend toward one- and two-child families continues. It is in this area that the traditional definitions of instrumental and expressive roles leave so much to be desired.

We therefore need to launch a whole range of studies that look at the way sex-role socialization is encompassed and provided at the moment. We have some studies going on in Aberdeen using walkie-talkies and tape recorders in order to obtain complete transcripts and recordings of mother-child interaction throughout the day. We have only just begun to look at one of the transcripts. Of course, we have a fantastic amount of material; it is very difficult to categorize and to analyze. In one situation, a grandmother had promised to bring some flowers for the little girl of the family, a four-year-old. On the Wednesday afternoon the grandmother couldn't come, but the grandfather was going to come, and so the little girl asked her mommie, "Will Grandfather bring the flowers?" The mother laughed and said, "Oh, I shouldn't think so." The little girl said, "Why?" And the answer was, "Well, gentlemen don't like to be seen walking along the street carrying flowers." This is the area we need to look at. It is important to reanalyze sexual and sex association in terms of sheer description rather than instrumental and expressive categories.

KAMM: I am concerned with the number of studies one has to undertake to obtain this sort of information. People who have been in the feminist movement have known all these things for such a long time. I don't mean to say sociology hasn't accomplished anything all these years; I have my own views on that! It seems to me that this approach is somewhat obvious, and that one should not spend so much time looking at the empirical data, but should analyze what we mean when we speak of the notion of sexuality and love, and seeing this as a game. Studying how little girls learn to play with dolls is really something that people have done already, or something equally as obvious.

What do we mean by love? What do we mean by needs? Is love based on insecurity? Is it a pathological phenomenon? Is sexuality and the notion of heterosexual sex also pathological? What sort of phenomenon *is* this? We need to raise the question whether the male and female can get away from roles altogether. How do we get people to choose to be neither, just to *be,* and to see things as outside of any role of any sort? Does seeing oneself in a role attached to either vaginal or male-organ function create too much insecurity, or not? These are the questions that have to be asked, something that has to be done.

GILL: It seems to me I could ask you a set of questions that would require you to specify precisely what ought to be done, but it also seems to me that those questions are of a sociological-philosophical-political nature. I would perhaps want to reiterate Lucile Newman's point, that the responsibility of the social scientist is to explain and to understand. I would not agree with you that enough of these studies have been done, or that we know enough about these forms of socialization and how some women are able to break out of the constraints to which you have referred while others are not.

What I would argue is essential at this time is to study the trends and to extrapolate from them, to envisage what is likely to occur in the immediate future, and to make some preparation in terms of reanalysis of socialization techniques that may help us prepare women specifically for the implications of the reduction in family size. I am assuming that the family is going to persist for a considerable length of time yet. I have no evidence, either cross-cultural or sociological, that would lead me to doubt this conclusion.

POLGAR: I am somewhat less shy about inferring from scientific data what you call the philosophical or political. An anthropologist named Earl Count has worked on a very interesting treatment of the development of, among other things, parentalism in the mammalian evolutionary line. This idea is not new; it has been around for a while, but many people don't appreciate it. I think that it still has something to say. Very briefly, you can see that the specialization of the primates within the mammalian line meant a greater investment, if you will, on the part of both parents. In studies of primates, we find a great deal of parental behavior on the part of the male. The big change for the prehuman and human primates starts with the establishment of a home base and the fact that food is not shared beyond the point of weaning. After weaning, in no primate is food shared between adults and young. It is shared within whales and birds, we know, but that is a different line of evolution.

Throughout most of man's biological evolution, which was as a hunter and gatherer, males did the "getting." Men got most of the proteins, and women got most of the carbohydrates. This may, of course, be oversimplified. Women really contributed the larger percentage of the total calories of the diet, but most of these calories were necessary to the establishment of the home base. They were a commitment to the very long embryonic and postembryonic development of the human infant, a pattern that requires a minimal kind of human sociality in which this biparentalism that Count talks about is highly divided.

Perhaps Margaret Mead will comment on that in our subsequent discussions. She not so long ago said that there is a further development along this trend that she ties up with population problems. She made no reference to Count. Nowadays, society is so complex, she says, and what we need is more inputs per child from adults. In other words, the adult-to-child ratio should be increased.

I don't like this negative talk about population explosion and that we should curb ourselves and have zero growth. What we need is something positive. We need a more educational, formative input from adults to children, and we need adults who wish to do this—men, women, human beings. This is the direction in which we have been going for tens of millions of years, and we should continue in this direction.

GILL: In my extended discussion I referred to the current trend in the United Kingdom in which middle-class couples recognize and define the necessity of providing play-groups for their children. Here is a demand emerging, a set of factors being recognized, requiring some action to be taken on the part of the usually most articulate part of the population. This demand represents an acknowledgment of the fact that children should be provided relatively early in their total life experience with very much wider horizons than the family can provide. Part of this, if we take Swedish experience as an example, would include the introduction of males into nursery school situations.

MAJOR: A new phenomenon has come to my attention from experience in law offices dealing with domestic relations in California: Unwed fathers-to-be are demanding custody of the child; they refuse to let the girl give the child away. I wonder whether this is paralleled in England, and/or whether it is a quantitative thing or a qualitative thing, and if any studies have been done on it.

GILL: The answer to all three questions is no, and nothing is being done. Unmarried mothers' organizations have sprung up on the British scene very, very rapidly in the past 18 to 24 months. Occasionally, you will find evidence of putative fathers asking to be recognized, and even going to the length of objecting to an adoption order, for example, but it is still relatively rare. I know of no studies underway at the moment, perhaps because putative fathers are always very hard to find.

MILNER: First, Dr. Chilman's paper covers the American point of view on the same topic as yours, and I would appreciate your comments on Dr. Chilman's discussion in the light of your British experience. Second, I hope you will react more explicitly to Miss Kamm's comments. There is, I think, perhaps much more than Miss Kamm herself realizes, a strong value position implicit in her comments: that somehow there is something very burdensome, something very bad, about being a parent. She has every right to such a value position, but to put it forward as a scientific position would be misleading herself and misleading us. It is just as possible to hold my value position, which is that it is one of the greatest possible privileges to be responsible for the development of an immature human being.

Part of our problem today is that parental roles, because of many pressures for all sorts of less-important things, have fallen into disrepute. One reason there is so much trouble among young people in our society is that the socializing function of the adult has been virtually thrown out the window and children have, more or less, had to rear themselves. There is a considerable body of research indicating that children have to *learn* to be human. If no one bothers to give them this opportunity, either through teaching or through providing models, they cannot become human, and they don't become animals either; they become something very sick! I'm sure Dr. Lieberman and I would agree on that point. Anyone who has direct contact with sick children and with related research data would agree. I repeat that Miss Kamm certainly has a right to her value position, but she must recognize the difference between some kind of reaction-formation within herself, perhaps, and more objective knowledge in the field.

GILL: To draw out comparisons between the United States situation and that of the United Kingdom would take a long time, I think. What I will do is take one example that comes immediately to mind. Anyone who follows the British political scene will have noticed that equal pay for women is being debated at the moment in the House of Commons. The government has accepted this as policy; indeed, discrimination in this area will be illegal after 1975 and is to be phased out. It is interesting to compare this with the American situation; I understand such legislation has existed in the United States for some time, and yet certain evidence seems to suggest that it hasn't had the impact that one might expect on the American scene, particularly with reference to certain rates of pay in lower socioeconomic group occupations. It will be very interesting to see how the British experience compares with this.

As is usual with the British model, state intervention, once accepted, is always carried through very much more thoroughly. A tribunal will be established, to operate after 1975, which will make it possible for legal action to be taken against firms found to discriminate. British precedent suggests that this approach will be successful. The gradual development of equal pay over the transition period, plus the force of legislative support and eventual legal intervention underlying the situation will, one suspects, insure that equal pay will begin to operate as of 1975 in the United Kingdom.

LIEBERMAN: It is said that the Spartan women had equality with their men, but, as someone has said, they had equality with subhuman beings. The question of sexual equality reminds me of couples who have in their enlightened fashion decided that they will both be sexually free. The problem is that the women don't enjoy the sexual escapades nearly as much as the men. The question here is whether there is a biologically innate difference that we are dealing with, or is it a social difference. And assuming equality does come, will it mean that the woman's sex becomes more instrumental or that the man's becomes more empathic and expressive? Do you see two different lines of development here?

DELL'OLIO: Could it be that it is a master-slave relationship in which the woman does not like to submit to more than one master? That is bad enough, but to have to submit to several is really quite oppressive; for the man, however, it is an added pleasure to oppress more women, more slaves, and to own more slaves.

KUNDSIN: What you have just said, Dr. Lieberman, has been disproved. If women are free and interested, they are just as sexually interested as men. I am very surprised you should utter such a prejudiced statement.

LIEBERMAN: I was reporting from people who have reported to me; I was reporting on my own clinical experience with couples.

EAST: Whatever your prejudice dictates, you find it there.

LIEBERMAN: I asked for a reaction to my question. I am glad that I got one!

JECH: I find Mr. Gill's paper absolutely ethnocentric and rooted in 18th or 19th century morality, really Victorian morality. For example, basic assumptions are never questioned. There is the basic assumption that every one of us will get married, and we are all going to have a family. Therefore, let us try to have a family of one or two children. He has not allowed that there is a possibility of free choice, that some young women or young men may never want to marry or have children. What I find particularly ethnocentric or culture-bound is all those implicit assumptions about a female career, the assumption that she must be a mother and have a career. Nowhere is the man mentioned. It is, then, a problem for the woman to find out how she can be a mother and a worker, both. The concept of family planning is based on the assumption that all girls are going to have families. And how is the female going to adjust to your work world, which is rapidly changing, while having the two children? Wouldn't this make her knowledge obsolete? I think such basic assumptions as these invalidate the entire paper.

GILL: I will try to deal with as many of the points that have been raised as I can. I want to refer first to Steve Polgar's remarks. There are some biological precedents and some biological realities that it is impossible to escape. To assume that the majority of women would choose not to have children and that we therefore must restructure a social system to take this into account is to my mind unrealistic. Also, the topic itself of my paper creates certain constraints: some consequences of mass acceptance of the two-child family.

DELL'OLIO: Isn't that the whole point of socialization? We are so bombarded by the message that happiness can only be found in this universe of two in the marital state with a nice family. This is a creation of the mass media, and is sold in every home and throughout one's daily existence. If we are talking about how we can deal with that kind of propaganda, then shouldn't we ask how we can deal with the propaganda that diverts human beings to certain channels? Why not start further back and ask how can we *all* be human beings?

GILL: Precisely. One of the purposes of my paper is to argue the circumstances around which choice will be effected. The contraceptive revolution we are facing requires us to insure that when young people are placed in a situation in which they must reach a decision about whether or not they wish to have children, whether or not they wish to marry, and how many children they may wish to have, they are prepared by their prior socialization experience for this type of decision-making.

KAMM: My point is that they have no choice. We see only a private system as the ultimate happiness. Everyone has a private home with private child care. We haven't talked about complex family situations or kinships in which people can have the pleasure of being around children without necessarily being the mother or the father.

GILL: The evidence at the moment suggests that any attempts to institutionalize alternatives to some form of nucleated family organization have been exceedingly unsuccessful. These are the data. The decision to move to another form of child rearing and socializing procedure seems, to me, to be a political one, a philosophical one, an ethical one. There is no trend operative in British society at the moment to suggest that this is a requirement or a problem that we will have to face in the future three or four decades. It is not something that appears to be a possibility.

KAMM: What is involved here is the difference between the research attitude and the action attitude. One says that research is a prerequisite to action, but it doesn't pretend to say what the action should be.

MILNER: The research person just says to the person who has to make the decision to take action, "This is what is known. You decide what should be done in terms of values and whatever other things are relevant, but we as research people only gather and interpret the data on which you devise a course of action." Many of us here are mixing the two realms of discourse; that is why we are in poor communication. It is not necessarily that we disagree with each other, but we are talking about two different things.

PROBABLE SOCIAL AND PSYCHOLOGICAL CONSEQUENCES OF AN AMERICAN POPULATION POLICY AIMED AT THE TWO-CHILD FAMILY

Catherine S. Chilman, Ph.D.

Dean of Faculty
Hood College
Frederick, Md.

The probable consequences of a population policy aimed at the small family will depend, to a large extent, on the basic philosophy underlying this policy and the programs that are used in attempting to implement it. If a chiefly technological-managerial policy and approach is used, then it is likely that the emphasis will be on promoting specific contraceptive techniques, the further development of effective contraceptives, the expanded establishment of free contraceptive services, and public education programs aimed specifically at further reduction of the birth rate. This kind of program might even be expanded, as some have recommended, to finding ways of putting contraceptive agents in the drinking water so that persons would have to take a counter-agent in order to have children. Permission for having children would be required by an official body that would assess the suitability of the couple for parenthood.

In order to create social acceptance of such an approach, it would probably be necessary to use a strong barrage of modern public relations techniques. This statement is based on my belief that our culture, our biology, our psychological needs, and experiences tend to unite to create a strong urge toward parenthood, in the magnitude of two or more children, on the part of most young people and adults in this country. Thus, strongly persuasive public relations techniques, stemming from a technological population policy, would be devised to promote the no-child or few-child norm as being highly desirable to the nation, and especially so to individuals. Public relations campaigns would probably emphasize the social status and material benefits to be gained from small family size or no children at all. It is likely that the no-child or one-child family would be extolled, along with the two-child family; the present size of our youth population strongly suggests that it would benefit the nation if the birth rate were depressed below the two-child norm, especially because it is very likely that not all of our young women would have fewer than three children.

In attempting to handle this problem in specific technical terms, it is likely that the advantages of limiting parenthood would be extolled along the following lines. "The 'in' people are those with one or two children. Keep your family small. Today's wives are slim, glamorous, and working at exciting jobs. They have the time, energy, and money for fun, travel, beautiful clothes, and luxurious homes. They and their husbands enjoy a honeymoon that lasts forever, with no heavy financial burdens to mar their lives."

As the norms change and less emphasis is placed on homemaking and child-rearing, it is likely that business and industry will put their production and marketing emphasis on adult interests. This emphasis is likely to increase the already strong, materialistic, hedonistic trend in our culture. Self-gratification through the acquisition of things will probably be increasingly valued. None of these things is meant to decry the need for lowering our birth rate and keeping it low during the coming years. It is to question the kinds of policy and programs that might well be used to accomplish this goal. This question pertains both to the overly technological, managerial, materialistic approach and to an approach that is focused too narrowly and specifically on population control as a separate entity.

This problem-specific, narrow philosophy, is already responsible for much of our current demographic difficulty. Although the motivation of our public health experts has been humane, their past efforts at home and in developing nations abroad has brought about a rapid reduction in the maternal and infant death rate without a concomitant expansion in resources to care for the resultant swift rise in population. This latter provision would not lie within the function of public health specialists, but it should have been recognized by program planners so that provisions might be made for this outcome. Quite naturally, this called—and calls—for a broader approach to population concerns than one which focuses only on birth and death rates.

This observation should be expanded to an even broader concept. Obviously, when maternal and infant death rates are markedly reduced, it is necessary to bring about widespread, effective use of contraceptives in the general population to prevent the usual result of overpopulation. Analysis of numerous related studies reveals that contraceptives are least likely to be adopted and used effectively by persons with the following characteristics: little education, low income, low occupational level, rural residence or rural origins.[1] Thus, if we wish to reduce population growth in this, or other countries, we must use what might be termed an ecological approach: one that takes into account all of the factors most closely associated with non-use or ineffective use of contraceptives. Programs and policies of this kind would include the expansion of education and employment opportunities, especially among the disadvantaged; provision for higher income for the poor; promoting the process of urbanization; and programs aimed at a more rapid assimilation of rural immigrants to the city. In brief, it is unlikely that the general population, especially the disadvantaged sector, will be strongly motivated to use contraceptives effectively and to limit family size unless their life situation and perception of real social and economic opportunities for themselves and their children motivates them to do so.

The technological, special family-size-limitation approach would have far greater appeal to the upwardly mobile or affluent than it would to the poor, because poor people have so little hope of getting important economic benefits from any effort they may make as individuals. This is one drawback to such an approach to population control; another drawback, as already mentioned, would seem to be that of further escalating a material, rather than humane, value system in our society.

This materialistic getting-and-spending orientation has already saddled us with many severe problems. One of these has been the increasing hostility and separatism of our society. The poor, especially the minority-group poor, are rightfully resentful of the affluence they see all around them, the affluent norm that is steadily dispelled over the airwaves in contrast to the meager, constricted nature of their own lives. The poor are also rightfully resentful when they hear that family-planning programs have a lot to recommend them because they cost very little and have high benefits in preventing the birth of more children who are likely to be dependent on public assistance. Such an argument is likely to have little appeal to the mother in poverty; understandably, she has little interest in saving tax dollars for the more fortunate.

This mother—and others like her—would be much more impressed by increased employment opportunities at good pay for herself and for her man. A good job plus a good income offers a powerful incentive for limiting family size. The good job and income is unlikely to appear unless large-scale public works programs are introduced, since private business and industry cannot absorb most of the seriously underskilled, undereducated poor.[2] If such jobs are to provide real, continuing employment opportunities, they must be combined with enhanced educational and training facilities, child-care provisions, and solution of transportation problems. There is considerable evidence that women who are steadily employed are much less likely to have large families, and this applies to women at all socioeconomic levels.[3]

All in all, a broad program aimed at reducing the birth rate and keeping it low would require a large investment of public funds in a diversity of programs planned for the general upgrading of families, especially poor and minority-group families. These programs are desirable in and of themselves, for a variety of reasons, of course. They have also been recommended as being basic to preventing and reducing such ills as mental retardation, mental illness, crime and delinquency, and civil disorders. This ought to be one indication that a sound population policy should be part of a broader policy, taking into account social, psychological, and economic factors affecting population size and quality.

The question of quality is an important one, all too often overlooked by the technologists; if it is recognized, it is apt to be seen as a matter related primarily to genetics and maternal and infant health. Although these factors are important, indeed, the best born and healthiest baby has little chance for a high quality of life if he lives in a family and society that is preoccupied only with the quantitative aspects of living. A narrow, quantitative population policy has a number of dangers, as I have suggested. Another that should concern us is the current preoccupation with prevention of extra or unwanted births, with little attention paid to the unique humanity and psychological dynamics of the individuals involved. Some of our programs would seem to say in effect: "We don't mind what you do with your sex life so long as you keep the birth rate down."

Although these are massive arguments for separating public policy from private interpersonal behavior, the matter is far from simple. As our nation inevitably becomes more and more a creature of government planning, programming, and financing, public policy becomes more and more the pacesetter for social values and norms. In a highly technical, closely knit but impersonal, megalopolitan society such as ours, the culture would seem to be determined more and more by the norms of the large, public group rather than by families, neighborhoods, and religious bodies. Since these social systems would seem to be steadily losing norm-setting effectiveness, the values upheld by public policy would seem to gain in potency.

Up to this point in time, government planners and policy makers have taken a largely quantitative view of social problems and their possible solution. The gross national product, the cost of living, unemployment rates, individual and family income, birth rates, illegitimacy rates, death rates, marriage and divorce rates, crime rates, and illness and disability rates have been the bellwethers.

This is highly understandable; it comes about partly because it is so hard to assess and measure the quality of life, social values, psychological status, ethical behavior, and the like.

Thus, population problems have been seen as a numbers game. If we accept the proposition that public policy and programs are becoming more and more influential in determining cultural patterns, if we accept the proposition that man does not live by numbers alone, then we get into the knotty problem of public policy and its effects on individual values and behavior in the individual's private life, including his sex life. For if our society (for this, increasingly read the Federal government) doesn't really care how a person behaves sexually so long as the birth rates, illegitimacy rates, venereal disease rates, and public assistance rates are kept down, then the whole issue of humane, responsible, and psychologically sensitive behavior between the sexes would seem to become increasingly irrelevant as a matter of social concern.

This would probably hasten us down the road to a growing, already apparent tendency toward mechanization and further commercialization of sex. Rollo May explores with particular poignancy the reasons and implications for this tendency, this emphasis on the perfection of the techniques for high levels of orgasmic achievement for both males and females.[4] He points out the apathetic, uninvolved mode of the day in an impersonal technological society in which massive human destruction is only a few pushbuttons away. Faced with omnipresent fear of death, faced with a sense of personal impotence imposed by an antihuman environment, individuals are afraid of deep, personal feelings one for the other. To love too much is to endanger one's self too much; thus, mechanized fun and games with sex provides brief, superficial relief from an arduously concealed dread of life and its too-close partner, physical or psychological death.

The antilife forces crowd in on us strongly today, teamed with an impersonal, mass society operating on a numbers game. The humanitarian ideal, which has played such an important counter-balancing force to material goals, would seem to be retreating in shattered defeat. The psychological reactions to this defeat can be seen on all sides. As the 1940s have been called the age of anxiety, and the 1950s the age of apathy, the 1960s might be termed the age of depression and despair. As a people, we appear to have passed from worry, to boredom, to surrender of the self to inevitable forces of doom; we no longer seem to believe we can handle our individual lives or our society in positive, life-oriented, hopeful ways. A technologically based population policy would seem likely to enhance such a trend.

This trend has been called antifamily by some, and some applaud this trend. They raise questions about the necessity and desirability of the family in the future. They argue that a profamily society has many disadvantages and dangers, including a continued rise in the size of the population. They further argue that not only must we improve the genetic quality of the population by master planning to determine who shall reproduce, but that we must also improve the physical and intellectual quality of the population by not leaving child rearing to amateurs (i.e., parents). They present, furthermore, a strong case for freeing mothers from the imprisonment of child care and housekeeping. Then, too, they point out that marriage is frequently a trap, and people should be free to "do their thing," and that the nature of our abundant society (including an overabundance of children) allows and indeed demands a wider diversity of individual choices: nonmarriage as well as marriage, serial partnerships, homosexual and lesbian arrangements, communal living, polygamy and polyandry, and so on. The sex revolution, as a part of larger technological revolution, has set us free, they claim.

Although there is much to be said for these arguments, although changing times call for changing life-styles, although patterns of the past have brought untold burdens of human frustration, guilt, and entrapment, it would be desirable if we could evolve gradually into psychologically conserving patterns, rather than erupt into personal and sex anarchy. My belief is that marriage, family, and parenthood will continue to be an important life-pattern for many, perhaps for most, of our people. Human beings have always had some form of family life. Family life satisfies deep human needs of both children and adults for love, tenderness, permanency, intimacy, a sense of individual significance, the need to give as well as to receive, and selfvalidation through membership in a small group. Out of the family experience comes values and traits that are important to society. The family is probably the chief source of humanitarian and nurturant values and capacities. And these values, I believe, should very importantly figure in population policies and programs.

Earlier in this paper, a forecast was given of the likely social and psychological consequences of a technological, managerial approach to population control. I plead for an approach that much more strongly includes humane, familial, nurturant components, not only as a matter of pronouncement, but as a matter of actual policy and program formation and implementation. Such an approach should emphasize enhancing the social, psychological, economic, and physical quality of life. It would be based on the premise that as a nation we care about the total well-being of all people, both males and females, at all socioeconomic levels and of all ethnic and national backgrounds. In respect to the sex lives of individuals, we must care as a society about the fulfillment and well-being of individuals as whole people, not just as potential reproducers. Thus, we should promote coordinated human services programs and centers, rather than isolated, specific family planning or even maternal and child-health units. A humane population policy would recognize the need to motivate people to have no or very few children, and it would lead from a social and psychological base rather than one that is exclusively material and technological. It would emphasize that there are many ways of being a respected successful person other than having a large family; that there are many benefits, other than economic ones, alone, to be gained from controlling family size. It would build on and enhance the human need to love, cherish, nurture, and protect by providing a large number of institutionalized outlets for this need: publicly as well as privately financed careers in the nurturing occupations of child care, medical services, recreational and educational programs, care of the elderly, and other community services. In effect, we need further enlargement and further public formalization of a trend that we already see: the community as the extended family.

In these policies and programs, we must give specialized attention to women, especially to those at the lower socioeconomic levels. We are already well acquainted with the frenzied despair of middle-class and upper-class women whose small families have freed them early in life for activities outside the home —but these actually are often far too hard to come by in a sufficiently fulfilling and significant sense. When lower-class women are similarly freed early in their lives by small families, their frenzy and despair will be even greater, for a number of reasons: Many are unemployed, and few have satisfying, adequately paid jobs. Then, too, their sense of personal significance is apt to be at a low level, and they have fewer inner and outer resources to raise their self-esteem, to give them a sense of direction in their lives. Moreover, they are likely to suffer more from culture-shock than other women if they do have no or very few children. The whole life-style of such women has generally been centered around their reproductive and child-rearing function, with male and female sex roles being rigidly defined. Self-expression and fulfillment as a person will generally be a difficult value for them to assimilate and act on.[5] Thus, from many viewpoints, special care must be taken to help these women cross the contraceptive gap.

For women in general, modern life and life in the future is not and will not be easy. Their guilt and confusion over their sex roles is still rampant and will continue to be so unless further cultural and institutional changes can be brought about rapidly. Traditionally, and to a large extent still, girls and women have been led to believe that motherhood is their chief *raison d'etre:* "That's why you menstruate every month, my dear; that's why you must protect your body; that's why you must attract a man and hold him; that's why you must set a good moral tone for yourself and your man; that's why you can't have a serious career—and as far as your education, that's so you can be a good wife and mother." But if you never become a mother at all? What if you choose not to marry or are not chosen? What if you have only one or two children? What do you do with all the female physical functioning, education, time, energy, and moral rectitude that you have left over?

Such questions aren't easy to answer, and I won't try to deal with them all here. However, we need to go much further than we have to date in according status and esteem to the single woman or the childless woman, in getting our concept of motherhood out of the shrine of selfless martyrdom and noble sacrifice and into the secular world of real employment opportunities adjusted to the needs of mothers. To do this, we must provide readily available low-cost home services and child care so that all women who wish to can play an integrated, relatively conflict-free role, as mother, employee, and community worker simultaneously, and with different emphases at different points in the family life cycle. Until now, we have mostly paid lip service to this conception and have left it up to individual families to go through the necessary related psychological, economic, and situational gymnastics to try to accomplish these multiple roles for wives and mothers.

If we truly want small families, *if* we truly want high quality child care, *if* we truly want to promote the overall well-being of the population, we have to get mothers off the numerous hooks on which they are hanging by making it possible for them to have a larger status and role in life than sharply constricted motherhood and grudgingly allowed low-level employment. This requires child care, but not only for very young children. In fact, this is not the main problem for many mothers of small families who enjoy functioning as full-time mothers when their children are little. A real and unrecognized difficulty is for mothers of school-age children. These mothers need both more part-time jobs and more facilities for care of school-age children, such as when the child is sick, or on vacation, or comes home from school before the mother does.

A humane population policy directed toward the quality of population, as well as the quantity, makes it possible for mothers to fulfill their maternal drives for nurturance and high-quality child care without sacrificing their opportunities to fulfill themselves in other ways when the period of full-time child care is over. Unless this is recognized and supported by public policy, the quality of child care and family life is apt to be eroded by an increasingly large number of women who are captive to home-bound jobs and functions that become more and more part-time and tenuous with the passing years. We are well aware of various forms this sense of frustration often takes: from suffocating maternal overprotection, to child neglect, to psychological depression and various forms of frequently unhealthy escapist behavior.

The need for a more humane, less exclusively technological population policy has been discussed thus far largely from the woman's viewpoint, and for this I apologize. I have fallen into the error that I so frequently decry in others—the error of conceptualizing a population policy and related programs as being female-centered. This kind of value-base impresses me as being grievous indeed and fraught with dangerous potential outcomes.

It would seem imperative that the plea for small families be addressed equally to males and females, and that related programs and services be equally addressed to them. The basic reason for this plea is that the fundamental nature of reproduction and parenthood is both masculine and feminine. By focusing attention only on women in such matters as contraceptive education, counseling, and services (as is frequently the case), there is an implication that men don't count as potential or actual fathers. This seems likely to undermine the male's sense of self-worth, responsibility, and significance in a pair relationship and function in this most central aspect of carrying out family life. Such an approach enforces an already damaging tendency to undermine the importance of the role of the lover-husband-father and to view males as basically exploitive sexual beings whose sexuality must be controlled in one way or other. Assumptions such as these have a way of becoming self-fulfilling prophecies, to the detriment of both sexes and to healthy marriage and parenthood.

One of the many reasons policy-makers and planners fail to see this point is a tendency to take a strictly medical view of family planning, with an overemphasis on the biological aspects. Particularly in this country, the prevalent view is that the best, most generally acceptable contraceptives are the pill, loop, or diaphragm. The condom is frequently overlooked, although it is widely used in many other countries. Even if the most generally used contraceptives in the United States are those employed by females, it doesn't follow that the male can or should be overlooked in family planning and related education and counseling. He counts as a person, whether or not he is the primary contraceptor.

The present contraceptive methods have potential social and psychological dangers as well as biological ones. Their nature, for example, puts contraceptive control entirely in the hands of women without the necessity of male knowledge or cooperation. This is a real revolution. For the first time in history, women have sole and independent control over prevention of pregnancy. This fact, along with emerging evidence as to the apparent superior orgasmic capacity of the female,[6] poses a very real, serious threat to the male's sense of importance. This sense is already under attack by social and economic changes that challenge his superiority, or even adequacy, in many other spheres at work, home, and in the community.

Unless we are sensitive to the implications of these developments and direct programs and policies to a full consideration and appreciation of the male's psychological needs, it is likely that our population policies and programs will cause more, or at least as many, social and psychological problems for men as might well be the case for women. We need new models for masculinity, just as we do for femininity. We also need a wider diversity of roles for men, just as we do for women. Men, too, will be affected by the no-child or few-child family. They, too, take pride in parenthood. For them, too, it meets psychological needs for loving and being loved, for a sense of importance, for an opportunity to protect and cherish. Thus, for males, as well as for females, we probably should provide a greater diversity of substitute human service outlets in both volunteer and employment capacities.

It is arguable whether males, innately, have stronger aggressive drives, on the average, than females do. I don't intend to get into the thickets of this argument. However, the weight of evidence seems to be on the side of higher levels of male aggressiveness. Contemporary society generally constrains and denies the aggressive drives of all its members except in reference to those of the tragic institution of war. It could be argued that for males, particularly, smaller family size could further constrict opportunities for expression of aggressive drives, of activity needs, and proof of physical prowess. This could result in a further escalation of hostility and aggression, as is already seen in our current waves of crime, strikes, and riots, or in the rising numbers of those who escape into drugs or alcohol. More public recreation, readily available and rich with opportunities for active involvement in sports and creative activities, would seem to be especially needed in the small-family, urban, mass society of the future.

The possible impact of the contraceptive culture and small family size on sex morality has already been touched on. Today, we have a clear need for a new set of sex morals. The moral codes of the past have simply lost their original base: to protect against the occurrence of out-of-wedlock pregnancy. The emergence of one form of the new morality—"sex with responsibility"—seems very sound, but can we pull it off? It has great potential, and there is much to be said for the view that sex should be one aspect of a mutual-partner relationship, marked by honesty, intimacy, commitment, and sensitivity, one to the other. In this view, for instance, women are no longer to use the withholding of sex as a means of trapping a husband. The new contraceptives force greater honesty about the real feelings between men and women and their real ethical values in that fear of pregnancy can no longer be used as a handy excuse to refrain from sex relations. These new ethics and new situations put great strains on the ego strength of both males and females, who are now required to control their impulses out of decisions made independently of fear or of the authority of firm social constraints.

These factors call for a very high order of moral development, a morality which places a priority on humane values, responsibility for self and others, compassion, generosity, and honesty. Such values must be deeply integrated into the self, if they are to be effective in the area of sex behavior under today's circumstances. Such a high order of moral development and integration is not to be expected of adolescents and youth.[7] What help can society, in its policies and services, provide young people as they work their way toward psychological maturity in today's climate? Open, honest, skilled, humanitarian, educational counselling, and health programs would seem to be among the requirements.

It is clear that the high level of moral development and moral qualities that are likely to be needed in our new society will not evolve unless our social policy and programs (including those of population policy) are based on a humane philosophy that employs, *but is not subjugated to,* technological knowledge. It is also clear that our population policy must be one integrated part of a much larger social policy that is based on a deep respect for and understanding of the many important positive aspects of the human drive to nurture and be nurtured, to express one's self, in part, through a deep identification with young life and its splendid endearing potentials. While this recognition most certainly does not and cannot mean that our social policy should encourage all adults to have children and as many as they wish, it does suggest that this life-giving and life-caring drive be recognized as being of utmost importance to the quality of society and that it be encouraged and cherished through socially approved and institutionalized means in educational, recreational, community service, occupational, and creative realms. If we do not adopt policies and programs along these lines, if we continue to take a public view of man as a dot in a frequency distribution curve to be manipulated by technical strategies into a more favorable position in demographic and economic tables, then, I believe, we will go more deeply into our current winter of discontent.

Needed Research

Evaluation

According to Bogue, the pressing social research need in the family-planning field is for a series of experimental programs in service delivery with a built-in evaluation component. He further remarks that surveys of family-planning knowledge, attitudes, and practice have provided generally sufficient information regarding the needs and desires for service on the part of the various groups in the population.[8] A major question now is, how can these needs and desires be most effectively met? There are many opinions as to what constitutes a good family-planning program and what methods are necessary, but little objective evidence is available along these lines. Bogue proposes a standard evaluation model so that studies can be replicated. However, there is lack of agreement among the research specialists in this field about whether or not sufficient experience and expertise have been developed to allow for a standard model at this time.[9]

Although a rational development and placement of alternate program strategies in randomly selected locales have a strong appeal to the logical experimentalist, the actualities of community functioning are likely to undermine such dispassionate logic. Communities tend to develop the kinds of services that seem appropriate for them. This sense of appropriateness derives from many factors, few of them purely rational. Through a diversity of program developments, a number of ready-made experimental situations present themselves; to the researcher it is a question of knowing what program models he is looking for and where to look for them.[10]

Follow-up studies are needed over a period of five years or more in order to ascertain long-range use of family-planning services. In these studies, research is indicated concerning the characteristics of: (*a*) those persons who are referred for services but fail to apply for them; (*b*) those who attend the clinic but drop out; and (c) those who continue to attend and to use contraceptives effectively. Differences in child spacing and family size between these three groups should be measured, as well as associated differences in social, economic, situational, program, and psychological characteristics. Information should also be sought from both men and women as to the reasons for their participation or nonparticipation in family-planning programs.

Social and Psychological Effects of Contraceptive Use

1. Research would seem to be indicated concerning the "social-psychological side effects" of family planning. Considerable attention has been paid to the medical aspects, but social and psychological factors are of equal importance. For example, what are the effects of small family size on the behavior and roles of women? What will women, who formerly made a life career of motherhood, do with the increased amount of time and energy at their disposal as a result of limiting family size? If they find second careers in the community and the labor market, what effect will this have on them, their husbands, and their children? (These trends already exist, of course; more extensive use of family planning will merely intensify them.) We know very few of the answers to these questions, especially as they refer to different socioeconomic levels and different national, ethnic, and religious groups.

2. Other social-psychological side effects that should be studied include the effect of contraceptive use, or non-use, on the marriage relationship and the stability of the marriage. Are there differential effects related to the use of different kinds of contraceptives? Are there differential effects associated with different types of child spacing? What are the effects of contraceptive failure on the marriage relationship?

3. What are the effects of planned families on children? For example, are there optimal patterns of family size and child spacing that seem to be highly associated with positive parent-child and sibling relationships, as well as with optimal child development?

4. What are the effects of contraceptive use—and the different kinds of contraceptives—on the attitudes and functioning of men? What are the implications for men of the newer contraceptives that women can use without the knowledge or cooperation of males? To what extent should men be involved in contraceptive counseling? Are the "mechanics" of contraceptives specifically a matter to be worked out between a woman and her medical counselor, or should the male partner be included in such counseling? Is reproduction control the sole or major responsibility or prerogative of women?

5. There is widespread concern as to the effects of simple, readily obtainable contraceptives on the premarital behavior of youth. There are also a number of prescriptions as to what is needed to help youth handle this situation. More needs to be known regarding the actual impact of contraception on youth behavior—in reference to both males and females—at different socioeconomic levels. Evaluative studies of the effects of such proposed remedies as sex and family-life education are also in order.

6. It is interesting that the chief concern seems to be about the effects of simple, readily available contraceptives on the *premarital* behavior of *youth*. It is widely recognized that this availability poses a number of questions of ethics and values to our young people. It would seem that similar questions would be posed to their elders in reference to themselves and to their possible extramarital and postmarital behavior. In effect, the married woman might be

exposed to considerably more temptation than the unmarried one since she, presumably, would be "on the pill" or equipped with an IUD anyway. Choosing such methods of contraception would not imply to her or others that she was planning to have sex relations outside of marriage. On the other hand, the unmarried woman, similarly "contracepted," would clearly be planning for nonmarital sex relations. Such planning may be more difficult to arrange and would seemingly be more difficult psychologically than would be the case for the married woman.

Education for adult sexuality has been suggested by a number of family-life educators. Developments in contraceptive information and availability would seem to enhance the logic of this suggestion. The allied research question is: What of the effectiveness of various research and counseling strategies?

Some Basic Social and Psychological Issues

1. There is considerable disagreement as to whether or not the "urge to reproduction and parenthood" is innate or culturally induced. There have been a few suggestions that individual women may innately vary in this regard and that such variation is associated with the length and frequency of the menstrual cycle. Physiological differences in women and their (possibly) associated differences in maternal attitudes and behavior might be investigated.

2. Somewhat along the same lines, animal studies might be conducted (especially with the higher order of mammals) in order to obtain clues as to whether or not there is an "innate" maternal drive. Experimental manipulations could be carried out, systematically depriving one group of female animals from reproduction and parenthood and allowing another group to reproduce. Would it make a difference if the nonmothers had no, little, or a great deal of contact with mothers and/or offspring? Would differences appear in behavior and physical functioning? Would the response of males be different toward the two groups? While animals are not directly comparable to human beings, some insights into the role of learned behavior might be gained from studies of this kind.

Sterility Problems

1. Family planning includes services to people who have apparent sterility problems, as well as to those who need contraceptive aids. What are the social and psychological factors associated with difficulty or inability to conceive or to carry infants to term? Clinical observations have been made along these lines, but systematic, long-range, multidiscipline research is lacking.

2. Various strategies are being employed in dealing with sterility problems. In the case of male sterility, one approach is that of artificial insemination. What psychological impact does this have on both husband and wife, on the marital relationship, on the development and personality of the child—sons being considered separately from daughters? How does this "solution" to sterility problems compare with other approaches, such as acceptance of childlessness or adoption in terms of impact on parents, the marriage, and—in the case of adoption—the children?

References

1. Chilman, C. 1968. Fertility and poverty in the United States: Some implication for family planning programs, evaluation, and research. : J. Mar. Fam. May : 207–227.
2. Cox, I. 1969. Employment of mothers as a means of family support. United States Department of Health, Education, and Welfare. Washington, D.C.
3. Schorr, H. 1966. The family cycle and income development. Social Security Bull. Feb.
4. May, R. 1969. Love and Will. Morton.
5. Rainwater, L. 1965. Family Design. Aldine Press. Chicago, Ill.
6. Masters, W. & V. Johnson. 1966. Human Sexual Response. Little, Brown & Co. Boston, Mass.
7. Kohlberg, L. 1964. Development of moral character and moral ideology. *In* Review of Child Development Research. Hoffman & Hoffman, Eds. : I. Russell Sage Foundation. New York, N.Y.
8. Bogue, D. 1966. Population growth in the United States. *In* Family Planning and Population Programs. Berelson *et al.*,. Eds. University of Chicago Press. Chicago, Ill.
9. Hauser, P. 1967. Family planning and population programs: A book review article. Demography. Summer.
10. Freyman, M. 1966. Organizational structure in family planning. *In* Family Planning and Population Programs. Berelson *et al.*, Eds. University of Chicago Press. Chicago, Ill.

LEADS ON OLD QUESTIONS FROM A NEW REVOLUTION: NOTES ON CUBAN WOMEN, 1969 *

Virginia Olesen, Ph.D.

Associate Professor of Sociology
University of California Medical Center
San Francisco, Calif.

> That is a problem now, too, getting married. I like to dominate my wife and that is not so easy any more.[1]

> I know I am married to an exaggerated case, but his point of view is very Cuban. The position of Cuban women is terrible.[1]

> . . . God knows there is something she can do. . . . In case you have not noticed it, there has been a revolution here and women do not have to put up with that kind of treatment.[1]

> I like to sleep with women other than my wife. . . . Of course it is because of the way we Cuban men are that the girls have to be careful. I say so because of myself. . . . Cuban women are resigned to this behavior from their husbands. They do not like it, they are simply resigned.[1]

> The Cuban woman is now being trained for productive work. This is a completely new situation.[2]

Introduction

To participate in a workshop on the impact of "free choice" on feminine life-styles and self definitions is to address a problem on which old theories, concepts, and findings guide and sustain exploration, but inevitably must give way to uncover and accommodate the unfound, the unthinkable, and the unexpected. Such exploration is at issue in this paper, which seeks to outline thinking and research in areas basic to the workshop, one such area being the appropriate and useful modes of thought with which to approach and understand the problem at hand.

Social and behavioral science does not lack concepts or theories that are both relevant and basic to the concerns at hand. Such useful and well-worn concepts as "marginal man" come to mind: Is not modern woman, at least in the United States, a case of "the marginal man," finding herself between the residual femininity of the last century and the modulated feminism of this? Equally attractive is the colonial analogy, currently in vogue among analysts of race relations: Is not modern American woman a type of freed colonial, rid at last of the burdens of male imperialism, but like many former colonials, now confronted with the vicissitudes of freedom and, in some instances, a lack

* This paper derives from the author's current research on changing sex role definitions and health care roles, which, in the exploratory stage, was funded by a grant from the University of California School of Nursing Faculty Research Fund, University of California Medical Center, San Francisco, Calif.

of preparation for that freedom? Yet another currently popular concept is that found in game theory as it ranges from Stephen Potter's witty insights through the sometimes forced analogies of certain psychiatric game theories: Is not the situation of modern woman, thanks to "the pill," a new game in which old rules have changed, the name of the game is different and "fun and games" implies new plays and ploys? Finally, a possibly useful concept is that of "the survival of the fittest:" Is not the arrival of ways of altering the female reproductive cycle another step in evolutionary development that grants modern woman not "free choice," but the bondage of responsibility for assuring "the survival of the fittest" in the evolutionary cycle? Each of these lines of thought illuminates certain aspects of the workshop theme that other lines of thought do not touch, but all channel and harden thinking along the logical patterns implied in the particular concept used. It would, therefore, seem more profitable and less foreordained to generate useful themes and ideas by first-hand examination of a society in which the customary arrangements for women and men have altered, in order to reveal ideas that are useful in the analysis of women's situations elsewhere.

No less than the analogies just discussed, analysis of a society in which sex roles have altered also carries its own logic and possible conclusions. However, when one starts from analysis of such a society, one starts from empirical substance, not from abstract concepts and theories. Nevertheless, one must recognize the guidelines that influence the selection of the society to be so analyzed: Is the society, with respect to women, undergoing dramatic change, as in China since 1947, or are the alterations proceeding less rapidly, as in contemporary Morocco? [3, 4] Are the perceived changes, whatever the source, associated with emergent strains between the sexes, to wit, the situation of the women of the new American left, who complain in verse that, "I make love and I make coffee but I can't make policy. Who's the garbage can of the radical man? It's me." [5] Is the extent of perceptible change and accommodation to it extensive, as in the familiar case of Russian women, or, conversely, very limited, as in the situation of certain Indian or Latin American social classes? [6–9] Are variables involved in change particularly visible and, therefore, readily available for scrutiny? This choice, alas, is not always possible. While modern China is almost prototypical with respect to the viability of such variables, the American social scientist is at present restricted by the dolorous facts of foreign policy.

Difficulties of another sort arise in considering certain societies in which dramatic change is perceived. In Israel, for instance, the situation is especially intriguing because of continuous and pervasive change, but the multiplicity of ethnic groups differing widely in their cultural proscriptions for the sexes—Yemenite or Persian Jews contrasted with Russian or Polish Jews, for example—make for analytic complexities.[10]

Ideally, though, and most particularly when it is not possible or desirable to undertake comparative analysis, analysis of issues of concern to this workshop leads to selection of a society in which change has been rapid and dramatic, where elements indicating emergent or reduced strains between the sexes are highly discernible, and where composition of the society allows meaningful analysis of wide sectors of that society. Contemporary Cuba, the women and men of that society, and variables in the author's research on other topics, seem to fill these requirements, and it is, therefore, to Cuba that this paper turns for materials which speak to the workshop issues.

The Natural History and Nature of the Research

It is, however, appropriate to briefly indicate the origins and nature of the parent research. Briefly, it originated in the National University of Mexico art gallery in March, 1968, when I by chance visited an exhibit of contemporary Cuban painting. What was striking was the overall excellence of the artists' work, which ranged through familiar, contemporary styles—hard-edge, pop, surrealist, expressionist, impressionist—and utilized a variety of sophisticated techniques, including *fumage*.[11] What was even more notable was that three of the 15 painters, Amelia Pálaez, Antonia Eriez, and Lesbia Vent Dumois, were women; three is scarcely an overwhelming number, but, nevertheless, a proportionately larger number than one would find in a comparable American exhibit, in which Helen Frankenthaler would most likely be the lone woman. In no way did the quality of their paintings suggest that they were window-dressing or token painters. Indeed, the level of their work was, if anything, superior to that of several men in the show. Nor was it, except in one case, heavily ideological, and that one, interestingly enough, was by the youngest woman, who was also one of the three youngest painters in the show, all of whom tended to paint in that way. More interesting still, their ages, 71, 39, and 35, suggested that their work both transcended and was part of the recent decade of great change. Who, then, were these women? How had they or other women fared? What, indeed, was the lot of women in contemporary Cuba? All these and many more questions sprang to mind in the contemplation of the paintings and led, in early 1969, to an exploratory project on changing sex and health-care roles, a project underway at the time this workshop was organized.

What follows here, then, is an analysis of thematic materials gathered in the early stages of this research. The data, though rich and provocative, are derived from such secondary sources as *Granma,* Cuban films, novels, government publications, statements in print and in person from reliable observers in the social science community, and retrospective statements in print from refugees whose observations seemed especially good reports of former conditions in Cuba with respect to the central concerns of this paper, putting aside, where possible, the ideological endorsements and indictments in such statements.

Clearly, this is a research technique that precedes, anticipates, and eventually launches field research in an accessible society, but it does not substitute for the richness of first-hand data gathering in Cuba. Nor, it must be stressed, is such secondary analysis intended as a substitute in the present research. The disadvantages, perils, and limits of such analysis are obvious, for there has been much to criticize, as well as to admire, in such work even when it has been done well, as, for instance, research on wartime Japan, or Eastern European Jewish villages.[12, 13] In spite of these shortcomings, this type of analysis is a useful and necessary preliminary for field work in an accessible society, and serves as a *sine qua non* for study of the inaccessible society. Moreover, it is also meaningful in its own right, as a way not only to hone the social scientist's ideas about the subject at hand, but to sharpen and sensitize a sense of data, possible sources of data, and ways of teasing out indicators and new questions that might elude the researcher who enjoys direct access to or immersion in the field. Additionally, comparisons between analyses done at a distance and those derived from detailed field work can usefully highlight advantages and disadvantages of these approaches.[14] Finally, it is a useful exercise in the sociology of alternatives, an attempt to visualize different approaches to problems as a means of stimulating our sometimes sluggish imaginations and as a means of linking our enterprises with those of our intellectual cousins, the historians, whose concerns and ours make detectives of us all.[15]

Cuba as a Case History

Selection of contemporary Cuba as a society in which to scrutinize issues central to this workshop stems from more than a chance museum visit or a workshop invitation. Within a very short period of time, a decade, there have been dramatic changes at wide and diverse levels in Cuban society. For this reason, irrespective of one's feelings about or response to the Cuban revolution, it must be granted that this decade in Cuba does indeed constitute a case of radical social change, and, significantly, radical social change that implicates sex roles in the most profound ways.

This point is more than academic: The Castro government in espousing the familiar Marxist-Leninist line on women's labor in the home, has sounded, at times, rather like an old-time and somewhat shrewish feminist in its pleas for women to enter the labor force, to look for work outside their homes, and to regard housework as a form of slavery imposed by the male-dominated capitalist society.[16] Moreover, the recent Cuban production of the feature film "Lucia," which deals with the heroine's changing role in the Castro decade, and the mixed reception accorded the film in different parts of Cuban society suggest that the Cubans themselves believe that the changes in their country bear directly on the matter of sex roles,[17] as the comments which precede this essay suggest.

It is the very pervasiveness of this change that makes Cuba especially attractive for the sort of analysis at issue. A rich array of relevant variables is in play: the nature of government, economic arrangements, educational and health care systems, socialization practices, the opportunity structure—indeed, the entire range of social, cultural, and economic institutions and systems. In sum, the wide transformation of the bases of Cuban life demands scrutiny.[18]

The extensivity of the changes, however, transcends the great alterations in the economic order, which certain viewpoints deem as primarily influential in the matter of women's roles and their choices. It is certainly the case that there have been massive changes in the Cuban labor force occasioned by loss of skilled personnel who have immigrated, the decrease in the supply of skilled agricultural labor, as well as alterations in such fundamental economic arrangements as the collectivization of industry and business.[18, 19] It would, however, be a mistake to accord economic factors the full weight of an analysis of changes in sex roles or the lack thereof, in spite of observations on women's work.[20]

Not only do factors at play exceed the merely economic, but the heavy emphasis on psychological elements of revolutionary teaching leads an analysis of women's roles and choices far beyond economic determinism and necessarily forces consideration of the profound moral implications of these emphases for self and personhood of males and females in that society. More specifically, and without going into great detail on the nature, style, and substance of these teachings, which have been brilliantly and effectively detailed elsewhere, the regime's attempts to inculcate the ideal of "the new revolutionary man," unselfishly devoted to country, energetically oriented to revolutionary goals, unwaveringly concerned for fellow man in Cuba and elsewhere, are not mere maneuvers in political socialization to sustain the decade-old regime, but constitute efforts at a profound transformation of the Cuban self, indeed, the Cuban culture.[18]

Cuba, thus, is a particularly striking case with which to analyze the implications of the observation that "the historical and structural features of modern society must be connected with the most intimate features of a man's self . . . which cannot be done by dealing only in microscopic observations."[21] The Cuban case compels us to attend to the interplay of these variables and to witness their interaction so that we may transfer our inferences to other situations both discrepant and congruent. In sum, not the content, but the process and structure of events in Cuba are at issue here. In vivid outline we are offered a glimpse of variables that are more obscure in less dramatic or less sharply delineated situations. To draw these variables out it is appropriate to sketch briefly the situation of women in Cuba during the years immediately preceding the advent of the Castro regime.

Sociohistorical Situation of Cuban Women

In the years immediately preceding 1959, Cuba enjoyed a healthy economic profile, an attribute unique among Third World nations, and among those nations, characteristic only of Japan.[22] Within both underdeveloped and developed nations of similar size, under 6.5 million in population, Cuba's gross national product (GNP) in those years was less than that of such countries as Finland, Switzerland, Denmark, New Zealand, Norway, or Venezuela, where the GNP was over $600 million. It stood on a par, in terms of GNP between $300 million and $600 million, with such countries as Ireland, Israel, Costa Rica, Lebanon, Panama, and Uruguay, and definitely outranked poorer nations whose GNP was less than $300 million, such as Albania, Saudi Arabia, Dominican Republic, Ecuador, El Salvador, Guatemala, Honduras, Iraq, Nicaragua, Haiti, Paraguay, or Bolivia.[23] It was not, therefore, an "underdeveloped" country in the usual sense, although one must recognize that apparent wealth was badly and unevenly distributed in the population.[24] What concerns us here is the part that women played in the labor forces of that time: What was the opportunity structure for women? How many women were in the labor force? What were their prospects as women workers?

In the Cuban labor force of the middle and late 1950s, there were few women, the number being around 17% of the economically active population over 14 years of age.[25] This small percentage points to the prevailing Latin norms that severely restrict and govern activities of females outside the domestic arena. Only since 1936 had Cuban women been able to vote, and only since 1940 had they been assured the legal privilege of owning property. Moreover, this small number suggests that women's occupational choices were limited, even for those bold enough to wish or to have to step outside the bounds of the culture's restrictions on women's work.

The types of occupational choices available to Cuban women varied in those years, however, and in ways that suggest that both the economic structure of the country and the maldistribution of wealth influenced the kinds of choices women could make in this sphere of their lives. Examination of a list of occupations shows that of all occupations domestic service numbered more women workers (89% were women)† than any other.[25] The occupational category with the next greatest number of women workers was that of teacher, where 82% were women, a situation not unlike other Latin nations, e.g., Brazil.[26] Clearly, the two occupations drawing most women represented radically different paths and choices available to women whose background provided or denied them access to an education for the opportunities at hand. This duality is apparent in the rest of the occupational list: Whereas almost half (45%) of social workers were women, as were a substantial number of pharmacists (34%), a significant number of women were also employed in such critical industries as food and tobacco (24%) and the clothing industry (45%).

Judging from this analysis, it would seem that for those women whose life-chances had included the possibility of education, a theme of some importance in Cuba since the 19th-century pronouncements of such feminists as Maria Luisa Dolz y Arnago, the society provided some chance for professional employment, albeit a limited one, judging from the sparse numbers of women in medicine (13%) or law (a meager 7%).[27] For those whose station was much humbler, domestic service or industrial work was their lot.[28] For those whose situation fell between these extremes, the occupational structure held open the possibilities of work in clerical areas, and large numbers of Cuban women were drawn to these, e.g., typists (53% were women), or telephone operators (23%); these were women who, in the vivid description found in a novel on Cuban life of the period, "waged a battle between penury and decorum, struggling to get a hold on the fringes of the middle class; too smart to stop at high school, too poor to go to college or train for a career; too proud to end her anguished pretense by either marrying into the declared blue collar class or becoming the mistress of a minor merchant or political upstart."[29]

To this picture of the variable opportunities afforded by the occupational structure of pre-Castro Cuba it must be added that agricultural work drew very few women (less than 2%), for it was regarded as being too heavy. Women who worked in pre-Castro Cuba, therefore, were largely the urbanized women of the cities, particularly those whose social station permitted them access to an education, which would, for some, lead to such professions as teaching, social work, and pharmacy. Such was the picture from the viewpoint of women's choices. To turn the picture around, it may be noted that even though women were only 17% of the labor force in the mid-1950s, their substantial numbers in such professions as teaching, in such significant support activities as clerical work, in such basic industries as tobacco work, which had utilized women since the 1850s, were clear contributions to the economy of the 1950s.[30]

These figures also point to the public sector of life for Cuban women during that period and suggest that as participants in that public sector, irrespective of Latin norms, they had already begun to emerge from the convent-like dwelling of the home before the Castro phase of Cuba's long revolutionary history. Indeed, during pre-Castro Cuba, and even earlier, there were some women, particularly in the upper and middle classes, whose activities at high political and professional levels gave them what has been felicitously termed, by Professor

† All figures that follow are based on the percentages quoted by Mac Gaffey and Barnett (REF. 25, pp. 343–344).

Richard Fagen, "a strong public character." Such women as Doña Socorro Mancebo, whose correspondence with Simon Bolivar advocated Cuban independence in the 1820s, Doña Maria Luisa Dolz y Arnago, 19th-century educator and feminist, and Terresa Casuso, student activist of the 1930s and later Cuban ambassador to the United Nations, come to mind in this connection.[27, 31]

At the same time, however, that Cuban women had begun to enter public life in small numbers, and along with the symbolic facts of these women of "strong public character," the mode of Latin culture as found in Cuba surrounded these and other women of all classes with norms and sanctions that both pampered and restricted their lives, that emphasized sexuality while condemning women for extramarital infidelities, that on all social levels made women subordinate to the Cuban male in matters of intellect, family life, and, of course, sexual response.[25, 33] A few relevant examples will illustrate: Common-law marriages, frequent in pre-Castro Cuba, particularly in rural areas, were more binding on women than on men: social visiting in city cafes was appropriate for men but not for women; even after marriage, women remained symbolically part of their father's family; adulterous behavior on the husband's part was not grounds for divorce unless it had created public scandal; marital infidelities on the male's part were expected and, indeed, encouraged, but similar behavior by a married woman was regarded as flightiness; in rural Cuba, women frequently did not sit at the same meal with their men-folk, but ate with the children.[25]

These behaviors were supported by much more than the influence of the Roman Catholic church, which in pre-Castro Cuba was significantly weakened and had had limited appeal, and that largely to urban women of the upper middle classes.[25] Such behaviors were thoroughly grounded in and nourished by the cultural themes of *hidalgoismo* and *macho. Hidalgoismo,* the courtly sense of nobility, was balanced by the theme of *macho,* the demand to display manliness in matters sexual, physical, and intellectual by defying convention, but with the type of style and flair that would earn admiration not only of women, but of other men.[25, 34] The enactment of *macho* in the Cuban setting was, and, indeed, still is, heavily implicated with notions of honor and shame that link the psychological aspects of Cuban sexual identity with the social and behavioral norms noted.[35]

Rather importantly from the standpoint of social pressure on Cuban women, these experiences of honor and shame derived not only from the proper male enactment of *macho* and *hidalgoismo,* but on the continued proper conduct of women in any male's life. Ideal women, chaste and hopefully, indeed preferably, sexually innocent, contributed to their own honor and the honor of their men through their decorous behavior. In such a society, it is not surprising that marital infidelity for males was condoned, even encouraged, and that there were well-established institutions for prostitution. Clearly, the cultural pressures on women and their choices redounded on Cuban men, too, and may very well have been part of the reason for the jump in the divorce rate (from 0.83 to 1.17) between 1962 and 1965, when divorce laws were liberalized.[36]

Quite aside from these observations concerning sexual behavior and its prescribed limits, the Cuban family in the pre-Castro years was thought to be a significant social unit for the rearing of children and the provision of a stable society. Family size in 1953 averaged 4.86 persons, with 4.35 being the norm in the urban settings and 5.75 the rural average, reflecting the very large families of peasants, families often headed by women.[25] Family planning and the choices it represented were not a factor in the lives of Cuban women, by virtue of, on the one hand, the influence of the church, however weak, and, on the other, the impress of the cultural themes previously discussed.

To summarize briefly the situation of Cuban women before the Castro years, it may be noted that their partial entry to the labor market represented for different classes differential access to the education necessary to pursue occupations other than those of service or very low skills. In spite of the contributions, both symbolic and otherwise, of women with "strong public character," the Cuban woman was strongly influenced by strong cultural themes, which, in demanding manly sexual aggressiveness from males, muted and diminished female attempts at sexual forwardness in choices other than those rigidly circumscribed by these cultural themes. The realization of personal honor and the penance of public shame were closely related for both men and women to proper enactment of these cultural themes.

The Current Situation

With respect to the occupational structure and opportunities now open to women for education and occupational placement, contemporary Cuba is characterized by a much wider range of choices than previously. Women, as well as men, have been the beneficiaries of the extensive literacy campaign of 1961, which, for many of humble station or what would have been thought of as humble station in an earlier time, has meant greater access to clerical work, from which they would have been barred in an earlier era by virtue of limited education.[28] Nor is it the case that education for clerical work is the major outlet for many women who wish to or have been encouraged to work outside the home. The nationalization of some 55,363 small private businesses in 1968 necessitated the creation of a managerial class, largely recruited from the ranks of housewives whose background or skills were suitable for this purpose.[37] Nearly half of all medical-school classes are now women, and women have begun to appear in such diverse pursuits as barbering, driving tractors, and agricultural work of the sort formerly deemed too heavy.[38]

Not only are more opportunities for work open to women, but many more women are at work. By Cuban estimate, the number of women in nonagricultural pursuits jumped from 90,000 to 370,000 between 1965 and 1968, an increase which they hope to continue with the addition of 100,000 more women in agricultural and industrial work in 1969, and which will eventually culminate, they hope, with one million women engaged in nonagricultural pursuits by 1975.[16] Assuming that the Cuban population remains somewhat stable, or increases only slightly (it was 7,833,000 in 1966),[36] this means that by 1975 one out of every seven Cubans would be a working woman. From the official standpoint, these efforts to bring women into the labor force are determined and dictated by the economic necessity to increase the labor pool as an economic resource. Such efforts are, moreover, attempts to involve Cuban women in the moral aspects of the revolution, to make them a part of creating the new revolutionary man, and to urge them to take part in bettering the nation.

Although it may be reasonably assumed that many Cuban women earnestly have taken up work as their own commitment to the revolutionary ideals, it may also be noted that economic pressures on the individual, which involve rising costs and stable salaries, have also prompted the move of many women to the labor force.[16] In the advent, then, of increased numbers of working women, we see the tensions between issues of *conciencia,* the amalgam of conscience, conscientiousness, and commitment to revolutionary ideals, and *egoismo,* the concerns for material matters or rewards.[39, 40] For some, these tensions play their part with respect to the types of choices women can and do make with respect to the types of family lives they and their husbands work out, as shown, for example, by the comments of a regional secretary of the Cuban Federation of Women who noted that: [1]

> I have been married two years. My husband was at Guantanamo during the alert and since I had been in Santiago at school just before that, we did not see each other for four months. Now he is at Banes and we see each other once a week. It has to be, it is no sacrifice. My ambition is to see our work succeed. . . .

Along with broadening the opportunity structure for women, necessitated in part by the economic and moral demands of the new situation, there has been an effort to institute the types of social services that women need if they are to enter the labor force, particularly women with families. Chief among these has been the establishment of nursery schools, which enable women to take full-time work or to undertake studies that will later lead to work.[38]

The wider participation of women in work, several-fold beyond the modest 17% of the mid 1950s, has also been accompanied by the further emergence of the Cuban woman with "strong public character." To the familiar names of Mariana Grajelas, renowned as the mother of an early hero (Antonio Maceo), and Ana de Moro Betancourt, another 19th-century feminist, have been added the names of women whose participation in various phases of Castro's ascent to power nominates them for martyrdom or heroic stature—for example, Olga Guevara, formerly a guerrilla fighter who is now a trouble shooter in mountain settlements; Celia Sanchez, Castro's personal secretary; and Haydee Santamaria, heroine of the attack on the Monchada barracks, now head of the cultural services, La Casa de Las Americas, who has been celebrated in song and in poem.[41] The emergence of these women as potent symbolic figures of strong female public character has paralleled the increasing prominence of the Federation of Cuban Women, an organization headed by Castro's sister-in-law, Vilma Espin, and an organization devoted to the eradication of the inferior status of Cuban women as well as their induction and integration into the new situation.

Although these themes have strongly emerged in contemporary Cuba, much of the cultural arrangement from earlier times appears to have survived with respect to certain emphases on women's roles. For one matter, the family unit continues to be regarded as critical in Cuban life. The positive view with which the society as a whole looks on the family, and especially on the role of mothers, is clearly reflected in the large sections of the Communist paper *Granma,* which devoted these sections to Mother's Day; one foreign observer noted that on Mother's Day he had witnessed Cuban bakers devoting their entire capacity, and perhaps even the entire daily ration of flour, to the production of special Mother's Day cakes.[19, 42]

This observation leads to the question of pressures on sex-role behavior and the matter of women's choices. In this connection, it is to be noted that the cultural themes discussed in the earlier section of the paper, e.g. *macho* and *hidalgoismo,* are still very much an influence on sexual behaviors and judgments, as witness the report about a former Monchada fighter, now a disburser of scholarships at the university, who is reputedly notorious among students for refusing to allocate scholarships to young women who are supposed to have slept with their boyfriends, apparently basing his judgments on the old standards of chastity and innocence.[43] Other informal reports of negative responses from Cuban husbands to such fashions as miniskirts suggest that the former ideals of honor and shame are still realized to a significant extent through the wife's behavior.[44]

With respect to choices in the matter of child bearing, because Cuba does not utilize the pill, the older methods of contraception, where accessible, must be relied on; abortions, although available, are not encouraged because a population increase to restore numbers lost through immigration and to assure a sufficient labor pool is clearly important to the regime. Studied efforts, however, to enforce productivity and to realize a higher birth rate have not been undertaken by the Castro government, even though there has been an increase in the birth rate. For this reason, the analysis of women's choices in this area remains one in which the cultural, economic, and social proscriptions around sex role and family, not the dictates of the regime, are the salient considerations. Interestingly, as recounted in the statements of some young Cubans,[17] an almost puritanical attitude toward sexual relationships exists among some of the young, although by no means among everyone. It certainly is not extant among the *campesinos,* whose large families on the one hand give assurances of future workers, but who on the other hand pose critical problems for food supplies in an economy of scarcity, in which crop lands once devoted to food have been increasingly taken over by sugar cane.[45]

The eradication of prostitution, the regime's attempt to do away with an institution to which many women of poorer classes had been drawn in pre-Castro Cuba, has been accompanied by official recognition that not all of the former traditions, most especially the *posadas,* inns where lovers could dally at leisure and in private, could be dispensed with, and that certain traditions around sexual behaviors would have to grow out of the mix of the old and the new. Castro himself has noted:[2]

> Traditions and customs can clash somewhat with new social realities and the problem of sexual relations in youth will acquire scientific attention . . . . All of this [discussion on prostitution] raises the future necessity, too, of approaching the problem of sexual relations in a different way. But we believe that these are problems of the future that cannot be determined by decree—not at all.

Women's own responses to the revolution, and to the meaning of these changes for them as women, seem somewhat mixed. Inferentially, based on findings showing that women workers had a more conservative response to the revolution than did male workers, the question must be raised whether or not women were prepared, or even willing, to realign their roles in accordance with the new times.[33] Moreover, in an earlier part of the Castro decade, mixed comments from women about the role of a queen in a Havana carnival suggested that women themselves had radically differing ideas about their place as women, either as symbols of female roles or as participants in the revolution.[46]

To summarize, a number of tensions seem apparent in the observations just noted: For one thing, the effort to bring women into the labor market, both as an economic necessity for the country and for individual gain, is in conflict with the continued emphasis on the importance of the Cuban family.

The sacrifices to enact *conciencia* and to create a new Cuba and a new Cuban man may well articulate choices for family rearing and planning that far transcend the conventional choices and modes of control known elsewhere. Much of the resolution of this tension may depend on the success of child-care centers. For another matter, although women had earlier begun to be active in the labor market, they nevertheless are newcomers; there are, as yet, no well-developed norms or themes with which to work out the resulting tensions and their impact on the cultural themes of *macho* and *hidalgoismo* or the effect of these themes on their arrival in the work force. Clearly, what is implied in this particular tension is not only an emergent set of ideals or values to cover this particular situation, but an emergent set of ideals that would be shared by males as well as females. As has been pointed out about the revolution in general, its political culture is still dependent on revolutionary arrangements, rather than deeply ingrained values and patterns.[18] Will these deeply ingrained values and patterns be in conflict with the moral aspects of the revolution, so that the Cuban woman is faced with choices for sexual and family matters that draw forth the old feelings of honor and shame, the new concerns for *conciencia,* or as yet undefined and undetermined feelings of satisfaction and/or resentment?

Implications For This Workshop

From the foregoing descriptive materials on Cuba, and Cuban women and their situation in a radically changed society, it is possible to outline a rough concept of "reciprocities" that might be useful in analyzing this topic with reference to American women. The term "reciprocities" is nothing more than a metaphor to describe the trade-offs among and between the multiple pathways being trod simultaneously by any woman as she confronts realities and creates choices in her life. For Cuban women, these reciprocities clearly involve the economic (with their entry into the public arena of the labor market), the social (implicated in that entry), the psychological (in sustaining or transgressing norms rooted in *macho*), the emotional (in the experience of honor or shame), and the moral (implicated in the interplay of *conciencia* and *egoismo*). The virtue of the metaphor is that it reminds us that our concepts must go beyond "the woman" or "the situation" and must account for the interplay of cultural, social, and psychological themes, for in the workings of such reciprocities are the genesis of further change.

To apply the metaphor to the American situation, much of the better literature on the working mother examines with greater care the reciprocities between her economic situation, her psychological response, and her social role as wife and mother. Only rarely, however, is attention given to the reciprocity between these factors and the moral dimension of where the working mother sees her place as worker, employee, or professional in the society at large.

In an area central to this workshop—family planning—one now hears middle-class people talk of choices in regard to family size being restricted not for the usual social and economic reasons of support and provision for the progeny, but for the moral reason of limiting one's issue so that all can enjoy and use the available social and natural resources. Such talk suggests that the concept of reciprocities, pursued as a sensitizing or analytic concept, could indeed be useful. If so, the Castro phase of the Cuban revolution will have contributed more to the cause of womankind than its proponents or detractors would ever have dreamed.

Acknowledgments

Helpful discussions with Lucy Cohen, Ross Danielson, Richard Fagen, and Arlie Hochschild, colleagues in various disciplines in various universities, are gratefully acknowledged, as are the contributions of Jane Tabata and Barbara Britts, participants in the aforementioned research project.

References

1. Yglesias, J. 1969. In the Fist of the Revolution. : 212, 256, & 259. Vintage Press. New York, N.Y.
2. Castro, F. Quoted in Lockwood, L. 1969. Castro's Cuba, Cuba's Fidel. : 94 & 106. Vintage Press. New York, N.Y.
3. Chin, A. S. 1967. Mainland China. *In* Women in the Modern World. R. Patai, Ed. : 421–433. The Free Press. New York, N.Y.
4. Forget, N. 1962. Women and professions in Morocco. Int. Soc. Sci. J. **XIV:** 107.
5. New York Times. 1969. Is motherhood holy? Not any more! May 18.
6. Dodge, N. 1966. Women in the Soviet economy. The Johns Hopkins Press. Baltimore, Md.
7. Brown, D., Ed. The Role and Status of Women in the Soviet Union. Teachers' College Press. New York, N.Y.
8. Narain, V. India. *In* Women in the Modern World. R. Patai, Ed.: 27 & 31. The Free Press. New York, N.Y.
9. De Marti, R. S. 1967. Spanish America. *In* Women in the Modern World. R. Patai, Ed.: 204. The Free Press. New York, N.Y.
10. Waagenaar, S. 1961. Women of Israel. : 11–14 & 21–28. Lonnie Kahn Co. Tel Aviv, Israel.
11. Universidad Nacional Autonoma de Mexico. 1968. Pintura Cubana Contemporanea. Departamento de Artes Plasticas. Mexico City, Mexico.
12. Benedict, R. 1946. The Chrysanthemum and the Sword. Charles E. Tuttle Press. Tokyo, Japan.
13. Zoborowski, M. & E. Herzog. 1962. Life Is With People. Shocken Press. New York, N.Y.
14. Mead, M. 1954. Preface. *In* Themes in French Culture. R. Metraux & M. Mead. : vii. Stanford Press. Stanford, Calif.
15. Winks, R. 1969. Introduction *In* The Historian as Detective. R. Winks, Ed.: xii–xxiv. Harper & Row. New York, N.Y.
16. New York Times. 1968. Cuba steps up mobilization of women for labor. December 15.
17. Yglesias, J. 1969. Cuban report: Their hippies, their squares. New York Times. January 12.
18. Fagen, R. 1969. The Transformation of Political Culture in Cuba. Stanford Press. Stanford, Calif.
19. Leontief, W. 1969. Notes on a visit to Cuba. New York Review of Books **XIII** (3): 17 & 20.
20. Boorstein, E. 1968. The Economic Transformation of Cuba. Monthly Review Press. New York, N.Y.

21. Mills, C. W. & H. Gerth. 1953. Character and Social Structure. : xix. Harcourt, Brace & World. New York, N.Y.
22. Fagen, R. 1969. Revolution for international consumption only. Trans-Action **6**(6): 10.
23. Sawyer, J. 1967. Dimensions of nations: Size, wealth and politics. Amer. J. Sociol. **73**(2): 158–160.
24. Zeitlin, M. 1969. Cuba—Revolution without a blueprint. Trans-Action **6**(6): 38.
25. Mac Gaffey, W. & C. R. Barnett. 1962. Cuba, Its People, Its Society, Its Culture. HRAF Press. New Haven, Conn.
26. Gouveia, A. J. 1967. Education and development: Opinions of secondary schoolteachers. *In* Elites in Latin America. S. M. Lipset & A. Solari, Eds.: 484–513. Oxford University Press. New York, N.Y.
27. Dolz y Arnago, M. L. 1955. La Liberacion de la Mujer Cubana por la Educacion. : 93. Oficina del Historiador de la Ciudad, Municipio de la Habana. Habana, Cuba.
28. Cuba Comision Nacional de la Unesco. 1963. Cuba—Education and Culture. : 51. (Unpublished document.) United Nations. New York, N.Y.
29. De Gamez, T. 1966. The Yoke and the Star. : 35. Bobbs Merrill Publ. New York, N.Y.
30. Foner, P. S. 1962. A History of Cuba. **2:** 137. International Publishers. New York, N.Y.
31. Foner, P. S. 1962. A History of Cuba. **1:** 112. International Publishers. New York, N.Y.
32. Casuso, T. 1961. Cuba and Castro. Random House. New York, N.Y.
33. Zeitlin, M. 1967. Revolutionary Politics and the Cuban Working Class. : 123 & 127. Princeton University Press. Princeton, N.J.
34. Castro, A. 1964. Hidalgoismo: The sense of nobility. *In* Sociology and History. W. Cahnman & A. Boskoff, Eds. : 462–470. The Free Press. New York, N.Y.
35. Peristaiany, J. G. 1966. Honour and Shame. The University of Chicago Press. Chicago, Ill.
36. Demographic Yearbook. 1967. : 124. Statistical Office of the United Nations. New York, N.Y.
37. Meso-Lago, C. 1969. The revolutionary offensive. Trans-Action **6**(6): 24.
38. Huberman, L. & L. Sweezy. 1969. Socialism in Cuba. : 40, 42, & 57. Monthly Review Press. New York, N.Y.
39. Kahl, J. 1969. The moral economy of a revolutionary society. Trans-Action **6**(6).
40. Georges, R. 1968. La sociologie et Cuba. Rev. Inst. Sociol. **4:** 779.
41. Fernandez, P. A. 1967. Three poems from "The Book of Heroes." *In* Writers in the New Cuba. J. M. Cohen, Ed.: 87. Penguin Books, Inc. Baltimore, Md.
42. Granma. 1969. May 12
43. Hochschild, A. 1969. Student power in action. Trans-Action **6**(6): 18.
44. Britts, B. 1969. Personal observation during a visit to Cuba.
45. Dumont, R. 1969. Castro's rash gamble. Le Monde Weekly Selection. December 10.
46. Miller, W. 1961. 90 Miles From Home. : 4. Little, Brown & Co. Boston, Mass.

Discussion

E. James Lieberman, M.D., *Moderator*

Olesen: This paper follows very closely Dr. Milner's charge to me to prepare a paper that would delineate a useful concept for thinking about the overall topic of the workshop. In delineating such a concept, one needs to look for materials that take one in a certain direction. There is a vast amount of such material around, and the choice of Cuba was not only fortuitous in that I happened to be working on it, but it is particularly useful and dramatic for it shows clearly some of the interrelationships between and among factors which, both humanistically and sociologically, must be considered as we talk about the problems at the heart of this workshop. My paper, therefore, is an exercise not only in presenting materials with which you may or may not be familiar, but it is also an exercise in concept construction.

TANGRI: Would you briefly enlarge on your concept of reciprocity?

OLESEN: I am not even sure reciprocity is the best concept. It is the word that came to mind after I had reviewed the basic materials and had put together the psychosexual variables operating in that culture, the political or wide-scale social variables of the nature of the society, the moral variables with the element of service to humanity, and the cultural variables having to do with *macho* and *hidalgoismo*. It seems to me we must ask ourselves: If we develop very strongly in one way, what is going to happen in other sectors of the system? I was very impressed by related materials, for example, in Dr. Newman's paper; she pointed out that if there are few sons in an Indian family, then the proper religious rituals cannot be observed. I think this is a good example of reciprocity.

TANGRI: Is what you are pointing to the system nature of the society, in that alterations in some part of the system are going to have repercussions or effects in other parts of the system?

OLESEN: I feel quite uncomfortable about using systems analysis in a societal context. One gets into the problem of open and closed ends and the whole question of equilibrium, et cetera, but I am not very keen on that type of analysis. Rather, we ought to try to think of sensitizing concepts that point our thinking in new directions on these points.

YGLESIAS: What is interesting in this paper is that it is an example of a solution that grows out of the nature of a particular society. This point leads me to worry about the type of research that has been described here; for example, the question of the two-child family. I was associated with a well-known research project called "The Child Development Program," which is being conducted in many hospitals in the United States. Women and children from poorer sections of the population—black, Puerto Rican, and so on, who were admitted to the clinics—were being studied prenatally and then through their 12th year. The nature of the research design caused them to be handled as objects. I was associated with this program not as a researcher but to do the public relations, and perhaps, as a consequence, I had a different approach to what was coming out of it.

Studies that extract the human being from his social setting or extract his family unit from the pressures of the whole society upon it are improper, I feel, in terms of the sociological, or medical, or, indeed, any perspective. Interdisciplinary studies can also make the same kind of error. The researcher amasses a number of papers, and the actual human beings involved are turned into objects, which either fit or do not fit certain theses that are to be proven by the investigator. What particularly interested me in your study was that it was done without your having been in Cuba; am I correct?

OLESEN: You are.

YGLESIAS: That the actual life forms could not be studied is a failure of the paper, and it is an obvious failure, admitted by the author. But seeing these forms of life, I think, would be the right way to study them and would reveal some of the answers to the questions that are being asked here. Are we completely held within the forms that we know now? What about a structure such as on the Isle of Pines, where an entire youth community is being established without any adults at all? This would be a marvelous opportunity to study the breakdown of the family, if there *is* a breakdown of the family. We don't really know whether this phenomenon does represent a breakdown of the family, nor do we know whether our current family structure is something for which we should or should not work.

Some of this kind of openness of approach should be applied to our society because we tend to forget that the middle-class family is not all of society. Those clinic patients who are being studied don't fit into any of the categories that we have been discussing.

OLESEN: I am glad Mrs. Yglesias raised this point about the nature of the research because it indicates one of the things we should be aware of in connection with the workshop theme. Admittedly, first-hand research has tremendous advantages, particularly for sensitive observers. Nevertheless, there are some very good reasons for doing secondary analysis, when one is for all kinds of reasons prevented from being immersed in the situation. There are other examples of secondary-sources research. One is the Zoborowski and Herzog study on Eastern European Jews. In this type of analysis one really has to put on a thinking-cap. One is constrained by not being there. But at the same time, one is forced into very rigorous and careful inspection of all the available data; one's logic and thoughts are brought to bear on the matter.

KAMM: I wonder about the application of the psychologists' notion of cognitive dissonance to your idea of reciprocity. For example, in Cuban society, how is one to evaluate the custom of Mother's Day? As you pointed out, there is the importance of having children, yet there is also the effort to create a society in which the woman is somewhat similar to the man in terms of the functions each performs, that is, one individual has the problem of trying to understand and to incorporate elements that would seem to be contradictory.

How does one manage this in our own society? Is it really possible to create a new notion of what male and female may do, what they may be, in a society that continues to maintain a patriarchal relationship? For instance, there is our notion of a male god. Is it possible to speak about psychological freedom within such a context? How can people get rid of one concept and still prevent themselves from developing all sorts of irrational solutions to such dissonant phenomena? It seems to me that this is part of what you were getting at with your notion of reciprocity.

OLESEN: Cognitive dissonance is a very useful concept; it is a useful way to speak for the moment about the Cuban case, even though I don't apply it in strictly psychological terms. Persons who do not fully espouse or enact the philosophy of the moral obligation of the revolution and who engage in behavior not defined as consonant with these moral obligations could very well be interpreted in terms of cognitive dissonance. For example, what does cognitive dissonance mean with respect to the types of psychological processes utilized to alleviate it? There is the case, for example, of norms related to sex-role behavior, to enacting the masculine role as it is called for in that society. There are men who do not wish to do that. Why?

To shift the discussion back to our own society, I wonder whether cognitive dissonance is not useful in thinking about some of the problems of women's liberation, or some of the other problems about family planning that have come up in our workshop.

KAMM: I was really concerned with the fact that so many of the solutions to such problems as have been raised here—for example, of males being resentful of women controlling conception, of women desiring to go out to work, or of males taking care of children—are artificial solutions. We tend to say that there is really no problem at all, rather than to come right out and totally reject a part of our society. I think this kind of denial has, for a long time, been a very important element in maintaining social stability. The role of religion in this context is another area with which one should be more concerned. Are not the notions of the ultimate power being the male and of trying to develop a liberal clergy contradictory terms? How can we become more rational unless we deal with the society as a whole? What I found fruitful in your paper was your willingness to approach this sort of problem.

OLESEN: We have to try to find concepts that take us beyond the particular woman, or the particular man, or the particular situation. We have to find concepts that are, perhaps, the next higher logical or theoretical level, in order to remove some of the old cognitive hangups, some of the old modes of analysis, and proceed to a point at which we can open new doors for ourselves. There may be some bad leads in these new kinds of concepts, but we must try to get away from the older, rather bracketed, type of thinking.

POLGAR: I wonder to what extent you can say that the changes you described in your paper are part of the Hispanic tradition, or that they are dependent on Marxist philosophy with Eastern European traditions of equality for women, and to what extent (and this is the point that interests me most) may these be examples of what we call jumps in evolution, or marked cultural change? I was, as were so many others, much impressed by Betty Friedan's argument that the movement for female liberation has dwindled in the Anglo-Saxon countries, that there was a big push for a while, and then it sort of slowed down. Maybe there is another big push coming.

DELL'OLIO: Would you specify the era?

POLGAR: The big push in the Anglo-Saxon countries was from approximately 1860 to World War II.

DELL'OLIO: What about post-World War II?

POLGAR: Its height was, perhaps, immediately post-World War I. Then it dwindled away in this country. This concept of evolution occurs to me because of the example of recent marked changes in the lives of Tunisian, Turkish, and Indian women. Even though these are, perhaps, mostly elite movements, they started from further back, but then moved forward faster during a particular short period of history. To what extent can we look at the Cuban experience in this kind of cross-cultural perspective? These changes are not smooth ones, and not all are revolutions, and may not need to be looked at in terms of political revolutions. It may be that cultural change happens in this kind of saltating way. The Cuban case of female emancipation may be an example of this broader process.

OLESEN: One of the most critical aspects of this particular research is that it is difficult to analyze. Whether one has or has not been in Cuba, the extent to which there were pockets of achievement and liberation before this most recent dramatic change is significant. My best sources suggest that, classically, there have been women from the upper-middle and the upper classes of very "strong public character." There were also, obviously, many women who were sufficiently well educated to take jobs as clerks and typists before the Castro takeover.

Is it a sharp, distinct change? Clearly, in terms of some figures, yes. In terms of some other things that are currently not clear in my own mind, I simply don't know. Perhaps, since Mrs. Yglesias has more information, she might comment. Although it is very easy to assume there has indeed been a very dramatic and radical change for the better in the women's situation in Cuba, there is some disagreement on this point by a number of persons whose observations fall in other sectors of the social spectrum.

YGLESIAS: From what I saw in Cuba, the situation is very mixed. The demands of the new system and of the economy forced a burst of freedom for women because they were needed in the economy. This, in turn, forced the formation of an extraordinary nursery system, as well as all the other things that freed women for the economy. There is also, on the other hand, the tradition of *machismo,* the very strong Spanish tradition of male supremacy, of women in a very subservient position. The traditional Jewish mother is pale compared to the traditional Spanish mother. There is that whole tradition that they must work against.

As you say, there is a difference of opinion as to how far the revolution really has furthered women's progress, or whether they are merely being used to fulfill certain economic needs. Whichever it is, forms are occurring there that are most interesting to study to find out what effect they are having on traditional family structures. For example, there are now huge groups of Cuban children who are living in school situations away from parents.

OLESEN: In this mix of levels and variables, one intriguing aspect is the whole moral quality of that revolution, the service to others, the sacrifice, and so on. By no means does this necessarily suggest a New Jerusalem for womankind in Cuba. It may very well turn out that the notions of sacrifice and devotion and pushing the revolution ahead mean more, not less, liberation. But I want to stress strongly the moral aspect of the situation in that society. This is a relationship we need to look at more in our own society.

EAST: Professor Olesen, you mentioned that prior to the revolution in Cuba, 13% of the doctors were women, as were 7% of the lawyers. Those figures are about double comparable figures in this country. About 6% or 7% of our doctors are women, and not because women don't want to go into medicine. Far more apply to medical schools than are accepted. With regard to women in politics, I was quite astonished to see so many in Cuba. I wonder if any of the anthropologists or sociologists here have any ideas as to what it is in American society that keeps women down.

L. NEWMAN: I would like to make one statement to underline some of what has been said. It is extremely important to examine this point of developing new concepts. I think I only touched on it myself. I think our necessary reliance on old ideas has got to go. We have really to "think new," if we are trying to build something different, which is what I hope this workshop is trying to do.

LIEBERMAN: You said the "system" model was not satisfactory to you. Would you include the term "ecology" as another system term, or, given the fact that the term comes from the notion of household and community, would you see this as a dynamic model that could answer our needs for reciprocity?

OLESEN: I think so. That term would be particularly interesting because of the physical and geographical variables it suggests.

LIEBERMAN: In connection with the necessity of keeping the human being human in our research, I heard Erik Erikson discuss the dangers of studying the person as an object. It was also Erikson's idea to develop a concept of mutuality as a kind of reciprocity. What is your reaction to this term, "mutuality"? Also, I was concerned with generativity, that the person in the here and now can empathize with a larger circle and be concerned with the consequences both to those he cannot see and to those not yet here.

OLESEN: I think mutuality would be a useful concept to work with. I didn't entertain that, although I am familiar with Erikson's idea of mutuality. Reciprocity, I think, implies a kind of exchange, whereas mutuality is a balancing concept. But this is quibbling over words, really. Anything that suggests the interplay of factors is perfectly suitable.

DELL'OLIO: It seems to me, the more things change, the more they remain the same. Nothing has really changed. Women are in the same double-bind they have always been in. We are worse off than slaves; all that is required of slaves is that they be docile and submissive and work. But we are *also* required to be loving and giving, and possibly educating, and possibly academic, and possibly professional, and also good mothers!

This dichotomy, this polarization, strikes me as being just as obvious in Cuba, perhaps because of the long road they have had to travel too quickly. The reason, it seems to me, that they have made more strides in the case of the professions is because formerly they were so oppressed. In this situation, exceptional women—exceptional either by education or by opportunity—were given more recognition. But in countries like the United States, where more parity is being achieved, there is a much more subtle but more widespread oppression, a drive to keep women down because they are coming up so fast.

The situation *is* reciprocal or mutual—but the balance never changes. Women are constantly put in the same double-bind of being the "whore-madonna," the achiever, the person who doesn't castrate—and at the same time they are expected to cope with every problem imaginable. *This* is what should be discussed in a sociological workshop like this: this terrible double-bind that we must live out our lives in, that so prevents us from achieving, that keeps us mentally debased and inferior, because we are not only treated as objects but we treat ourselves as objects. Even here, in this workshop, we talk about ourselves as objects.

OLESEN: This is precisely why we need a new kind of language. One of my criticisms here is the rhetoric of the workshop itself, even its title—and I would include my own paper in this criticism. Everything is being related only to women. There is more than just an impact on women. We have to move away from that cause-and-effect kind of thing, that stimulus-response model, and begin to look at something where all the balls are being juggled in the air at the same time.

DUNBAR: When the younger elements have protested this narrowness, we have been told it is because we possess a different set of values, that we are throwing out family concepts. We are not doing that. What we want to do is to challenge the sterile and ossified basic approach, to challenge the language, the type of jargon that everyone is so completely accustomed to. That is the proper area for research.

OLESEN: That is what my paper is really about; it is a new way of looking at the whole problem.

KAMM: But no one is looking at the male role!

CURRENT AND EMERGING OCCUPATION-CENTERED FEMININE LIFE-CAREER PATTERNS AND TRENDS *

Cynthia Fuchs Epstein, Ph.D.

Columbia University Bureau of Applied Social Research
New York, N.Y.
and Assistant Professor of Sociology, Queens College,
Flushing, N.Y.

The roles of American women—and the problems they cause—have long been the subject of both the popular press and the behavioral sciences. Currently they are the subject of furor by the women's liberation groups that have recently sprung up on campuses, in professional circles, and in some cities. The issues, once academic or therapeutically focused, have become torrid and "sides" are becoming polarized. But there is no doubt that change has occurred, and that more is in the wind. Young women, attractive and talented, are challenging the norms attached to women's traditional roles, and are asking why the classic sex-role division within the family must be maintained, and in particular, why the expectations attached to women's home-based roles are not altered in the face of the growing demands of their careers.

It is no mystery that the problems women face in meeting role demands attached to their many statuses † are critical components of their commitment to work and their general participation in the more demanding professions. Clearly, only a minority of women have occupation-centered lives. A woman's orientation has, of course, been typically home and family centered, even if she has had an occupation. It is useful to view some of the role problems of American women within the analytic framework of status and role-sets, for then we can identify the general social processes that act to define women's life-chances and options—which are malleable, and which are not.

The Status-Set

The array of statuses that all people have generally determines their behavior and expectations in life. Robert K. Merton, who first conceptualized the notion of status-set and who has since investigated the dynamics of status-sets, indicated that some statuses are of greater weight than other, insofar as they may limit or permit acquisition of other statuses.[2] Within any given status-set, certain statuses may limit the performance of others (one may not be a priest and a father). In addition, attention may focus on a particular status so that other statuses may be given little recognition (the midget who may also be a

* This paper is a revision of sections in the author's books, "Woman's Place: Options and Limits in Professional Careers," University of California Press, 1970, and "The Woman Lawyer," University of Chicago Press, forthcoming.

† Status is defined as a social position that is institutionalized, e.g., mother, physician. As Goode points out, "role" and "status" have often been used interchangeably[1]

competent administrator). Merton has labeled the first *dominant* statuses. The latter are termed *salient* statuses.

People grow accustomed to certain combinations of statuses. Introduce a woman into the male domains where high finance or law are dealt with and immediately the "system" suffers a shock to which it must adjust. Male activities, from playing golf to meeting in a "men only" bar, man-to-man talk and deals, all operate in an arena of exclusivity. The status of "man" and the status of "banker" are the compatible statuses; that of "female" and "banker" are viewed as inappropriately paired in this culture. These views are rooted in cultural expectations and themes, and they are reinforced by the statistical frequency with which they appear. Thus, the woman who chooses the unfamiliar combination is a deviant and considered peculiar. My research in the past few years has centered on women who sought these combinations. They, like all other American women, face the consequences of being deviant.

Let us look at the preferred status-set for the American woman and the attached demands of time and performance: For a woman, her sex-status is the primary and pivotal status that determines much of her life course and her identity. She is a wife and mother, a daughter, and perhaps a sister. She may, but is not likely to, become a doctor, lawyer, engineer, or university professor. The feminine life-career means a core of statuses around which revolve a host of role relationships. As mother, she is called on to interact with children and their friends, teachers, the pediatrician; it is likely that the list increases with class position as the mother shepherds the child to dancing classes and museum lectures. These role-demands are structural "givens" which must give way or become redefined for women who assume occupational roles.

Given the assumption that everyone in a society must cope with an over-extended role network,[3] we believe that women probably have fewer structural mechanisms than do men for coping with the over-demanding network revolving around women's sex-linked statuses and occupational statuses. Some do manage to make the culturally unexpected statuses-sets congruent, but because it occurs so infrequently we suspect it is a sociological accident. Some of these cases are reported later in this paper. The woman may, of course, by dint of flexible personality or shrewd analysis, make her status-set congruent by a number of mechanisms.

Hierarchy in the Status-Set

The woman's status-set, as any other, is subject to hierarchy as established by the values of the society. For women it is clear that obligations attached to family statuses are first in priority, with the duties of mother overriding most other role obligations, and with those of wife coming second. The woman's occupational status of almost any rank, comes later. A role-strain problem is created for women because in the general culture, occupational roles normally come ahead of family roles.

The man, on the other hand is shielded from conflict "by the existence in his environment of a hierarchy of values which preclude, for the most part, the necessity of conscious decision. Unless family needs reach crisis proportion, the demands of his work come first. And neither he nor his wife is faced with problems of choice in a condition of crisis."[4] Professional people in particular are expected to channel a large proportion of their emotional as well as physical energies into work. One need never apologize for working if one is a man; in fact, if he spends "too much time" with his family, he is considered something of a loafer.

There is complementarity between a man's duties and obligations as a husband, and those in the occupational sphere. A good earner is a good husband. If he earns an adequate living for his family, he has nearly fulfilled society's demands on him, and, depending on his social rank, he is permitted a wide range of behavior by which he may fulfill his other husband-father roles. For example, he is admired if he does carpentry at home, but he does not lose face if he hires a handyman to do the same tasks. He can play ball with his son if he is athletic, but no one will hold it against him if he instead reads stories or works on science projects with his child. He must, of course, show *some* interest in his child to be considered a good father in our society, but unless the child gets into serious trouble it is usually the mother who bears responsibility.

Expectations about what is an "adequate" amount of time to be with his wife are also imprecise, and a man's other activities, starting with work obligations, but including clubs, hobbies, politics, and informal male social get-togethers, all are legitimate reasons for cutting down on this time. Assuming that the husband is not spending time away from home to be with another woman, the wife is given little legitimation for objecting to his absence. The wife who does object, who demands that her husband remain home, is likely to be labeled a nag by her husband or neighbors.‡ In addition, the husband may feel free to be away from home, from the children and the house, knowing that his wife is there to take care of things, to supervise the children's activities, to manage the house.

For the woman, by contrast, there is no such thing as spending "too much time" with her family and the quality of her role-demands as mother and wife are such that they intrude on all other activities. She remains on call during any time spent away from the family and, if she works, many of her family tasks must be fitted into what usually would be work time. The woman who works must deal with two conflicting priority systems (the occupational demands are not lowered for the woman although she may consider them second in importance), and she may often find herself under strain to perform both roles adequately.

It is often assumed that women's professional commitments deflect her from her home obligations and vice-versa. A man may find that being a husband supports his occupational role.[3] Edwin Boring and Alice Bryan have observed in a study of factors affecting professional careers of women psychologists that "women averaged 14.1 hours per week on familial or domestic activities as compared with 10.6 hours for the man. Three or more hours per week were spent on child-training and guidance by 29.4 percent of women, on physical care of children by 24.5 percent, and on special problems of children by 10.2 percent."[5] And, "nearly all the men are married, and a married man usually manages to make his marriage contribute to his success and prestige. Most of the married women do not receive the same professional support from their husbands and the unmarried women have no husbands."[6]

Add Reisman's observation of the married male professor's advantage in having a wife, "who even if she does pursue a part-time career, guards her

‡ In extreme cases of "neglect," wives may be permitted to complain, but clearly the absorption of the man in his work is not considered intolerable.

husband's productivity and performance in obvious and in subtle ways, just as her husband's secretary or the woman librarian . . . speeds him on his way." [7] Thus, the man's status-set is complementary and reinforcing and the woman's is not.

Role Demands and Institutional Pressures on the Woman in American Society

Limitations Placed on Occupational Roles by Family Roles

In some occupations there is no conflict between the demands of work and the demands of family. In others there is conflict, but socially sanctioned means of resolution exist, which are accepted by both partners, as, for example, in medical practice. Such occupations as professional musician may create problems for the man with a family. Professional expectations do not meet at all with lay expectations, and there are consequent difficulties for the musician (Ref. 8, p. 116). The family, as an institution that demands the musician behave conventionally, creates problems for him of conflicting pressures, loyalties, and self-conceptions. His response to these problems has a decisive effect on the duration and direction of his career (Ref. 8, p. 119). Thus, we see that there are role demands on all family members that limit and channel their participations in other institutions. Here we are concerned primarily with the family role demands on women.

What then are the role demands on the wife which lead to conflict with her possible or actual occupation roles? The American conjugal family system puts heavy obligations on the woman, especially in the middle class. Indeed, the work involved easily constitutes a full-time occupation in spite of the observations of Parsons§ and others who claim that the American woman has little to do. The American woman faces impediments to career beyond the stress she may feel as a result of wife-mother obligations. Many of these impediments stem from the same roots examined in the preceding section, and hence overlap with role-strains attributable to the wife and mother status. Some involve the power and authority structure in the American social system; others approach the problem from an investigation of the pressures and requirements from other social institutions.

Vested Interests

Hacker,[10] Goode,[11] and others have indicated that men are loathe to grant women opportunities to challenge their power positions in the occupational world and other spheres. Their opposition is not ideological; it stems from rivalry for power and the man's consequent suspicion of encroachment. Hacker claims that discriminating against women arises from the "present contravention of the sexes," and outlines the types of opposition men display in the face of this threat.[10] However, women as well as men may have interests in keeping certain occupational spheres male and will levy pressures on women to be occupied only with their homes.

§ Parsons states that the "domestic aspect of the housewife role has declined in importance to the point where it scarcely approaches a full-time occupation for a vigorous person." [9]

Who stands to lose, if the woman divides her attention between occupation and home? Husbands, housewives, and children, perhaps. The husband may be apprehensive if he believes his wife would and could outrank him in occupation or level of success. He might need her to work toward his own success, to be available for business entertaining, or to free him from time-consuming tasks (shopping for clothes, planning trips, maintaining links with his kin, and administrating the home).

The husband has a lot to lose if his wife works. Because he is in an economically dominant position (breadwinner) in the household, he has a great deal of power and is often the ultimate decision-maker. The wife's income can undermine the basis for his authority over both her and the family as a whole. The husband of a working wife may feel genuinely deprived compared to other husbands he knows and may well be absolutely deprived; he may, for example, have more household tasks to perform. There is also the element of sexual competition from the other men his wife encounters in the course of her work.

Can there be a wife-substitute as there are mother-substitutes? Even if the husband agreed it is unlikely that the wife would be willing to find a substitute for herself, and the surrogate-wife is hardly an institutionalized role in society. Thus, the husband may make do with less by choice or resignation, even though it is hardly in his interest to do so. Here we have highlighted the *lack* of payoff to the husband of his wife's working. There may be, of course, considerable advantage to him in terms of shared interests, a "halo effect" on the husband of his wife's success, the luxuries added income may buy. The husband may also not feel any loss because his wife performs all roles with deep commitment and high energy.

Housewives may see the working woman as a threat to themselves. The "threat" is varied; career women are seen as competitors for their husbands (the working woman, though hated, may also seem more glamorous); and as models of some superior competence who make more domestic women question their own choices of life style.

Parents, who usually derive satisfaction from the mobility of a son, may not feel the same reward from a daughter's occupational success. The career woman-daughter sometimes must be explained away, or apologized for, although this may be contingent on the daughter's performance of the more traditional female roles. There may be "after the fact" recognition (the parents may not assume she will become successful and therefore may not support her, but once she has "arrived" they feel a deep sense of pride).

Children, more than any other group, may see no personal advantage in the diversion of their mother's attention to other tasks. This attitude is apt to vary, however, with the social environment of the child. We would expect those who are reared with other children of working mothers to experience no sense of relative disadvantage. However, those who grow up in communities where only a small percentage of mothers work might be expected to exert strong pressures on their mothers not to work.

The Stratification System

One serious impediment to the woman's participation in work comes from her dependence on her husband or father for status classification. The United

States is something of a closed caste system for the married woman. When the woman achieves a job that is of higher rank than her husband's, confusion may arise as to what social niche to place her in. The same is true to some extent for the woman who outranks her husband socially by birth. A husband can raise a lower-ranking wife to his level without overly disturbing the stratification system, provided, of course, that she can assume certain social tastes and graces appropriate for the rank. But when the husband is of lower social rank, he will rise only with difficulty, and may cause distress in social relations due to the absence of norms on which those in the wife's group may base their interaction with him.

Institutional Pressures: The Economy

A striking social obstacle to the successful combination of work and family roles for women may be due to pressures for their participation in other institutions. The most obvious demands are, of course, those made by the family, and these have been described. But changes in the economic structure of American society have also generated pressures for the participation of women in other unique ways. David Reisman overstates the case, perhaps, but he identifies this tendency in his description of America's shift from an age of production to an age of consumption.[12]

Women are the main agents of consumption in American society. Of course, there is a "which came first" question here: Do American women, because of more leisure time, devote themselves to pursuing the marketplace, or do they have to devote more time to it because the economy, built on consumption, obsolescence, and replacement, depends on this essentially feminine activity? There is no doubt that, whether or not this activity is an intended or an unanticipated consequence of our system, prosperity and production would probably falter if women were to spend more time in the marketplace of ideas rather than that of furniture and housewares, and on personal adornment. (Of course, it is also part of the wife's role to adorn herself and her home as a symbolic attestation to the husband's rank. Thus, their activity in this area increases with socioeconomic level.) Betty Friedan, in "The Feminine Mystique,"[13] asks: Why is it never said that the really crucial function, the really important role that women serve as housewives is to buy more things for the house? In all the talk of femininity and women's roles, one forgets that the real business of America is business. But the perpetuation of housewifery, the growth of the feminine mystique, makes sense (and dollars) when one realizes that women are the chief customers of American business.

There is no doubt that a large part of the culture is built around consumption. Shopping is a popular activity, legitimized by the value attached to clever buying habits, to finding the bargain. This activity is time-consuming, but the product seems to be valued more than the time expenditure. This is possible because of the large amount and large variety of goods available in the society and the great deal of money and credit available for purchases.

In contrast, Soviet and Chinese society are not characterized as consumer societies. They do not have the array of goods to consume, and therefore the consumer's role does not have to be filled by any social category. This, of course, frees women for labor-force participation because their family role obligations are not as broad in scope as in the United States.

The Professional Woman

The obstacles described in the preceding sections may be described as "current," although there is some indication that revaluation of many of their components is going on. In the course of my research on women professionals during the past eight years, I was able to identify certain patterns of life-style which worked for those who successfully combined work and family roles and which might alert us to some adaptations women have made, and which have been possible even under the present structure of the social system. Certain of the findings of my study of women lawyers, for example, compared with other studies of women in professional careers, showed first of all, that a combination of roles was possible, although evidence also showed how the role obligations of each role limited choice in the other.[14] I have chosen here to report the combinations of professional and family roles and their consequences for life-choices.

Marital Status and Motherhood

Almost two-thirds (33) of my sample of 54 women lawyers were married at the time they were interviewed. Four of the women in the sample had been divorced (or had obtained annulments) and had not remarried; four were widowed. Thus, three-quarters of the respondents were or had been married. On the other hand, about 15% (eight) had been divorced, probably a high percentage for a group of middle- and upper-middle class women.

The proportion of our sample married or remarried at time of interview was somewhat higher than the percentage reported for all women lawyers by the United States Census, as TABLE 1 indicates. This may be partly because the census includes large numbers of single women lawyers working for the government in Washington, D.C. The census figures record higher percentages in both the "single" and "divorced" classifications than does the New York sample. A greater percentage—83%—of Rita Lynne Stafford's sample of women lawyers cited in "Who's Who" (REF. 18, p. 217) fell into the ever-married group and proportionately fewer in that sample—16.5%—never had married. Apparently, women lawyers who achieve unusual success (which makes them candidates for listing in "Who's Who") are more likely to be married than those who do not. All of the lawyers in our sample who were partners in firms were married, and proportionately more (but not significantly more) of those making more than $16,000 a year were married—35% compared with 30%.

Women lawyers seem to marry or remain single in about the same proportions as women in medicine and engineering. They marry in greater percentages than women in academic life. (About one-half of Rita James Simon's sample of women Ph.D.s were married and one-half single.[19]) However, women lawyers, like other women professionals, are less likely to marry, or to remain married, than are their male counterparts in any of the male-dominated professions.

Evidence does not indicate that the high frequency of single professional women is changing, although this may be so. Alice Rossi claims that younger women in engineering, science, and medicine are less likely to be single than are older women in these fields (REF. 20, p. 73–74). Because our sample was small and its median age was high, it did not include enough young women to test whether or not they were less likely to be single than were their older colleagues. The Michigan study of women lawyers graduated between 1956 and 1965 listed 69% of that sample as married, a greater percentage than shown by the census, but less than the 83.2% reported for the sample of male law graduates of the same period (REF. 17, p. 1065).

Some of the older single women in the sample claimed that World War II had been instrumental in depleting their generation's pool of eligible suitors. It is probably true that the shortage of men as dates, together with the career opportunities created by the shortage of male lawyers, meant that some of these women invested in their careers to the exclusion of marriage. This may also be partly responsible for the fact that women in the sample married late, on the average, although we do not feel that it was a major cause.

Age at Marriage

Women lawyers marry late. Of the lawyers in my sample who ever married (76%), about half (19) married after the age of 26. Stafford similarly found that her sample of eminent women lawyers were late in marrying; more than two-thirds married after they completed professional training, and more than 80% after college (REF. 18, p. 341). This pattern of late marriage applies equally to women in such other male-dominated fields as medicine, science, engineering, and dentistry (REF. 15, pp. 3 & 1010). Women engineers tend to marry "in the late twenties to early thirties" (REF. 15, p. 3). Stafford found 60% of the doctors and 60% of the lawyers in her sample married after graduate school. Women in "female professions" tended to marry a little earlier. Percentages of those in educational administration and nursing administration who married after graduate school were 58.7% and 46.2% (REF. 18, p. 341). It is considerably later, on the average, than for women college graduates in the United States, who today most frequently marry at the age of 22.[22]

TABLE 1

COMPARISON OF MARITAL STATUS OF WOMEN LAWYERS IN NEW YORK CITY, NEW YORK STATE AND THE UNITED STATES

	New York City	New York State*	United States
Single	24.1	16.5	32.2
Married, spouse present	61.1	62.4	45.6
Separated, divorced, or widowed	14.9	21.2	22.1
Divorced	7.5	5.9	9.6
Widowed	7.4	11.8	9.2

* As listed in "Who's Who."

Among those in the sample who were married, there seemed to be a direct relationship between earlier marriage and the tendency to leave practice. Although the respondents in active practice were divided equally between those married before the age of 26 and those who married later, 83% (five) of those who had left practice had married before the age of 26 and only one had married later.

Professional endogamy seems to be a favored marriage pattern for women in professional life.|| Close to half (45%) of the women lawyers in our sample who ever married chose lawyer husbands, and Stafford's sample of eminent women attorneys reported 51% married to attorneys (REF. 18, p. 322). Two-thirds of the women in our sample were married to professional men.

Although it is difficult to generalize from the limited number of cases in our sample, marriage to a lawyer did not guarantee marital success or professional continuity. Of the seven in the sample who had ever been divorced, two had been married to lawyers, and of the four who left law practice permanently, three were married to lawyers (one was single). One respondent who had divorced a lawyer husband felt they had been competitive with each other, something feared by many women not in practice with lawyer husbands. Another divorced respondent had practiced before marriage and only returned to her legal career after the divorce. Work in the same profession probably supports a good relationship, but can easily become an area of tension if the relationship is poor.

Children

In spite of the fact that the most intrusive demands on a woman's career most likely result from motherhood, almost all respondents who married had children, and generally as many children as other married women of their generation. Of those who were married or had been married, 85% (34) had children, and 60% had two or more. However, respondents tended to have their children at a much later age than is common. Almost half had their first child after the age of 26 and more than one-third of this group had their first child after the age of 30, when most American women have borne their last child. This is partly because the respondents married late. The comparatively late age at which these women began bearing children did not seem to affect significantly the number of children they had. One- and two-child families were common for the generation most of these women matured in, and, as noted, three-quarters of those having children had two or more.

None of the childless women in our sample stopped working (although some had left law for other jobs), and 85% of those with children were practicing at the time of interview. Of the women with children, as many were working at full-time jobs as at part-time jobs or not at all. (This was true as well for most of those with three or more children.) There was no relationship between the age at which these women had their first child and their present work status.

The Michigan study showed a strong association between maternity and retirement from law, yet close to one-half of those with children in my study were working full-time. One-quarter of the women lawyers with children were not working and another quarter were working only part-time. More than one-

|| Rossi presents figures from studies of women engineers, physicians, and scientists (REF. 19, p. 77–78; REF. 20, p. 894).

quarter of all full-time employed women in the study were married and had children—most of them (81%) under seven years of age (REF. 17, p. 1065).

The evidence of our study and the others cited indicates that although maternity is probably a primary reason for defection from law practice, or a reason why women often tend to curtail their working schedules, it certainly is not predictive of retirement. Apparently, women who desire to continue their practice find ways to do so, or are in situations where the pressures of child-care do not overcome their motivation or capacity to work.

It is interesting that the findings relating to career, marriage, and child-rearing seem to be similar for women in other male-dominated professions. Although some professional women, because they are single or childless, fail to possess the complement of statuses usually associated with the status of a mature woman, many or most of them manage to handle the array of role demands that flow from being wives and mothers, in addition to their professional status as lawyers. A study by the Society of Women Engineers of its members showed that they were equally likely to be married or single, but that if married, they had an average of three children (REF. 15, p. 13). Married women physicians studied by Rosenlund and Oski (REF. 16, p. 1010), similarly reported an average of three children. The women physicians working 40 or more hours per week had as many children as those women working 20 hours or less.

Choice of Practice

My interviews with women lawyers sought to determine whether motherhood altered their choice of particular kinds of legal practice; male lawyers with children are, of course, found over the entire spectrum of legal work. The respondents with children seemed to be distributed over a fairly wide range of types of practice, from private partnerships to large firms and judgeships. About one-half of the women with children were in their own practice or in partnership with a husband or father. However, this type of practice was typical of the entire group of respondents. The relatively small number of cases in our sample did not permit broader analysis to establish if motherhood altered selection of types of practice or specialties. From interviews during the pretest of the study, and from accounts by respondents of the careers of other women lawyers, it was suggested that these factors may not be directly related, and that intervening variables, such as age at birth of first child, husband's profession, and initial specialty, may account more for the kinds of practice women lawyers tend to have. The age at which a woman has children seems to be important to the choice of practice, because she has greater flexibility and acceptability if she has established her reputation in a firm before the children arrive. She may also become more committed to professional work and be more loathe to leave her career to become a housewife. (However, several of our respondents did retire on becoming mothers and then worked only intermittently after ten years or more of full-time practice.) In addition, some positions of high prestige, such as judgeships, are apt to come at a point in the life cycle when children are sufficiently grown so they do not require the type of care that is likely to intrude on a work schedule. The universe of women judges is not large, but three whom we had contact with, or information about, had children; two others were married and childless. In any event, having children may be considered an asset at these later stages. The woman who is a mother is considered more "normal" and the significant others in her professional-role network need not be concerned about excessive demands on her time by them. For some kinds of legal work, political activity is useful. Many women with children continue political activity even during the years they practice in a limited way, developing contacts and knowledge that will return professional rewards later.

The Michigan Law School study of women lawyers [17] generally substantiated that women with children seem to be clustered in private law practice. The women in the Michigan sample who continued in full-time practice after the birth of a child were heavily concentrated in firms with four or fewer members, the smallest unit the questionnaire designated. Of the married women with children, 40% worked in these firms, compared with only 25% of those married but without children (REF. 17, p. 1066). There are probably good reasons for women lawyers to choose private practice while their children are young. It offers considerable flexibility in time schedules and selection of cases. Of course, private practice may be demanding because it requires strenuous work to build, but women lawyers tend to be satisfied with more limited practices, and may be less concerned with expansion of their practice early in their careers. The large number of women in small firms which are not solo practices may also reflect the large numbers of women lawyers in practice with their husbands. In such cases, the woman has considerable work and time flexibility, and has a partner with a personal interest in aiding her professionally if her home demands should become pressing.

It is clear that women lawyers marry late and marry less than nonprofessional women, but that most of those who marry have children. They tend to marry men in the professions, the majority marrying other lawyers. This is probably partially a function of the opportunity structure, which brings them into contact mainly with male lawyers, and of the fact that their minority position in law school and the profession increases their visibility to a pool of eligible spouses. Professional endogamy is characteristic of married women who are professionals. For lawyers, as for women in other professions, this probably is both a function of access, as noted above, and of the fact that those who marry men in their profession may have gained a friend and supporter in an otherwise obstructive world. Husbands engaged in similar activities (or in shared activities in cases where spouses share a joint practice) presumably will understand the problems posed by work and will assist where possible. (Probably those whose husbands were not supportive would have been the ones who had dropped out of the profession.)

Although the single women and married women without children have more male-typical career patterns (more of them work full-time), those who have married, or who have married and had children, tend to achieve the same or higher levels of success in terms of income and attainment of high legal statuses. However, those with children tend more to be engaged in private practice, which indicates their dependence on a more flexible and independent time schedule than that required by childless lawyers. The relative success of married women probably shows that characteristics that underlie their capacity to make a career successful also indicate social skills which made them marriageable. The many who were clever or skilled enough to "make it" in law could lean on their skills to "make it" in the other arenas of life, and to interweave the obligations of their various statuses in a workable way.

I believe that what these materials suggest is that combinations of home and occupational roles can be maintained where there is some complementarity of interests between spouses, particularly in the occupational sphere, and where the structure of the work can be bent to meet the flexible time needs of women. Probably more widespread alterations in the social structure are necessary to create work conditions that mesh with people's other needs and wishes, not for family demands only but for leisure, privacy, and personal interests. It is the unusual woman who manages to be career-minded and also have what is, at least today, considered to be normal—a husband and children. The adjustments that will make it possible for *usual* women to choose this option may be coming.

References

1. Goode, W. J. 1960. Norm commitment and conformity to role-status obligations. Amer. J. Soc. **66:** 246–58.
2. Merton, R. K. 1957. Social Theory and Social Structure. : 52. The Free Press. Glencoe, Ill.
3. Goode, W. J. 1960. A theory of role strain. Amer. Soc. Rev. **25:** 483–496.
4. Bailyn, L. 1964. Notes on the role of choice in the psychology of professional women. Daedalus Spring : 700–710.
5. Bryan, A. I. & E. Boring. 1947. Women in American psychology: Factors affecting their professional careers. Amer. Psychologist **2:** 3–20.
6. Boring, E. G. 1951. The woman problem. Amer. Psychologist **6:** 679–671.
7. Riesman, D. 1963. Introduction. Academic Women (J. Bernard): : xxiv. The Pennsylvania State University Press. University Park, Pa.
8. Becker, H. S. 1963. The Outsiders. The Free Press of Glencoe. London, England.
9. Parsons, T. 1954. Age and sex in the social structure of the United States. *In* Essays in Sociological Theory. : 89–103. The Free Press. Glencoe, Ill.
10. Hacker, H. M. 1951–2. Women as a minority group. Social Forces **30:** 60–69.
11. Goode, W. J. 1964. The Family. Prentice Hall. Englewood Cliffs, N.J.
12. Riesman, D. 1964. Abundance for what? Amer. Soc. Rev. **29.**
13. Friedan, B. 1963. The Feminine Mystique. : 206–207. W. W. Norton. New York, N.Y.
14. Epstein, C. F. The Woman lawyer. University of Chicago Press. Chicago, Ill. In press.
15. Society of Women Engineers. 1963. Profile of the woman engineer. New York, N.Y.
16. Rosenlund, M. & F. Oski. 1967. Women in medicine. Ann. Nat. Med. **66:** 1008–1012.
17. White, J. J. 1967. Women in law. Mich. Law Rev. **65:** 1051–1122.
18. Stafford, R. L. 1966. An analysis of consciously recalled professional involvement for American women in New York state. Unpublished Ph.D. Dissertation. New York University. New York, N.Y.
19. Simon, R. J., S. M. Clark & K. Galway. 1967. The woman Ph.D. Soc. Prob. **15:** 221–236.
20. Rossi, A. S. 1965. Barriers to the career choices of engineering, medicine or science among American women. *In* Women and the Scientific Professions. J. Mattfield & C. G. Van Aken, Eds. Massachusetts Institute of Technology Press. Cambridge, Mass.
21. Diamond, M. C. 1963. Women in modern science. J. Amer. Med. Women's Assoc. **XVIII:** 891–896.
22. Population Reference Bureau. 1964. Marriage and the coed. *In* Population Profile. (Mimeo.) Washington, D.C.

Discussion

E. James Lieberman, M.D., *Moderator*

EPSTEIN: We have a member of the department where I teach who is known as the "hippie professor." He wears boots and fringed jackets and has long hair, which is now in a ponytail. You can recognize his followers among the students because they now have their hair in ponytails too. He advocates a change in society generally. He is our left of "the Left." I gave him an article that I had written about women. He said to me he had been mulling over the problem of change in the role of women and that he was interested in my article. But the idea sort of disturbed him. I said, "Why you?" He said, "Well, that would really shake up things."

When women say certain things very quietly, somehow the same message doesn't get across. Women are at a disadvantage in that if they do walk around in fringed things, they are not considered revolutionary, but slobs, especially if they are beyond a certain age. But the terminology used shouldn't put off those people who are concerned with change in the social structure. Even if you call it "change in social structure," it really means the same thing as revolution.

KAMM: Just the same, I am concerned with the use of words. For example, I am disturbed that the term "reaction-formation" was thrown at me when I asked people to describe what they meant by parenthood and by love. Phrases like "the parent's role" are being used. I have nothing against such phrases if they are defined. Does the parental role mean that one gets satisfaction out of being an authority-figure? Does it mean that one can teach others to be like oneself? Does it mean one provides bribes for certain sorts of behavior?

EPSTEIN: You are mixing sociological and psychological variables. When you talk about a role, you don't talk about the kinds of satisfactions you get from it; you are talking about what society says one ought to do, whether one is doing that thing called being a parent. That is all it means. As a concept, it raises such issues as, if that particular thing called the role of parents is ascribed, what are the possibilities of the range of norms attached to that particular role? Norms constitute a range of whatever behavior is considered permissible and what behavior can do. We are trying at this point to address ourselves to variations that are possible. Perhaps it is not so terrible to look at the range of variables that have been active both in our own system and elsewhere.

It disturbs me somewhat that, with the exception of Dr. Olesen's paper, we haven't explored sufficiently the vast amount of data we have about the playing out of the sex-roles in different societies. That nobody has even mentioned the Soviet Union seems rather strange, at least to me, because there you find enormous discrepancies as compared with our society in percentages of women not only in the labor force, but in occupations that are defined as being male occupations in our society. It is not surprising that they happen to be the prestigious professions. However, we do know that the Soviet women in those professions are, typically, not at the top level. They are not only performing these particular roles in the occupational sphere, but they are also performing the traditional roles. That also seems to be true of the few women in those professions in our society.

The lawyers I studied as part of a broader study of married women in the professions showed sex-difference patterns consistent with other professional samples. Among women lawyers, 32% are single as opposed to 8% of male lawyers. Among women in the sciences, 45% are single as opposed to 9% of the males. Among women physicians, 31% are single as opposed to 7% of the males. That may be changing. But if such women do get married—engineers and doctors, at least—they tend to have an average of three children while they are, in fact, doing everything else. They also tend to marry later than other women, which probably means that if you are going to have a career, you have to get your training first.

OZER: Are these data based on questionnaires returned? Are the marriage-rates reported a little low, perhaps because those who have married and have not continued with their careers did not respond to the questionnaire out of guilt or out of a feeling that they may look bad? Was there any correction for this possible bias?

EPSTEIN: I was citing census data. Of course, census data are a big problem because they are now ten years old. Of the percentages I quoted, those on numbers of children came from two studies, one by the Society of American Women Engineers of their own members, and one on married physicians, reported by Rosenlund and Oski. Simon reported similar findings for her particular sample of Ph.D.s, and I found the data valid for my group of women lawyers.

One would want to do more research, especially now, because of what I think is happening. The research I was associated with was old as of nine months ago, when there were very few organizations, for example, pushing the woman's role at all. Last April, one could say that there was almost nothing going on among women except a few things here and there in the colleges. Since then, there has been a congress in which 15 women's organizations have been involved. The New York University Law School, during the time I was studying lawyers, had an enormous upsurge in the number of women in the entering class. This number had gone from a tiny percentage to 48 people, close to 18%, I believe. I understand that this proportion has since gone up to something like 36%. But this may only reflect the effects of Viet Nam. If so, we can probably expect a decrease in the future. Ten years from now, conceivably but not probably, women might be relegated back to the home and completely cast out of all professions. This is not really likely, but it *is* conceivable that the government could completely ban the use of birth control.

We see this constant movement back and forth in the eastern European countries. First, they free abortion laws completely, and a woman can get abortion on demand. Then, for example, Rumania says, "It is terrible. The birth rate has to go up, and no more birth-control information should be disseminated." Of course, there is always resistance on the part of the population, and there are many alternative ways of coping with the problem. But still, changes and shifts in government policy are terribly important. We haven't addressed ourselves to that topic yet—to really changing the course of things. We need to look not only at acceptance of change on the part of the population, but also at an analysis of legal changes.

SASSOWER: I am the former president of the New York Women's Bar Association. I think I am reasonably qualified to confirm some of Dr. Epstein's perceptive observations, and I would like to do so. Certainly the number of women lawyers has sharply increased—not as much as we would like to see, but certainly more and more women are turning to the study of law. In 1955, my law class finished with, I believe, seven women. The entering class of freshmen at the same law school in 1970 has about 86 women.

The percentages are on the rise, but concomitantly, too, the personal development of the recent enrollees is a very serious problem. These young women, unlike their predecessors of years back, are not willing to sacrifice the more traditionally feminine roles such as marriage and motherhood. They resent very much being torn apart. What they are seeking, and what they hope to arrive at in the not-too-distant future, are real solutions to the present necessity of leading a "split-level" existence. These young women, who are representative, I believe, of young future-professional women in general, are interested in real, active change. They want no more symposiums, no more workshops and reports and seminars; they want a material change in the status of women.

GARDNER: It came as a pleasant surprise to me to read some of the data in a study of discrimination against women at Columbia University by Ann Harrison Payton. One of the statistics cited is the increase in doctorates awarded to women from 1956 to 1968. In every year there was an increase, so that the proportion has gone from 4.6% in 1956 to 24.3% in 1967–1968. The pattern suggests that this phenomenon of increasing participation by women at postbaccalaureate levels may not be a function of Viet Nam, although the trend has accelerated since the war started.

KUNDSIN: I regret to report a very different experience. I have investigated statistics at Harvard Medical School, and the number of women has dropped in the past four years. In their place, we have a very high percentage of black males. Blacks have been encouraged to enter the medical school, but not women, white or black.

KAMM: Dr. Gardner, did you notice that in the Columbia report you referred to, there is an indication that women have more trouble finding positions once they get their Ph.Ds? In the 1940s, 15% of the women were getting doctorates at various institutions, but when they looked to see how many women are professors now, they found that there are something like 0.7% in certain fields. It is getting jobs that really becomes important.

EPSTEIN: One might predict that when Barnard College becomes part of Columbia's total structure, sharing faculty and so on, the percentage will drop even further, although the absolute number might increase for Columbia University as a whole.

KAMM: Even at Barnard, the number of women full professors is minimal compared with the number of men as full professors.

EPSTEIN: You have to remember that there is a slimmer pool of eligible candidates. You can't deny the fact that the problem starts far earlier in the educational process. There is not really that much discrimination.

KAMM: This raises the question whether women's colleges and universities should not try to compensate for discrimination at supposedly nonsegregated universities and attempt to exclude men from their faculties completely.

GILINSKY: The paradox that emerges from the report cited by Dr. Gardner is the one that Frances Kamm has just pointed to. More women are getting a superior education and are being accepted by graduate schools, yet when they receive their Ph.D.s, they are not given jobs in anything like the proportion of women who have actually been trained.

EPSTEIN: Simon's data dispute that. Her data show that women, once they have achieved that particular degree, are in fact, employed and producing.

CHESSLER: But they don't get tenure.

OZER: Dr. Simon's study is most interesting in that it is the first I have seen that breaks down the statistics for married females, unmarried females, and females with children. As I interpret her data, although the productivity of all categories was the same, there was a negligible difference between the success of unmarried females and males. However, in the case of married females, and especially married females with children, their tenure, rank, and salary, although not productivity, were considerably lower.

We may debate the issue of whether or not employers discriminate between married and single females. I tend to think they don't but that what is acting here is the ego development of the female. For example, it is possible to maintain that in the case of a couple who are willing to relocate to a city where the husband is given the optimal position (rather than to one where there is an optimal position for both of them), we are not seeing something institutionalized in the hiring procedures. What may be institutionalized is something in that particular family and in the development of the ego of the male.

We have mentioned the mass media. In regard to this, I doubt that many men identify with the Vitalis commercials, or any of the other commercials on television; therefore, such commercials don't affect their egos. Yet the Vespré commercial apparently threatens many women, particularly those who have not yet developed ego strength in their own field. Their insecurity is in marked contrast to the ego strength of many of the young women participating in this workshop. I would like to talk more about sex differences in ego development in our culture.

The real point of Simon's data was that the difference between single females and males was negligible. Therefore, unless we accept the hypothesis that employers discriminate against married rather than single women, and I tend to believe they don't—

TANGRI: I believe they do.

OZER: Then it is institutionalized in the family rather than in employment.

EPSTEIN: I can cite a small indicator of social change, a one-case example: Through a friend at Columbia, I was informed that this year, when potential faculty candidates for next year were being reviewed, the delegated committee was presented with a married couple who were both in the same field. Obviously, husband and wife were applying together in order to come to New York together. After review of the applications, the woman was offered a job and the man was not. This is a radical departure from what has happened previously, partially, I think, because the judgment would have been made by those offering the job that such a reversal would be too threatening to the family, and they would not want to be instrumental in this.

POLGAR: In Europe and in Asia, women work at the top and at the bottom of the social structure. There is a great deal more equality in India. Women are carrying pans on their heads in construction work, and so on. The highly educated women, for example, doctors, also work. But in between there is very little. In the United States, the "in-between" is the big proportion of the total social and occupational structure. A certain number of gains were made, but women's gains were then siphoned off into what we call women's occupations.

I wonder if within the United States there may have been a series of developments, social-historical-economic forces, that might bring about a radical change. Perhaps as a by-product of this liberal democracy, there is a pattern that allows women to get so far but no more, which is similar to the process of allowing blacks to get so far but no more.

EPSTEIN: I reject any single-factor explanation. You can say that affluence does it for American society: We can afford to have a large part of our work-force potential, people who are talented and useful, put out to pasture, so to speak, which other societies cannot afford, and so women in other societies have made radical jumps. An example may be the Soviet Union, where so many men were killed during World War II. They have had to make use of their reserves of manpower. This is not a good enough explanation, however. Ideology obviously has a bigger role to play. Considering the framework in which equality takes place in the Soviet Union, it is important to note that a woman who stays home is embarrassed by being labeled a social parasite. Therefore, in order for her to alleviate her embarrassment, she is motivated to seek a career, and considers doing so a matter of course. In our society, we have just the opposite situation; it is an embarrassment to explain why you are working. If you, as a woman, want to climb the ladder of achievement, you must establish that you are still feminine. So you start to bake bread to show you haven't lost your female accomplishments. It gets to be quite exhausting.

Simultaneously—and I do like a systems approach here—our whole service population is falling apart, and so the middle-class, educated, women must do the domestic service-kind of tasks that they never had to do before, like cleaning and scrubbing, because there simply isn't anybody else to do it. So if you want to free women, you must seek other kinds of solutions.

To turn to another point. I am now doing some research on black professional women. I find they are faced with a very special set of conflicting and contradictory motivations and problems. Black women professionals, and particularly those who are married, are closer to making an equal contribution to their families; their pay differential is not discrepant—for bad reasons. That is, black women professionals are paid as much as the males because the males are kept down! But now many black men, and the loud white people who are on their side, are saying that black women should step out of the professional-level area now and give the men a chance, as though the men don't have a chance because the women are there. So what may be considered a good model, as something the white middle-class should aspire to, is being undercut.

MEDNICK: What do the women whom you have interviewed say about this attitude on the part of the militants?

EPSTEIN: They are a little bit torn. Some of them say, "I fought my way from the bottom, and I have worked and worked. This was necessary to get where I am, and I am not going to step down right now." But many of them are torn. For example, some who have administrative posts in hospitals are bringing in a lot of young black men now, and they say, "I feel that I ought to give the job to the men in preference to any woman." Here we have a very interesting and, I think, very thorny kind of convergence of political and cultural factors.

In conclusion, what I tried to do in my paper was to analyze the network of problems and forces that interact to affect women's participation in various spheres. The extent to which one becomes too committed to one-factor explanations really limits the perspective considerably.

CONTRACEPTION AND FEMALE JOB-CHOICE AND CAREER PROSPECTS

David Chessler, M.A.

Department of Economics
Lehman College
Bronx, N.Y.

Since the mid-19th century, if not earlier, the American labor force has included an increasingly large proportion of women. If anything, the participation rate of women has been increasing at an increasing rate since World War I. Yet women are still concentrated in low-paying jobs, particularly in the clerical field, and are grossly underrepresented in most professional and managerial occupations. Furthermore, women suffer from another form of discrimination: they are often paid less than men who do the same job. A detailed discussion of this issue can be found in almost any standard text on labor economics.[1, 2] Schultz [3] and Snyder [4] suggest, among other things, that by some measures the amount of income inequality for all race-sex groups may have decreased over the decade 1951–1960, possibly indicating a lessening of such discrimination.

It is the purpose of this paper to examine, mostly on a theoretical level, some of the ways in which new methods of contraception may affect the female job picture. As the statistics show, the entry of women into the labor force is not a new phenomenon. Indeed, it may well be that much of the present research in contraceptives is due to the, perhaps belated, realization that women are productive members of society outside the home, and there is, therefore, an economic need to permit them to have their children at such times as will interfere the least with their market occupations.* Certainly it is recognized that labor force opportunities may affect family size.[5]

Recent work on female labor force participation rates over the business cycle seems to indicate that for most families at this time the wife is a supplemental worker, one of whose functions is to stabilize family income by entering and leaving the labor force to compensate for fluctuations in the income of the primary wage earner (the "added-worker hypothesis" of Woytinsky [6]). On the other hand, these same studies show that women are still very sensitive to changes in their prospective earnings, and will tend to enter the labor force in increasing numbers as their potential earnings rise (the "discouragement hypothesis" of Long [7]). The best measurement for the actual magnitudes involved are to be found in Mincer's report [8] for the National Bureau of Economic Research.

Some trends in the composition of the labor force as a whole seem to give some hints as to why women are being drawn into the labor force in increasing numbers. In jobs involving manual labor, brute strength is being replaced

* There is a long-standing controversy as to whether invention (as distinguished from innovation) is induced by economic factors. For our present purposes, we should recognize the possibility that this induced invention may have occurred, without denying that it may not have.

by skill and dexterity, permitting women to compete more effectively with men. The increasing need for education of workers improves the earning prospects of women who have these skills even more than men do; women have up to two years more median schooling, depending on age and race (for those now in the labor force).[1, 2]

On the other hand, the need to leave work when having a baby decreases a woman's potential earnings by making her a less suitable candidate for on-the-job training, and for placement in a position of responsibility. The fact that the greatest increases in female labor force participation in recent years seems to be occurring in women older than 35 years of age (that is, whose families are completed) lends some credence to this argument (REF. 9, p. 181). It is younger women whose husbands are most likely to suffer unemployment, or to be engaged in low-paid employment (REF. 9, p. 168), so one would expect younger women to have a stronger added-worker push into the labor force.

It thus appears that increased availability of contraceptive and fertility drugs and devices must have the effect of increasing female reliability as workers. The effect of this would be to increase the potential earnings of women in the prime child-bearing years, and add an increased-earnings pull to the added-worker push, and thereby tend to increase their labor force participation. Women who choose the option of delaying child bearing will be able to arrange to have their children during natural hiatuses in their careers (such as unemployment—involuntary or while changing jobs—or long vacations) or when it is most convenient for them. They and the women who choose the option of having their families early will find their potential earnings increased by the relative certainty with which they can avoid "accidents."

For the family as a whole, certain trends will become more apparent. It already appears that in many families, particularly older ones, both spouses share the economic burden. It seems likely that the wife's increased earning power will cause an even greater amount of such sharing in the future. It is not clear that this will cause a decline in male labor force participation—no such trend is apparent, except perhaps for men over 55 (REF. 9, p. 181)—but it does seem likely that the rise in female earnings will cause an increased demand for leisure among men. Because the price of leisure time is earnings foregone, the increased earnings of the working wife will compensate the family for the decreased earnings of the husband who is decreasing his hours of work. Thus, the family will be able to spend more time together. Furthermore, the increased earning power of the wife will raise the opportunity cost of having her work in the home, and decrease the relative opportunity cost of having the husband do some of the work. Thus, there will be an increasing trend toward a more equal distribution of all the family burdens between the spouses as the effect of contraception begins to make itself felt. This is an application of the analysis of Prof. Becker's theory of allocation of time, which treats the production of final consumption as occurring in the market (through the earning of income) and at home, and deals with the substitution between home- and market-produced goods. Applying the same sort of analysis to "production" within the family unit suggests that the "shifts in role," or shift in who produces the particular final commodity (such as education of children), will tend to take place as described above, in response to the economic pressures (whether or not the family consciously responds to the economic pressures).[5, 9–11]

It seems unlikely that women will, in the forseeable future, earn as much as men, despite the slightly greater education of those in the labor force, although the educational difference is declining or even reversing (REF. 9, p. 190). Still, with contraception eliminating unplanned leaves to have babies, and permitting child bearing to be suited to the requirements of the job, many of the reasons for the alleged lower productivity of women will be eliminated. As women's earnings approach parity with men's, women will be less likely to change jobs because their husbands do (that is, their income will be more of a factor in the family budget, and its decision to move). So something approaching parity does seem possible in the long run.

Clearly, however, some reduction in male incomes would further raise the female participation rate, although such a trend (as discussed above) does not appear to have begun. Also, the addition of more workers to the labor force must lower the wages of existing workers. Similarly, reducing the cost of child-care facilities would probably change the parameters of Professor Mincer's model, and raise the ultimate female labor force participation rate. Such a cost reduction might occur as working wives become more common, setting up a demand for child-care facilities large enough to permit the realization of economies of scale; such discussion, however, is plainly far afield from the purpose of this paper.

REFERENCES

1. BLOOM, G. F. & H. R. NORTHRUP. 1969. Economics of Labor Relations. 6th edit. : 15–16 & 250–251. Richard D. Irwin, Inc. Chicago, Ill.
2. HENEMAN, H. G. & D. YODER. 1969. Labor Economics. 2nd edit. : 32–34, 49, & 543–544. Southwestern Publ. Co. Cincinnati, Ohio.
3. SCHULTZ, T. P. 1969. Secular trends and cyclical behavior of income distribution in the United States, 1944–1965. *In* Six Papers on the Size Distribution of Wealth and Income. L. Soltow, Ed. National Bureau of Economic Research. New York, N.Y.
4. SNYDER, E. M. 1969. Comment. *In* Six Papers on the Size Distribution of Wealth and Income. L. Soltow, Ed. National Bureau of Economic Research. New York, N.Y.
5. BECKER, G. S. 1960. An economic analysis of fertility. *In* Demographic and Economic Change in Developed Countries. Princeton University Press for the National Bureau of Economic Research. Princeton, N.J.
6. WOYTINSKY, W. S. 1940. Additional Workers and the Volume of Unemployment in the Depression. Social Science Research Council.
7. LONG, C. D. 1958. The Labor Force Under Changing Income and Employment. Princeton University Press for the National Bureau of Economic Research. Princeton, N.J.
8. MINCER, J. 1962. Labor force participation of married women: A study of labor supply. *In* Aspects of Labor Economics. : 63–105. Princeton University Press for the National Bureau of Economic Research. Princeton, N.J.
9. MANPOWER REPORT OF THE PRESIDENT. 1966. Table A–13, p. 168; Table B–2, p. 181; & Table B–11, p. 190. U.S. Govt. Printing Office. Washington, D.C.
10. BECKER, G. S. 1965. A theory of the allocation of time. Econ. J. **75:** 493–517.
11. BECKER, G. S. 1962. Irrational behavior and economic theory. J. Polit. Econ. **70.**

OUR SPECIES LEARNS TO BE HUMAN: SOME SOCIETAL AND INDIVIDUAL LIFE-CAREER IMPLICATIONS

Florence A. Ruderman, Ph.D.

Assistant Professor of Sociology
Brooklyn College
Brooklyn, N.Y.

Introductory Remarks

To begin with, I believe mine is the most delightfully obscure assignment of the workshop: "Our species learns to be human. . . ." Let us assume that we are fairly clear on "our species." But anyone at all in touch with the field of education in its current social and intellectual turmoil knows how difficult it is to define "learning," or to come to any agreement as to what we mean by it. How do we learn? What makes learning possible? Why do some learn and others, in similar circumstances, do not? Is all learning the result of similar neurological processes, or are there different types of learning? How much of learning is a function of external, or environmental, factors; how much of internal—genetic and congenital, physical and emotional—factors? We are only now beginning to realize how complex the matter of "learning" is, and how far we are from a full understanding of it.

Now add to this another small word, "human," and we have compounded our difficulties enormously. Throughout all of the ages of philosophical as well as scientific, and proto- and pseudoscientific, speculation on the subject there has been little dependable knowledge and little agreement on this among observers and theorists. What does it mean to be "human"— in fact, what do we mean by the question? I began by saying that we can probably agree on our species. Well, then, one approach is to say that all that ever has been or ever is observed in our species is human. On this basis—and to bring the discussion around to our major concern, "feminine self-definitions and life-styles" —we might say that any and all forms of behavior, life-styles, values, goals, that ever have been or are being adopted by members of our species are "human." That is, any kind of behavior—living, values, goals—is human if it has ever been observed in our species.

But such a definition will probably not satisfy us. And there are a number of reasons for this. Probably, most of us feel simply that some forms of behavior, some values or goals, are more "human" than others. I shall try to avoid the more controversial aspects of this subject, and will cite only those about which we could probably come to fairly wide agreement. In the lifetime of some of us there has been, on a scale unsurpassed in history, massive, systematic savagery. Because this has recently been the subject of some popular "ethology," let me say at once that animal analogies add little to our understanding here, because there *are* no animal analogies to these events. Nor does the hypothesis, emanating from the same quarter, that the advance of technology and modern warfare, which makes it possible to kill or maim at long range, explain concentration camps, crematoria, the tortures of ghettos, prisons, or slave labor camps. The peculiar horror here is not simply the massive scale, the goals of annihilation, torture, and degradation for their own sake, but also that these activities were carried out at *close range,* "personally," and often by those who had previously been neighbors and associates of the victims. The perpetrators of such deeds were, and are, human beings; shall we therefore call these goals, and these behaviors, human? On one level, presumably, we must. Yet, if we have come together to discuss the possibilities of "learning to be human," we probably mean by "human" something more, or something else, than simply that which has ever been manifested by human beings, individually or collectively. We have in mind, however dimly or inarticulately, a conception in which certain modes of feeling and behaving are considered human, while others are not, or are less so. In short, we mean by "human" not simply whatever a human being *might* do, but rather, what we think a human being *should* do. And if we speak of "learning" to be human, then we imply also the belief that, to an unknown extent, human beings have the capacity to *make* themselves: to *become* something in accordance with personal or societal or cultural ideals.

Briefly, then, not everything human beings do will necessarily strike us as "human." While this is probably a point most of us will accept in regard to massacres, torture, etc., the difficulties will become clearer if I suggest that, in regard to family relationships, sexual behavior, personal life-styles, perhaps the same point can be made. Here, objections are immediately raised. Killing affects others—unwilling victims—but sexual behavior, life-styles? These are personal, private matters, and here, surely, whatever we freely choose to do is "human." However, there is hardly any aspect of personal behavior without implications for society, and hardly any that can be modified, on a large scale, simply at will. Whatever we do affects others, regardless of our intentions; all behavior exists within certain biological, cultural, and societal bounds that cannot be readily transcended.

Here, we are dealing with questions which appear in sociology under a number of guises. I have already indicated that we have in fact no sure definition of "human" other than a purely biological one, referring to a species, or a purely operational one, meaning whatever human beings have ever done. I have also suggested that most of us feel in the term "human" something which implies judgmental criteria (better or worse, more or less), or something to be striven for. Here we are in the realm of *values.* And this has been a controversial sphere for sociology throughout all of its history in a modern form. I will mention only two major approaches. One is reflected in Max Weber's belief that sociology (or science generally) cannot give us "values," that these must come from our philosophy, religion, and culture, although, of course, sociology (and other sciences) can help us to understand the sources and implications of our values and can help us select the most effective means to achieve particular values.[1] In contrast, there is Emile Durkheim's belief that the living and functioning of a society can be likened to the living and functioning of a biological organism, and the sociologist to a doctor. Just as the doctor, drawing on the biological sciences, can tell us what is good or bad for our health (meaning biological survival and also optimum biological functioning), so the sociologist should be able, and one day will be able, to tell us what is good or bad for the health (survival and optimum functioning) of a society.[2–4] Unfortunately,

Durkheim's analysis breaks down at the point of defining societal health, or optimal functioning.*

For decades, the dominant sociological view has been in favor of Weber's approach. Today, the general social climate is increasingly skeptical of and even hostile to the idea of a "value-free" sociology or "value-free" science at all.† And within sociology, the hope that we may some day be able to provide a scientific basis for evaluating societal forms in terms of their adequacy in meeting basic human needs—or their correspondence to "basic human nature" —never died out. Recently, Amitai Etzioni has returned to the question: Can sociology (and other sciences) hope to provide answers to just such questions as are implied in my topic, "learning to be human?"[5] Can sociology attempt to define "basic human nature" (as the biologist defines the basic elements of our biological nature), and tell us which family patterns, which definitions of our roles, which forms of child rearing, are most in accord with this nature? Can it tell us which social forms are most in accord with societal health, or "optimum social functioning?" I do not pretend to have definitive answers to these questions, but I shall try to delineate some of the elements of what I take to be basic human natures, as well as some of the biological, societal and cultural factors that I think set limits on the amount, or type, of change possible in family structure, definition of sex roles, and so on.

Today (and not only at this workshop, of course) we are hearing more and more that the family (or the monogamous, or nuclear family) is obsolete. Contemporary sexual relations are not in accord with human sexuality, and especially female sexuality. The "isolated" nuclear family provides an unhealthy climate in which to raise children; we should have collectives or communes, day-care centers, etc. We have heard, from all kinds of spokesmen—more often, women—that women are oppressed and exploited; that both within the family and in social life generally they are discriminated against, not allowed to develop freely and fully, to participate as equals and so on. This oppression and exploitation is usually laid at the doorstep of men; being stronger and more mobile—unhindered by menstruation, pregnancy, childbirth, lactation—men early acquired power and created cultural norms and social institutions to enforce and legitimate this power. In essence, then, men and women are alike; the differences between us are only those that society (and that means of course our upbringing and all social influences from birth on) imposes. This view does not deny that the differences may *become* real, but it entails the assumption that they are, in principle, external; they are internalized through socialization; and they involve an alienation of women from their own "human nature." Thus, the little girl soon learns that she must be demure and modest, that her goal in life is to marry and have babies, that certain interests, studies, occupations, etc., are "unfeminine," that she must

* Societies usually maintain continuity, in some sense, over such a long time that notion of societal "death" is problematic. But health or optimum functioning is always an issue, and Durkheim's discussion of what we mean by it and how we determine it, seems almost completely useless now.

† There are two issues here: (*1*) Can scientific work be conducted without being vitiated by the general social and culture values of the scientist, or of his setting; i.e., is "value-free" science possible? (*2*) Can science, by investigating and answering values (in "value-free" fashion) provide a scientific basis for choosing among values? Can there be a normative science? I am concerned here chiefly with the second question.

allow a man (or at least her husband) to feel superior, etc., etc. In this paper I want to suggest that while there is indeed much truth in this view, it is nevertheless superficial. We are dealing here not only with socially imposed patterns, but also, I suggest, with elements of human nature and of society or social organization itself. These elements may be ineradicable—they may be of the essence of human and societal life—or they may be modifiable only through slow (and uncertain) processes of social and biological evolution.

At this point, let us note certain parallels between the "female liberation movement" (or the antifamily movement) and other movements, political as well as more purely intellectual, of the day. "Women's liberation" is very much part of the climate of the times, and has many of the same ideational characteristics that can be found in some of the revolts of youth, of blacks, of the poor. Some of these common characteristics are: (*1*) little clarity or agreement on what the positive goals are, with much more emphasis on the negative, destructive goals (overthrow the establishment); (*2*) the belief that, somehow, once the establishment (or power structure, or whatever) is overthrown, something new and better will necessarily arise in its place, and we needn't be overly concerned now about what it will be; (*3*) the assumption that differences between groups or classes—here, the sexes—are either superficial or superimposed, that they have no intrinsic validity and are not determinative of potentialities; (*4*) the belief that the individual is by nature good and that therefore whatever the individual chooses (limited only, if at all, by the right of others to live and to escape direct physical harm) is legitimate, right; we may all "do our own thing;" and (*5*) the correlative belief that society is evil, that socialization and social norms and institutions are per se threats to human freedom; that society (if it must exist at all) must serve whatever purposes the individual wants, but can itself make no claims on him.‡

Before going further, I want to make clear certain theoretical predilections of my own. I have no claims to a developed theory of "basic human nature" or of "societal requisites" (features without which a society cannot exist). But I think the evidence—from sociology, psychology, biology—points strongly toward certain conclusions. I believe there are certain broad limits to what is possible, humanly and socially. I believe that no definition of "human nature" can be attempted or serve any theoretical purpose that does not include the idea that there is no human nature without a society, that society by definition entails institutions and norms, and these entail a certain logic and force of their own. I am not only making the obvious point that no individual can exist without a society (i.e., that we need others for support, shelter, etc.), or even that human society is essential for a child's normal physical and mental development, but also the more difficult point that we need societal and cultural attachments, *with their concomitant restraints,* for a sense of self, for a sense of meaning in life, for the possibility of personal achievement, fulfillment, or satisfaction. "Basic human nature," I suggest, entails a need for limits, for imposed definitions, for authority. It can be suggested that much of the present turmoil—generational, sexual, racial, etc.—is due not so much to dissatisfaction with particular norms and institutions, as to an absence or weak-

‡ In some of these movements, these last two principles are not applied, at least not to those societies or groups seen as possessing the truth; here, the right to subordinate all claims of the individual, in the name of a higher or truer understanding of his interests—or of a historical process—is affirmed.

ness of ties to norms and institutions, to an absence of all internalized authority. It is less frustrating to struggle against one's attachments, against distinct requirements, than to float in an almost complete absence of framework or structure. Societies that increasingly deny the validity of all particularisms, all social ascription, and in which all allegiances and attachments are weakened (through technological and demographic as well as ideological change)—and this is happening all over the world—provide the seedbed for essentially nihilistic revolts. This is at least one source of the fury of white middle class youngsters, who have not had to struggle or strive for anything, who have never been subjected to anything—but can't stand our repressive society. Similarly, I suggest that much of the present "feminine revolt" can be traced not so much to an imposition of roles or norms that are not in accord with personal desires or basic human nature as, to a great extent, the reverse—the *absence* of any socially provided definitions, or structural framework, that gives distinct meaning to being a woman (or a man). It is not that a "feminine role" has been imposed from childhood, but rather, that our society (and to some degree almost every society) has largely stopped "imposing" *any* roles, *any* identifications, *any* distinctions. As a result many of us have no way of knowing what we want, or what we are. Such a sociocultural vacuum may itself be, I suggest, in conflict with human desires—with "basic human nature."

Briefly, I am saying that society must give social significance and direction even to primary biological identity. The awareness of anatomical sexual differences comes very early in life; with this must come the beginning of a sense of its social meaning, social definitions, the range of possible roles and behaviors. It is society that must define for us and channel innate biological needs or drives; without this, we may in fact not even recognize them. And it is in this process that the individual learns that there are social implications even in private, "personal" characteristics and actions. This, I think, is one definition that we can give to such a question as, "How do we learn to be human?" It is, how do we come to understand who we are? What are our drives and needs, and how do we learn to express and meet them in socially responsible ways? These are, of course, not simple questions, because in the absence of adequate and appropriate socialization and institutional patterns our personal drives or longings may appear to us or be socially manifest in distorted or even wholly inauthentic forms. To sum up: I believe there are basic human needs, which are not only the obvious "physical" ones. Etzioni,[5] for example, has listed extension of affection and recognition of achievements, or personal recognition; I have added the need for social identifications—including *a social definition of our sex*—and a need for authority, for limits. We need to understand, in social and cultural terms, the meaning of our sexual identity. Societies may differ in the extent to which the meaning and structures they provide correspond to "basic human nature" or allow for a range of variability. But a social definition—of male, and of female—is a necessary element in the development of a social self, and an essential component of social order, of social organization. If we are concerned nowadays with how to "humanize" society (to make it more responsive to the individual, or to "basic human needs"), perhaps we need also to be concerned again with how to "socialize" the individual, that is, how to make the individual aware that he is dependent on society for an understanding even of his own "nature" and that all of our actions affect others, and society as a whole. The trend of our society generally (and this is reflected in our scholarly and scientific work) is to deny the second element. Perhaps this is a reflection of how far we still have to go to "learn to be human."

Some Relevant Considerations

What does all of this mean in terms of the present "female liberation" movement, equality of the sexes, and so on? There are many points which need to be considered. Let us group them under three headings: biological, cultural, societal. These are fairly arbitrary groupings, with obvious overlap. But they are all "real;" and in each of these spheres, I shall suggest, there is evidence that some of what is now being fought, or rejected, is in fact necessary and perhaps even ineradicable.

Biological Considerations

Have women simply been "discriminated against," oppressed, exploited? Is there any reason to think that differential treatment ("discrimination," if you will), including a restricted range of roles, exclusion from certain spheres, lesser pay for the same job, lesser likelihood of promotion, etc., is anything other than prejudice, or a result of men's greater strength and mobility? The usual answer here is that anatomical differences, and asymmetrical roles in regard to reproduction, have provided the traditional basis for alloting "outside" roles—the instrumental and leadership roles of society—to males, and for restricting females essentially to the domestic sphere. It is women who conceive, carry, bear and nurse the young, and they who are primarily concerned with their care and upbringing. By extension, then, women are assigned the "nurturant" functions, for the aged, the weak, for society generally.

If this were all, we would still be justified in attributing some degree of inevitability, or inescapability, to the division of labor and associated "discrimination" by sex, with its implications of female inferiority. But we might also be tempted to ask whether the different involvement in reproduction is not rapidly becoming an outdated determinant of social ascription. Today women can choose whether or not to become pregnant. The risks and disabilities associated with pregnancy and childbirth are not as great as they once were. Nursing need no longer tie a woman to the house. Families are small, and a much smaller part of a woman's life today is occupied by pregnancy, nursing, and child care. We are even being told that test-tube babies are in the offing. And at the same time, the male's greater strength and motor capacity are steadily losing their social significance, as neither work nor mobility are now primarily dependent on physical attributes. All of this means that, superficially, sex might seem to be an increasingly irrelevant factor in assigning social roles, socializing to patterns of behavior, and so on. But we should also consider that the sex differences that are manifest—both anatomically and in reproduction—are only, so to speak, the top of the iceberg, that far more pervasive "inner" differences of mentality, temperament, drive, innovativeness, are associated with these "external" sex differences. Sexuality is more basic and more diffuse than sex. It works through a complicated endocrinological system, a hormone structure that makes male and female not simply the identical thing packaged differently (with the differences in structure and reproductive functioning largely "incidental"); rather, it makes them, in their nature, in their very being, alike yet unalike—to some small but critical degree, essentially, qualitatively, different.

This is not a field in which we know very much as yet, although it is an area of vast social significance. But some facts are known, and are relevant here, and a few should be reviewed: Sex is a crucial element of differentiation throughout the animal kindgom. In human life, a difference in the nature of "maleness" and "femaleness" is manifest on the level of sperm, e.g., in the highly disproportionate production of male cells; it continues through the greater frequency of conception of males, the greater vulnerability of the male fetus, male neonate, and so on. And from birth (if not before) differences in behavior in response to inner and outer stimuli are marked. Male babies sleep less, are more restless, cry more, demand more attention, are more "unconsolable," and so on. Female neonates, despite greater tactile sensitivity, show greater placidity and contentedness. Recent discussions of the apparent relationship between the XXY chromosome pattern and a propensity to crime point to the Y—male—chromosome as a factor in aggressiveness, violence. Our increasing (although still very limited) knowledge of drugs that affect mental and emotional state similarly suggest that sex-related substances affect us, however subtly, on many levels of feeling, perceiving, behaving.

We can trace further dfferences. Very early in life, differences between the sexes appear in verbal ability (usually greater and developed earlier in girls), in social skills, and passivity and docility; in abstract conceptual and spatial thinking (greater in males, and manifested in ways apparently "uncontaminated" by cultural or social influence); in drive and persistence; in objectivity, innovativeness, and intellectual creativity. There seems to be a far greater inner pressure, a creative tension, driving males. This is found over and over again, in tests and observations of school children, in comparisons of productivity and "scope" of male and female professionals, etc. In short, before we ascribe everything to oppression and exploitation, to convention and socialization—or even to the unequal burdens of reproduction and child care—we should consider that more basic, intrinsic differences—inescapably bound up with life itself—may provide males and females, typically, with a different interior climate. To put this as strongly as I can, I think a scientific attitude itself requires, if not actually the belief, then at least recognition of the possibility, that as universal a distinction—through virtually all forms of life, through aeons of evolution—as that of sex cannot be simply a limited, "functionally specific" difference, affecting only reproduction in a narrow sense and completely independent of the rest of our feeling and behavior; that it must, particularly in as complex a creature as man, be associated with subtle and far-ranging differences, from the level of biological functioning to that of personality and mental organization.

I do not mean to suggest that any limitations should be placed on men—or women—in choosing their fields of endeavor or styles of life. It should also be clear that there is within each sex a wide and overlapping range of abilities, potentialities, etc. But I do mean to suggest that there are general differences, and that these may be more basic and more pervasive than we are likely, in the present climate, to be willing to grant. Perhaps we should consider, too, that just as the male seems to have greater physical vulnerabilities than the female, from conception on, so too there may also be greater psychological vulnerability. This is suggested not only by the aforementioned facts, but also by such well-established facts as the greater proneness of males to crime, suicide, and many forms of personal and social disorganization. I would like to suggest that perhaps assuring, structurally and ideationally, a special place or significance to maleness itself is an essential component of social organization, i.e., of society. In any case, if, indeed, there are, on a biological basis, differences associated with sex and affecting inner state, mental and emotional drive, etc., on the average, or in the aggregate, then it is probably unavoidable that societies will take account of this, building it into cultural definitions and institutionalizing it in norms and social structures.

Before leaving this section, I want to point to a few other relevant facts. Certain differences in behavior and basic needs (again in general), such as the greater importance to males of initiative—including an initiating role in sex—may also have deep biological sources. The male's greater need to be, or at least feel himself to be, the initiator in sexual encounters seems to be deeply ingrained, biologically. In animal species in which the female may be as powerful or as aggressive as the male, she nevertheless becomes docile and passive during the rutting season; in silver foxes it has recently been found that there is a genetic relationship between multiple periods of heat and docility. In some species, ritualized gestures of submissiveness—assurance of absence of threat—on the part of the female is a necessary prelude to copulation. And in our own species, the sudden increase of female sexual demandingness, generally associated with "the pill" but probably having more complex social causes, has been creating problems of male resentment, and even a rise in clinical impotence. Certain other differences in behavior and basic needs—again in general—such as the male's greater need for dominance, for recognition, for achievement, probably also have profound (if obscure) biological bases. So deep may these roots be that it may be a social threat, i.e., a threat to the stability and strength of a society, to block the need for achievement, recognition, a place in the "outer" world, on the part of males; such a threat does not exist when such needs—on the whole much weaker, and often nonexistent—are blocked for females. Again, I suggest that "learning to be human" may mean learning to understand and accept such differences. It may mean learning to recognize and accept our own potentialities and limitations, and learning to accept, and adapt to, the special needs and vulnerabilities of others, and in particular, others in our own families—husbands, children. For many reasons, a greater adaptiveness must come from us—not from them.

Cultural Considerations

If we now leave aside biological differences or those aspects of behavior that can be traced to a biological basis, we have still the elements of culture to deal with. Of course, cultural forms are themselves to a considerable extent elaborations on the ideational plane of observed—or assumed—biological facts; but the cultural elements can have a life of their own, and, indeed, this is inevitable, and this, too, corresponds to something "human." We need to have beliefs, ideas, a sense of meaning, about who we are and what we are. All cultures have elaborate beliefs about sexual differences, about appropriate sex and family roles, and so on. Certainly cultures can and do change; and I have already suggested that I do not, by any means, consider all cultural forms, all beliefs, ideas, etc., equally valid or sound. But we may ask whether a universe of human cultures—I refer to all of the beliefs, religious, philosophical, or whatever, that assign not only different roles but an essentially different nature or character to men and women—can be readily overcome, or simply dismissed as mythology. We are sometimes told that there have been matriarchal societies, societies where the men are the babytenders and housekeepers, while the women are the leaders or rulers. In fact, there have not been. It is instructive to look at those modern societies where allegedly the greatest strides have been made toward equality of the sexes, freeing women of the burdens of the family, etc. If we look at these societies, we see that the departures have been more apparent than real. England has long had a tradition of the strong-willed eccentric (and wealthy) lady, but it is a male-dominated society to an extraordinary extent. The same is true in Scandinavian countries. The situation in countries with a revolutionary background is even more revealing. In Russia, women overwhelmingly work, and are represented in fields we tend to think of as male (this includes not only professions such as medicine and dentistry, but also heavy physical labor); yet in all fields they are concentrated in lower levels and in subordinate positions. Perhaps even more to the point, although Russian women—married women, mothers—are pressed, both by official doctrine and economic hardship to work outside the home, all aspects of domestic work remain theirs as before, including the cooking and cleaning, the long hours of waiting in line to buy food, and so on. In other words, Russian women are working more and harder than ever, but the inequality in status and in domestic burdens remains. And the cultural ideals of the revolution—of complete equality of the sexes, of the freeing of the bonds of family life, of the state taking over domestic and child-rearing functions—have been quietly laid aside. The Israeli *kibbutz* is a fascinating and, in many respects, successful experiment, but here, too, there are points that must not be overlooked. It is only a small minority of the Israeli population that lives in *kibbutzim;* and, despite the early ideology of supplanting the family, the *kibbutz* succeeded precisely because—whatever the verbalizations may have been—crucial elements of the cultural background of the members proved stronger than the Marxist ideals; the *kibbutz* clung, in the last analysis, to a strong morality and ethic, including a "puritanical" sex and family ethic. In recent years, even those elements of traditional family life and sexual differentiation that had been weakened, have reappeared or been reinforced; *kibbutz* children now spend more time with their parents and in some *kibbutzim* may sleep in their rooms; and the *kibbutz* now typically assigns men and women to different roles on the basis of sex. It is the women who work in the kitchens, the laundries; it is they who are the children's nurses and teachers. In fact, so strong is—apparently—the hold of cultural elements that define certain spheres of life, as well as certain ways of acting, feeling, etc., as essentially "male" or "female," that we may venture the prediction that no matter how revolutionary the society, no matter what its attitude toward the family, it will sooner or later revert to cultural differentiation and some degree of social ascription on the basis of sex. These cultural elements, too, are facts of life, part of being "human." We may even wonder if they do not correspond to a basic "human need," and whether a culture that did not elaborate differences by sex—one of the most fundamental ways of providing meaning, identity, and channeling aspirations and longing—could possibly be maintained, in any society, for long.

Societal Considerations

All societies require that certain functions—certain roles—be fulfilled. Even the most primitive societies have a division of labor, and even such primitive societies as hippie "communes." These essential functions include both so-called integrative, expressive functions—including those concerned with physical care, emotional support, socialization—and instrumental functions: leadership, control, defense, production, etc. We are increasingly being told that women can fill the latter roles as well as men (or at least, that they could if they were brought up to believe they could), and that men can and indeed are eager to assume housekeeping and child rearing roles. I know of absolutely no evidence for these assertions, or even of anything to suggest the possibility of this, on anything like a mass scale and an enduring basis. I think such statements, especially when they come in the guise of scholarly or scientific knowledge—unsubstantiated and, apparently, rarely challenged—are misleading and irresponsible. I repeat, I know of no evidence that, on a large scale, women could (or even want to) assume roles or primary responsibility in the economy, government, etc., or that any substantial numbers of men want to become full-time babytenders and housekeepers. I do know of considerable evidence to the contrary. In my own research, for example, I found that situations in which fathers are the major child-care agents for working mothers are generally unhappy situations (for all); that men in such roles tend to be embittered and resentful, and also, not irrelevantly, to perform poorly. And in those situations in which father does not work, while mother does—i.e., where there is a virtually complete reversal of roles—there is almost always a high level of tension and conflict. And, on the other hand, I found that while many women are genuinely committed or dedicated to their outside occupations, many more simply enjoy the change in routine, being "out," and so forth. The general level of commitment to work is quite low and undependable.[6] In short, the prospects that we can, or should, attempt, in the forseeable future, any mass reversal, or even statistical equalization, of roles of men and women seems to me highly illusory. Perhaps, instead, we should reconsider the possibility that the traditional division of labor may be—certainly not in all cases, but in the aggregate—not the result of injustice and alienation, but the result of an interaction of societal needs and "basic human nature:" men's and women's own intrinsic desires and aptitudes.

Finally, what about the possibility that child care and related functions may be turned over to institutions, such as day-care centers or other facilities? I do not doubt that in the next few years we will see a growth of day-care centers, of all sorts and under all kinds of auspices. But I strongly doubt that they will become a major mode of substitute, or supplementary, child care and child rearing; and I doubt even more strongly that facilities of this sort will literally "supplant" the family, in our society or any other, for any substantial proportion of the population. Actually, we know of no society where such arrangements are common, and this includes even societies with strong socialist or collectivistic traditions, and where communes have for long been visible and admired; and we have no evidence that such arrangements can work at all satisfactorily, for large numbers of children, outside of small, elitist, highly motivated, highly disciplined, homogeneous groups (or subsocieties). There is a great danger that, after decades of resisting all forms of group care for young children (as a result of misinterpretations of "hospitalism", etc.), social workers (and others) will now jump on the "group care" or "*kibbutz*" bandwagon (on the basis, again, of misinterpretations and such limited studies as Bettleheim's recent book on the Israeli *kibbutz*[7]). Just as a woman's assuming a dominant or aggressive role in the home or her becoming too occupied outside the home and relegating her husband to housekeeping and child care may threaten his identity, so a mother's continual absence from home during a child's formative years, and his relegation to unwilling or unsuitable child-care agents—or to not yet fully tried and understood group arrangements—may threaten the emotional and even physical security of the child. We have no conclusive answers to the many problems in this field, but the evidence is still very powerfully in favor of dependable and close maternal child care, within a stable "nuclear" family, for optimum development of the child, and for effectiveness and order in the society as a whole.

Conclusions

In this paper, I have deliberately played devil's advocate, and deliberately stressed those elements—biological, cultural, social—that I think militate against drastic change in sex roles, or in the structure of the family. In all of these contexts, further points could have been made, all tending in the same general direction. Am I saying, then, that no change is possible, or that no changes are needed, that we must all resign ourselves to being suburban housewives, dumb doras, or—if we work, typists with college degrees, or any of the other unhappy stereotypes of the contemporary female? No, but I am saying that to "learn to be human" means to learn to recognize our own limitations—they are not always the result of oppression or discrimination—as well as to understand our genuine aspirations and desires, which are not necessarily what the lady militants or academic or literary authorities tell us they are. To "learn to be human" means also to understand that we are all inescapably part of a number of social networks, and that what we do inevitably affects others, often those who depend on us, and who are in one way or another peculiarly vulnerable to our actions and attitudes. It is a kind of infantilism to assume that we need suit only ourselves, if others depend on us, or that through the intervention of some magical mechanism, our personal needs and desires (even assuming we genuinely recognize and understand them) necessarily coincide with those of our family, or of society. It is an unhappy, but inescapable, fact of family life—of social life generally—that the needs of different members of a group may conflict. Finally, "to learn to be human" means that we may have to learn to make choices with greater awareness of their implications, and with greater understanding that not everything may be equally, or simultaneously possible. I think we have a wider range of choices before us than ever before. We need not restrict ourselves to certain fields, certain occupations. We need not become suburban housewives. We need not marry at all. We need not have children. Neither must we have "careers." Our problem becomes acute when in fact, we either do not know what we want (and this is very common) or when we want everything; when we want the same professional status, salary, promotions, etc., as a man—but are unwilling, or unable, to apply the same drive and commitment to our work; when we want to be simultaneously married and single; when we want to have children, but do not want to care for them; when we want a family life with its security and warmth, but without its sacrifices and obligations; when we want to "do our thing," in disregard of any societal claims on us, while demanding that society make it possible for us to do this.

Basically, then, I am saying that we now have more freedom to select among life-styles. But we should be aware that whatever "style" we choose implies certain restrictions and certain sacrifices, that it entails a long-range, constant commitment, and the necessity to assume responsibilities. A "career," for example, is an increasingly possible life-style, but it requires lifelong dedication and the sacrifice of some freedom, and some degree of domesticity. To be married, to have children, and to combine this with work, or with a career, is also increasingly possible—but there are likely to be conflicts and competing claims. These are the inevitable results of inescapable biological, social, and cultural facts, not of exploitation, the power structure, etc. We should be aware of the likelihood of such competing claims and pressures, and, in my opinion, prepared for some measure of subordination of personal interests and desires to those of husband and children. To be married, and have children, and not work, may well continue to be the "life-style" of the majority of women; here the need is likely to be one of finding suitable outlets for unused energies and talents. Perhaps many of these women should work, or should develop some lifelong commitments or interests outside the home. Finally, an increasing number of women seem likely to drift, in and out of marriage, in and out of casual liaisons, in and out of motherhood (or pregnancies), in and out of jobs, in and out of causes and movements. It is hard to call this a "life-style," although it is becoming more common. These women, I think, are the more obvious casualties of an age in which we have forgotten (or will not accept) that "learning" means that there are things to be taught, and that some must do the teaching, and that to be "human" means to be willing, and able, to accept limitations, responsibilities, long-term commitments, social discipline, and even sacrifices.

References

1. Weber, M. 1949. Science as a vocation. *In* The Methodology of the Social Sciences. E. A. Shils & H. A. Finch, Eds. The Free Press. Glencoe, Ill.
2. Durkheim, E. 1938. The Rules of the Sociological Method. The Free Press. Glencoe, Ill.
3. Durkheim, E. 1957. Suicide. The Free Press. Glencoe, Ill.
4. Durkheim, E. 1933. The Division of Labor in Society. The Free Press, Glencoe, Ill.
5. Etzioni, A. 1968. Basic human needs, alienation and inauthenticity. Amer. Soc. Rev. **33**(6): 870–885.
6. Ruderman, F. A. 1968. Child Care and Working Mothers. Child Welfare League of America. New York, N.Y.
7. Bettelheim, B. 1969. The Children of the Dream. The Macmillan Company, Collier-MacMillan Ltd. London, England.

Discussion

E. James Lieberman, *Moderator*

Kamm: Professor Ruderman, I would like to question some of the data on which you based your paper, or at least have them clarified. You seem to rely heavily on Lorenz-type fixed-action patterns. I am wondering why you make the leap from this lower-animal behavior to human behavior so central in your analysis. Professor Milner's paper appears to be different on this point; she specifically attacks this reliance on fixed-action patterns, and places more stress on developmental-type studies.

Second, I wonder whether the conclusions that you reach don't really amount to a sort of "Valeria Solanis" approach to the male sex. What you are saying, in essence, is that men are so immature—you use that as a moral statement applied to the biological perspective—that they cannot be made to change their desire to dominate, their desire to be aggressive, and so forth, and that women are the ones who have to adapt, because that is the way they are constituted, to be adaptive. You suggest that we can be at least honest about this relationship. But then, of course, the cognitive framework gets all mixed up. Once a man knows I am only humoring him, that I am indeed really superior, once he can no longer feel dominant, I am wondering whether the Valeria Solanis approach will work.

LIEBERMAN: What is the "Valeria Solanis" approach?

MILNER: She is the girl who shot Andy Warhol. She started an anti-male organization whose name I can't recall.

KAMM: The organization is called SCUM, which stands for the Society for Cutting Up Men, which is Valeria Solanis' major contribution to political theory. I don't think this is something to be laughed at! If there is so much biological evidence that males are so weak and so immature that they cannot deal with honest presentation of the female in her full potential, then Valeria Solanis' solution is that we must do away in some fashion with the male sex. So, I don't see what is so amusing here; the only suggestion Professor Ruderman has is that we have to keep doing what we have been doing; we who are the superiors must adapt to the inferiors. I do not think this is a very good revolutionary principle.

You mentioned one other point, that it is important for society to assign functions in terms of sex, and that no society could possibly exist without that. But at the end of the paper, you suggested that there are so many individual differences that sometimes there are exceptions to this rule? I was wondering whether you classify these exceptions as hormonal imbalances, and if so, why are there so many hormonal imbalances? The fact that women have two breasts doesn't necessarily mean that they behave in one particular way. If we are going to relate more complex behavior patterns to underlying physical differences, how is it possible to maintain the very stable society that you would like, which enforces a tremendous amount of security? If we do allow for individual differences, it will make people insecure.

RUDERMAN: First, let me deal with what seems to have offended you. As I listened to you relate what you saw in the paper, I didn't quite recognize it. Your first question was in reference to the justification for using biological data or material from the animal kingdom. After all, we aren't rats or cats or chimpanzees and so forth. Certainly we are *more* than animals; but we are *also* animals. If we didn't have certain things in common with the animal kingdom, we wouldn't today have the pill, for example. We wouldn't have a lot of the drugs and other things that we rely on scientifically and technologically. In other words, we have developed these things because we are able to act on the assumption that in certain respects things are the same in the animal kingdom as they are for us. There are certain physiological and other similarities. How far this goes, how determinative it is, I am not sure, and I don't know that anybody is. But I don't think we can dismiss it. Within the past few years, for example, there has been a great deal of discussion about diurnal rhythms, about our built-in clocks. Certainly man has been able to transcend something of a biological nature in this instance, and yet he has done so at a certain cost. All I am suggesting is that in the realms of sexual behavior and family behavior there may, similarly, be very complex kinds of things built into us that set limits to the kinds of changes that we can bring about very readily or very easily.

I also don't see any necessary contraindication to utilization of data from the animal world whenever we seem to see parallels in human behavior and in developmental studies. Not because there aren't other sides to this, and not because the book is, in effect, closed, but simply because it is to a great extent an unpopular view now, I deliberately stress this, and I wish to put it strongly: When we find something to be universal or nearly universal in the animal kingdom—certainly among all species that have sexual forms of reproduction—and when we find it to be universal or nearly so throughout all known human history, then I think we are entitled at least to speculate that it may have a very profound basis, and that it cannot be completely overcome. And, if it is overcome, it would take a very long time, and it would be a long process of evolution, not revolution.

Here I will depart from biological material and go into sociological material and tell you that in regard to revolutions in family structure, as with political revolutions—as distinguished from the process of evolution, which takes tens of thousands of years—the revolutions are frequently wiped out within 10 or 20 years. This happened in Russia; this happened in Israel. You can make revolutions, but they don't necessarily stick!

DELL'OLIO: Perhaps such revolutions didn't work because they never did entirely reverse and equalize the process. The process was never thoroughly completed. It was only begun, and perhaps the real failure of the revolution was that there was no real revolution, no basic structural revolution, so the basic inequity between male and female continued. There is a presumption in saying the revolution failed because of underlying biological factors. We don't know that. I submit they failed because the changes were never really completely adjusted to by the society that attempted to implement them. Men remained in positions of power and continued to manipulate society and to suppress females while giving them such minimal freedom as letting them work along with keeping house and having children. Maybe that is why these revolutions failed, because they were betrayed! Perhaps this is what will happen in Cuba.

RUDERMAN: This is essentially a utopian argument. We have only certain kinds of data at our disposal. These data have come from scientific studies and from historical cases and so on. On the basis of whatever we do know, these attempts have been made. You can always say the trials haven't been good enough. But there have been trials over and over again. In the Israeli *kibbutz* there were genuine trials; and it is not true that in Russia women were given the right to work side by side with men, but then were always told, "O.K., now you go home and take care of the house." That was not the case.

DELL'OLIO: Women were left to take care of the children of others.

MILNER: The grandmothers did it.

RUDERMAN: At the beginning of the Israeli experiment, both men and women shared equally in all functions. But 20 or 30 years later, there has been a reversion to the traditional pattern; now the men drive the tractors and women work in the kitchens and laundries. But it didn't start out that way. A change was tried. You can always reject any trial because there wasn't enough of a trial, if you want to. If it went on for 20 years, you can say, "Well, it should have gone on for 40 years." But this is a utopian kind of thing. Why didn't it go on? Why did the reversion start? What I am suggesting is that this situation is not somehow an historical accident, but that there is something intrinsic in "human nature" or in the structure of society that is not easily overcome.

OLESEN: In the *kibbutzim* that you are referring to, Dr. Ruderman, are you speaking only of the oldest ones like Degania, or are you referring to the whole span of *kibbutzim*? How, then, do you account for the inputs of new people and new cultures which would have brought new elements in there? Your position assumes a consistent situation from 1899 or 1901, whenever it was that Degania started, to 1970. That has not been the case.

L. NEWMAN: I would like to raise a question about a statement in your paper, mainly because, I suppose, I'm the "house anthropologist" at this workshop, and our role should be to expand the data a bit. I'm referring to the section where you said, "I want to point to a few other relevant facts." I want to relegate the facts in this case to some realm other than fact. I've already referred to my nonacceptance of certain concepts of ethology. I don't believe that men have to be dominating and have the initiating role, and I would like to point out certain field work done by other anthropologists which might broaden our perspective a little bit. For example, Philip Newman at UCLA, my friend but no relative, has done field work among the Gururumba in New Guinea. Sexual aggression is always carried out by females. The males are notably Victorian and prudish and are never sexual initiators. When western males go to visit the Gururumba, they always think they have died and gone to heaven!

This is an extreme example and a marginal society. But I would like to suggest that the idea of sexual aggression is rampant among women and is also rampant in India. Men in India believe women to be the sexual aggressors. That country has a large population and is not a marginal society. I don't see male sexual aggression as a biological "given." I would also suggest that women do not have a corner on compassion either, and that the myth of selflessness that we have in the Western world about compassion in women is a part of the way we go about adapting to whatever our situation is. I am not saying that there are no biological determinants whatsoever, but I do think the material we have comparing animal behavior with human behavior is almost useless as far as this kind of discussion is concerned.

SASSOWER: I wonder if you would make some analogy between the reversion you refer to in the Israeli family structure and, for example, the backsliding of American women during the 1950s from their former high accomplishments during the 1920s and 1930s.

EAST: I suspect in all the instances where women in the recent past have been given new roles, they were *given* new roles and so they were still being objects for use by the state. I suspect that women will become fully human and fully equal to men only when they demand it. Only that way will they become autonomous human beings. Women in Israel didn't become autonomous human beings because the state decided how things should be. They had no more sense of controlling their own destiny than they had before.

GARDNER: I would like to comment along the same general lines as some of the previous discussants. I was particularly taken aback by this passage in your paper: ". . . learning also to accept and adapt to the special needs and vulnerabilities of others, and, in particular, others in our own families—husbands, children." I would like to suggest that this is precisely what this society is telling us to do. I reject that as a solution for my being in exactly the same way that blacks are rejecting it. I just don't think you can ascribe a certain kind of role to a whole class of people.

KEIFFER: I wish to take exception to another portion of Dr. Ruderman's paper. I think that Professor Ruderman does a great injustice to both the female liberation movement and the revolts of the blacks and the poor by suggesting they have certain common characteristics. It *is* true that they have certain common characteristics, but the characteristics they have in common are not those that she suggests they have. For instance, the first example given—that there is little clarity or agreement on the positive goals, but much more emphasis on the negative destructive goals —I don't think is true. A great deal of time in both movements *is* spent in thinking and talking about what society is going to look like—"after the revolution." There is a great concern for alternative life-styles, for alternative ways of behaving. It is not just tearing down the old, but providing something new and better. There *are* positive goals, and there *is* concern about what the society will look like once these changes take place.

Also, the assumption that differences between groups or classes is superficial or superimposed: It is probably true that we would accept that this *is* a basic assumption of these revolts. And, you say we believe that the individual is by nature good, and therefore whatever the individual chooses is right. I don't think that is the case, at all! The individual is neither good nor bad, but has a capacity for either. We are not Hobbesians or Millsites, or whatever. We believe that people are socialized into certain forms of behavior. Society is not evil, per se, but forms of socialization and the process of socialization based on sex are wrong. What we want is a society that allows individuals to develop to their fullest potential in all ways. I'm not referring to everybody "doing their own thing," but to a society that allows people to develop fully. You cannot do your own thing when doing your own thing is maiming or oppressing others.

HEIDE: My challenge to this paper is so fundamental that I could not begin to detail different items. If we take women and men as they are now, if we accept behavioral differences that now exist, and then begin to document and perpetuate them, we are in trouble immediately. If we are talking about innovations, and different ways of looking at people, and creating a new society, we have to take those things that are common human traits, and recognize that the differences within the sexes are greater than the differences between. This does not deny those differences that are real, but it challenges those that we have been *told* are real. We have taken them as given, and they may indeed have been so programmed into us that we don't really know what the biological differences are. Once we start looking at men and women as separate entities, we further emphasize these differences, rather than concentrate on the common traits that transcend such divisions.

YGLESIAS: In discussing role differences between males and females, you state that women desire to be in leadership positions, but that, in fact, their own intrinsic desires and aptitudes go in the opposite direction. What are the data on this? Where was this generalization culled from?

TANGRI: I have two comments. First, your statement about males' greater need for achievement is not borne out by any of the literature on achievement. If you review it, you will find, if anything, that there is no way of comparing the achievement measurements of males and females on the scales that we now have. They just don't work for females, and it has nothing to do with their need for achievement. That statement is scientifically wrong.

MILNER: The studies in this area have been culture-bound.

TANGRI: Second, you state that certain things are the inevitable result of ineradicable biological, social, and cultural factors; this is, on the face of it, unscientific, because anything that is cultural is not ineradicable. Culture is a human creation, and therefore can be un-created by human beings. Biology is something else.

MEDNICK: I would like to ask about the basis for the data on the reversion of the *kibbutz* style of life because I don't have that impression at all. There are many *kibbutzim* that still hold to the same kind of pattern. I have seen women driving tractors in Israel.

POLGAR: I agree with Lucile Newman's statement about the obligation of "house anthropologists;" and I don't think you know your anthropology—or your biology. I do not believe there is any evidence that the greater tendency of men to crime, suicide, and many other forms of personal and social disorganization is biologically conditioned. I particularly take issue with the idea that assuring a social-cultural definition to maleness itself is a functional prerequisite of human organization. This notion has more to do with my quarrel with the functionalism approach in sociology than anything else I could pick out. I don't think you have a leg to stand on—a male leg or female leg.

OLESEN: I have a kind word for Dr. Ruderman. There *is* something very important in this paper. We do not know where the cultural thing begins and ends; we don't know where the biological thing begins and ends. But there is the fundamental biological fact. I share everyone's objections, by the way, Dr. Ruderman, and probably more strongly than the others. But nevertheless, this fundamental point is very well taken. It had not yet been raised at this workshop, and the fact that it has now been brought up and that the participants had this strong reaction is in itself very positive.

RUDERMAN: I will try to handle all the questions about the *kibbutzim* at the same time. First, there are differences; there were differences from the start and differences all along, and there are differences today. Those who came from the left wing in the early days—and they were the majority—came knowing what they wanted to do. They had an attraction to nationalist and Zionist ideals, as well as

Marxist or socialist ideals. And they knew that one of the things they were going to try to do was bring about the equality of the sexes; they were going to try, if not totally to destroy the nuclear family structure, at least radically to alter it. This is why they set up special quarters for the children instead of letting them grow up in their parents' quarters. Women's roles in the *kibbutz* were not ordained by the state, as was suggested in one of the questions.

If we look at the original *kibbutzim,* not at the later generations that came, perhaps with different motives and different ideals, we see that they went through a process of change. The change was to move closer to the traditional kind of family system. Furthermore, if you read Talmon-Garber's papers about these original idealistic settlers, they haven't given up their *kibbutz* ideals completely; there is frequently an expression of something like regret, especially on the part of the women. They look around them and see other families, *not on the kibbutz,* living in that traditional kind of family system, with their children being brought up by their mothers, home with them all day, and there is frequently some feeling that they have lost out on something. So there has been a reversion to closer family ties, a strengthening of both the nuclear family and of extended family ties, as well as a reversion to traditional role distinctions.

EPSTEIN: Talmon-Garber's point was not that. Her point was that they looked with regret precisely because they had not gained anything. The women in the *kibbutz* said, "We have not gotten what we were promised, which was equality, and we also don't have the children. We are in the laundry doing laundry for everybody."

RUDERMAN: Why didn't they get their equality originally? The *kibbutzim* started out with the men as likely to be assigned nursery jobs as the women. What has happened through time is that all these traditionally female jobs are now held by females.

EAST: Who made the assignments?

RUDERMAN: All the decisions in the *kibbutz* are made by everybody voting: every member has one vote.

EPSTEIN: The women did not vote themselves into the laundries.

MILNER: It is quite possible that they did; that is one of the problems.

RUDERMAN: You are wrong; they did, although you may find it hard to believe. To continue to another question, "Why this backsliding?" to use the questioner's word. Why do we find this in the *kibbutz*? And why do we also find some kind of decrease in the proportion of female Ph.D.s? I suggest that we find just this sort of problem over and over again in the most diverse kinds of settings. Maybe there is something quite profound at stake. Maybe there is something underlying this.

MILNER: I think there is too, but I am not at all sure that the matter is as simple as you suggest it is.

RUDERMAN: I don't claim to have any final answers, but I wanted these elements to be part of our thinking. I speak of both cultural and biological things as being possibly unalterable, and the objection was raised that perhaps biological things are, but cultural things certainly are not. One of the discussants has already given a good answer to that. Culture and biology, as far as we can tell, are intimately related. If we assume that there is some kind of biological basis to the patterns that all cultures have developed, and if you are prepared to grant that some aspects of biology are unalterable, then perhaps the corresponding elements of culture are also essentially unalterable.

Men and women have more things in common than there is differentiation between them. I think that is true. I assume that we are both members of the human race. There is certainly more that unites us than separates us, but some of the things that unite us, by the way, are the complementarities of our differences. I don't think we can afford to overlook that.

OUR SPECIES *LEARNS* TO BE HUMAN *

Esther Milner, Ph.D.

Department of Education
Brooklyn College
Brooklyn, N.Y.

Perhaps the most important knowledge we have about man for social purposes concerns the role of experience and learning in human development. As a member biologically of the human species, the nature and the quality of our humanity and our individuality are *not fixed* at birth. Contrary to most other, lower, forms of life, we do not fulfill our innate species potentials merely as a result of instinct or of maturational unfolding. We begin to learn to be human shortly after birth through our experiences with, and the conscious teachings of, older persons who have already been made human by *their* social experiences. When compared with the lower animals, man exhibits three general classifications of behavior: unlearned behaviors we share with other mammals; learned behaviors we share with other higher mammals; and learned behaviors we share with no other form of life.

Species-determined patterns of physical growth play a basically important psychological role during our earlier years in three ways particularly: They impose limits on *what* we can do, experience, learn *when;* they make the infant and young child totally dependent on other, more mature, persons for his continuing existence; and, especially during the first several months of life, they impose, as a result of the mammalian principle in our species' dual genetic inheritance, the necessity for certain kinds of direct, "gut-level" experiences with another responsive human being if later patterns of psychological development are to emerge and develop normally. If such "responsive relationship" experiences are provided during this early period, innate developmental forces are able to take firm hold and to provide a natural impetus for increasing maturity; psychologically healthy children require no "pushing" in order to grow up (and certainly, for disturbed children, such pushing is a most ends-defeating incentive for growth). Genetically determined individual growth patterns also play a fundamental role; they impose limits on the nature and the quality of each person's experience and learning at every stage of his development, and as a result have much to do with his individual uniqueness.

But the consistent *direction* of individual behavioral development is from expression of behaviors that are determined by innate maturational forces relatively uninfluenced by experience, to the expression of behaviors that emerge only as a result of highly individualized experience and learning. Freud, whose therapeutic work with upper-middle-class adults led him to an almost exclusive interest in the role of early emotional frustrations in later psychological development, did not adequately appreciate the role of culturally determined learning, both in these early experiences and in later development.

* This paper is a reconstruction composed of excerpts from two monographs by the author. See REFERENCES 4 and 5.

Underlying this developmental shift from maturation to learning as the dominating force in the development of human behavior are certain developmental changes in the human nervous system. The direction of these changes is from little or no direct involvement of the higher brain centers in the behavior of the newborn child, to those centers' participation in nearly all human functioning beyond the sheerly vegetative processes in the mature human organism. It is not a young child's "natural stubbornness" or his possession of "original sin" that can be held accountable for his "refusal" to comprehend and to behave at the more mature level we may desire. His innately determined stage of neural development and his directly related level of experience make it either difficult or impossible for him so to behave.

Paralleling this pattern of nervous-system development and of the shift in determining dominance from maturation to learning, is a trend from a very small repertoire of distinctly human and individually unique behavior patterns in the infant, to a very large repertoire of distinctly human responses, organized in highly individual patterns, in the biologically and socially mature adult. Very early behavior, which occurs at a stage of development when the higher brain centers are barely functioning, and when the infant's learning has scarcely begun, is characterized by lack of physical and emotional coordination and control. His complete dependence on others at this stage accounts for his development of some degree of what I have termed *existence anxiety*. When higher brain functioning and attendant learnings have begun but are not advanced, primacy of self-centered motives, lack of inner-directed emotional control, incapacity to delay voluntarily the satisfaction of basic bodily needs, incapacity to see oneself as one among many, are all developmentally characteristic of the older infant and young child. As such, they are thoroughly normal behaviors for this developmental period. To insist that a child behave more maturely than his developmental status permits him to behave is to instill in him anxiety and hostility.

Such more mature and exclusively human behaviors as self-directed communication through spoken and written language, more complex abstract thinking, the more subtle emotions and appreciations, increasing self-discipline and self-direction, ability to conceive of and be controlled by goals and concepts beyond our immediate personal welfare, increasing organization and individuality in the ways we perceive, structure, and react to reality, are all mediated by neural circuits inclusive of the now-functioning human-principle higher-brain centers, i.e., behaviors that develop as a result of our learning, chiefly of socially derived learning. Presence in adulthood of behaviors typical of early childhood are, except during moments of extreme stress, not normal for most people because they are not imposed by developmental and intellectual limitations, as they are in the child. When they are so present, it is because the adult was not allowed to behave as a child when he was a child; or just the opposite, because he was given no real opportunity to learn adult ways of behaving as he became developmentally able so to behave.

The overall developmental trend from dominance of maturational forces to dominance of learning in individual behavior has an innate basis directly related to the pattern of development and functioning of the human nervous system. As such, this trend is biologically characteristic of the human species. Our humanity is a constantly emerging phenomenon, in both a social and an individual sense, in the light of this circumstance.

However, a very important "but" must be inserted here. At every stage of individual development, the role of learning is particularly complicated by two considerations: individual differences in constitution and environment, and the effects of strong and prolonged inner tension. Wide variations in such a personality characteristic as social maturity exist at chronological maturity because there are wide individual differences in the experiencing-learning process through which each of us becomes at once human and unique. The interaction of individual and constitutional and environmental factors contributes to individual differences in this learning process.

Because the major source for what we learn, including what we react to emotionally, is the human environment into which we are born, the core responsibility for the younger generation's progress toward humanity, individuality, and inner integration rests squarely on the shoulders of the older generations, who represent and reflect the society into which the new generation is born. Whether we are aware of it or not, we teach our version of humanness and our social values and practices to younger persons through our relations with them—not through lip-service, word-magic, admonitions—whether these relations involve direct personal interaction, or are indirect, as in the case of adult-controlled mass media. At the same time that we so teach, we provide them with the social experiences from which their own unique personalities are derived.[3]

Contrary to popular belief, the survival and the perfectability of the human species do not depend primarily on biological laws of natural selection operating on a simple individual basis. The circumstance that the pattern of development of the human nervous system makes individual experience subsequent to birth of major importance in human development, complicates matters for the human species.† This circumstance means that the advancement of the human species, including the wide possibility of inner psychological health among structurally normal human beings, has, at our evolutionary level, come to depend on social factors. To put it plainly, our species' advancement depends primarily on our capacity to develop, and constantly to redevelop as environmental changes require it, humanity-promoting forms of child rearing and social living.

Individual self-hood is not merely impossible apart from society; there is an intimate relationship between the inner life of the apparently autonomous adult and the society in which he has grown up. Here, again, there is a circular relationship: In order to improve himself, the individual must improve society; in order to improve society, the individual must improve himself. This is not to deny the possibility that a few unusual adults are, in their maturity, able to achieve inner functional integrity, apparently in spite of the functioning of their society. But even the particular personal "salvation" such individuals attain bears the ineradicable marks of their background of socially derived experience.

The respective roles of learning and of emotional stress in individual development make it possible to develop a yardstick for evaluating a simple

† Here is why the popular pastime of the semi-knowledgeable, to apply lower-mammalian data on the expression of a complex instinct such as sex or territoriality directly to man, must be considered just that—a pastime. Here is why, also, genetics investigators who speak of being on the verge of controlling the genetic makeup of man and thus, by implication, of man's behavior, are revealing the limitations—and grave dangers—of scientific over-specialization.

society or a subculture within a complex society. We can arrive at the "humanity quotient" of a particular culture or subculture by asking two related questions: To what degree do the *actual* values and practices of the various aspects of this society promote the growing individual's emerging humanity and inner integration? To what degree do they help him outgrow his earlier, developmentally imposed immaturities, no matter what his level of ability and perceptiveness may be?

I submit that when the dominant working values of a society are:

> that it is all right to offer for sale, and keep on selling more and more of, anything that people of any level can be induced by any means to buy;
> that individual and group immediate self-interest come first;
> that immediate expediency and self-interest are adequate principles on which to base major economic, political and personal decisions;

then that society does not merely have a low humanity quotient—it has already traveled far along the road back to barbarism (REF. 4, pp. 148–155).

I prefer to put one of my basic "social realities" in the form of a question. It has been implied that physical and intellectual effort and opportunities for practice provide the stimulation that is essential for the growing child's rounded development, as well as for the maintenance of mental alertness and physical tone throughout adulthood and old age. Can we carry the present technological trend towards eliminating any and all physical and mental effort in the individual's daily round of living so far as to promote human deterioration?

I believe, as another "basic reality," that there are psychological limits to the degree to which the social functions and responsibilities of the human individual can be delegated to specialists or to gadgets and machines. When we surrender the active exercise of certain functions at particular stages of our development, we give up the essential building materials from which our individual personality is structured. The exercise of the "universal parent" role, the "creative citizen" role, and the "moral responsibility" role provide, among other social functions, these psychologically indispensable experiences.

Let me use the current fragmentation and specialization of the universal parent role as an example here. We may have no question that nursery-school teachers, social workers, group workers, guidance counselors, marriage advisers, audiovisual teaching aids, educational television do a much more competent job on those services that, in a less complex age, every socially mature and responsible adult performed for younger relatives and friends as these roles were required of them. Nutritionists recommend vitamin pills as a supplement to, not as a substitute for, a basically adequate daily diet. So I have no question about the value of such specialized professions as I have enumerated —if they are seen as having a supplementary rather than a substitutive function in our complex society.

We can no more afford to give up our active exercise of the universal-parent responsibility so far as our own personality development is concerned than we can afford to give up the exercise of such other basic human relations as friend, husband or wife, son or daughter, father or mother, productive worker, leader, follower, and still expect to fulfill our particular potential for humanity and for individuality. And we cannot give up the exercise of our responsibility for passing *ourselves* on to those younger than us and still expect *them* to become human beings. It is through their interaction beyond the early years with (preferably) a wide variety of other human beings that children develop a rich and complex personality. So much daily human interaction centers around economic transactions and mutual services of various kinds that the delegation of these transactions and services to machines eliminates a very important source of social learning for the child. The images on the television screen, a major source of stimulation for children today, can never compensate psychologically for this loss of responsive social interaction (REF. 4, pp. 160–161).

Certain delinquent-parent patterns, although representative of families far apart on the economic scale, have not only a crucial parental personality characteristic in common—immaturity—but also an outcome of that characteristic of major social import. Some, if not all, of these parents' children were not wanted, especially by the mother; they were conceived and born either because of vulnerability to social pressure (including religious belief) or because of ignorance of or unwillingness to utilize anticonception measures—and they continued to be unwanted after birth.‡

When medical and psychiatric researchers and criminologists broaden their research designs to take into controlled account such complex developmental influences, we shall have documented what many students of human development now strongly suspect: that a substantial proportion of a wide variety of social incompetents—alcoholics, drug addicts, the chronically ill, criminal psychopaths or sociopaths, prostitutes, so-called sex criminals and attackers of women—have a crucial characteristic in common: they were unwanted by one or both of their parents, after birth as well as before (REF. 4, p. 76).

The two following principles relate to the communication aspects of human interaction, aspects that are postulated as fundamental to the undistorted development of the "human principle" in human development. One concerns the circumstance that there are two relatively discrete avenues or levels of interpersonal communication among human beings, the "gut" or somatic level, and the verbal level, a circumstance deriving from the operation of the mammalian and the human genetic principles in the development of individual members of our species. At birth and for some months thereafter, the infant experiences his world primarily through direct somatic contact; hence, others' communications with him occur through direct physical, usually skin-to-skin, contact. As his mother cares for him, she communicates to him her gut-level reactions; the words she coincidentally speaks represent sound patterns that have meaning for him only in relation to what is occurring at her somatic-motor level.

As speech emerges and develops in the child, it becomes a meaningful avenue of communication for him to the extent that the words he learns actually express his feelings, and the degree to which they do is a function of two factors: the appropriateness and promptness of his mother's responses to his preverbal efforts to communicate his needs and feelings, and to the degree of coincidence between her gut and verbal reactions to him during his first several months of life. This proposition implies that speech and language development proceed more smoothly and with fewer regressions in the child whose mother's responses to his preverbally expressed needs have been both

‡ The implication of this commonality for conservative moralists both within and without the church would seem to be clear: women have truly formidable, *albeit quite unconscious,* ways of striking back at a social order which denies them the right of control over their own bodies and individual destinies.

prompt and appropriate and whose gut and verbal levels of reaction to him have coincided, than in the child where these circumstances have not obtained. This implication must be stated as a reasonable hypothesis, pending its focused investigative testing. Beyond childhood, the degree of convergence and/or divergence between the individual's gut and verbal levels of expression bears a relationship to this order of his early experience. Generalized, cultural and subcultural factors also have an impact here, but not as potent a one.

The other principle is a further elaboration of the gut or mammalian level of communication enunciated previously: the "interpersonal feedback" or "resonance" principle. As the growing person relates to his immediate environment, primarily his immediate human environment, he alternates between taking into self what is occurring "out there" and going toward the other person, adjusting to his reactions. This alternating process has been noted and analyzed by various theorists.

I prefer to place this alternation of environment→individual and individual →environment within the broader framework of the process of human communication, conceived as a *mutually regulative* process that is directly analogous to the operation of the feedback principle in complex automated systems. This approach applies especially well to the nonverbal, somatic or gut or mammalian level of communication. In any interactive human diad, the incipient, unverbalized, somatic reactions of the one ordinarily call forth a similar set of incipient, answering responses, also somatic, on the part of the other, which in turn evokes a reactive, gut-level response in the first member of the diad—and a fundamental communication tie is established, a tie that determines whether communication also occurs at the verbal level—or only words are exchanged.

As the prototype for all later human interaction and communication, such a tie must be established between the mother and her newborn, *as yet only mammalian,* infant. At this early stage of cortical functioning, the tie is established through direct somatic contact of the mother with her child because the infant is able to experience the external world primarily through the skin senses. Studies of the effects of early sensory deprivation, Harlow's skin-comfort concept,[1] clinical evidence, all lend credence to this formulation. This prototypical communication tie is the foundation for the child's unconscious, gut-level attitudes toward self and for later meaningful verbal communication.

It also appears to serve an even more basic role. The infant member of the dyad has, at this early stage, no objective awareness of his own identity, but he *is* able to register on others that he exists. He does so through his demands for satisfaction of his urgent vegetative needs and demands, of which he is not aware and over which he has no control. The adult member of the child's first communication system has a special and a fundamental responsibility in this situation. When she reacts to her newborn child's demands responsively and appropriately, she is not merely keeping him alive physically, she is also reflecting back to him *that he exists;* the mother's appropriately responsive reactions to her babe's first overtures to the external world that he has so recently entered constitute for him his first—and at this stage his only—concrete source of information that he has identity.

If one member of this first interaction system habitually does not react responsively and appropriately, the result is similar to one key component of a feedback system that does not feedback accurately; cumulative distortion in the system occurs—and although the original defective component may be either the adult or the infant, it is usually the immature half of the diad who is wrecked as a result.

A not atypical example, unfortunately, in the middle-class subculture of a defective adult component of this first communication system is the young woman who has been taught all her life not to express, nor even to acknowledge to herself that she experiences, strong spontaneous emotion, especially strong negative feelings. Such a person has typically also acquired a verbal posture of warmth towards, and acceptance of, others because of the sex-role stereotyping of her subculture. But behind this socially accommodative facade is confusion about her own identity and her own feelings; that is, her gut-level reactions are frequently at variance with her verbalized posture (a split which can occur only in the human species) and she is not even aware that this is so. When a person with this personality organization has a child, especially her first child, she is very often unable to accept any of the normally negative feelings she may have towards her infant because "mothers are supposed to love their children." As a result, she is very likely to feed back contradictory reactions to her child: she maintains for others *and* for her cognitive self a verbal posture of love and acceptance, but at the somatic level she is communicating very different feelings to her infant—who is exclusively dependent upon her for reflection of the fact and the nature of his existence. It is not difficult to visualize—but may be very hard to establish experimentally—the effect that such a dual set of behavioral cues has on her child (REF. 5, pp. 281–285).

Most of the following suggestions (concerning measures that are conducive to the prevention of psychological disorder) have been influenced by what is probably the most serious of our society's many cultural contradictions or discontinuities: our country's current tendency to devaluate the child-rearing and -caring roles and responsibilities collides head on with the wealth of evidence documenting the fundamental importance for individual human development of the mothering and fathering processes.

This tendency expresses itself overtly as well as covertly at both the individual attitude and mass communications levels; two of its more concrete manifestations are the lower social status accorded those occupations that are child-care centered, and educated women's own reactions to the relative worthwhileness of traditionally feminine versus traditionally masculine roles and responsibilities. The former manifestation was succinctly expressed in a letter from a professional nursemaid of British background in the May 1965 *Harper's* (p. 14): ". . . This is a thing-oriented culture. Growing is not tangible. One cannot chart the child on a sales-graph. People who care for children are not social equals and are not to be paid salaries comparable with those of other professions."

There is a great irony in the second manifestation. Educated American women are caught in a bind between their own attitudes toward the lesser merit of the traditionally feminine functions and the circumstance that if and when they do act out their culture's values and assume occupational roles that are traditionally the province of men, they rather quickly find that a double standard of evaluation and of rewards of their work obtains, a circumstance that a number of recent discussions have begun to air openly; Dr. Ruth Kundsin's article [2] is an especially articulate example.

My emphasis on the fundamental importance of women's mothering function may give the impression that I am in favor of women's return to their traditionally restrictive venu of "*kinder, kirche, und kuchen.*" Not at all. When girls and women have full access to all the social, occupational, and intellectual opportunities of their society and, as a direct consequence, freedom of individual choice, they will be much more likely to develop the mature, integrated personality mode that is a prerequisite to adequate exercise of the mothering function. They will then be able to evaluate realistically the relative merits of the various occupational and personal roles available to them. A great many will, as a result, discover for themselves the tremendous personal satisfactions accruing from growing a human being. More and more women will so arrange their individual lives and, through appropriate political activity at local and national levels, help to arrange the economic, occupational, and educational practices of their society so that they will be able to do full justice to both their time-limited biological and related social responsibilities and the continuing cultivation of other facets of self.

Voluntary programs of population limitation are, and will increasingly, aid and abet the implementation of this cultural change. It will shift the emphasis in child rearing even more toward quality than quantity, and will not only place a premium on the greater participation of women of all social levels in the decision-making processes of our society, but will allow them more time for such activities.

In the meantime, and in addition, there is a genuine need for practical programs that will serve to assure all children a physical and emotional environment of a minimal level of stability for the first six years of their lives. In this country, the extension of already existing agencies, which are intended to strengthen and supplement the role of the family, is undoubtedly a more acceptable approach to our citizenry than the creation of entirely new child-nurturing institutions (REF. 5, pp. 345–346).

REFERENCES

1. HARLOW, H. F. 1960. Affectional behavior in the infant monkey. *In* The Central Nervous System and Behavior. M.A.B. Brazier, Ed. Josiah Macy, Jr., Foundation. New York, N.Y.
2. KUNDSIN, R. B. 1965. Where are our women in science? Harvard Med. Alumni Bull. Winter.
3. MEAD, G. H. 1935. Mind, Self and Society. University of Chicago Press. Chicago, Ill.
4. MILNER, E. 1968. The Failure of Success: The Middle-Class Crisis. 2nd edit. W. H. Green, Co. St. Louis, Mo.
5. MILNER, E. 1967. Human Neural and Behavioral Development: A Relational Inquiry, with Implications for Personality. Charles C Thomas Publ. Springfield, Ill.

DISCUSSION

Emily Moore, M.A., *Moderator*

KAMM: I would like to know what you mean by "gut reaction" and the responses that infants depend on from adult figures. You seem to say that there has to be some figure that is present, and it must be a mothering figure. I would like to know the extent to which men could be mothering figures, and whether some of the experiences that are required for the child to develop are simply a sensation that can be produced by some sort of nonhuman stimulus in the environment. For example, there are the Horlow monkey studies, which indicated that schizophrenia results when the little monkey-child has no blanket. But when they put him in a rocking chair, he was no longer schizophrenic because he needed something approximating the mother's rhythmic heartbeat to be maintained. There could also be a nonhuman stimulus for human infants. I would like to know how far one can go with this. That is one basic question.

OLESEN: One thing that concerns me is your comment concerning the responsibility of the older generation. That may be true in early childhood, but the point very quickly comes in the developmental cycle when lateral socialization is more important than the values that are transmitted by the older generation. Would you like to comment on how you see that fitting into your thinking?

TANGRI: I have a general comment on your point about how we teach our version of humanness and values to younger persons through our behavior rather than merely through lip service. This admonition has often been used as an argument that social change, if it is going to come about at all, has to come about slowly, because it takes a long time for people to alter their basic mechanisms of behavior, response-sets, and so on. We tend to think that children learn more from example than by preachment, but I am not sure that we really have data on it. In certain situations, a child will take both sources into account and arrive at some sort of solution for himself. That is, social change goes on even if the older generation cannot make itself over into an image it espouses but can't carry out itself. You don't have to wait endless generations to see social change come about—as far as behavior is concerned.

MILNER: I will start with Dr. Tangri's comment, the last. You seem to have misunderstood my motivation on that point. I was addressing myself in my book, from which these passages were drawn, primarily to what was, in my mind, an irresponsible parent generation, a generation that did not want to be parents. That is, they preferred to abscond from the practice of the parental roles. My intent in making this point was to try to get across the fact that children do not just grow like Topsy. We are learning that the human aspect of our genetic potential as a species, in the sense of higher parts of the nervous system that are unique to the human being, is present only as potential at birth. It is not functioning at birth; it unfolds after birth, and at the same time it is unfolding, it is unfolding in a social milieu. It was my motivation to get across to the adults that they can't subscribe to the notion, "We are going to put you in a cage and shove food at you, and somehow you will turn out to be a human being." My whole thesis is that we are a form of life that must *learn* to be human, and if we don't have any human models available, we do not become human.

By taking the point out of context, I feel you are missing what I was trying to get at. I am bawling out an adult generation that, because of the way they were programmed by the Depression, felt it was far more important to get the material and status things of life to make up for *their* parents' hangups. In the process of doing so, a great many gave up their responsibility for raising their children, especially the fathers. Many of the younger generation have reacted against the kind of parenting they had. I don't mean to be critical of the younger generation. I mean that there was really nothing else they could do as growing organisms who needed to have certain kinds of experiences at certain stages of their development and were not given them. I think the hostility being expressed by so many young people today is very well justified in terms of both their family experiences and the overall tone of our society, which to me is that we adults want to "do our own thing" like any teenager. We want to spend all our time satisfying our own immature needs, and we refuse to take responsibility for the optimal growth of the next generation.

To get back to Miss Kamm's comments. We're in a sort of "brave new world" era where, among other things, we are replacing human organs with artificial ones. Obviously, as we study this most complex thing that has ever been found, the human organism, psychologists are going to be able to abstract certain subsystems from it that we can then to some degree mimic in an artificial sense. Therefore, some say, in true "brave new world" fashion, "Let us get rid of the human caretakers who program in a lot of static we don't like. Let us just use a machine to perform what was formerly a human role. Then maybe all these other individual hangups that come from the human source can be eliminated."

I am suggesting that I am not satisfied with some rough approximation of this marvelous thing called interpersonal communication. No computer and no communication system of an artificial nature can even *begin* to approximate the real thing. I am saying, if we have got the real thing, let's use it and develop it and perfect it as much as possible, not say that because there are certain faults and problems associated with it, let us then get rid of it entirely, let's throw out the baby with the bath water. The early interpersonal communication aspect is what is basic in the mothering process, whoever does the mothering—mother, father, grandmother, or foster-parent.

I would prefer to focus on the issue of constantly learning more about the nature of our being as human beings, so that we can relate this knowledge to our society and in turn keep on constantly trying to perfect our society and our ways of raising children. We must keep on trying to improve our behavior and our society, not the reverse, which is what we seem to be doing today. Because we are dissatisfied with ourselves and with what is going on today, we reject the imperfections of the human organism and we say: "Let us make something else, another kind of organism. Let us monkey with it—that is a good word—and somehow create something on the biological level which is different." I say we are by nature a social form of being. We cannot become fully human without interaction with other people. If this is one of the things Professor Ruderman was trying to say, I agree with her. This is our nature as a species. We are programmed to be social, so let us try to have the feedback improved.

Each older generation has a responsibility to provide the kind of learning experiences for each new generation that will create a better generation and hopefully, this can be a cumulatively better process. I prefer this approach to the one I've referred to, where, because we have failed in a particular generation, some want to apply the kind of reasoning people like Aldous Huxley warn us against. The irony here is that it seems to be certain groups of women, of all people, who are fighting harder to achieve the "brave new world" type of society than anybody else.

There was one more comment, from Dr. Olesen. Would you repeat it?

OLESEN: I was raising a question about the role of the peer-group in socialization. The socializing role of the parents becomes very diluted after a while.

MILNER: It is again a question of emphasis. I have had contact with disturbed children. The developmental progression socially is that the child needs a stable relationship with adults in the earlier stage. That early stage must be completed in a positive sense, so that the child can next go on to develop relationships with his/her peers and profit from them. The reverse evidence suggests—and here the concept of imprinting comes up—that if the experiences needed at certain stages of development are not provided, the child is not released to go on to the next developmental stage. So he becomes fixated and keeps running after the adult as if he were still two or three years old even though he is now 10 or 12, because when he was an infant and young child he didn't have the initially stable attachment. But *with* that kind of initial, predictable, dependable support, the child can then go on and relate and learn a great deal from his peers.

Someone mentioned efforts at bringing up children entirely in a peer-group setting. If this experiment involves youngsters who have already developed this basic communication tie in the earlier years, and have developed basic trust in other human beings as a result of the kind of early relationship they had with adults, there may be some positive outcomes. But, I submit that a baby who has been treated like a machine and never had any predictable reinforcing human interaction would be autistic within a very short time. We are not entirely sure of the roots of autism, but I suggest that trying to raise a baby by machine is the best program for infantile psychoses that you can get. We are, at birth—and this is a point I tried to make in my paper—dominated by what I term the mammalian principle; that is, at birth, we humans have an incomplete mammalian nervous system. It is not like other mammals because they, for example, the chimpanzee, are more advanced in neural development at birth. In the human being, all the higher parts of the nervous system, those parts that allow for uniquely human behavior, are completely nonfunctional at birth.

We are living at a time when everybody is getting into the act with all sorts of quick solutions to all sorts of things; for example, because some children can be taught to read at age three, then let us make all kids read at age three. I am concerned about this trend toward very early, artificial intervention in children's lives. I submit that if we do not wait until we determine the effects of such intervention at 15, 16, 25, and 35 years of age, we may find that we have, perhaps, programmed something quite negative. Perhaps if we force development before a child is ready and we divert energies for growth in artificial directions, something else is going to give. But we cannot know that within two days or a month or even a year of the experiment.

I felt strongly enough about this particular research trend to write a letter about the social responsibility of the psychologist *qua* researcher to *The American Psychologist* a year or so ago. One of my arguments was that, whether it is drugs or some new learning method involved in a study, researchers have no right to publicize their short-term findings as some new panacea until the longitudinal dimension is worked through: What kind of kids are they going to be at age 16 whose lives we have intervened in at age two? Until we check this out, we can't say anything with certainty.

I have one more point to make, that we are a very complex form of life and a very malleable one. We need to decide the kind of adult we want to have. Do we want a tribal personality? Do we want a person who is going to be programmed to do what the state wants him to do, or do we want a person who in adulthood will be able to make some of the most complex and difficult decisions there are? To decide on the kind of life not only he himself wants to lead, or she herself, but to take responsibility for how a society is run, for how the next generation is going to develop? First we have to ask, what kind of personality do we want at maturity? Then we say, how do we create this kind of personality? I prefer to do this kind of thinking than to start from the reverse end, which comments like Miss Kamm's suggest: "Let us fiddle and see what happens; let us try it." There may be some merit in this approach, but let us fiddle with a little more concern and respect for what may be the outcome!

DUNBAR: I have several comments. One is that I feel that my reaction to the institution of the family doesn't come from rebellion against the family. I don't come from the milieu you were talking about, the spoiled children. I come from a sharecropper family. The family doesn't really exist there, you see, because it takes money to support a family. People destroy each other in such so-called families.

My objection to the family is that, first of all, it is a dead institution. We are talking about rebuilding something that died along with a class that has died. We have a decadent class that still rules, but it is dead, and it is taking the world with it in genocide, in racism, in sexism; and it has to be destroyed and with it, its basic unit, the family. That unit is based on the private ownership of children. There has been no question at this workshop about whether children should be held privately. The basic problem is that children are arbitrarily abandoned to whatever womb they happen to come out of. That is the most absurd thing I ever heard of, particularly in a society that condemns a good percentage of its people to utter, desperate poverty. In your paper, you talk about reinforcing the private family, instead of providing child-care facilities. I think it is sick and evil to think in those terms.

My other point concerns irresponsible parents. What I have seen of supposedly irresponsible parents are mothers working themselves to death to fulfill those obligations as parents that Margaret Mead, the anthropologist, and that Benjamin Spock, the baby doctor, told them they must fulfill so they would not destroy their children.

The result is what we have. Women were brainwashed; they were fed this rubbish in Spock's book and *McCall's* and *Ladies Home Journal* in the 1950s. There was then a move to the suburbs, to these white ghettos, where the children were isolated from each other. No wonder the kids want some kind of collective, something to hang onto. No wonder they don't trust the system. It completely betrayed their parents. They believed their parents, and they shouldn't have, but they couldn't see beyond them. I think the people who are to blame for this should be questioned about it, and not the individual parents, who are trying their best.

MILNER: Actually, we are not disagreeing. I don't think you are reacting to *my* paper; I have already said what you just said in a somewhat different way.

DUNBAR: How do you feel about the nuclear family?

MILNER: That it is in a mess at the present time, but we don't throw out the possibility that it can be improved or supplemented in some positive way. My paper ends with the statement that we need to have a great many child-care facilities to make up for families that have not done what they should.

JECH: And who wants the results we get from the private family?

MILNER: We don't have to have the "private family;" we do have to have *some* form of the family because of the biological nature of the human species, in which the baby is absolutely dependent at birth. If no one looks after the baby, it will die.

GARDNER: I would like to say in support of Dr. Milner that she is saying precisely some of the things that her critics have been saying. For example, at one point, it seems to me she is saying that society will be sick as long as mothers are forced to rear children that they did not want to bear.

DUNBAR: What about the children who may not want these parents?

MILNER: Then those children should be provided with good care aside from the family.

DUNBAR: And at two years old they say, "I don't like my parents. I want child care." It has to be an institution.

MILNER: Of course.

KAMM: First of all, I think I was misunderstood. I wasn't saying I was in favor of various artificial approaches. I just wanted your opinion about them.

Second, what people are objecting to in your paper is that the nuclear family is set up not only for the raising of children but for the maintenance of some sort of relationship between the husband and wife, and between society and the family. It drains off certain energies that might be directed against an irresponsible society by having the man come home and release himself in the family situation. It provides for the glorification of the parents as authority figures as well as a means of communicating the culture. It has provided women with a way of living vicariously through possessing their children. It has provided for ways out of people's insecurity. It is a basis for people coming together. This parenting function that you think is very important is really much more than just responsibility or consideration for others in a responsible society. As it is now, it consists of bribing a child to behave in a certain way for a certain thing called love.

When people are happiest relating to this one thing, this child they feel they have produced, this kind of relating is not the highest form of relating that you seem to think it is. It is not people judging each other as people, trying to take part in the growth of someone else, as you suggest; it is, rather, fulfilling lost opportunities for one's own growth by way of another individual. What you are saying is not necessarily wrong; I just think that you are not really saying anything specific. I don't think the nuclear family is the best way to get the sort of personality that you want. I don't think that there are any specific instances in which it is any better than some other ways of bringing up children. Also, when a child is brought up in the nuclear family, later as a creative individual, how can that person talk back to an authority figure, and in that way relate to this authority figure not as such but as a human being? How can that person not be bribed and not have some repressed tendencies that will result in other characteristics you dislike?

LADER: I want to say as a male—and, I guess, an older male—that I agree completely with Miss Dunbar, and I suspect maybe there is a silent, or not so silent, majority of males who perhaps agree with her estimate of the nuclear family a lot more than we may think. I believe what she is driving at is correct, and that it isn't a question of firming up or bolstering the present family, the nuclear family. For those who want to bolster it, fine; but I think what society and the law must do, as she pointed out, is to make child-care facilities available as a complete option, not just in emergency situations. What we have to drive at is a full-time setup for child care and after-school play centers all over the country. In other words, these options must be available for those who are growing up today. There might be a dozen options. If they want the commune, fine. If they want to use the child-care center, fine. If they want to use the marriage license, fine. I think all these options must be provided by society. I am not sure that we are ever going to be at a point where we can say one child-rearing approach is more ideal than another.

Obviously the first step is to make sure—which we certainly haven't done yet—that no child is brought into this world against the will of the mother. This first step involves contraceptives and complete repeal of abortion laws. But beyond that, we have to institute this complete child-care approach immediately, so that a woman can have this alternative.

I would like to suggest from my personal experience that the male isn't always at fault. The husband may want very much for his wife to have a complete career and full self-expression. My wife, who happens to be an opera singer, is a very good singer, better than I am a writer, but my problem is to try to give her this opportunity. It is extremely hard without child-care centers, *et cetera,* and with the domestic-help problem that someone already noted. It isn't possible to give a woman a chance to live a full life unless society provides these facilities, and it is society's obligation to do so immediately.

MILNER: I would like to say something that is substantially the same as what Mr. Lader said, but in a somewhat different way. I get the feeling that some of the younger people want to replace one old dogma with one new dogma. My basic point agrees with Mr. Lader's—that what we really should be fighting for is a wider range of choice.

Believe it or not, a great many women—and possibly the majority of women—really want to have children and to raise them themselves. If they do, they should be permitted to. There are a great many other women who don't want children at all, and if they find themselves in an embarrassing accident, for the future child's sake I hope very much they can get an abortion; I personally identify with the unwanted child in such a situation.

The communication among us gets very poor when some keep saying it has got to be all *this* way, in response to what used to be all *that* way. Let us be pluralistic, as was suggested, but let us be honestly pluralistic. Let us not say that just because we don't like certain aspects of the nuclear family we should impose our preferences on people who still do like it and find great fulfillment in being a father or a mother. Let us have a wider variety of possible life patterns, so that a greater variety of needs and behavior patterns can be fulfilled. This is what helps to make us a complex, open society, and not a totalitarian or a tribal society.

There is a certain element of bad faith among those people who assume, even before another person starts to talk, that just because that person is over a certain age or is a college professor or whatever, that he or she must automatically subscribe to a certain kind of dogmatic position. If you start out with that kind of premise, it becomes very difficult to have a really worthwhile interchange.

COMMENTS ON THE "POINTS OF DEPARTURE"

Virginia Olesen, Ph.D.

Associate Professor of Sociology
University of California Medical Center
San Francisco, Calif.

It is more a measure of their excellence and productivity than an indication of their shortcomings that one can point to three major themes lacking in most of the papers prepared for this workshop. These three themes should be included as themes for planning any subsequent conference:

Provocative Cognitive Styles

As is implied in the very title of the workshop (and this volume) the perspective for the most part is that of viewing woman as receptor into which changes are poured and as tablets upon which changes are writ. Although not necessarily negative, this viewpoint is limited in terms of what can and cannot be said, and it might be profitable to depart from it in favor of other perspectives. Recent reversals in thinking about child rearing, e.g., that parent-child socialization is reciprocal, are examples of overturning familiar modes of thought and the profit that can accrue from such reversal.

Several papers hint, in passing, at a provocative theme, e.g., the potential power to be exercised by woman in an area in which she utilizes devices that she chooses and controls (unless, of course, access to such devices is to be controlled by licensure more fully than is presently the case with prescription-controlled devices.) Another provocative theme, suggested in several papers, is the notion of the consequences that flow from choices made by woman. As an actor on her own choices, as originator of the very consequences that emerge from those choices, woman is not passive, but is creative and acting. Analytically, this perspective generates very different viewpoints than does the implied view of woman as passive receptor.

Research in Genetics and Biochemistry

Before the end of the 20th century, it well may be that man's most profound discovery about himself, the full unlocking of the genetic code, will have been accomplished or will be very close to realization. It is scarcely possible to envision the implications of this achievement, much less its bearing on the topic of this workshop, yet some speculation, however fully or partially informed on this issue, is critical to the issues of any conference that might spring from this workshop. What issues of control, choice, and consequences spring from man's knowledge on how his very life is shaped? Where will woman, her life-style, her career, take her place in this new genetic epoch? Will there even be differences between men and women as culture presently defines them?

Philosophical Implications

Few, if any, of the papers are informed by an image of society, although there are hints scattered in a number of places about possible images of society in which women exercise choices on fertility. Perhaps the implicit theme in all the essays is that womanly exercise of this choice generates the good society, the benevolent society, the creative and liberated society. Is this indeed the case?

Equally few papers are informed by an image of woman, except, as noted previously, as a passive beneficiary of technological, social, economic, and, now, biochemical change. Perhaps this is the result of Westernized scientific thinking, with its implicit cause-effect model. Perhaps it derives from deeply rooted structures in the language in which these papers are written.

What does seem striking is a consistent theme of concern for the moral aspects of the person, and from this standpoint the papers arrange themselves into a variegated, but generally coherent, statement on the philosophical implications of this technological change for women. Ultimately, as suggested in several of the papers, and fully articulated in a few, the philosophical parameters proscribe viewpoints in which self and society are seen as intimately and reciprocally interrelated.

Part II. Feminine Life-Career and Personality in a Free-Choice Society: What Are the Most Desirable Models?

POSITION PAPER: MODELS OF SEX EQUALITY *

Alice S. Rossi

Baltimore, Md.

Pluralist Model of Equality

. . . In the case of sex, the pluralist model posits the necessity of traditional sex-role differentiation between the sexes on the grounds of fundamental physiological and hence social differences between the sexes. This is the perspective subscribed to by most behavioral scientists, clinical psychologists and psychoanalysts, despite the fact that the women they have studied and analyzed are the products of a society which systematically *produces* such sex differences through child-rearing and schooling practices. There is no way of allocating observed sex differences to innate physiology or to sociocultural conditioning.

. . . Coupled with this is the further assumption, peculiar to American society, that child-rearing is the exclusive responsibility of the parents themselves, and not a community responsibility to assure every child a healthy physical and social development, as it is for example in East European countries, Israel and Sweden. This belief keeps women tied closely to the home for the most vigorous years of their adulthood. The "new" look to a woman's life-span, now institutionalized by over one hundred centers for continuing education for women in the United States, does nothing to alter this basic assumption, but merely adapts to our lengthened life-span: women are urged to withdraw from outside obligations during the child-bearing and rearing years, and to return for further training and participation in the labor force when their children reach an appropriate mature age. The consequences of such late return to active work away from the home are a lower income, work at levels below the ability of the women and withdrawal for the very years all studies show to be the peaks of creativity in work—the 20s and 30s.

Why does American society persist in maintaining erroneous myths concerning female sexuality, contrary to research evidence, as it does in urging women to believe their children's development requires their daily attendance upon them, again contrary to research evidence? I believe the answer lies in the economic demand that men work at persistent levels of high efficiency and productivity. To free men to do this requires a social arrangement in which the family system serves as the shock-absorbing handmaiden of the occupational system. The stimulation of women's desires for an affluent style of life and a bountiful maternity—to be eager and persistent consumers of goods and producers of babies—serves the function of adding continual pressure on men to be high earners. The combination of pronatalist values and aspirations

* This paper is extracted, with permission, from the author's article, "Alternate Models of Sex Equality," published in *The Humanist,* Fall, 1969.

for a high standard of living has the effect of both releasing and requiring men to give heavy psychic and time investment in their jobs; and requiring women to devote their primary efforts and commitments to homemaking: as a result, the broad sweep of many an American woman's life-span is caught by the transitions from Bill's daughter to John's wife to Johnny's mother and Billy's grandmother. . . .

Assimilation Model of Equality

. . . Feminist ideology is but one variant of the assimilation model, calling upon women to seek their place with men in sufficient numbers to eventually show a 50-50 distribution by sex in the prestigious occupations and political organizations of society. The federal government has served as a pace-setter for the economy in urging the appointment and promotion of competent women to the highest civil service posts and encouraging private employers to follow the federal example by facilitating the movement of women into executive posts.

The feminist-assimilation model has an implicit fallacy however: no amount of entreaty will yield an equitable distribution of women and men in the top strata of business and professional occupations for the simple reason that the life men have led in these strata has been possible only because their own wives were leading traditional lives as homemakers, doing double parental and household duty and carrying the major burden of civic responsibilities. If it were not for their wives in the background, successful men in American society would have to be single or childless. This is why so many professional women complain privately that what they most need in life is a "wife."

The assimilation model also makes an assumption that the institutional structure of American society, developed over decades by predominantly white Protestant males, constitutes the best of all possible worlds. Whether the call is to blacks or to women to join white men in the mainstream of American society, both racial integration and a feminist ideology accept the structure of American society as it now exists. The assimilation model rejects the psychological theses of innate racial or sex differences implicit in most versions of the pluralist model, precisely the assumption numerous blacks, women and members of the younger generation have recently been questioning and rejecting.

Hybrid Model of Equality

The hybrid model of equality rejects both traditional psychological assumptions and the institutional structure we have inherited. It anticipates a society in which the lives of men and of whites will be different, not only women and blacks. In fact, it might be that this hybrid model would involve greater change in the role of men than of women, because institutional changes it would require involve a restructuring to bring the world of jobs and politics closer to the fulfillment of individual human needs for both creativity and fellowship. From this point of view, the values many young and women subscribe to today are congenial to the hybrid model of equality: the desire for a more meaningful sense of community, greater depth of personal relations across class, sex and racial lines; a stress on human fellowship and individual scope for creativity rather than merely rationality and efficiency in our bureaucracies; heightened interest in the humanities and the social sciences from an articulated value base; a social responsibility commitment to medicine and law rather than a thirst for status and high income—these are all demands for social change by the younger generation in our time which are closer to the values and interests women have held than they are to the values and interests of men. They represent an ardent "no" to the image of society projected to the new crop of male technetronic futurists: a machine and consumption oriented society that rewards technological prowess in a "plastic Wasp 9–5 Amerika" to use Jerry Rubin's colorful phrase. . . .

. . . The new breed of academic women will ask, as many young students are now demanding, that the quality of teaching, the degree of colleagueship with students, the extent of service to both an academic institution and its surrounding community, become part of the criteria on which the productivity of an academic man or woman is evaluated. No one has conducted research on academic productivity with this enlarged net of criteria, and it is a moot point whether men would show greater productivity than women if such criteria were applied. . . .

Conclusion

A pluralist model of social equality is implicitly a *conservative* goal, a descriptive model that accepts what exists at a given point in time as desirable and good. The assimilation model is implicitly a *liberal* goal, a Horatio Alger model that accepts the present structure of society as stable and desirable, and urges minority-groups to accept the values and goals of the dominant group within that system as their own. The hybrid model is a *radical* goal which rejects the present structure of society and seeks instead a new breed of men and women and a new vision of the future. . . . An analysis of sex equality may start with the reality of contemporary life, but soon requires an imaginative leap to a new conception of what a future good society should be. The hybrid model envisages a future in which family, community and play are valued on a par with politics and work for both sexes, and for all the races, social classes and nations which comprise the human family. . . .

POSITION PAPER: OUT OF THE FRYING PAN—?

Esther Milner, Ph.D.

Department of Education
Brooklyn College
Brooklyn, N.Y.

The more I think about certain sectors of the still crescent "new feminism," the more their quite unconscious subscription to the masculine mystique *—and the many negative social ramifications of that subscription—impels me to adopt the role of devil's advocate. Because the gist of that advocacy is directly related to the question, "When women may at last freely choose, what *are* their most desirable life-styles?", this bit of "deviltry" is being tied to the "great debate."

It seems to me that some activist-women's thought processes are so boxed in by their pressing gut-level reactions/agonies, that they are fixated on the most immediate and apparent source of their problems—men's scapegoating of women. Many are especially bitter about male reluctance to accord women genuinely equal opportunities in the occupational world at a time when status in that world has become the primary source of feelings of individual self-worth for increasing numbers of women, as well as for men. I have no quarrel with the limited, short-run goals of equal occupational opportunity and equal access to the decision-making levels in our society for women, as long as these goals are recognized as being limited and short-run. As for the resurgent tendency among many men at this time in United States history to "put down" women,† those young women who have been most sensitive to, and negatively affected by, this currently omnipresent tendency have not recognized that such male behavior is related to a broader sociological situation/process, a situation that affects men even more directly and pervasively than it affects women.

Activist women will not be able to understand what is happening to women

* By which I mean, in essence:

1.—the *wish* for, and the institutionalized plus individual practice of, power/control over nature and other human beings;
2.—the general-societal conviction that those activities that implement this wish and this practice, whether intellectual or directly physical in nature, are of the highest societal worth and prestige;
3.—the contemporary, typically American, expression of points 1 and 2, which is to approach traditionally competitive or status oriented situations, whether they be economic or institutional or interpersonal in nature, as if they were a competitive sport or game. Such situations, like an athletic contest or a game, are engaged in only to be won; if possible by following the rules, if necessary by any means at hand that work.

† That men, especially young men in the process of "finding" themselves, are psychologically prone to do just this is acknowledged. Why they are is only partially accounted for by the kind of sociologically oriented analysis that is developed in this paper. A rather complex social-psychological "bridge" would have to be built to provide a more adequate explanatory structure; such an enterprise would require another entire position paper—at the very least.

nor why they themselves are so angry/unhappy until they focus their analytic perspective on realities beyond the nearest billboard or television commercial or abortion-death. Further, that as long as they center their rationale and their rage on another equally victimized group rather than on underlying realities, they are not merely also scapegoating, but they are diverting their magnificent energies from the "main bout." In so doing, they are being reactionary, first, in the broader societal sense, and second, they are serving admirably the interests of the politically reactionary groups of our time and country—very much as the few black militants with their ideology and tactics of black-white confrontation are doing.

The sociohistorical situation/process I have referred to cannot be conceptualized within the traditional capitalist, free enterprise vs. communist ideological and political polarities; in my eyes, today's functioning versions of capitalism and of communism are but the two sides of the samc obsolete coin. Rather, my thesis is: As a result of the convergence of at least three developments of our time and place—the rapid spread of the second industrial revolu-

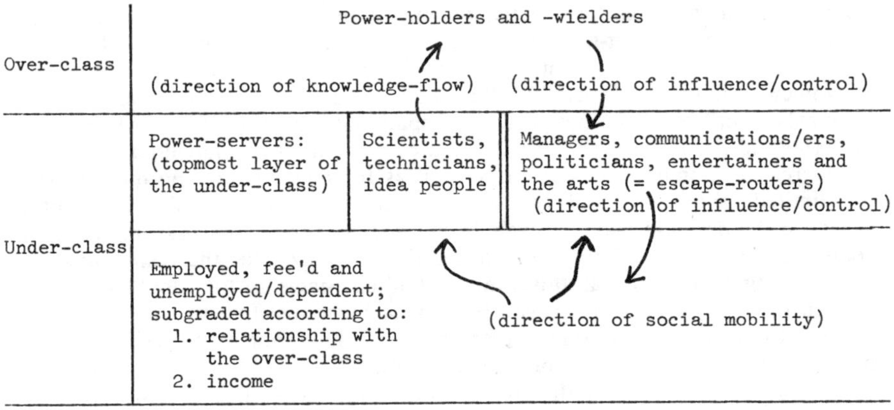

FIGURE 1. The new feudalism: the technocratic, power-centralized society.

tion of automation-cybernation-global communications, increasing population and attendant urbanization/suburbanization, and concentration of economic, political, and information-gathering and -dissemination power in increasingly fewer hands—a mass, power-centralized technocratic society is now in the rapid process of emerging in the United States. It is my further thesis that we are now, and have been for some time, in a period of transition from a former power-diffused social structure to the new power-centralized social structure just described.

It is an old sociological principle that during periods of major societal transition, the sequence in which the various old-structure social groups are displaced, structurally and psychologically, is, first, the already marginal groups, and, next, the more centrally located groups. Today's marginal groups in our country are the very poor and unskilled (a large proportion of whom happen, at this point in our history, to be people of color); women; adolescents; the elderly. Of all these groups, contemporary women bear the additional burden of being doubly displaced; the urgent world-wide need to slow down population growth is peaking during the same period that the new technocratic social order is surfacing in our country, so that women are being shorn not only of the economically productive roles they once had but *also* of their traditionally primary social function of child bearing and rearing. The psychological concomitants of that double displacement are already evident; the "new feminism" is only the reaction-formation symptom most exploitable by the mass media.

FIGURE 1 embodies my current picture of the structure of the technocratic, power-centralized, essentially feudal society currently emerging in the United States—a society that, ironically enough, many activist women, by diverting themselves and others from the underlying disease process of our time, are inadvertently expediting. Those who *so* resent (as I do) women's under-representation and utilization in the decision-making and otherwise really meaningful roles in United States society should analyze just where in this schema they would like to place themselves. Among the intensely competitively chosen few, who are or will be directly serving power, either as knowledge developers or as managers or escape-routers? Or are you willing, more realistically perhaps, to settle for being in that section of the under-class which is or will be caring for or protecting the other, larger, demented-dependent-criminal section? (Doesn't anybody read Aldous Huxley's "Brave New World" anymore?)

DISCUSSION

Margaret Mead, Ph.D., *Moderator*

MEAD: I have a general feeling from the point-of-departure papers that we are terribly focused on ourselves, that we look at other countries only as giving us a little information about what we are not or might be, that we are very, very contemporary, and that women's bodies are apparently just like men's except when they are having babies. It is as if women could push a button and turn into women, and then, when they were not going to have any more babies, they could push another button and become exactly like men. One of the assumptions seems to be that in the future we will produce men as much like women as much of the time as possible.

I was asked the other day by some students what I thought my major contribution had been, and I said, "Living a long time, because I have been able to go back and study societies that I studied 40 years ago, and that is very useful." This point may also be true here, because my mother was a suffragette, and I was exposed in my childhood to the fights for women's suffrage. I learned on antisuffrage monologue that I used to recite on appropriate occasions. It is still used today: "If women get the vote, they will vote exactly like their husbands and nearly double the existing vote." Do you like that argument? If not, take this one: "If women get the vote, they will vote exactly opposite to their husbands and divorce will stalk the land." There is a wonderful passage in which St. Paul said, "Let your women keep silence in the churches." The participants in this workshop are ready, and anxious, to speak out.

DELL'OLIO: This discussion is on the feminine life-career and personality, in society, and what are the most desirable models. My feeling is that there are no models. The whole difficulty of feminists today is that we are searching for a path in uncharted territory, and that is such a difficult thing to do.

MEAD: You are sharing that difficulty, of course, with young men. There are no models today for either sex.

DELL'OLIO: Right. But a change in sex roles is much more difficult for women whenever there is a change.

OZER: Some years ago, a book by Jessie Bernard on academic women made me very, very angry. There were three model-vignettes in it, as I remember. One of them happened to be a good friend of mine. Here was my model of Eve, who had been very successful until she married, and she started having babies and was now working about two afternoons a week. As far as her reputation in the community was concerned, she was a fine academician and a most fluent teacher. Yet her academic status was much lower than her husband's. This irritated me terribly because I was then a graduate student at Stanford, and I wanted to be a scientist. Where was there an ego-ideal for me? Everyone would say to me, "You are going to go home and have babies. You are only going to be a research associate." Today I am 30 and I am my own ego-ideal, and I am very happy about it. The first time that I said, "I will be a professor," I was told I was completely ridiculous. Well, I am not a professor, although I had the opportunity to be one. At the moment I am an Established Investigator of the American Heart Association and doing my own research, and this is what I want to do.

But what are the choices one makes when one is completely free? I feel completely free. I feel that my relationship with my husband and with other people is completely free. The role of children is very important, and in my own case, if my husband and I do decide to have children—and perhaps the next five years will tell—they will be children who will be raised with both parents interested in equal participation in their growth and development. But at this time we work very hard and we do not know if the leisure time we have now we want to give up to spend in the presence of small children. The fact that everybody else has children and we do not does not disturb us. We will make this decision independently.

As you grow older and become more sure of your work and of yourself as an individual, the idea that you may be very different from everybody else you know just does not disturb you. I hope that, through our mass media, we will help give young people the confidence that they will grow out of the age they are now in, a period of ego-identity difficulties, and that it won't matter at a later time in life whether or not they had an ego-identity problem earlier on. They are their own ego-ideals. I hope that most have confidence that at least one woman has been active in probably every profession there ever was and that there are possibilities if one wants to reach for them—that things are not precluded. Perhaps that will make the pain and difficulties I see among young women today—I am active in the Washington women's liberation group—not as bad as it was when I was a little younger.

MEAD: It is awfully easy, though, because one has had an easy time of it oneself, to feel that nothing needs to be done. You know, you owe your chance to the fact that other women worked very hard before you, or else you would not be working where you are, and you would not have a Ph.D. For example, I had a professional grandmother. If everybody could have a professional grandmother, it would be much easier for them. But they have not got one, and it is hard to get one, retrospectively.

OZER: The things that women's liberation people today assume existed for a great length of time, to me existed as a result of the Depression followed by World War II. For instance, during the Depression, both of my parents had to work, because whoever could get work, worked. My father had been a widower, so there were my father's children during the years that he was widowed, and he had ample experience at housekeeping and child raising until he met my mother. Therefore the role-identities in that house were a little different from those in other families. After the Depression and after World War II, people wanted to show they had made it by having a large number of children and doing well by them with only a single wage-earner. This kind of thing, the feminine mystique, doesn't go far back. Maybe we are now on the downslope.

MCLAUGHLIN: I am a newspaper-writer by trade. There has been something very much unappreciated by this group. My freedom did not arise from anything except the W.P.A. The W.P.A. came into the school system in 1932 and 1933 bearing the message that if you worked hard enough you could be anything you wanted to be—short of an opera-singer, perhaps. I came from a family that had high I.Q. and low opportunity. The war brought my family into the city of Boston, where I had an opportunity to have a scholarship and therefore to go through college. It is not appreciated here that women can work today just as hard as they want to. They can enter any profession they want to. There can be an increase in Ph.D.s, there can be an increase in job opportunities in the marketplace, and there can be equality of pay.

DUNBAR: That is not true. The statistics show quite otherwise. Overall, there is a 40% difference.

MCLAUGHLIN: Let me finish my point, despite some possible error on my part. The great inequality for women today is inequality of opportunity for *promotion*. We can all enter the market, whether it is the factory level or the professional level, but the woman who thinks that she is going to get to the top is very much mistaken. She may be a first-class private or a sergeant or even a lieutenant, but she is never or hardly ever going to be a captain, and this is something we need to look at. In Boston—and I think Dr. Kundsin will agree with me that perhaps there is greater cultural lag in Boston—I don't know of a woman editor in journalism unless she is on the woman's page, and I don't know of a woman head of an academic department unless she is in a woman's college, and I don't know of a woman head of a medical service unless she is in a woman's hospital.

I would like to say to this young woman from Washington, like the woman in Betty Friedan's book, "Where were you all when I needed you?" In the 1950s, when I was starting out, there was not this kind of acceptance of the working mother; there was not this kind of acceptance of the working woman at all. I very well remember sitting at the family dinnertable and having an in-law aunt say to me, "When are you going to stop putting the almighty dollar before the interests of your children?"

MERRIAM: I am a writer. There is an anecdote about Margaret Fuller, I believe. She said one day, "I accept the universe," and the response was "Madam, you'd better!" We had better accept the fact that the young people of women's liberation have arrived, are here, are going ahead whether those of us who have been around before are going to join them or not. There must be some reason why this movement has suddenly burgeoned after being dormant for years. You cannot keep up with it; it is going in geometric progression. I find it very exciting.

Why are they interested in these issues? I don't think they are just pulling them out of thin air. What was said before about the need for women's opportunity for promotion remains. But it is not as easy to get started as Mrs. McLaughlin suggested. Women have often been linked with Negroes in their struggle for first-class citizenship. Women and youth are also similar. Not only are the young men I know finding it very difficult to get jobs, but it is very difficult for young women to get jobs on any level, whether they want to be stenographers or sales clerks or anything. I think there are also quite substantial pay-differentials. If you look at some non-union supermarket clerks, you will find that the women who are doing the heavy work behind the counter, just as heavy as the men, are not receiving the same pay as the men are. You will also find this in other occupations.

Perhaps some of you saw the same television program I just did, with Ann Bancroft as the many women in the life of a man. It was touted by *The New York Times* as a magnificent program. It took me back 100 years because it showed every stereotype you can think of with respect to a woman's role. It may be that the young women coming forward now are rediscovering some of the things that we did earlier, but I think it would be dreadful if we talked about a generation gap. We do not have a generation gap. We might have some kind of communication gap between some of us who may be 20 and some of us who may be 50, but we do have linkages that we must find. We all have intellectual smog around us, but please let's not beat up on the young people who are being radical. Let us try to understand why they have come to this workshop and see what we can learn from them.

REEVES: I would like to comment on Alice Rossi's categories of conservative, liberal, and radical goals. I want to make an analogy of these categories with Mannheim's utopias. For the conservative type, the utopia is today. For the liberal, if a thing is unfair, then you can list the reasons why it is unfair and then say the utopia will be when we make it fair. The radical takes readings in present reality and says that we need a future utopia and we are going to get from here to there in this way. We have been talking on all these levels at the same time.

There should be some way of organizing our thinking, at least along philosophical lines, so we might say, for example, "I am a conservative in this sense. I think the utopia is today. I just want to get in there. I would like to get those jobs. I think they are great. I have been denied these jobs, and I want a movement that will get me in there." Second, the liberal approach: "Never mind the job market. Never mind whether there is technological unemployment. Never mind whether we are trained for the right things or not. It is not fair. We are going to make a movement and get in there. Anybody who keeps us out is going to be taken down a peg, because we are angry." Third, the radical approach, which is really the sociological approach. You take a look at reality and say, "What is going on in the world and what are the things we can do to solve these social problems?" It seems to me that there is no organization of our ideas, and we are supposed to be academic people, trained in ideas.

RUDERMAN: Dr. Mead, on the basis of my own paper, I wonder how you can say that we all feel male and female are essentially the same thing, just packaged differently.

MEAD: Because you did not give a single detail of how they were different.

RUDERMAN: I would be very interested in hearing what you would have to say on exactly this point.

MEAD: There was a great deal of discussion in these papers of the ways in which women could function in the work-world, just as there was in the report of the President's Commission years ago; the major emphasis was on work and on careers. Careers can be defined as the things you would pay people to let you do if they did not pay you to do them. Academic people have careers, but most women work, just the way most men work. And there was far more emphasis on people being allowed to do the things they want to do than there was on the number of women who have to work outside the home.

I did not feel the black woman was represented in these papers, or any other minority-group. I felt the materials were very confined to the United States, and very confined in history, and that there was almost no discussion of woman's psychological and physiological makeup. As I said before, you press a button, become a female, and produce a baby; press another button and stop. There was no recognition of women's rhythms being so different from men's. We may damp them all down, we may treat the menopause as a disease—as the medical profession would like us to—we may take a pill until we are ready to menstruate again and get the nest built, and then we work toward making women as much like men as possible. That is one possibility.

But another possibility is to recognize a great many other things. Breast feeding was recognized only as a contraceptive measure. We don't know what the relationship of breast feeding is to women themselves or to the children. We don't know the relationship of not having children to the possibility of cancer, and there is a good deal of evidence that there is a great relationship. Women would have a perfectly good right to say they would rather risk cancer than not do what I want, just as I think men have a right to smoke if they want to smoke themselves into an early grave. But we ought to be considering the relationship between the new world we are undoubtedly moving into and the population explosion. We ought to consider a good many other things about women's physiology that we are not considering at all.

GARDNER: I would like to respond to your definition of career, because I think that is where "it's at." You defined a career as what you would pay people to let you do if they would not pay you to do it, and that is what the woman's movement is all about. Women want to do things that they are not paid to do. None of the things that women are allowed to do are regarded as of great worth in our society. In fact, I have a career, and I would pay to be allowed to do it. Women are demanding the right to do things that have not traditionally been regarded as women's work.

MEAD: But this is equally true of men. Very few men have careers. Most of them just have jobs. There has been an overemphasis on that very fortunate section of the human race who really want to do something so much that they will make any effort to do it, and very little emphasis on the very large proportion of the human race, male and female, who have to work to stay alive and who have no relationship with a career at all. This is the thing I am worried about.

GARDNER: I really think that the proportions of men who are allowed to do what they would like to do are so much greater than the proportions of women—

MILNER: That is debatable.

GARDNER: —and that is what we women should be concerned about.

HEIDE: I don't know whether to call myself a learning expert or an expert learner. I think where "it's at," to use today's vernacular, is in terms of our value system, the kind of culture we have. Few people, I think, would dispute the fact that we have an androcentric culture. Concomitant with this fact is that we have valued those things traditionally associated with male activities. This has certainly shown up in the behavioral sciences, where we have a proclivity to be thing-oriented and to quantify, to measure that which is visible. And I think that has had its effects.

MEAD: Do you know that every single culture that has ever existed has valued the male activities more than the female? It did not make any difference what these activities were—even dressing dolls—if the men did them, they were valuable.

HEIDE: I agree. This is the way the world has been. I would not disagree that it has also been difficult for men to find their identity and that most men have jobs and not careers. Men very often have to conform to somebody else's image of what it means to be a man, and women have to conform to somebody else's image of what it means to be a woman. It is this kind of stereotype hangup and the relative overvaluation of one kind of stereotype as against the other that permeates our culture and our lives. I would like us to concentrate on creating the kind of society in which we have some idea of what it means to be a person who also happens to have important elements of sexuality.

MEAD: I think this is the first time in history that we really have a chance at it, because this is the first time in history that society has not been scared to death that there would not be enough children and has therefore insisted upon high reproductivity. Now every society is in various measures going to be insisting on lower reproductivity. This is, therefore, the first time that societies will be able to let women be persons and men be persons. They have never let very many men be persons either, but they have let more men be persons than women.

HEIDE: May I add a point that I neglected to make and wanted to? However effective, universally available, and safe, and so forth, any contraceptive device is, it really won't make much difference in the birth rate until women have significant alternative roles to motherhood. I would like to suggest to people who are concerned with overpopulation that perhaps one of the best things they could do is support what we have called the "women's liberation movement," which may turn out to be a "*human* liberation movement"—and they should seriously support it.

NAG: I want to comment, Dr. Mead, on your remark that this is the first time in human history that we are not concerned about having large numbers of children. If we talk about the period after every cultural revolution, or neolithic revolution before that, as far as we have evidence now, as long as the people were still in the hunting-gathering stage, they were concerned about having too many children. Examples are the Eskimo society or some Australian societies in which they were, often with some approval from the society, committing infanticide.

MEAD: That is not incompatible. I have worked with societies in which there is infanticide, and they can still be worried that they are not going to have enough children, because the child they kill is the wrong sex or the wrong sequence or something, but they still worry.

NAG: People in all societies are concerned about having too many children or having too few children. That means they have an idea of what family-size they should have. In many cases, they have taken drastic steps to control it. We do not have very good evidence, but at least in societies in which people are nomadic, it seems there is concern about spacing.

MEAD: But they are afraid that babies will die, because so many of them die in all those societies. In developed countries, however, they do not die. The ones who are born live, and that is the sort of thing I am emphasizing.

KAMM: People usually start off with recollecting the personal, and then they go back to the theoretical. I'd like to try both. The point about values is extremely important because what has struck home to me in my own development is that our culture, as a whole, hates and fears women. There is a notion of the female as some sort of infectious disease. She is out to castrate, or she is a vicious sort of creature, or she is Catholic, or she is bad, or she is babylike, or she is a pussycat. This permeates our whole culture. And the idea of her power a a mother—once men realize how important the mother-role really is, they don't like that either. If a man doesn't want her to be a dominant figure in the marriage, and she plays along with this wish, sooner or later he realizes she *is* only playing along, and that she is really more dominant than he is.

No matter what you allow women to do, men somehow dislike them, and there is a resistance to honesty in the relationship between men and women. Look at our religion: We have male gods. Even feminists go to church and to rabbis. We have religions in this day and age that will not allow women to be members of the clergy because women are supposed to be bloody and dirty.

MEAD: They menstruate.

KAMM: Men have discharge.

MEAD: That only worries Mohammedans.

KAMM: I think the point that has been generally overlooked is that there is a tremendous fear and hatred of women in our culture. It seems to me that we place so much emphasis on the sex roles because they are oversimplifications in response to our insecurity. They are two obvious distinctions and therefore the easiest way to generalize roles. This is perhaps what Professor Ruderman was referring to. Any complications create insecurity because then people have to begin to look at each other as individuals. The fact that we have tremendous and pervasive insecurity should, it seems to me, be a basis for social philosophy.

The fact that men seek to possess or to dominate is a paradigm for all other sorts of oppression. Is it insecurity that makes a woman desire this so-called thing, love, from someone who supposedly regards her as an inferior? Is it a seeking of regaining humanity by the identification? These are the sorts of notions that people in women's liberation are trying to figure out. Why do these things happen?

I would like to see a new type of personality and much more of a sense of people relating to each other as individuals. But we have to recognize that so many of the institutions we value so highly, such as the notion of love or of sexual sex, are expressions of people relating to one another not because they want to respect each other or to communicate, but because they are deeply insecure. And they need to fit into each other because of their insecurity.

MEAD: Don't you think a pregnant woman, or a woman after her baby is born, needs somebody to look after her?

KAMM: How does she react to pregnancy? Is she afraid of it, of the physical fact of dying? If so, that is a nominal response. If she seeks a male figure because this man is a god figure, a rational figure, nobody can help her. Of course we can seek to help each other, but must people consistently feel that the only reason they are needed or wanted is because they serve some sort of function for one another? I don't think these are the best bases for a relationship.

I also want to introduce another issue, the notion of sexuality. If female sexuality is essentially clitoral as opposed to vaginal, what are we going to do with heterosexual sex? There is a large population that is homosexual. Is sex, heterosexual sex or any kind of sex between human beings, primarily a psychological relationship? Or is there a physical element as opposed to a communicative one? This whole realm of sexuality, which seems to be the binding force between men and women, has to be looked into at this stage of the game.

MAJOR: I was very much taken by Nancy Reeves' paper, which I believe to be most comprehensive and in-depth in approach because it showed a sense of history. With the emphasis today on the physical sciences and with the diminution of the value of humanity, I feel that it brought into focus the issue at hand. The women's liberation movement must be seen in this historical context. In addition to the fact, Dr. Mead, that this is the first time in human history in which we are not fearful of not producing enough children, it is also the first time in history that we would be able to feed everyone in the world if the social organization were brought up to date. I therefore think our fundamental need is to refashion our concepts of the universe in which we live.

We are living in a space capsule going around on its axis. We have to understand the world in which we are living, whether we are thinking about going to the moon or the population explosion or the selective affluence in which we live. We are also living in a time of duality, of the terror of extinction of the human race, and when we women struggle for our own liberation, it is impossible to separate it from working for the survival of the human race, male and female. So it is the time of affluence, and it is the time of the bomb, and it is the time of the pill; and it is the time of the black man and woman, and the Mexican and Puerto Rican; and it is the time of liberation. Unfortunately—or perhaps it is very good that this point was raised early in the schedule of the workshop—our discussion has thus far centered on this one objective and around the individual. It is my hope that we will be able to see these issues in the larger, universal, context of today; the hope and the fear.

EAST: I am Executive Secretary of the Department of Labor's Interdepartmental Committee on the Status of Women. I hope for the future that human beings are so constructed that one role-model for men and one role-model for women is not necessary—that we can have a multiplicity of roles, because from what I have observed there are really very wide variations in personalities, temperaments, desires, and needs among men and women. The differences among men and the differences among women on almost every psychological variable is greater than the differences between the means of each sex. I don't know if human beings are so constructed that they can tolerate this wide variation of role-models or not. I hope they can, because if we can, human beings will be happier. My own two daughters are very different in their needs, and I hope the world of the future will be such that each of them can recognize her full potential.

I am concerned in my job with the nitty-gritty, and my knowledge is more in this field. And I wonder about our legal system, a system under which women are required to receive longer prison sentences than men in some states. Our Supreme Court has never held unconstitutional a law that discriminates against women. In 1969, in Pennsylvania and in Connecticut, laws under which women have been sentenced for years came to light only because we had a poverty program, and through it, lawyers who were willing to fight to the highest state courts for the rights of women. In Pennsylvania, when the case reached the Superior Court, which is the intermediate appeals court, six judges out of seven held that men and women were different and that therefore it was logical to require longer sentences for women than for men for the same offense.

MILNER: What offense?

EAST: In this particular case it was a felony, and a man and a woman were involved in the same crime. The woman was a prostitute who had lured a man into a room, and her colleague had robbed him. She was only 19 years old, with no prior offense, and he was an older man with a prior conviction. The lower-court judge had to give her a longer sentence than he gave the man. But in Connecticut, 200 women were released from prison when the Supreme Court of that state held that the law was unconstitutional.

MEAD: In England, they are retiring women earlier than they are retiring men.

EAST: Some of our private pension plans do this, but our public plans do not. Also on the economic side, women earn about 60% of what men earn, and these are women employed year-round, full-time. Women who are high school graduates, employed full-time, year-round, earn less than men with fewer than eight years of education. I do not know what lies back of this; I get awfully curious about it. One-third of all the families in poverty in this country are headed by women, and yet our training programs for the unemployed give preference to men. Women who are heads of families get less preference for training than do adolescent boys.

The highest unemployment rate of any group in this country is 33%, and this is the rate among black girls 16 and 17 years old. Has anybody ever stopped to think what the options are for these girls? If a 16-year-old girl who is a high-school dropout cannot get a job and her family is on welfare, what does she do to eat? Or what would a white girl in that situation do to eat? She turns either to prostitution or some other crime, or she has a baby of her own and gets on welfare. Can you think of anything else she can do? We have boys' clubs in Washington supported by the Police Department, so that poor, pre-adolescent boys can get skilled training and sports and so on. We have nothing like that for girls. There is not a girls' club in Washington except for two that are run one night a week by a policewoman who does it on her own time.

These are the things that bother me even more than some of the abstract concerns about women that we've been discussing. What are we going to do about these girls, 16 and 17 years old, who cannot get jobs?

SASSOWER: I would like to supplement Mrs. East's remarks by offering some additional statistical information with respect to women judges which may be of interest. When one points to the difference in treatment of women litigants, it is interesting to consider who is imposing this punishment. Hardly a woman. There are very few women judges in this country, probably fewer than 0.5% of our federal judges. In the Empire State, of which I have particular knowledge, there were approximately 750 judicial positions at the time I became President of the Women's Bar Association. I learned at that time that there were only a handful of women judges, fewer than 25!

In 1968, the legislature of New York State, which we like to think of as a pace-setter, a leader in the march for social justice in this country, created 125 new judicial positions. This event was generally regarded as an unrivaled opportunity to bring about some remedy of the tremendous imbalance that existed in the state with respect to giving minorities representation on the bench. At that time there was a great deal of talk in the press about the right of Negroes and the right of Puerto Ricans to be represented on the bench, but the press was silent about the right of women to be included in that representation. It finally got to a point where it was more than I could bear, and I called atttention in the press to the serious omission that had been made by the press with respect to the right of women to be represented. Notwithstanding the fact that I wrote the New York papers and my letters were published, you will be interested to know that the 125 positions were filled as follows: 123 men and two women, one woman in the city of New York and the other outside the city of New York. Who was it who said before, "Where were you when I needed you?"

I would like to bring this comment up to date somewhat by recounting a conversation I had just yesterday with a representative of the Mayor's office in connection with some recent appointments made by the Mayor. Are any of you aware that seven judicial appointments were just made by the Mayor? They were not new positions but were a result of a reshuffling caused by creating new positions. One of these appointments went to a woman and, I am pleased to say, the woman was first vice-president of the Women's Bar Association during my presidency. In the course of my conversation with the Mayor's representative, we reviewed the Mayor's appointments since he took office. Our step-by-step tally came out to this grand total: two reappointments of women and two new appointments of women. His closing comment, put seriously, was: "We think the Mayor has treated the ladies very nicely." I'll let all of you decide whether the Mayor has treated us very nicely!

At one point in our conversation—and I am quoting it without identifying the individual involved—he said no one could accuse the Mayor of being an antifeminist. This was really a little more than I could take, so I said if this meant he liked women, well, women would return the compliment. But if this meant he had given women the recognition that their talents and abilities have qualified them for, I can only point to an item in the newspaper, dated February 18, 1970, about a group of women working in the city administration who sought an appointment with the Mayor. They had been promised an appointment with him, but they got Deputy Mayor Aurelio instead. In answer to their request that they be permitted to submit resumés of qualified women for responsible positions in the city government, he said that "no statement in response to their request would be forthcoming." These are exact quotes from the item.

MILNER: There is a certain degree of usefulness in documenting, as we have in the last few contributions, the extent of discrimination against women. It exists, and no one is denying it. The subsequent topics and roundtables of this workshop are expressions of that recognition. But I hope that the discussion does not continue along this line. Despite Miss Dell'Olio's feeling that it is impossible to project the future, the opportunity is here to try to—what shall I say?—take the positive approach. If we do not have some goals that we think are worth working toward, we develop a kind of nihilism that not only destroys us, it helps further to break down and destroy our society.

MEAD: Aren't you assuming that we want a world in which women can be as full persons as men?

MILNER: I am not proud of a woman who works on biochemical warfare just because it is a good-paying and high-status job. I'm not proud of what's-her-name—is it Wells?—who has made it on Madison Avenue, manipulating us in the mass media. None of you seems to care about the social impact of a position, just so long as women get their share of recognition. We have to live in this world, as anyone does. I am far more concerned about a world in which we can live constructive lives, not just that we have as much recognition as men, no matter what that recognition may represent.

MCLAUGHLIN: One of you repeated my words, "Where were you when I needed you?" I say even now, "Where are you? Where are we as women?" I am reminded of the quote from Pogo, "We have met the enemy and they are us." We have to recognize that the past is prologue. It was implied that women would be treated more fairly if there were more women judges. I was once a news reporter, and let me tell you that there were woman judges who meted out the same sentences that the male judges did, even when the law did not require it. I know a woman judge who said there was a difference between the alcoholic man and the alcoholic woman, and that it was a worse crime for the woman than it was for the man. In Massachusetts, with our Puritan tradition, we have a crime called "lewd and lascivious cohabitation." It is our worst, most condemned crime, short of murder. A man can receive up to five years for it, but a woman can receive an indeterminate sentence, which means until she is "rehabilitated." The one person who for 25 years stood between change of that law and its continuation in Massachusetts was a woman, Senator Leslie Cutler. The reason was that her husband had been carried off from her by a very attractive young nurse. This is the kind of thing we really have to face up to. We have to face the fact that we are among our own worst enemies, that the education of women has to change, and that the education of society has to change, very, very fundamentally.

FISHMAN: Doesn't that mean we should be considering that change is also necessary for the men in our society? If life-styles for women change, mustn't the men's life-styles also change?

MEAD: Both. I don't know whether some of the younger participants to this workshop would agree, however.

DELL'OLIO: This bothers me, all these double-binds that we are constantly being presented with. On the one hand, there seems to be a lot of doubt by some in this workshop that there really is discrimination against women, so that all of a sudden some are on the defensive and say that people in general are discriminated against. Then we hear that we should be looking for solutions, and that it is not a good idea to talk about how we are in uncharted territory. Then we went back to, "Let us not exclude the men." We are hearing how women will imitate the men, how there are female judges who will condemn women to longer sentences. This sort of thing has been happening since Hera and Zeus.

Enough already! It is our life. We have to get our education out of the control of men. So long as we are controlled by men, nothing is going to happen. We cannot plead with men, "Please find some other ways to fulfill your lives and get off our backs." There has not once been raised in this workshop the idea that there might be an inherent fallacy in interpersonal relationships based on needs, that there might be something sick and parasitical in this sort of thing. Perhaps society should feed and clothe us and provide work so that we can relate to each other in a different way than we do now. You may need someone when you are sick, for example, or have just had a baby. But just a need to be taken care of by someone else is parasitical.

I am sick to death of worrying about men. Men have oppossed us since we were born. If they are in control and if they are oppressed, let them start a male liberation movement. I am tired of constantly having to worry about men. Let them worry about themselves. They need us to prop up their egos. Even if they are sick and destructive to themselves, there is still some power gratification in them. We do not even have that.

UNIDENTIFIED SPEAKER: Miss Kamm, if Dr. Masters and Mrs. Johnson had heard your comments about the clitoral versus the vaginal orgasm or the comments on the same subject in the liberation-movement literature that I have seen, they would not have said they would write the next book in English. They would have at all costs written the last book in English. This kind of idea that you brought up with regard to sexuality—

KAMM: It was a question, really.

UNIDENTIFIED SPEAKER: O.K. The question of interpreting their work is not that there is a clitoral orgasm, but simply that there is stimulation, and an orgasm is an orgasm. I don't understand your reference in this context to heterosexual relationships.

KAMM: What I was questioning is that since people are relating sexuality to functions other than that of reproduction, and that sex is a mechanism of communication, wouldn't this shift the emphasis from complete heterosexuality to other forms of relating to people? Do we want to come to someone with a desperate desire, or is this desperate desire something that is bad to have? Do females want to relate to females? How do men want to relate to men? If part of the problem of men's relationships with women is that perhaps they do not like women, perhaps they see them as inferior and do not really enjoy being with them, then perhaps certain homosexual behavior we see today in our society may serve a compensating function.

OZER: There seems to be some dichotomy between some of the facts that have been referred to here. Some say freedom exists to a certain degree if you will only exert yourself. Others say, "But how *can* we exert ourselves?" I wonder, Dr. Mead, if you would comment on cultures in which freedom exists, but individuals are afraid to assert themselves because they have been taught not to? Then we can proceed to deal more sensibly with such individual variations on this theme as discrimination in jobs and the discrimination of being oppressed, of being kept down.

MEAD: What we are really talking about here is that in many cultures there is a possibility of reversal of role that very few people take advantage of. For example, in Bali there is no objection, actually, to a woman being a musician, but most women are not. And when the Balinese started to be modern painters, one woman started to paint the way she actually saw things, that is, in perspective. But everybody else was painting conventionally, and the men stopped her quite rapidly and told her perspective was wrong and got her back to the traditional style. If, at the time she started to paint in perspective, several other women had also started to do so, this might have been enlarged to a point where a whole new women's art might have emerged. So you are talking about the chinks in a particular social system. The pertinent question is: Are there chinks in the system that people can get through?

GILL: I would like to return to the issue of sexuality. America is the home of theoretical development in sociology. It is here that we find some of the most illuminating developments coming out of the area of deviance and how this relates to heterosexual activity. American investigators are finding that heterosexual activity is reciprocity and exchange—mutual exchange of sensuous relationships, of aspects of behavior that provide reciprocities and mutualities of a whole variety of types and conditions, extending from a purely sensuous exchange, ranging through to verbal communication at its highest level. It seems to me that this aspect of the interactionist perspective needs very much more careful analysis. We are already aware it is being written about.

Jessie Bernard reminds us that the sex game, or sex as a game, is something that we need to look at very much more carefully. We need to be aware of the indirect, nonverbal ways in which heterosexual activity is first mooted, how it gradually develops to greater degrees of intimacy, resulting finally in sexual exchange of various sorts. What part do these relationships play in the total social system, in the total area of social relationships? It seems to me that these questions are much more important to ask than whether the heterosexual relationship is facing any sort of instinctive opposition. Of course it is not. It is based on a situation that is determined by the cultural constraints we place on heterosexual behavior.

MEAD: You may not realize, Mr. Gill, how much the general position that was derivative of Freud has been popularized in this country. Freud's dictum that a woman does not have a vaginal orgasm and that in this she is somehow defective has been very heavily popularized. Nobody who knew anything thought it really was so, because we have had the contrary evidence of many, many cultures. But this statement of Freud's was heavily propagandized in this country, and so Dr. Masters was a great liberator, just as Robey and Havelock

Ellis and Freud were great imprisoners who thought they were Santa Claus, telling women what they ought to have.

KUNDSIN: I am associated with the Harvard Medical School. I wonder whether we realize how much women are under a man's influence. At Harvard, the male doctors do not respect their female peers; in other words, they do not give them comparable, equal-status positions. How then can they respect their women patients? I believe that a woman patient does not get the same understanding and care that a male patient does. If they do not respect women, it is impossible for me to conceive how they are going to take care of them. So I totally agree with the young woman who said that we are so imprisoned that we do not even think about these things.

Then I also think about our representation in the legislature. We do not have any women there—or so few that they are our token women. How can these few represent a woman's point of view? Another matter was just brought to my attention: I am working in the field of venereal disease. The case-worker at the hospital, a woman, told me about the many scholarly books that have been written about male homosexuals, but that no one has thought enough about female homosexuals to write a book about them; they are totally ignored.

MEAD: The State Department worries about them.

KUNDSIN: You said, let us look for the chinks. I am not going to look for chinks; I am tired of looking for chinks.

MEAD: I did not say "let us." I was responding to Dr. Ozer's question about available opportunities. As I see it, we have to have enough expressions of emotion to be sure that we understand the different currents in society by age and by occupation and so on.

MILNER: We have to move beyond this.

MEAD: But we have to begin, if possible, to define the situation that we are working with in terms of the future, as several of you have mentioned, and work toward some kind of a better world. If you want to have one of these idealistic statements that women are going to be better than men, all right; but I think you should be planning to go further, to go somewhere, and at present we are not going anywhere that I can see.

DUNBAR: I want to make a couple of points. One is about this assumption on the part of many people that men are persons and that women want to become persons like men are already. I do not agree with this. What I am talking about is creating a new human being. In comparing the present state of male and female in the world, and particularly in our own society, the female is the better model for the future than the male. You have to differentiate between present reality and actual consciousness. I think the consciousness of the female, the consciousness of the black person, and the consciousness of the oppressed peoples of the world make all these people the better models.

It so happens that white American males, particularly of the upper class, have the position of the oppressor over the vast majority of other people. This is a role that destroys. For these men to re-do themselves will probably require psychiatry; they are a mess. But I am interested in masses of people, not individual psychology. I agree with Dr. Milner in that I do not want to see women simply accept the male model. We have to go beyond that and develop a new model; we have to talk about female consciousness.

I do not like us to talk about getting child-care centers to get rid of women, because one of the greatest things that should be conditioned into women, and men as well, is something called maternal love. Maternal love should be a generalized trait, not reserved only for one's own child. Women simply are more like that than men are. I see a woman, I feel comfortable; when I see a man, I feel tense. That is a personal reaction, I know, but it has to do with the fact that men may kill me; I don't get attacked on the streets by women very often.

MEAD: They are doing it all over New York. Women are attacking other women on the streets, in case you are interested.

MILNER: In what way?

MEAD: Spitting at people and throwing things at other women in supermarkets.

DUNBAR: This is an instance of women incorporating a masculine model. It is not a widespread phenomenon. I agree to this extent: In the middle and upper classes during the 1950s, some mothers tried to give their daughters freedom from the things that oppressed them. So they did not train them to do housework or to give them the values or the ability to make it in the men's world. They left their daughters with nothing.

MEAD: I am now very wary of saying this is the first time in history for something—but it *is* the first time in history, so far as I know, in which we have let educated men near babies. Heretofore we have had dozens of intermediaries, eunuchs, grandmothers, servants, and so on. Right through history, with women being the breast feeders and therefore having more contact with the babies, both men and women have been brought up by women initially. But in the last 20 or 25 years we have been letting men also take care of babies. This has meant that at least some of today's women and men have had close cherishing care from both sexes. We now have the possibility of both men and women being brought up by both men and women, which would make a very major change in the world if it were spread around far enough. This, as I understand it, is something some of you would approve of, but you, Miss Dunbar, would not—is that right?

DUNBAR: You are right. Change has to be on a wide scale within a social revolutionary process. I don't think just having men share in the private care of children will do it, at least not in the nuclear family, where parents have the right to own their children. I do not want men to have that right. I am talking about transforming the values I spoke of into social values on a social scale, not the further privatizing of the situation. I think this will require, first of all, a total change in the economic basis of this society. I do not think there is any way to patch up the society as it is. Right now, we have a choice, but the ruling class is not really ruling. It is running on borrowed time, and ashes is where it is taking us.

Unless you see the situation in this larger context, in fact, in the international context, we can't get anywhere. Look at China, for example, the largest populated country in the world, one-third of humanity. It is so far advanced beyond where we are; they are looking toward a new humankind, a new social relation, things we have not begun to think about. We have so much to learn from them.

MEAD: I do not know just which phase of China over the last 25 years that you are speaking about. Women have been in and out of the home several times.

EPSTEIN: We do not know anything about what is going on in China. I doubt if you have data on family-interaction patterns of the kind we would need to have.

DUNBAR: There are some very good things—Fanshen, for example.

EPSTEIN: Fanshen was done in 1947. It was just recently reissued in paperback.

DUNBAR: With a revision.

EPSTEIN: It was revised only in the sense that the printer reprinted it. Even if you take Jan Myrdal's material—he went to only one village—it is interestingly anecdotal, but it does not give you a real taste of what is happening among 700 million people. We do know as sociologists that the worst oppressors are people in the lower social classes. The people most against the liberation of women are, typically, the uneducated.

DUNBAR: You mean oppressors of women?

EPSTEIN: Yes. You get the worst kind of behavior in terms of physical aggression in the lower classes. In fact, for every class level, the chief amount of aggression is at the lower part of that level. We also know that lower-class mothers are more likely to hurt their children, reflecting not that beautiful quality of sensitivity of warmth you seek. I do not think we are going to find good models in the lower strata of society; I wish we could.

DUNBAR: I was speaking of consciousness, not behavior. I said people have to behave as they do now because of economic and social pressures on them.

EPSTEIN: "Consciousness" is an empty term; it is not a fruitful concept. If you can discuss it in some way that really opens our eyes, I for one would like to see it.

DUNBAR: How do you explain the black revolution going on now?

MEAD: One of the things that is well worth considering is what happened to women in the Russian revolution. Before the revolution, there was a great deal of emphasis on women's full participation. After the revolution, when peasants became increasingly important, women were given less of a role in Russia. On the whole, emancipation of women throughout history has come when women were in a superior and privileged position and not the other way around.

HEIDE: That is true of all revolutions. Revolutions do not originate as proletarian revolutions; they originate among the bourgeoisie.

NORTH: I am a part-time journalist and public-relations writer. I felt terrible when Dr. Epstein said that the worst oppression was in the lower-class family, and I feel obligated to stand up to say something about that. As someone said earlier, one-third of the poverty families are headed by women. Lower-class women are the most liberated of our women, mainly because they have to live without a man and make their own way.

EPSTEIN: I said most child assaults occurred among lower-class families in the statistical sense. I did not say that all lower-class women assault their children.

NORTH: Statistics can be used in a damaging way; the statement was derogatory. But if you want to talk about damaged children, you should also talk about damaged psyches or personalities.

Also, when we talk about oppression of women, we get into a lot of self-pity. We've had a recounting of the Book of Horrors; that sort of thing is demoralizing. We should address ourselves to the direction in which we have to move. Despite the opinions of some, I do not think this direction is against men. If we are going to free anybody, we have to free both of us. We have to evolve some kind of program for women that is also going to free the men from that oppression; otherwise we will never get anywhere. I found from this discussion that we are what men have made us; we are what our men are. There is a world out there where men themselves are not free, and we are not going to be any freer than they are; let us not kid ourselves. So if we are going to address ourselves to freeing women, we address ourselves as part of whatever overall freedom-movements there are going to be; there cannot be a separate program for women and a separate program for men. Women have the vote. We are part of a peace program. We do not go to war, true. But if we want to organize as women, we organize with the same goals that are going to make men freer and give greater economic freedom to our families as well.

HEIDE: Miss Dunbar, we have opposite positions on this matter of child rearing. Although I have not got great expectations for men, I don't feel too hot about women either. Something I would like to see come out of this workshop would be a resolution by this group to the effect that men and women should indeed share in the raising of children, especially when the cybernetic revolution frees us to work only part-time. I don't think parents should own children just because they can have them; I happen to believe in communal care for children. I think the best qualities of humanity are androgenous, so that male and female should equally raise children without their identifying with any of the older, sex-limited models. As long as only the women bring up children, child rearing is going to be a down-graded situation. Despite my pessimism about the parental adequacy of both men and women, some suggestions in this direction should be made by sociologists. When we try to do it in the women's liberation movement, men say, "You want to castrate us." They do not want to help raise the children—that is women's work, meaning that it is degrading. So the feminists are put in a bind. When we make positive suggestions, the men say we are castrating them; when we do not, then we are accused of not making any positive suggestions. One of the reasons that there has not been a great deal coming out of these discussions is that the feminists feel rather inhibited about making any positive suggestions.

MEAD: We are going to have to be very careful not to downgrade women's work while we are making these statements.

HEIDE: I do not downgrade it, the men do. The only time they talk about how great it is to be a mother is when they are trying to convince you that you should stay in the home.

OLESEN: In support of Dr. Epstein, the studies of prejudice show that one of the seedbeds of prejudice in our society is the lower-middle class; it is the hotbed for fascism, if you will.

The point I really want to develop spins off from Dr. Milner's earlier attempt to get us on to the future, and also from something Dr. Mead said about the levels of difficulties that come out of the catalogue of woes that have been recited here. The implication in everyone's comments is very strong that if these things are to be achieved, the golden doors next year of the New Jerusalem will really be in Jerusalem. I am not going to question that very strong assumption, but I do think we need to think about the kinds of assumptions we have been making here.

We also need to play around with the sort of society we want. Is it a society in which we have rotating husbands and wives? Or is it a society in which we have the Mormon style of marriage? Or is it a society in which we have a national service corps so as to keep everybody out of bed and in the potato fields until a certain time of life? We need to move on to this kind of playful projecting about the society of the future. Most of our discourse is focused on the individual, but I would like to see us generate some wild, far-out ideas about the societal level, at least as a beginning.

FAVA: I am a sociologist. I thought that this was what we were here for, and not necessarily in a playful spirit—to deal with the matter of the two-child family and its relationship to the life-styles of women. I don't think we have dealt with it yet. It seems to me what we are here for is a professional aim, and I have been disappointed because I have not seen very much of it. You can see a psychiatrist for a personal catharsis. If we want to deal with the topic that we are presumably dealing with, let us get down to cases. Our discussion thus far has been on an awfully low level, the sort heard at a cocktail party or down in the laundry room. If we are concerned with the cause of women and the cause of society, we will not do ourselves any service by this kind of intellectual charade. All of this has been a kind of intellectual prologue to the dance; let us get to the dance.

FISHMAN: May I ask, in keeping with Dr. Fava's comments, by whom the children are going to be cared for in our society, and what options can we identify for our young people as to their goals and purposes?

ROLLIN: I would like to suggest that we might start our brainstorming with the assumption that the only thing that no woman can do, so far as I know, is to be a sperm donor, and the only thing that no man can do, so far as I know, is to be the incubator of the human embryo or to be a wet nurse. I am not trying to be facetious. I would not want to go along with providing models for our youth; they are trying to develop their own models. With that kind of basic assumption as a start, can we address ourselves to this task in terms of what kinds of models are possible, and not be too constrained by the models we have known?

KEIFFER: I am a social-psychologist. I would like to ask this group what it conceives to be a "free choice" society. *Can* there be a society in which there is free choice to be anything you want? If everybody had free choice, maybe everyone would want to be the same thing.

MEAD: But that would be free choice.

KEIFFER: But would it be a society? Isn't there something about society that precludes free choice?

MEAD: We have enormous degrees of free choice today, fantastic degrees of free choice compared with any other society in the world.

WAXENBERG: I think we have come to the point where each person here ought to look at his and her own life and career and remark on the possibility that there has been a great deal of free choice in it. Can we think about how we want to go on exercising that? And how do we want to help other people, particularly young people in the educational system, get the idea that that system has actually got a lot of degrees of freedom in it?

KAMM: First, I think it is wrong to say that this discussion has been catharsis and that we should go to psychiatrists. People have been giving examples of social problems and not of individual difficulties, even though they have chosen to speak in individual terms.

Second, with respect to the notion of free choice, children should not be brought up to believe that simply because their sex organs are different, they are going to have to choose different life-styles. That is the only point that has to be made at this stage.

Of course there are certain things society needs, and we are going to choose individuals to spend their whole lives doing these things. This idea of specialization is very prevalent, and especially with respect to certain good things that we want to do and that take a long time in doing. The idea of certain functions that we can all benefit from by sharing, such as Roxane Dunbar brought out, is good, that is, the mother-care function. But what disturbed me in the Ruderman paper was the idea that we can never recognize our innate natures if we are not conditioned into them at a very early age. If these characteristics are innate, why do we need conditioning? Even if there are hormonal differences, is it societally functional to start modeling a very young child according to the hormonal value she is going to have 20 years later? What about the young female's abilities as a human being at that early point?

Third, with respect to the relation between men and women and women and women. The relations between women and women have to be looked into, especially in our society. A tremendous number of young women are going to resist any sort of sex-role change because they are bound up with men at this point in their lives. There is an insecurity in dealing with other women because of the idea of competing for men. There is also the element of sexuality, the element of security—the economic base of the family. If we are looking at mechanisms for change, we have to concentrate more on how women relate to other women.

The feminine role has not been analyzed sufficiently with respect to the sort of defense mechanisms that the woman uses to protect herself against the outside world. The lesbian phenomenon might be interpreted as a political reaction; how is it that some women admire other women more than they admire a superior male in our society? I am not recommending that we become lesbians; I am just saying that we need to look at these phenomena.

COMBS: I do not want to take on the whole women's liberation movement, but I think that in asking questions about what direction we are going to move, and how we are going to bring about this change, we have to have some idea about the nature of a society and how it moves and what process is going on. We might very well ask who is going to implement the blueprint that anybody draws up.

There has been a lot said about the man's world and that men make the world. Most men in our society are reared by women, up to a mature age as a matter of fact. Our personalities are fashioned by our mothers. If we come up with hatred toward women, sometimes I think it is displaced hatred of the mother and her disciplinary role. Men and women participate in the making of their institutions; and if the functionalism theory of society is correct, they get a maximum number of rewards through this joint participation.

There is no question that cultures follow their own development, and that at certain times we come to a point where the social arrangements designed to solve the problems of the past are dysfunctional for the present. It has already been pointed out that when revolutions occur, the changes that come at the top peter out after a while because individuals, in pursuing their own lifestyles and maximizing their rewards, work out their relationships and come to some agreement. It is all of us who participate in this process, and we cannot pass blame, except in a revolutionary sense, on the leaders of society. Societies grow democratically by one method or another, and we live in a society which has, it seems to me, probably the maximum resources to move things in a democratic way.

MEAD: We have been letting men into the feminine positions as we have been letting women into the previously masculine positions. I do not think most people would disagree that this is one of the things we are moving toward.

DELL'OLIO: Where do you see it?

MEAD: Men taking care of children? All over this country for the last 25 years, men have been taking care of children every night and weekends. They have given up chances at promotions, they have given up a good proportion of their professional work, because they were home in the suburbs taking care of children.

L. NEWMAN: May I also say that young boys often are baby-sitters now?

JECH: We have forgotten the larger social setting. Free choice—did I hear free choice? Most professional women are non-married or have been married and divorced. They have to be single, because it is extremely difficult to do justice to both a career and to homemaking. So where is the free choice when we look at society, at the reality-picture at the present time? Just because there are exceptions and there are some males who are baby-sitters and some males who have love for children or who are saying, "I have been deprived of fatherhood; let me have it at least on Sunday afternoons," that is not to say that we are institutionalizing any kind of change. Children by the age of five have had not mothers or fathers, but 80,000 hours of television. As for technological unemployment, females are at present technologically unemployed. They can be economically introduced only if the entire system were changed, economically and politically.

Another perspective is, where is the power? Even if we convene this workshop at The New York Academy of Sciences, do we have any real power? Did someone say we have the power to vote? What power does that represent today? I understand that Eugene McCarthy was given a majority, but he did not win the election. We know that, at least in principle, the majority of the people do not agree with the war in Viet Nam. Regardless, it still goes on. We should go back to Nancy Reeves' paper about the technology that has gotten far away from the control of human beings. The cybernetic revolution is here. We could restructure it, but not one of us has the power to do so. We have kindergarten and elementary schools where, at a very tender age, children are divided into a male and a female line. One is told to be aggressive and the other dependent. And this pattern is enforced every day through all kinds of mass media. How can we say, let us have free choice, when the patterns of choice are only one of two, sexuality or being real people? Or even the need for cooperation: we are not a cooperative society. I am talking about ego; even each of us has to get up and express her ego.

REEVES: Are we perhaps committing a logical fallacy in discussing women as a single category? There are more differences between women of different races, different countries, different historical periods, different economic brackets, than between men and women of comparable countries, historical periods, *et cetera.* So we start talking about women and then we talk about women models, and each of us has a picture in his or her head. But that picture is not generality. If you are talking about people on Riverside Drive on Sunday, you may not necessarily be talking about coal miners on Sunday and you may not be talking about the Kennedys on Sundays. There are all kinds of gradations to this concept of women, this concept of men.

I wonder whether we should just stop talking of the roles as bisected, the hemisphere of the orb of the world fitting into two hemispheres based on the most obvious physiological differences that were evident to our ancestors. We are at the age of genetic engineering. I wonder whether, in addressing ourselves to the potential models, we might just think that this particular one, the sex dichotomy, is today irrelevant.

MEAD: We might even concentrate on thinking about the children and how these children are going to be brought up. We would still be rather feminine if we took the trouble to think about the children. One of the things that disturbs me about this situation is that it is so focused on one particular group called "women," and a rather small number of them at that, at a period in history when the problems are so urgent.

If we were to shift our focus and ask, "How are we going to bring up the smaller number of children?" this would have all sorts of implications. Women will not have to spend so much time on reproductivity; men won't have to spend so much time supporting reproductivity; society will be able to accord more freedom to both sexes to do a variety of things. But to repeat, let us ask, "How are children who are going to be the next generation going to be brought up? How are we going to protect them and care for them?" Might this possibly be the most feminine and universal thing we could think about?

Part III: Impediments to Women's Development of New Self-Definitions and Life-Styles

POSITION PAPER ON CULTURAL AND PSYCHOLOGICAL IMPEDIMENTS: ARE MENTAL HEALTH PRACTITIONERS CONTRIBUTING TO THE PROBLEM?

Wilma Scott Heide, M.A.

American Institutes for Research
Pittsburgh, Pa.

Clinical standards of mental health reflect stereotypic sex-role expectations of the larger culture so that women are judged to be mentally healthy if they are more submissive, more easily influenced, more easily hurt, less independent, adventurous, competitive and objective than healthy men. Women who conform to this immature standard are eupheuristically considered "feminine." To aspire to the ideal maturity of sex-unspecified traits of an achievement-oriented democracy not based on ascribed sex roles, the female who develops her fully human potential risks the labels of "masculine" or "deviant." Relatively few women perceive this reality and manage to finesse the expectations; most don't.

The statistics on mental illness are fascinating but do not tease out the incidence and prevalence of women and men who agonize through to some adjustment to historical and therapeutic sex-role expectations regardless of their incompatibility with individual needs and potentials. Adjustment to the status quo does not reveal to the diagnostician and practitioner the enormous price of the double standard. A single human standard that values all traits that make one functionally self-confident, independent, caring, growing, *et al.* seems an ideal mental health goal that needs to be made realistically attainable.

The challenge to mental health practitioners is to make the ideal a reality. An examination of cultural values and our androcentric language itself reveals that the words female, woman, and she are derivative words for people who are *not* derivative. Rather recent, though little-known, research reveals that the primal human embryo up to six weeks is female, not male, which has implications for the enormously pervasive Adam's Rib mythology. Practitioners are challenged to hang up their socially learned sex "hang-ups." Relevant traits of true maleness and femaleness will prevail as in other animals. Frustrated human potential in the search for "femininity" and "masculinity" may be a significant component in the etiology of mental illness. Mental health researchers, practitioners, and educators are urged to relate to clients in terms of ideal personhood, which transcends gender.

The reality is that the television commercial, "You've come a long way, *Baby*," provokes no national outrage at the symbolic reference to adult women in language appropriate to an immature organism. The problem is that immaturity is expected of women. Mental healthers are challenged to cease being part of the problem and instead become part of the solution. Women *are* people.

POSITION PAPER ON STRUCTURAL/INSTITUTIONAL IMPEDIMENTS

Roxane Dunbar

Southern Female Rights Union
New Orleans, La.

The November 21, 1969, issue of *Time* reported:

> Although 51% of Americans are female, women face many of the problems of a minority. Only 1% of the nation's engineers are women, 3% of its lawyers, 7% of its doctors. For the same jobs, women's pay is often less than half that of men, and nearly 1/5 of employed women with a B.A. have jobs in such categories as clerks, factory workers and cooks. Moreover, the status of American women is, in many ways, deteriorating.
>
> Median wages and salaries of fully employed men were $4713 in 1957, compared with $3008 for women. In 1968, men's income had risen to about $7800, or 65%, while women's had gone up to 4550, or 51%. The gap is widening.
>
> In the past ten years women have lost 50 seats in state legislatures. Margaret Chase Smith is the lone woman in the U.S. Senate, and there are only ten Congresswomen, compared with 17 in 1960.

TABLES 1 and 2 show the United States Department of Commerce, Bureau of Census, reports of comparative statistics for men and women in the labor force as of 1960. Men often ask, scornfully, why women don't get out of the house and go to work. The statistics shown tell part of the story why. TABLES 1 and 2 do not list other job categories to which women are relegated, such as prostitution, playbunnies, go-go girls, and marriage. No statistics are given for the poor subsistence that women are given for their jobs as housewives and mothers.

TABLE 1

COMPARATIVE STATISTICS FOR MEN AND WOMEN IN THE LABOR FORCE, 1960 *

Occupation	Percentage of Working Women (%)	Annual Income ($)		No. of Workers (Millions)	
		Female	Male	Female	Male
Professional	13	4,358	7,115	3	5
Managers, officials, and proprietors	5	3,514	7,241	1	5
Clerical	31	3,586	5,247	7	3
Factory workers	15	2,970	4,977	4	9
Sales	7	2,389	5,842	2	3
Service	15	2,340	4,089	3	3
Private household	10	1,156	—	2	—

* United States Department of Commerce, Bureau of Census.

The division of labor and resources by sex constitutes a system of *sexism,* which is the oldest form of institutionalized oppression. The roots of sexism have long been obscured by the dialectics of history. Different races and nationalities have been oppressed for centuries at a time, continuing into the present day, but the subjugation of the female sex by the male has gone on for thousands of years. Time and the dialectical interactions of civilization have served to hide the caste oppression of females by means of ancient traditions, refined and modified, or exaggerated and rigidified.

TABLE 2

MEDIAN ANNUAL WAGES BY SEX AND RACE

Workers	Annual Wage ($)
White males	5,137
Non-white males	3,075
White females	2,537
Non-white females	1,276

Sexism can not be revealed by any superficial or traditional examination of society. To understand sexism, we must reexamine the foundations of civilization. To destroy sexism, we must fight, as females, separately and collectively, for the unity of humankind. We must change attitudes and material conditions.

DISCUSSION

Melvin Tumin, Ph.D., *Moderator*

Biologically Rooted Impediments

McLaughlin: I am the Public Relations Director of the Massachusetts Eye and Ear Infirmary in Boston and I am a medical writer. Our roundtable first considered the age-old question of basic hormonal differences between men and women, to see whether or not these were truly fundamental sexual differences and whether or not they were a genuine impediment. The hormone androgen occurs naturally in both males and females. Dr. Waxenberg reviewed some of his research for us, in which this sex hormone has been identified as responsible for the phenomena of sexual arousal and orgasm in both men and women. Androgen has been popularly identified as a male hormone because it is present in larger quantities in men. However, he said, and we generally agreed, that behavioral differences as a result of differences in male-female hormones are not real, in that they do not constitute any meaningful expression of basic sex differences—and that this circumstance needs to be more broadly communicated. We also examined the question of who is biologically sexier, males or females, and rather quickly agreed that this was really a dead issue. The sexual-arousal potential is equal in both men and women, it was agreed, although differences may still obtain in frequency of sex contact, which is probably due more to social than to biological factors. Dr. Garai stressed that men are primarily genitally involved in sexual relations, but for women sex is a generally more widespread, whole-body type of response.

We also talked about sex assignment, and what the biological roots of that are. Dr. Waxenberg brought out that if children are mislabeled because of undescended testes or other reasons, their psychological, or rather psychosexual, development is not reversible after 18 months of age. In this general catchall of sex-assignment, other matters were brought up. One was the issue: What are the naturally innate characteristics of men and women? Dr. Gardner described some of her own research, which showed that male rats have, under certain experimental conditions, a strong parental-nurturing characteristic. In this research, colonies of young male rats were given injections of testosterone. It was found—and this result is reproducible—that 15% of these rats will, under the influence of testosterone, retrieve rat pups, build nests, and care for the pups; and that as the level of testosterone declines, they revert to the pre-testosterone type of behavior.

Pregnancy was identified as a biological impediment only in the sense of an unexpected or unwanted pregnancy. It was felt that with improved and more reliable contraceptives and their more widespread use, pregnancy need no longer be considered an impediment. There is a remaining obstacle, however, in that the physical changes that occur during pregnancy are still not accepted institutionally. For example, women, particularly teachers, often have to leave their jobs when their pregnant state becomes noticeable.

Menstruation was discussed as a biological impediment. Menstrual difficulties remain the major cause of absenteeism at school and at work. We considered whether menstruation is really natural or not, that is, whether it is a biological necessity. Work done by Dr. Charles Flowers of Chapel Hill was referred to in this context. He has put about 300 women on the pill, but on dosages that do not permit breakthrough bleeding. As a result, these women menstruate only once a year. He has gone into the possible background of this phenomenon, noting that in tribal societies women do not menstruate very often during the child-bearing years because they are either pregnant or lactating. He sees the monthly menstrual cycle as a product of advanced civilization. We decided that this whole question, whether menstruation is biologically natural or unnatural, should be further explored by research.

We barely touched on two questions, whether physical strength is somewhat less in women and whether or not that is a biological impediment. Without going into this subject in depth, we felt that what the female might lack in bodily size or strength she made up for in muscle fineness or dexterity. Nor did we explore in depth whether or not there are certain psychological factors that are innately characteristic of women, such as the often-voiced opinion that women are by nature more emotional and less stable.

Finally, we turned to the question of who owns the baby. The woman has the closer biological relationship with the fetus. Does this constitute an adequate basis for possession? What is the biological legacy here? Our final, overall view was that matters that have been traditionally considered biological impediments are not truly so, that these faded as they were explored, that they are really wrapped up in mythology and not in fact. But we conceded that the real biological differences between males and females are not clear, and that a great deal more research is needed in all aspects of female functions, physiological as well as psychological. We concluded that research into female functions was probably the most neglected area of research thus far considered at this workshop.

GARDNER: May I give further information on maternal behavior in normal male rats? This was accomplished in a small proportion of the total sample by delivering minute amounts of testosterone directly to the medial or lateral preoptic area. When this dosage was delivered appropriately to the right place in the brain, male rats displayed all the components of maternal behavior that they were capable of displaying. These were fully developed rats, and had had a normal life history as males. What was expected as a result of this direct brain stimulation was that they would mate more readily, but what developed was that they took care of baby rats instead of eating them.

TUMIN: Does that suggest that the male rat is normally a cannibal, unlike the female?

GARDNER: If not chemically interfered with, male rats have a greater tendency to eat baby rats than to place them in a nest or to build a nest around them.

EAST: The Public Health Service does a yearly survey on time lost from work because of illness. They find it is 5.6 days a year for women. For men, 5.4 days is the average. The average for women includes time lost because of childbirth, complications of pregnancy, menstruation, or anything else.

MCLAUGHLIN: I did not want to suggest that menstruation was causing women to be absent from work more than men are absent from work, but only to identify this as a major cause of absenteeism, and therefore as a subject that is worthy of a great deal more research. How do you account for the consistent finding of certain industrial surveys, such as that of the telephone company, that menstruation is a factor in absenteeism?

EAST: Maybe their problem is one of boring jobs, and the boredom contributes to this pattern of absenteeism.

MCLAUGHLIN: I still think the issue needs a lot more study.

TUMIN: I am sure the males participating in this workshop have a wonderful piece of serendipity to bring home. Having heretofore permitted my wife certain indulgences 12 times a year, I can now go home and say to her she is entitled to one only once a year, because it isn't necessary.

DELL'OLIO: I would like to recommend that a particular research study be done on the degree to which menstruation does indeed contribute to absenteeism from work. Studies might be conducted among the female armed forces over a period of 30 or 40 years. Training films I have seen have a very directive attitude toward female indulgence in this area, and the incidence of any kind of absenteeism in the women's armed forces is practically nil. So it would be interesting to discover exactly what the results are in those situations where there is high motivation not to be absent.

MCLAUGHLIN: Several studies have shown that premenstrual changes in fluid balance and so forth do play a role that is detrimental to the efficiency of the female. Studies have demonstrated that a woman does less well in tests if she takes them at the time of the premenstrual phase of the cycle, that there are certain emotional changes, and that depression is quite common during the premenstrual phase as a result of high levels of progesterone. I know that in France, for example, if a woman commits a homicide during the three days prior to menstruation, it is automatically considered second, rather than first, degree murder. It is a significant phenomenon and should be much more thoroughly studied.

POLGAR: The group that just reported apparently considered only unwanted pregnancy to be a biologically abnormal state. I have a student, a male physician, an epidemiologist, who is writing a treatise on the subject of pregnancy that departs from the premise that even wanted pregnancy is an abnormal state. That is, he considers pregnancy, any pregnancy, to be a pathological state, physiologically.

UNIDENTIFIED SPEAKER: Is it really pathological?

POLGAR: It is pathological in the sense that changes in fluid balance, and all these other things which are not ordinarily normal, occur. He objects to the circumstance that all the textbooks of obstetrics treat pregnancy, if it is uneventful, as a normal alteration of female physiology. He says the alteration is not normal from the physiological, the epidemiological, and even the sociological points of view.

CULTURAL AND PSYCHOLOGICAL IMPEDIMENTS

MCMURRAY: If we assume that there are certain impediments to the development of women, then we first have to define the goal toward which we should be striving. Our roundtable decided we should be trying to achieve a humane society in which each person is treated as a human being; treated equally and in terms of his or her own individuality. Each person should be responded to in a loving manner; there should be mutual respect and understanding of one's own and others' needs. We recognized that there would have to be changes in the roles of men as well as women in this kind of society. Also, women must be productive units in such a society and now most are not.

Moving from that frame of reference, we began to look at the kind of society we now live in. In this area, there was some general agreement around the main thrust, but some disagreement around specific issues. For instance, it was agreed that the society we now live in is dysfunctional, that it is based on a highly diversified division of labor and is exploitative, that it has a discriminatory system of rewards and punishments based on one's role in this highly structured situation, that in this context women are exploited, as are people who belong to minority groups, as are people who may be young or who may be old, and that this society is, as one participant put it, "based upon a male-supremacy concept, in which the white male is the patriarch, and every other person in the society must be subservient to him."

In this society, there are expectations of what a woman should be, socially and sexually. These expectations impose on many women a role they would not otherwise choose or accept. Many individual parents try to keep from imposing sex-stereotyped personalities on their children, but cultural patterns of socialization work against them, and these sex-delimited patterns become ingrained. We must realize that these impediments are culturally imposed. It has been found that the critical period in the death of high aspirations in girls comes in adolescence. Their aspirations are downgraded, in part, because of their attachments to the opposite sex and as a result of the cultural stereotype that since the male is the breadwinner she must subjugate her desires to his. In part, this also has to do with the fear of pregnancy, forcing girls into early marriages.

We recognized, however, that there are women who are able, in spite of this kind of socialization process, to achieve a sense of their own humanity and individuality. One participant termed this type of person as a deviant in terms of the kinds of goals our society sets. There was a research suggestion that we take a look at deviance in that context, that is, at the kind of woman who pursues a professional career and attempts to achieve, on the basis of her own recognition of her worth rather than what our society says she is worth. What kinds of input has she had and does she have in her life to make her the kind of person she is? Might we also use this particular situation as a basis for getting ideas about the kinds of strategies that are necessary to move deviancy to becoming more socially acceptable, to become, that is, the main thrust in the society, rather than deviant?

We also need to develop a body of knowledge about the history of sex relations, as well as a history of intrafamily relationships, especially with respect to the role of the male, of the female, of the parent, and of the relationships between parent and child. And, to achieve the humane society that is our goal, we need to attack not only the psychological and cultural impediments to woman's development, but we also have to work for change in the man's role *vis à vis* women and society.

The question about the kinds of strategies necessary to bring about the kind of society we want was then raised. It was in this context that we took a critical look at the feminist movement—or perhaps we should call it the neo-feminist movement. Some participants felt that todays' feminists were really engaging in a battle of the sexes. After some consideration of that charge, we came to accept that the contemporary feminist movement was trying to draw attention, through the use of confrontation, to some of the more subtle discrimination that goes on in this society. It was felt that these confrontation techniques were genuinely necessary as a means of helping women, as well as men, understand what is actually going on, and what kinds of changes need to be made.

Finally, several topics were suggested for research in this general area. I present them in summarized form: What is the effect on the female ego of living in a male-supremacist society? What are the pressures on adolescents with respect to sex-role ideals? How is the young male affected by stereotypic sex differentials? What is the process of individual development among women who pursue professional careers as an apparent matter of course?

MILLETT: I'd like to elaborate on two points that were insufficiently stressed. Concerning the effects on the female ego of living in a male-supremacist society, just how damaging to the female ego is this situation? As for the impact on adolescents of our ways of socializing male and females into their roles, does this process cause stress and conflict that does not result in better adaptation, but actually amount to the oppression of people? What kind of permanent damage is done to the personality by these pressures?

I also suggested a theoretical framework that was completely omitted from the report. We should look at the situation of the sexes as related to a patriarchal political system in which males dominate all avenues of power. This dominance, this differential status and role, is effected from earliest childhood on through the socialization process. We cannot discuss the relationship between the sexes knowledgeably until we arrive at a theoretical understanding of racism or colonialism as an additional manifestation of male supremacy—to understand that all these things are interrelated.

EAST: Another point was made that I think should not be lost. There is a double standard of mental health among mental-health practitioners. While the leaders in the field have, no doubt, abandoned this type of thinking, the practicing clinicians and those who write for the popular press have not. They put forth a standard of mental health for males that would be considered mature for human beings. But the standard they promulgate for women is immature; it would be considered immature for the male to behave in these ways.

STRUCTURAL/INSTITUTIONAL IMPEDIMENTS

GILL: Our roundtable focused its attention on three situations. The first area that we examined was child-care institutions, mainly confining our attention to the situation in the United States. We agreed that there is a dearth of child-care facilities for both lower- and upper-income groups. This situation was particularly true, it was suggested, for middle-income women. When we broke down day-care nursery facilities by age-range, using birth to two years and two to five years and over, we concluded that for all income levels, services for the child between birth and two years were hopelessly inadequate. However, some alternative surrogate parents associated with extended family patterns were available, particularly in lower-income groups.

It was recommended at this point that *both* parents share the responsibility for the provision of child care, therefore enabling both to go out to work if they so wished. In this connection, it was suggested that when a man applies for a job, he should be asked how many children's care he is responsible for; this procedure should be institutionalized. Without such a provision, the current situation, where only the woman is responsible for child care, would be perpetuated.

We then attempted to define some research projects in this area. Out of a very diffuse discussion, three such projects emerged:

1. The suggestion was made to utilize school-strike situations for research purposes. What happened during the recent school strike in New York City among families where both parents are normally at work away from the home? Anecdotal evidence was given of children being brought into office situations and of the whole range of difficulties created by this emergency.

2. It was mentioned that under the Lanham Act during World War II in the United States, nursery-school facilities were set up in various urban communities. It was suggested that interviews might be conducted with women who had used such facilities, to investigate their opinions of how effective, or otherwise, these services were.

3. Professor Nag questioned the apparent assumption that no alternative child-care arrangements are currently available in the United States. He noted that in other societies there are such common familial arrangements as care of children by grandparents. Might not this pattern be promoted in the United States as well? Should not a study be done on this possibility?

The group then moved on to consider what we described as time-space and allocation of facilities in familial situations. Provision of services in the total social system, it was stated, are arranged on the assumption that a woman, or at least somebody, will be permanently present in the house during the day. Repairmen, for instance, expect to find somebody at home when they are called on for service or repairs. This implicit assumption was seen as a further impediment to women's self-realization. In Sweden, a system has been introduced in which women, usually above the age of 35, are trained to go into homes to handle various emergency situations; this arrangement is somewhat analogous to the system of "home helps" provided in the United Kingdom.

Discussion then turned to the real problems posed by urban geography. In American urban life, the locations of occupation, home, school, and shopping all tend to be separately located, and often very far apart. This pattern again necessitates some sort of permanent household figure. We again referred to the Swedish situation, where people associated with a particular factory stand in for employees so that their women workers are able to take time off during the normal workday to purchase groceries and to do other home-related errands that they would otherwise have to make a special allocation of time for, either within or without the workday.

Next, we examined the problem of patterns of sexual behavior. Are there impediments to women's self-realization because of culturally accepted patterns of sexual behavior? Despite the contraceptive revolution, it was suggested, there has been no real examination of sexual roles and sexual socialization. Dating is still male-dominated, and other norms and regulations surrounding sexual behavior continue to be based on concepts that are now irrelevant. Women are still treated as sexual objects; little attention has been directed toward sex as a communication mechanism.

Finally, it was argued that the status and position of women should not, and in a sense cannot, be discussed in isolation from the rest of the social system. This issue is a socio-structural problem that affects all other elements in the social structure, so that, again, as a research possibility, much more effort needs to be directed at the examination of female sexual and sex-role socialization in the early years of life. The restrictive life-styles and life-chances characteristic of the position of women today are implanted at this early stage, and the details of this process need to be understood before there can be any possibility of changing it.

CHESSLER: In addition to the Swedish system where people come into the home to perform services, reference was made to the French system of the concierge, where a person has the responsibility of administering a home, admitting repairmen, and so forth, without any actual occupant of the home having to be present.

KAMM: The idea of a man also being responsible for children should be taught in daycare centers. We have to watch out that the old patterns of socialization are not followed in these new facilities. It was also suggested that not only the state, federal, or local governments, but also the business and educational institutions for which people work should be responsible for the creation of day-care-center systems. If men were not required to register the number of children in whose care they shared, it would be more difficult for women to obtain positions in these institutions, since the employers would be likely to feel that they would have to have a greater expenditure of money for day-care centers if they hired women. Such a male-registration procedure would thus equalize the liability for men and women.

With respect to the time-space concept, I objected to our fixation on the idea that there is a home, that there is a nest that two people are going to build, and that there is shopping that has to be done and plumbing and so on to be taken care of. I, as well as others, have suggested that most of these private-home functions should be taken over by a specialized service in the community, a service which would take the responsibility for checking on the plumbing and electrical facilities and so on. Such a service could be professionalized and so provide people with a release from the nuclear-family situation.

My third point is related to sex-role behavior. Those behavior patterns are begun extremely early through education as to goals, dress-behavior, and so on, behavior patterns that are expressed by the parents as first models. There should be new potentials for bisexual relations. We need to investigate the possibilities for homosexual—female to female and male to male—interactions also.

MERRIAM: When trying to break down the institutionalization of time-space patterns, it was also pointed out that because the hours for such cultural facilities as museums and libraries are set chiefly during the daytime, it isn't only housewives who are penalized by present patterns. Men, and women who work, are also penalized by the stereotype that the stay-at-home woman is the receiver of "culture." So we perpetuate the caricature of the garden-type woman who reads books and gives book reports and admires paintings. A perfect example of this sort of thing occurred on the "Today" television show when Mrs. Nixon was being interviewed. She was asked, "What kinds of paintings do you choose for your collection?" and she answered, "Only the greats." She claimed that these interests break up one's workday, that she gets "a little lift" through music and painting. We pointed out in our discussion that we could do away with some of these stereotypes and that this would be done by breaking up present time-space patterns.

JECH: I don't think the point was made strongly enough that we don't know enough about the effect of the dearth of child-care centers in the United States on the status of American women, that there should also be cross-cultural studies on this issue, and that we need to find out more about what is happening in other countries in this area.

I would also like to mention that some in the group took the present isolated nuclear-family situation for granted and were satisfied with a kind of bandaid approach, where supplementary services of various kinds would be provided. We did not examine the really fundamental underlying issue, the necessity to do away with the nuclear family.

This leads me to my third point: Do we require stereotypic concepts of people? Do we have to have a stereotype before we can see an individual? Galen, a German anthropologist, has distinguished between the many and complex "instincts" of man and the few basic instincts of the lower animals. Doesn't this difference have implications for the way we organize our social systems? Why should human beings have to divide people by such gross categories as color and sex? If such distinctions are necessary, can we plan for better relationships between needed roles and the social structure as it new exists? What kind of social structure could be developed, economically. politically, socially, and educationally?

POLGAR: The idea of tying together transportation research and the time-budgets of different categories of individuals may not have been stressed sufficiently. I remarked on the fact that American sociology was way behind Polish and French sociology, and someone also mentioned Russian sociology, in this respect. We felt that this problem was a highly relevant issue within the broader context of both child care and the time-space allocation of facilities in our society. As someone else pointed out, even the science-fiction stories one reads do not show a conception of vastly different social arrangements between people; this business of the little nest recurs again and again. I suggested that one way in which we might push ourselves into highly innovative ideas for research and action that would get us away from this little nest of services would be to try to write science-fiction stories in our minds.

GENERAL COMMENTS

MILNER: I would like to comment on the report of the roundtable on structural/institutional impediments. The need for child-care facilities for working women was referred to several times. As a college teacher who works with adults in evening classes, I would add higher-education institutions to the list of places that should have such facilities. They could then better serve those women who, having taken time out to start their families and who, having given their children a secure start, return to college to complete their education and prepare for a career. A rather concrete instance of the need for such a facility occurred during the first class of the last Spring term of one of my courses. A young woman came up to me at the beginning of the class to say to me, "I can't stay tonight because I'm having baby-sitting trouble and I have to go home as soon as possible. I came only because I wanted to get at least the basic introductory material for the course. I'm sorry." If we want to help women continue their education and prepare for second careers, child-care facilities should be attached to educational institutions that serve adults.

I also wanted to refer to the father's role in sex-typing. Much of the information on this topic is out of date; even the developmental textbook dated 1969 that I am using in one of my courses does not include the newer research and understanding in this area. Contrary to the older, Freudian orientation, the father has been found to play a key role in not only his son's sex-typing but his daughter's as well. That is, it is the father who plays a key role in socializing the girls into the culturally traditional feminine behavior patterns. When we talk about needed changes, one of them may well be to get fathers to change their ways of interacting with their daughters.

This circumstance seems to me to have certain broader and rather important ramifications for professional women. During a conversation with Sylvia Fava a year or two ago, in connection with the problem of discrimination against women with respect to promotion to the higher academic ranks, she made a point that has been echoing in my mind ever since. She said: "If anyone should be playing a leadership role in protesting discrimination against women in the academic world, it is academic women themselves. Yet, with very few exceptions, they do not. It would be interesting to do a study to find out why academic women do not play such a leadership role." I've since developed a hunch that the father's role in sex-typing is at least part of the answer to this puzzle. Most academic women are of at least middle-class background; they grew up in a traditional middle-class family with a dominant father. In fact, such a woman is in academia probably because she identified more with her father and his values than she did with her mother and her values. But in connection with this identification, she was also seduced into the belief that if you are a nice girl you never take issue with a man; you get what you want through *indirect* tecniques. You certainly don't stand up and directly and openly disagree with a male authority-figure.

So we have to include the father as a major socializing person in at least the middle-class family situation. We cannot discuss most of the issues that have been raised thus far in terms of women as apart from men; these are interactive roles, certainly so far as child rearing is concerned.

TUMIN: During a coffee break, I could not help but overhear various discussions. In one, I heard someone comment to the effect that this workshop had a very uptight audience, that one could hardly feel free to speak because the academic jargon seemed not to be able to confront the realities of the situation. Would anyone say that we have not gone near the bounds of important discussion, and why?

JECH: It is not so much that we haven't gone there, it is just that the state of science today is a highly specialized and technological one, so that in many of our roundtables the emphasis over and over again is to do some specialized study. There is a resistance to look at the larger picture, to look at the implications of the overall structural arrangements of our society. We also have a tendency to do studies with animals and to say, "You see, the sexes among animals are very different and therefore men and women are different, and therefore we should provide structural social arrangements that cater to this difference."

TUMIN: Could you say concretely what a structural study that took the larger realm into account might look like?

JECH: Such a study would take into account certain basic assumptions, for example, concerning such biological factors as pregnancy, illness, and physiological changes before and after we eat. Should we call each of these a pathological state? When people drink alcohol, should we call that a pathological state? When people have orgasms, should we call that a pathological state? Are investigators looking at these things from a culturally stereotyped point of view and does their research serve only to reinforce these stereotypes? Can we, for example, look objectively at the way we socialize children from the time they are born?

TUMIN: If I understand you, you are saying that our science is itself sufficiently culture-bound as to be unable to grasp some of the fundamental problems, and that to do so would require distancing oneself from the assumptions of one's culture.

JECH: And the reason why we seem unable to disassociate ourselves from our culture is because we perhaps suffer from the romanticized idea of ultimate happiness being the nuclear family, the love-situation, in which the female depends upon the male. We have no conception of other life-styles. Not one workshop paper referred to the fact that certain young people would not want to have a two-child family; they would not want to have a family at all. As for sexuality, heterosexuality is to us the norm. Maybe *that* is a pathological state.

TUMIN: One of our workshop participants is one of the country's most distinguished family-sociologists, William J. Goode. He supposedly specializes in what might be called academic jargon, although *I* think it is academic clarity. Will you comment, Dr. Goode, on the charge of cultural parochialism and near-sightedness in research on sex and the family?

GOODE: It is literally not possible for anybody to live up to that billing. The quantities of materials presented at this workshop are so complex that I can't imagine making a statement that would do justice to each of the areas discussed, let alone do what you have asked me to do, that is, make an over-all statement that would be reasonably intelligent. I won't state it in jargon, but I can't state it in good English.

On the one hand, there is considerable militancy represented at this workshop, which I not only approve of now, I have been approving of it for a number of years. It has been a strain on me that my women graduate-students at Columbia weren't worth the time and trouble I gave them, and I gave them a lot of attention, simply because they didn't go and do the work I had prepared them to do. They dropped out—got seduced by marriage, and all the rest of it. In this new militancy, there are a great number of proposals being offered. Most of them are directed at some kind of liberation from stereotype, from rigidity, from discrimination, and so on. We also know that these problems go back to quite early, primitive experiences. But the basic fact is that you can't implement most of these proposals without a radical reorganization of the society itself. And therefore, as a consequence, it almost makes no sense to talk about some of them.

But I do want to emphasize that I still think the militancy will have some immediate effect on all of the short-run solutions too. If aspirin will get rid of the pain immediately, for God's sake, take aspirin. If a doctor wants to fight a disease, he will begin by doing something on an interim basis. There are many kinds of short-run measures that I think will be useful, that in fact will get women jobs, will create more day-care centers, and the like. All of these things are good. So there are some short-run solutions one shouldn't sneer at as a kind of temporary solution only because the large-scale and longer-term thing must be very different.

Now on the large-scale perspective, on the other hand, I am going to keep defending love. I don't want people only to knock it. It isn't just a one-way domination situation, it is a *double* domination situation. It is much more complex than even that, and if you want to get data on it I think you could find much more interesting relationships than have been described. There are a great number of beautiful relationships that involve other than the domination element, though that may be one component. I, for one, do not want to live in a place where someone like a concierge takes care of a lot of things in my private life. I don't want my food cooked, for example, by any institutional arrangements. But that is a very personal set of values; it is politics in a broader sense. I am simply saying that there are more desirable elements in an intensely personal style of life than the "1984" pattern, with all its impersonality.

PART IV. DIRECTIONS OF, AND STRATEGIES TOWARD, CHANGE

POSITION PAPER: ON THE FORMATION OF RESPA

Esther Milner, Ph.D.

Department of Education
Brooklyn College
Brooklyn, N.Y.

It is hereby proposed that a new national, voluntary, membership organization titled "Regional Environmental and Social Planning Association" (RESPA) be formed. A brief rationale underlying this recommendation follows.

This statement assumes an acceptance of the general proposition that the rapid rate of spread of the present-day technological revolution has resulted in an urgent need in this country for a kind and a manner of planning that goes well beyond the restricted and fragmented varieties of planning currently practiced. It further assumes acceptance of these more specific propositions: that there is an imperative and growing need to go beyond the heretofore economically delimited planning practiced by individual corporations and by the federal government to consistent inclusion of environmental and social planning as well; and that in existing public attempts to deal with environmental and social problems, there is an urgent need to go beyond local (city, county, state) planning and application units to a unit that is adaptive to the scope of the majority of the problems involved, i.e., that is regional in scope.*

Given the acceptance of these propositions, the question that must immediately follow is: *How should and can social and environmental planning best be done in a political democracy?* It is here maintained that if this question is not raised, and broadly based attempts to answer it not made, within the next very few years, Americans, by their default or inertia, will be permitting our country's present drift toward becoming a completely technocratic society—in which all important social and economic decisions are made by narrowly specialized technical elites in the employ of big government and big business and industry, and imposed from the top down—to proceed unchallenged and unimpeded.

It is therefore proposed that the United States go beyond present *ad hoc* and specialist- or politician-dominated governmental planning procedures to the innovative development of a broadly based, citizen-participative planning process that is as permanent as our present elective machinery and that functions in complementary-*cum*-integrated fashion with it. Immediately correlative is the further proposal that there be equally innovative developments in public education from preschool through college, to provide for the acquisition of the attitudes, knowledges and skills basic to everyman's and everywoman's competent participation in such a recurrent process. Precisely what form each of these two innovations should take is itself a problem for broadly based discussion, experimentation and decision.†

* Precisely what these regions should be remains to be determined. It may well be that the size and geographic composition of a particular regional unit should vary according to the particular problem at issue.

† The suggestions concerning the basic shape of the former, primary innovation are given in the final chapter of the author's recently republished book, "The Failure of Success, the Middle-class Crisis." W. H. Green, St. Louis, Mo., revised edition, 1968.

As with any major social innovation, the best way to begin is *to begin,* in this case through the political process, ideally. But there are practical and persuasive reasons ‡ why the pattern typical of many previous human-welfare innovations should be repeated in this instance; individuals ahead of their time form pioneering private organizations to provide a particular social service needed by a particular group/community/area, and after these agencies have demonstrated their usefulness, general citizen response eventually sees to it that a public agency is formed to provide the service.

For all the foregoing reasons, the time has come for the formation of a national, open membership, voluntary organization dedicated to: formulating the details of the proposed planning process, as well as the nature of its public-education (including mass media use) concomitants, both preferably by application of the very planning processes it hopes to develop; and to promoting these innovations' widespread acceptance by the American public by all legal means possible.

That is, RESPA shall be open to anyone who (*a*) pays its (hopefully modest) annual dues and (*b*) subscribes to its core purposes, as enumerated. The first practical steps toward implementing this proposal are here seen as: the formation of a transitional governing board (to be succeeded within three(?) years of RESPA's formal inception by a ten(?)-member board elected by its membership; and the drawing up of a tentative constitution by the transitional board, this constitution to be passed on to the eventual elected board for formal consideration, revision, and adoption.

‡ Among others: (*a*) the proposed innovation is as yet decidedly controversial among the majority of Americans primarily because of their lack of awareness of the nature and of the social impact of the technological revolution of our time; and (*b*) the institutional/structural obstacles to its inauguration are formidable.

DISCUSSION

Sandra S. Tangri, Ph.D., *Moderator*

What Are Alternative and Supplemental Sources of Self-Regard and Satisfying Alternative and Supplementary Ways of Spending Daily Time among Women?

HEFFNER: Unfortunately, our roundtable got no further than the first half of the question; we paid very little attention to various alternative ways of spending time—alternative, that is, to most women's present child-centered life-style. We did mention that because we live in a highly technological society where machines are taking over the routine manual and mental labor functions, both women and men will have more time on their hands. But before solutions can be found to this problem, changes will have to be made in the society itself, most particularly, we felt, in allowing women to have a greater sense of their own self-worth and greater self-consciousness.

Most women, we decided, don't have many sources of self-regard. They don't have many opportunities to feel themselves important, functional people aside from the mother-role. Part of the problem here is that our self-image comes not only from our experiences in our family as we grow up, although the family does play a major role. You will find families where a child is given a full sense of equality, but when the girl goes out into society at large and meets the full impact of her peer group and the mass media and religion, what she got in her home will be at least partially destroyed. We think that society is definitely male-oriented; that the norm of our society is male, and that, therefore, women are essentially deviant. The female position has always been a subordinate position. Feminist and suffragist movements are invariably ridiculed. We've been treated as a footnote to history, rather than as an integral part of history. In having no indeterminate word for human being, our language enforces this way of thinking; we speak of "man" and "mankind," which tends to leave out "woman" and "womankind." Rather than this sex-linked word "man," we would like to see another word that could be substituted to mean human being. Literature has usually presented the human condition as a male condition. Rather than having a woman as the symbol of the human condition, she is usually portrayed as the mistress or the wife or the mother, the person who is always acted on, rather than acting on.

So the first and basic effort must be to strengthen the female ego. Today, sex prejudice is the only acceptable form of group prejudice left in this society. It is necessary to make it totally unacceptable in this society or any other society. Changes must be made in the educational system. Women have to be made aware, consciously aware, of themselves as worthwhile human beings. The feminist movement is, in a real sense, a humanist movement; it is not just searching for female rights but for all human rights. We have to interact more as people, as human beings, rather than as man or woman or black or white or Jew or Christian.

We also brought out that pressures, both political and economic, have to be put on advertisers, the mass media, the schools, even parents, not to allow them to make women this sex object, subordinate type of person. We believe that the present economic and political system cannot maintain its status quo if women are given their full rights as human beings, and that once woman is given her full rights, there will have to be fundamental changes in society. The vested interests are, of course, going to fight this because they have their powerful position to maintain. Political action on the part of professional—that is, deviant—women is necessary to bring about these changes. Nonviolent militancy may also have to be used.

One other point: Many men say to women, "You have the most important role in the world, the role of raising children." But unless women's consciousness is expanded, unless she has higher regard for herself as a person, the process of socializing children will not go on in the best possible way for either the children or a just society.

MILLETT: We also looked into such other avenues of change as public schools and universities. We also examined ways in which we can put pressure on the media, including logging hours of television to check the proportions of male and female participation, and who speaks the most. A group I am associated with had alarming results when we conducted such a study. Also, one way you can put pressure on advertisers is to threaten to dump their products in Central Park; they get terribly upset. And we continued to talk about one of the points Mrs. Heffner mentioned, that it is impossible to have sexual equality in a class-structured society that is racist, imperialist, and bent on war; thus we must make very drastic social changes if we hope to bring about any real sex-related changes.

OZER: We suggested that those of us who are connected with the academic world should demand that admissions to academic institutions be on the basis of achievement only, and that hiring and promotion policy be on a sex-proportion equal to the graduation-proportion of the highest degree.

SASSOWER: It was also recommended that we follow one of the techniques employed by the civil rights groups; specifically, to direct attention to and pressure against restrictive legislation against women in New York State. We should initiate legislation to set aside such restrictive laws, much as was done in various civil rights actions in the South.

WHAT STRUCTURAL/INSTITUTIONAL CHANGES ARE NEEDED TO FACILITATE NEW SELF-IMAGES AND LIFE-STYLES AMONG GIRLS AND WOMEN?

FAVA: The key things our roundtable discussed were the kind of formal norms that earlier generations of feminists fought against, rather specific kinds of female-discriminatory norms in the culture, such as legal discrimination. We indicated that the current generation of neofeminists, or whatever you wish to call them, are more concerned with informal norms, so that there is a gap sometimes—a generation-gap, if you will—between earlier generations of feminists and the current one. Someone pointed out that the reaction on the part of the current generation of militant feminists is essentially a reaction against the feminine mystique so prevalent after World War II in our society. We moved on to a long discussion of formal norms as expressed in law, and indicated some of the ways, in which these norms still discriminate against women.

Jessie Bernard reported a particular "first" arising out of a committee that she has been a member of, which is dealing with uniform marriage and divorce laws. These laws, as you know, are still handled by the individual states; there is no uniform, federal, set of laws. She reported on the current movement toward "no fault " divorce. This recourse becomes complicated if there are children involved, but if there are no children there is, in effect, no necessity to have any grounds for divorce. Someone pointed out that this would seem to imply that there are no marriage-norms to be faulted! Dr. Bernard went on to report that the possibility of having no requirements for marriage, not even age, was examined by the committee. They also discussed whether or not every applicant for marriage should be required to have exposure to contraceptive information at some point before marriage. We then discussed the role of the state and the extension of the state's role into the area of marriage and of family and sexual relationships.

There was further discussion of the still-current laws that are discriminatory against women, and I will simply list some of these: various laws restricting women's ability to get certain jobs; instances where women are to be fired in case of pregnancy; the legal necessity to take the husband's name to obtain certain rights; domicile rights—the wife has to go where the husband goes; prostitution laws; laws relating to "community" property; sodomy laws; abortion laws; jury-duty requirements. One final point that was made related to the married state. If we are going to move to a real liberalization of the divorce laws, for example, this will imply minimum or no requirements for marriage, and raises some fundamental questions about whether or not we need marriage to begin with.

MOORE: We continued, starting with the discussion of the family and the purposes of the laws that have been enacted; we seemed to focus, as a result of this concern, almost entirely on the need for child care. If the purpose of the family is primarily the care of children, what do you do when the institutions now present are changed? Dr. Polgar suggested that the reason for studying legal restrictions and institutional problems related to the older child-care institutions was that it might give us some understanding of possibilities for change. The labeling of certain forms as deviant defines what the acceptable forms are. We examined causes while discussing change. For instance, why did the state interfere in lineage activities? Because it was in the state's interest to strengthen the marriage-bond in order to weaken lineage; the loyalty of the couple is, accordingly, tied to the state, thus cutting across lineage lines. This analysis helps us to understand why the state was interested in matters that we now consider a matter of bedroom privacy.

We also discussed vertical vs. horizontal care of children, that is, whether children should be moved from institution to institution at different stages in their development, or whether they should progress vertically within one child-care institution. In discussing alternative arrangements for child care, the question was raised: What about provision of such facilities by industry, business, and universities, so that parents can be with their children at various times during the day? This arrangement becomes difficult when a male and a female parent's places of work or education are geographically separated. This point led us to focus on four aspects of child-care institutions:

1. Financing—the state should either pay for, or at least subsidize, centers at a geographic location near both the father and the mother.
2. Staff—hopefully, men as well as women.
3. Supervision-inspection, i.e., who sees to it that what happens to children in these facilities is good—many state-run institutions are so poor that they are little better than custodial.

4. Constituents, i.e., to whom will such services be made available—children of all social levels, not just for working parents, whether of low or middle income.

It was suggested that if this is done on a private basis, such arrangements would have to be remunerative. Coordination and integration could probably be done only by the state. Then the parents of a particular community could and should control whatever the state was financing in child care. With respect to research possibilities in this area, we ought to have a better look at what is good about good child care and what is bad about bad child care, aside from the obvious things. Also, just what might be transferred from the good examples to the broader scale, when publicly provided child care is recognized as something not just for welfare mothers but for the entire community.

With respect to the issue of assertiveness, it was suggested that girls are trained to be submissive in all our social institutions. It is difficult for them to make themselves visible. The mass media play a role here, perhaps, although we have to be careful about assuming that the mass media really are influencing our choices and our images. Someone suggested that we should focus on the school guidance counselor, who usually influences students to choose "sex-appropriate" careers. A further complication here is that the girl is amorphous on her career-identity, tending not to decide what she wants to be until she knows whether and whom she is going to marry, but the boy, in contrast, tends to have more crystallized ideas about his occupation at an earlier stage. Two very practical suggestions were made. First, that if we felt a specific broadcaster's portrayal of the female image was not what we thought it ought to be, we should protest that station's renewal of license. Second, that we ask President Nixon to appoint to the Federal Communications Commission, if not a woman, at least a feminist, i.e., someone who would insist on proper portrayal of female roles.

These two television-related suggestions led us to raise further fundamental questions: Should television be educational or merely a reflection of the current state of the community? Who controls television? How should pressure be applied to bring about change in this medium? Someone pointed out that even a situation-comedy in which a so-called dominant female is destructively assertive toward men, in which, that is, a woman is manipulating the poor bungling male, is demeaning to both men and women. It was suggested that we could perhaps seek out the scriptwriters and try to influence them. We should also pay more attention to teens-audience magazines, because the presentation of stereotypes in these magazines may be crucial at a developmental stage when role identity is being formed. We ought, in summary, to look into media responsibility in the area of sex-role identification.

In regard to availability of medical care and family-planning assistance, it is generally assumed that middle-class persons have access to good contraceptives, and that it doesn't really matter what they are because where there is a will there is a way. In actuality, there is a whole spectrum of willingness and readiness among middle-class persons to pay whatever costs are entailed in order to remain unpregnant. Contraception is, therefore, not just a problem for the poor; there is a range of problems in contraception for the middle class as well. We noted, for example, the rate of "unwantedness" in the United States. Westoff's investigations show that half of a national United States sample of nearly 5,000 married women studied between 1960 and 1965 admitted to not wanting at least one conception. This percentage doesn't take into account those babies already born who might have been unwanted but were not admitted to have been such to the interviewer. Now that we have these wonderful coitus-independent contraceptives, we are all supposed to have total control over our fertility. This is simply not so. Until abortion is readily available to all, and contraceptives that are completely effective and acceptable are available to all, we will continue to have only partial control of our fertility. And because of current ambivalence over desirable family size, the differences between three acceptable children and two desired children might be removed if we had a truly total system of fertility control.

Mr. Chessler commented at this point on his paper. As far as the job market is concerned, we noted that despite increasing numbers of positions for women in the traditional job categories, there has not been much progress in terms of additional types of positions open to women. In fact, in some areas of employment there has been some retrogression on this score; we still find only token women here, there, and everywhere. There is scarcely a position any longer that women are not represented in, but in many instances the women involved are the pioneers, the lucky, or the unusual. The real breakthrough doesn't come until jobs in each of these categories are possible for the nonexceptional woman, just as they are for the nonexceptional man. We also noted that when a job category begins to be dominated by females, the prestige and median salary of that category tends to decrease; and the reverse also holds. Finally, we noted that the United States is the only country where gains for professional women, and for women in many other occupations as well, have actually been lost over the last 20 years. There has, for example, been a decrease in the proportion of university instructors.

CHESSLER: Our discussion of the labor-force situation indicated that there is room for a great deal of research in just what jobs women hold and in what fields, what positions or responsibility they have, and what their salaries are. There are some statistics now available on these indices, but not nearly enough.

How Can Resistive Public/Male Attitudes and Women's Self-Attitudes Be Changed?

COMBS: I find that there is a good deal of overlap between the excellent report of the previous roundtable group and our notes, probably because there is always an interplay between the institutional level and direct efforts to change attitudes. It is a two-way street; a certain change in attitudes is necessary before you can bring about institutional change, and the institutional changes then reinforce, or may reinforce, the development of, or further change in, individual attitudes. Our roundtable first listed the theories relating to attitude changes that might be relevant. We are indebted primarily to Dr. Judith Long Laws for this list:

1. The expectancy-value theory, which holds that it is important to change role-expectancies by reinforcing attitudes. But it is, at the same time, also necessary to change the structure that will reinforce these expectancy-value attitudes, because if the expectancies are out of line with what can actually be implemented, both disappointment and a loss of the attitude tend to result.

2. The functional theory, which holds that attitudes serve a socially adjustive function.

3. The informational theory, which is that people will change their attitudes on a purely rational basis if you give them sufficient information and show them that certain attitudes *are* rational.

4. The social-learning theory, which holds that if you control learning experiences by changing the incentives, you will change the attitudes and the behavior that goes along with these incentives. Part of what is involved here is the role of modeling, that is, what we learn without exhortation if we have appropriate models to emulate. A negative example of this point is our current absence of women in public positions; this circumstance makes it difficult for both males and females to develop acceptant attitudes toward women in public positions.

5. The theory of cognitive-dissonance, which states that if you change behavior by any means, you may also bring about a change in attitude because the individual has a need to close the gap between overt behavior and inner belief. Kelman's model, for example, has three aspects; the first is overt compliance, brought about by a system of socially imposed rewards and punishments. The role of identification then feeds into the process; that is, people identify with someone who is esteemed and who has the desired attitude. This, in turn, leads to internalization of the new attitude so that it is consistent with other attitudes that are approved by the important people in one's group or society.

We then moved from this rather academic discussion to suggestions for various practical, applied ways in which related attitudes might be changed, and here we weren't at all systematic. Many of the things that were pointed out in the previous report are relevant here. One suggestion was that individual women, through their influence on particular men, can increase the number of supportive males, that is, males interested in the development of women as individuals with their own careers. An effective way to reinforce women's sense of status—another suggestion—is to have all-women discussion, or "rap," groups which would center on their problems, their needs, their concerns, their demands, their sense of self, so that they will be able, through their interaction with other members of the society, especially the male members, to bring about a change.

Some considerable attention was given to the role of communications, that is, to require that the mass media disseminate information about the status of women and the inequalities that exist on the one hand, and to provide data on the abilities of women on the other hand. Also, to insist that programming on television project a more positive image of women, as has already been mentioned.

In the educational arena, we should have more instruction in self-understanding for both boys and girls, especially with respect to their roles in society. The issue of governmental intervention was also raised. Here, of course, you have some difficulties because you must have a certain amount of consensus before you can get public figures to act. In addition, we talked about the necessity of having watchdog groups monitor and react to prejudicial programs and ads in the newspapers and on television. The women's liberation movement itself is helpful because by increasing the status of women it will change children's perception of women and of men as status-bearers. Let me elaborate on this idea a bit! It was mentioned that men probably are the models that are envied and imitated by the growing child simply because they are the status-bearers in most families. But as you increase the participation of women in high-status jobs, children will see their mothers as well as their fathers as desirable models.

Finally, it was pointed out that the various theories of attitude-change are themselves areas for continuing research, especially with respect to our present area of interest. We also discussed the need for cultural studies to try to discover why differences in male and female roles exist; that is, what are the cultural underpinnings of these differences?

TANGRI: As a participant in this roundtable, I would like to add something. Rap sessions for men were suggested as a parallel to women's rap sessions, particularly if a liberated man could be found to lead such discussions and to involve others with them. Men need this sort of thing every bit as much as women do, if not more, and we need them to go through the same sort of change process that we need to go through ourselves.

KEIFFER: Another thing we need to do is to get to the women's magazines that propagate bad or one-sided images of women. Women read these materials and are very much influenced by them. We have to begin to confront them about what they are doing.

CALDERWOOD: I have started a journal called *Feminist Studies*. One of the issues looks at the essential assumptions of the disciplines—not the content, but the methodology.

What Should Be the Respective "Change" Roles of Parent Education, Public Schooling, the Mass Media, Arts and Letters, Social Planning/Governmental Programs, and Political Pressure/Women's Groups?

GARDNER: Our roundtable was unable to consider the whole topic, but we did give serious attention to the combined roles of government and the mass media, and as a result we formulated a resolution to be presented to this workshop. During the previous report, one of the members of our roundtable said to me, "It appears there were not four roundtables but only one." And, in truth, there is a lot of overlap, so I will eliminate some of the things I was going to say that were already mentioned and simply add that we agreed with the other things that were said. We did, however, come up with something important and unique to our roundtable. It is a resolution that we would like this workshop as a body to adopt. I present it as a motion at this point:

> We demand that the Federal Communications Commission adopt as one of the criteria that must be met by an applicant for a license or for a renewal of a license, the requirement that broadcasts not depict persons unfairly or disparagingly on the basis of sex-identity, as well as not on the basis of race, religion, or national origin.

One of our participants pointed out that the FCC is supposed to do just this; it is part of its mandated job. We suggest that this workshop demand that the FCC carry out its obligation under the law.

TANGRI: After we have heard this final report and the discussion of it, we can make this proposal one of the items of the general discussion to follow. We can then examine its appropriateness and determine whether a vote on it can be taken.

GARDNER: I accept that procedure. To continue with the rest of our report, we spent a substantial portion of our time on the respective change-roles of parents. Myrtle McGraw was very concerned that young people be given a learning experience involving actual contact with the developing human being, that seeing what a baby is like as he or she grows and changes should be a necessary part of the education of every human being. She has implemented something like this at Briarcliff College. Anselma Dell'Olio forcefully supplemented this suggestion with the proposal that we should also have parental education for persons who are at present parents or are about to become parents; that such education is of utmost importance; that such an educational program should stress especially the tendencies of parents to be manipulative; and that parenthood does not confer automatic "ownership" of one's children. She suggested that all modern techniques of education be used toward this end, including the audiovisual. Someone indicated that we should make use of encounter sessions and sensitivity training for parents to help them overcome the manipulative and exploitative tendencies of parents with respect to their children.

Myrtle McGraw took strong exception to this proposal. She said, "Many parents have had a lot of parent-education, and this has served to wreck many of them as parents by creating anxieties rather than securities." Her feeling was that we need to know much more about what we are trying to produce in the way of optimum human development before we get too directive about what parents should be. At this point, Frances Kamm said that possibly what we should do in educating parents is to focus not on what parents should do, but on what parents should not do, since some of these "nots" are very well established. That "parents should not be possessive of children" was emphasized again and again.

It was also stressed that parents should not bring up sons and daughters differently, that they should be educated to raise them in the same way. Wilma Heide suggested that we may need to emphasize for a while what have been called "female values" in training parents. Miss Kamm called our attention to the need for parents to consider what it means to be little in a world in which there are big people who are making all the decisions. And further, to consider what it means to have to compete with other little people for the attention and the care of big people. Anselma Dell'Olio pointed out that the tendency for childhood to receive so much emphasis is a very recent development historically. Evelyn Kott said certain stimuli surrounding children need to be changed. She gave as examples pictures that accompany toys. Models that have to be put together by the children themselves always depict a little boy doing so. Children are identified from birth by the color of their clothing and the color of the room they are introduced into. Perhaps dress should be neutralized, so that it isn't necessarily always pants on boys and skirts on girls. One person suggested that maybe each sex should alternate wearing pants and skirts every other day, because we don't want to eliminate female images and values, but to have both sexes have the best values of both sexes. Mrs. East suggested that we might have the PTAs present in their newsletters a series to show how parents produce undesirable effects in this area, particularly to show some of the specific consequences.

One unanimous conclusion of our roundtable, in addition to the FCC proposal, was that feminist groups should be supported by *all* groups pressing for social change. Many reasons were given for this recommendation: Feminist groups have figured out what to do and have taken action; they provide a haven for women who are considering what they are and what they might like to become; they are consciously self-interested. For all these reasons, they are catalysts for change in our society and we should support them. And finally, Mrs. North suggested that public schools ought to have a curriculum which includes "her story" as well as history. In fact, at a time when our public-school curricula are so concerned with presenting the sociology and the cultural contributions of various minority-groups, there is still no provision for presenting what women have been, what women are, and what women might become.

DELL'OLIO: We also recommended that public accommodations be sex-desegregated. The lack of public toilets for women in certain bars and restaurants, for example, is often used as an excuse not to admit women to such places. On the manner of dress, when we brought up the value of dresses vs. pants, I pointed out that it wasn't a very radical ideal to advocate pants or slacks for girls. They are being worn in the most conservative offices and in high schools and colleges all over the United States. I doubt that dresses have any value at all; they should be abandoned.

MILNER: They're *much* cooler in the summertime.

KAMM: In this culture of ours, the stereotyped presentations of women are not confined only to the mass media, but are also given in the theater, in arts and literature, and even in rock music. Also, one of the functions of feminist groups is not only to concentrate attention on women and to bring women together to help them with their problems, but in a sense to create a subculture in which the creative activity of women who haven't had such an opportunity before can be released. Also, we need to be wary of what will happen when the government steps in to provide day-care programs and employment and so on. Materials and mass media programs put out by government, by women's bureaus, etc., have thus far been a force for reinforcing the old stereotypes.

As for sex-education in the schools, the need to bring up boys and girls who as adults are inwardly free to be spontaneous does not mean they don't need to learn about sexual functions. One of the most important things that schools can provide today is a scientific approach to this matter. Yet, such organizations as SIECUS have the tendency not only to present the objective facts about sexual functioning but to overlay them with discussion about how to go about dating, how to go about creating strong families, how to go about preventing illegitimacy, etc.—all the stereotypes we want to get away from.

I also want to point up the difficulty of getting support funds. The question of women's rights and men's liberation is being ignored by the foundations and other organizations that have money to fund action and research programs. There are feminist organizations already in existence, such as one in Washington, which are having difficulty getting money anywhere. We also mentioned various action-type approaches to dealing with some of the problems described; boycotts are an example.

GENERAL COMMENTS

TANGRI: We have a resolution before us.

REEVES: I would suggest that copies of this resolution be sent to status-of-women commissions throughout the country, particularly those at the federal and state levels.

J. BERNARD: Is it part of the FCC's charge that they must do this? If it is, then I think we should state as part of the resolution, "in line with your legislated mandate," to emphasize that they have not been doing their duty.

EAST: They have not accepted this as part of their mandate. Although they have an obligation to enforce the fairness doctrine, they have acted only against race and ethnic-group slurs; they've never interpreted it as applying also to sex.

J. BERNARD: Then it should be put in the resolution as an essential part of their mandate.

OZER: I think we have to be more specific. Many people think that depicting a woman scrubbing the floor in a television ad is not discrimination and wonder why we are insulted by it. We may have to be broader and say that there has to be more flexibility in the formally stereotyped sex-roles shown in television ads and programs.

GARDNER: The people on the FCC are undoubtedly aware of the pressures for this change. They've been informed by Kate Millett and NOW and other groups that the Commission isn't doing its duty. They know what should be done; it's just a case of bringing pressure to bear on these people.

FISHMAN: I am confused about various aspects of this resolution. Does the present law need to be changed?

EAST: The law under which the FCC operates does not need changing. Its present mandate is sufficient.

SASSOWER: Terms should be defined more precisely, particularly when most of us are agreed on what is and is not fair in regard to women and their representation in the mass media. To say women shall not be presented unfairly will require a judgment. The term itself is so vague and has so many conflicting interpretations that it loses its meaning. I would suggest an amendment that defines unfairness in terms of presenting women in a passive or subordinate or dependent role; then I think it could be reasonably enforced.

EAST: I'm afraid to change the wording; I got it from an expert in Washington.

MILNER: May I make a clarifying suggestion ? This resolution could not be transmitted to the FCC in the name of The New York Academy of Sciences because of the Academy's policy in such matters, but it could be sent from a group of undersigned individuals, so I would like to put forth this somewhat modified motion: that we accept the wording of the resolution as it was presented, and that we add a supplementary statement saying that we deplore the kind of sex-stereotypes that are depicted in the media, and give a few examples as guidelines.

TANGRI: I sense agreement on this suggestion. I think we are ready for a vote on the version of the original motion.

[*The resolution was moved, seconded, and passed unanimously.*]

TANGRI: For the record, the persons who have volunteered to write up the additional clarifying statement are Mrs. Heide, Dr. Gardner, Mrs. Sassower, Dr. Ozer and Mrs. East—a committee of five.

JECH: We should pass another resolution recommending that colleges and honorary societies and so on write into their bylaws no membership discrimination on the basis of sex. Women are presently excluded from membership in certain honorary societies.

OLESEN: I have a comment on the kind of action advocated earlier by

Miss Dell'Olio. We have to think very carefully about the kind of things we really want to accomplish and what the costs might be. For example, the sex-desegregation of public rest-rooms would deprive another deprived group in this society—namely, homosexuals—of a private place for making contacts. This pattern has been well established in the sexual research done at Washington University in St. Louis.

POLGAR: I would like to comment on the report of the roundtable on public attitudes, as well as on an implication in some of the other reports. The general tone was that one needed to have a change in public attitudes before there could be a change in institutional structure. The various recent liberation fights have taught us that the thing to aim at in terms of strategy is to try to change institutions, and that in the process of the fight to change institutions, the attitudes will also change. This is a conclusion on my part based both on the examination of research findings and from practical experience in the fight for birth control.

KAMM: One thing that has not been mentioned which is important to many people is the discriminatory nature of the tax structure. Also, if we want to encourage women to leave the oppressed situation in which they are at present, we should consider the possibility of reparations. Take the example of a woman who has spent most of her adult life taking care of her husband and her children, who now wishes to go into the world outside her home for which she is not ready. She should be provided with an educational program as reparation for all those isolated years. Again, the Equal-Rights amendment. which has never been passed, is something that should also be dealt with. Some mention of Title VI as it applies to the educational system has been mentioned; this too should be looked into. Also, two important institutions have not been dealt with at all. One is the marriage-contract; it is not explained and women do not know what they are signing. The other is the institution of religion as our foremost stronghold of male supremacy.

GARDNER: One of the statements in one of the reports, that women should try to increase the number of supportive males, is bothering me. I'm very tired of hearing what women should do. *Males* should try to increase the number of supportive males. As a parallel to this point: when we take what we have done to blacks seriously, we address ourselves to changing the behavior of whites. Similarly, males should get busy on the problem of women's rights. In fact, men in professional life are also being exploited in the present society, and it is very hard for a woman to put this point across.

TANGRI: That was my point. I said, in fact, that my husband carries on an informal educative process outside the classroom with his male graduate students. That is why I made the point about male "rap-sessions."

MILLETT: We could make an infinitely more intelligent kind of proposal than the one about desegregating toilet facilities by considering the possibility of supporting the Equal Consent law, so that present laws against homosexuality will be repealed. Another related point—laws against homosexuals also affect heterosexuals, although no one seems willing to admit this. A great many sexual acts are forbidden by the state which are really nobody's business.

POSITION PAPER ON ADDITIONAL DIRECTIONS AND STRATEGIES REQUIRING EXPLORATION: SOME EGALITARIAN ALTERNATIVES TO ANDROCENTRIC SCIENCE

Wilma Scott Heide, M.A.

American Institutes for Research
Pittsburgh, Pa.

The objectivity, rationality, and instrumental effectiveness of physical science and scientists are everywhere evident. Most scientists are men. Behavioral science and scientists have followed the model of physical science in methods and membership by sex. The methods and orientation have been androcentric. The subjective, emotional, expressive orientation and traits often considered "feminine" have been almost absent from behavioral science, as have women themselves. If, to be human, all are bisexual to some degree, then does it not follow that to have a fully human behavioral science, the totality of humanness must include the presumably "feminine" and the life experience of females themselves?

Behavioral science needs new models of methodology, orientation, and participation that extend beyond the instrumental objectification of the physical sciences. Including the excluded groups of young, poor, blacks, and women will provide egalitarian alternatives to androcentricity that should liberate even behavioral scientists from stereotypy and false notions of objective reality. Models of science must be created for the future not limited to the physical model of the past.

The excluded groups not only promise fresh insights but existential reality that has its own objectivity with implications for behavioral science. Today's gut rhetoric of the outsider, the dissenter, becomes tomorrow's cerebral process. But why wait? Women today and to come also have insights for human behavioral science. We need a more egalitarian society and science to fully benefit from their contributions.

DISCUSSION

Catherine S. Chilman, Ph.D., *Moderator*

SOCIAL-PSYCHOLOGICALLY ORIENTED APPROACHES TO FERTILITY LIMITATION

LAWS: Our roundtable was concerned with the issue of feminine identity, not with contraception as a narrowly technical problem. When we summarized what we knew about fertility limitation, we concluded that a woman's working, having high educational levels, a good income, and many options or sources of satisfaction in her life all added up to a very strong determinant of small family size.

We began in a very ethnocentric way, talking about career women, but we eventually broadened our perspective and talked about all working women. We did not really distinguish among the various categories of working women because we saw a job as one of the sources of positive self-esteem for women, and working women at all socioeconomic levels do have smaller families. We considered working women to be deviant in terms of present cultural norms in the United States, and we addressed ourselves to the determinants of such deviancy. We discovered, first, that various kinds of anomalies in the standard nuclear family structure would produce these deviant women, and we made a note that perhaps it was valuable to have anomalous nuclear families for that one reason. Second, we had a great concern, but relatively little information about, noncollege populations, and we identified that as a major research priority, particularly as it related to career women as deviants. So the first major category of our discussion was deviant women.

Our entire discussion was oriented toward research, so anything I mention as a topic should be considered a research suggestion. Before we went on to the second category, we talked about female time-perspective as a researchable topic and also the possibility, just in passing, of developing a decision-model or model of the feminine life-career.

The second category departed from the question: Are there any other alternatives for women than a career? We had already decided that a career was an alternative to being defined entirely as a wife and mother. But we had some difficulty determining what there might be between two rather diverse life-styles, that of a private family-life at one extreme and that of a career in the sense of full-time occupational involvement at the other extreme. None of us knew very much about it, but we suspected that there is an alternative way to identity involved in the life of hippies and the possibility of communal living. Then we talked about a more conventional form of noncareer work, voluntary activity, and included paraprofessional work that women might be involved in, paid and unpaid, in the larger community. We talked, just in passing, about secondary organizations, and included political movements there. We talked about sensitivity and encounter groups, a recently developed technique for the solution of some of women's needs for self-affirmation. And we talked about radical departures from heterosexuality which go along with, but are distinguished from, departures from the nuclear family, that is, about homosexuality. Finally, we got around to the topic of the happy housewife and concluded that there may be some, indeed, and that they probably ought to be studied too—although nobody volunteered for that assignment! But we did raise the question of the woman who is contented, for whom the socially sanctioned, family-centered role is, in fact, consistent with her own desires; what kind of second career does she have after her family is complete and grown, or at least half-grown?

UNIDENTIFIED SPEAKER: Alcoholism.

LAWS: We did not suggest that. We decided we did not know enough about motivations for and against motherhood, and that this area ought to be studied anew—our third category of discussion. Similarly, marriage as a very important, self-defining act and important life-commitment was referred to. There are different ways of "being" within a marriage, and different ways of thinking about marriage. We do not really know for sure what that decision means, and we would like to study that. Finally, we noted that, in this context as in others, there is a tendency toward an indeterminance of identity in women. This situation is very commonly related to waiting around to see whom you will marry. It is related, further, to the time-perspective question, in that young women often do not plan their lives beyond marriage.

The foregoing analysis is obviously a value statement on our parts. We preferred a model of women that corresponds to the self-initiated, high self-esteem, involved with one's work kind of "deviant" woman we talked about under the first major discussion heading.

Our concern about there being opportunities for nurture by men, by single women, and by older women whose families had grown was the fourth category of our discussion. This idea implies that nurturing does not take place only in the private family nucleus. We didn't pursue this any further than someone's suggestion that we look at foster homes as a research population where child-rearing takes place and where, by definition, it is not a proprietary relationship, legally if not psychologically.

Next, we talked about men, in several possible research contexts: (1) men as the partners of achieving women; (2) men in work-relationships with women; (3) supportive men—we were almost as interested in the notion of the supportive man as we were in the notion of the deviant woman. In addition to wanting to study supportive men, it was very much the feeling of our round-table participants that we wanted to make some kind of public statement of appreciation that there are such men. My own suggestion is that this workshop as a whole might wish to recommend the fostering and developing of more such men, at least as much as we want to foster and develop more "deviant" women.

Our final discussion is "other points," or "miscellaneous." We talked about the psychological uses adults put children to, particularly the use of children as an extension of the self in women. We saw this pattern among women as a substitute for the extension of self through further identity development. We also looked at the structural conditions that would facilitate a greater flexibility of life-style for women. We had some difficulty in being specific about these conditions, but they could probably be summarized as conditions that limit family size, conditions that permit women to get a good education, and conditions that permit them to work and to use the skills they have acquired through education. All of these factors would permit women to have a more flexible life-style than at present.

MERRIAM: On the point about supportive men, I suggest that such men form a Douglass-Blackwell Association, in honor, first, of Frederick Douglass, who was a great supporter of women—his last public act was to speak at a women's meeting in Washington—and in honor, second, of Henry Blackwell, who was the husband of Lucy Stone. It seems to me that such an association might be appropriate.

LAWS: Such groups are needed, because such men are likely to be anomalies in today's world.

REEVES: I would like to speak to the concept of career and to make the point that we are thinking too exclusively of professional women. Most of the women who work in nonskilled jobs do not consider themselves and cannot be considered career women. Their motivation for going into the job market is usually not a form of self-expression but an economic necessity. This is a fact we have lost sight of, and therefore we make extrapolations of self-fulfillment through work that I do not believe to be valid.

CHESSLER: I would also like to question the term "deviant," since over 40% of the labor force is composed of women.

CHILMAN: I am speaking now as a member of this roundtabe. What we intended to denote by this term was high-achieving, career-oriented women. Today, it *is* deviant for a woman to be very highly achieving and very strongly committed to a career.

CHESSLER: Such women may be deviant statistically, but in the larger, sociological sense, even the other types of women are deviant insofar as the determination of our normative structure is concerned.

CHILMAN: It depends on what norms you perceive. The norms are changing.

EAST: In the age-bracket of 20 to 25 years, almost 90% of women work.

OLESEN: I would like to make two additional suggestions for research. This roundtable report omitted entirely the notion of social movements or of historical events as they relate to the present ferment among women. If you want to look at the women's liberation movement as a unique historical event, the apparati of historical analysis are available; if you want to categorize it as a social movement, then you can utilize sociological means of looking at it. It seems to me to be just such an event and just such a movement, and is, on both those bases, worthy of study.

I am offering a second suggestion in the utmost seriousness, although it may cause some amusement. We have been hearing that we live in a man's world. I would like to point out that none of us women really knows what a man's world is like. Methodologically, it is very hard to get inside that world. Since we live in an era when style of dress permits a kind of "passing," I would suggest, both as a demonic exercise and as an aid to a sluggish imagination, that an investigator have someone pass as a man for a while, like the people who blackened their skins to see what it was like to experience the invidious inflictions upon black people. This is an important phenomenological suggestion; I offer it very seriously.

GILL: Just one pedantic point: Someone said that the average family size of women who work tends to be lower than the average. The United Kingdom experience does not suggest this to be true in certain socioeconomic groups. To depart from Professor Olesen's point, one area of research that is absolutely fascinating is to present people with babies and young children up to the age of 18 months and declare them to be boys when they are girls and girls when they are boys and then accumulate people's reactions. People tend to say when you tell them the child is a boy, "Isn't he vigorous! He has a nice strong chin. Looks just like his father." And if you tell somebody else that the same child is a girl, "Isn't she sweet! What a nice smile!"

NAG: I want to raise a very broad topic that is also researchable: why Americans of various classes still want children. If we try to guess why people in other countries who work want children, men and women both, some of the reasons that come to mind are security in old age, that a son has to be there for some religious reason such as ancestor-worship, and so on. In America, none of these reasons evidently applies. This question is not only mine; many sociologists are puzzled by the fact that in America both men and women still want children.

UNIDENTIFIED SPEAKER: They want babies; they don't want children!

NAG: That comment does not answer the question. As long as American men and women want three or more children, the world population problem will never be solved. Thus, an important, and researchable, point is to find out the motivation among American men and women for having children at all, as a preliminary step to finding out how to limit or reduce that motivation. There seems to be some change in this area only recently. During the last four years I have met three or four young women who have told me, "We don't want any children." But this has been an exception.

UNIDENTIFIED SPEAKER: I don't think you appreciated the distinction between wanting babies and wanting children.

KEIFFER: I would like to suggest some of the reasons that people want babies and even children, because I think some people do want children. One reason is the narcissism of it, the reproduction of yourself in something smaller. That is why some people refuse to adopt children; they want their own flesh and blood, their own genetic sort of reproduction of themselves. Another reason seems to be related to the fact that Americans do not touch each other very much. We are not a "touch" society; it is frowned upon. Babies are the one human creature that one can cuddle and fondle. Animals, pets, are popular for the same reason; nobody puts you down for stroking them either. So I think one of the reasons that people want babies is that it gives them an opportunity to hold another human being; the only other way available to us is in the privacy of the bedroom in sexual intercourse.

MILLETT: I would like to call your attention to another phenomenon that is becoming a social and even a political movement. This may terrify you, but it is composed of homosexuals and is called the Gay Liberation Front. How is this movement organized politically and sociologically? What kind of brick wall of social hostility does it come up against? What will its effect be upon our society; particularly, what is its potential effect upon sexual stereotyping and sex-roles? There seems to be a concern to break down sexual stereotyping and sex-roles. One direction of doing so comes through the women's liberation groups, of course, but the Gay Liberation Front may also have something to offer. But I think this is something you would be very unwise to do anything about right now.

UNIDENTIFIED SPEAKER: Are you suggesting studying the Gay Liberation Front or its effects upon the population?

MILLETT: Studying the Gay Liberation Front as such.

UNIDENTIFIED SPEAKER: You do not anticipate the difficulties that people who have tried to study women's liberation have found, that the groups do not want to be studied?

MILLETT: I cannot believe that is true. *I* have been studied time and again, mostly through "planted" volunteers.

THE INDIVIDUAL LIFE-CAREER AND PERSONALITY IN A MACHINE-SERVES-MAN SOCIETY

MILNER: The individuals who originally signed up for this roundtable discussion decided when they met that they would prefer to join one of the two research-oriented roundtables, and did so. Thus, this important, future-oriented topic was not discussed.

ADDITIONAL DIRECTIONS AND STRATEGIES REQUIRING EXPLORATION

YGLESIAS: Our roundtable topic could have taken us almost anywhere. We began with a diffuse discussion in which we were trying to tie suggestions for possible research to the presumed aims of the workshop. We tried to touch on areas that had either not been sufficiently developed or had not been touched on at all in previous discussions. The first was the subservient position of women in religion, but we did not pursue that in any detail. Then we considered the problem of the nature of research projects involving human beings and the nature of the subjects. Who is studied in these projects? What about the dehumanization that occurs within very large, long-term studies of this kind? A positive aspect that may come out of such projects was mentioned: The consciousness of the women being studied may be raised to the level where they themselves recognize that the problems that they are facing are real ones.

Next we discussed the contribution of the younger women participating in this workshop, both those who are more concerned with activist areas of women's liberation and those who are more concerned with the research aspects of the problems related to women's liberation. Why had they not been asked to prepare major papers? Some of these women have had very interesting experiences organizing other women; for example, there is Roxane Dunbar and her work in New England and the South, yet she was not asked to report. We have a representative of the New Feminist theater participating, but that activity was not reported.

A research-project to study the extent to which "mental health" as currently defined is a function of compatibility with traditional sex-role expectations was suggested. Or, to state the issue in reverse, to what extent is mental illness a function of incompatibility with traditional sex-role expectations? In terms of economic aspects, the impact of changes in this area on women's roles was not sufficiently discussed, although it should be thoroughly investigated.

We also discussed the possibilities of new organizations or new conferences that could bridge the gap between activists and researchers. The cross-fertilization of researchers and activists is an enriching phenomenon, and this very valuable element should be maintained in future conferences. Perhaps such future meetings should not have papers prepared solely by academicians and given to passive listeners; perhaps various views should be given on each subject. The orientation of such conferences should be a problem-solving one. A number of questions related to this proposal were raised: How effective was this workshop for the activists? How can participants tie awareness of problems together with the resources to study them further? And how can we disseminate the knowledge we have gained to other women?

On this last point, some specific ideas were suggested. One was the need for a medical journal for women—not for specialists but for women in general—so they can better understand their own bodies and as much medical knowledge as is related to their own functioning as is available. Another point in favor of such a journal is that people in related disciplines need to have access to much deeper and broader research on menstruation, pregnancy, childbirth, and lactation than is currently available either in the medical literature or in women's magazines. We also considered the idea of a communication center, a central setup of some kind, as a continuation of this workshop, and a newsletter until such a clearing house could be established. A lecture bureau to supply information to the general populace through the public schools was also suggested. There is a need for courses on the status of women in general, as well as for courses on specific areas; both types could be developed in such a communication center. Where such courses are being given at present, those giving them have been finding that there is not enough information available.

The question of the funding needed to amass this wide variety of information and to make it available in one place to both lay persons and specialists was discussed in some detail. We formed a subcommittee to prepare a related resolution for presentation to this workshop. The problem of greater availability of related past studies and of government-funded research was also raised and will be included in this resolution.

GARDNER: We present for consideration and urge the adoption of the following resolution, which we believe to be consistent with the purposes of this workshop:

Economic, political, and social equality of the sexes is an objective that remains far from realization. Although there is a considerable body of research that directly and indirectly bears on the factors influencing this goal, it is clear that far more work on it is urgently needed.

More specifically, some examples of high-priority research that should be done include:

1. Investigation of social influences, such as the media, schools, churches, discriminatory government legislation, and the sex-role-sterotyping assumptions of social and behavioral scientists.
2. Investigation of the relationship between fertility rates and the allocation of roles in the family.
3. Investigation of the disparity in our culture between the apparent deference accorded the female sex and the real commitment of resources to the serious study of women as people.
4. Study of the extent to which "mental health" as currently defined is a function of conforming to traditional sex-role expectations, and, conversely, to what extent mental illness is a function of nonconformity to traditional sex-role expectations.

We accordingly urge a major national commitment of resources and priorities for support of research in the research-areas enumerated, training of new researchers, establishment of new related centers of learning, and development of a mechanism, such as a national clearing house, for the orderly collection and dissemination of information related to the above concerns.

CHILMAN: May I suggest that particular emphasis be given in the resolution to grants and supports to women as researchers. Many of the studies that have been done about female development, women's roles, and so on, have and are being done by men. There is a strong tendency in the granting mechanism for the men with the big names to get the grants. Research, including how one poses the question under investigation, is heavily affected by the perspective of the person doing it. It is often said, for example, that when middle-class investigators study the poor, they build in lots of biases as they do it; they cannot help doing so. Also, Alice Rossi's experience in having to attach her study to a bigger piece of research to get a grant is rather illustrative of how she had to fight to get any visibility and to get the funds. I am not suggesting that women who are not qualified be given grants, but that there are many qualified women who could carry out such research most appropriately.

GARDNER: Steve Polgar has just asked whether we should add "including qualified women." This indicates to me that we really ought to mention something about feminists. Why am I so insistent on specifying feminists? Just as there are—or, rather, have been—two kinds of blacks in our society, so are there two kinds of women; there are women who are "turned on" to this problem and there are women who are not. So we cannot just say women, we have to say feminists. By feminists, I mean people who are actively working for the economic, political, and social equality of the sexes. Rather than add "qualified women," I would like to specify "feminist women" or "feminists."

MILNER: How about the term "qualified women investigators"?

GARDNER: No, because that does not imply that they are feminists.

MILNER: The term "qualified" make possible further definition of what the qualifications should be, so we might say later that a qualified women investigator must have certain attitudes toward women.

UNIDENTIFIED SPEAKER: I would like to see the term "qualified feminists" used, the "qualified" taking care of the professional criteria that are to be met, and the "feminist" taking care of the point of view of the researcher.

FISHMAN: As I understand it, one of the purposes of this workshop is to reduce sex-stereotyping in professional and other activities. That is to say, we've stressed that men can be nurturing agents and that a man does not have to be competitive or aggressive or support a family by himself. We should therefore try not to specify male or female aspects of behavior in this resolution.

OLESEN: Although I am profoundly in sympathy with the point you are trying to make, I think your approach gets us into a very murky area. It is like saying that Communists are best qualified to study Communists. I think it would be both dangerous and ultimately self-defeating for women to insert a qualification about "feminists." "Qualified women investigators" is as far as we should go.

GARDNER: We were not restricting the training of new investigators to the feminist group; rather, we were insisting that a particular group be included.

FAVA: We ought to remember that there may be more than one way of being a feminist. I think it would be a mistake to restrict the term to those who participate in militant movements.

GARDNER: I repeat that such a phrase would not restrict; it would, rather, insure the inclusion of a group that has not been included heretofore.

POLGAR: We are, I think, reenacting some of the bend-over-backward arguments that I have heard time and time again when it comes to admissions criteria. What is involved here is just a recommendation on spending more money for research and researchers, so it is not crucial to this particular resolution that this issue be resolved. I suggest this wording: "that new investigators be recruited without any prejudice according to sex!"

CHILMAN: Dr. Polgar, I have been on the other end of it in the government-granting mechanism, and have found that there is a strong tendency to accept an application with an illustrious name on it; if so-and-so is in charge, it must be good. Women have not had equal opportunities to achieve this automatic response that so-and-so gets. Also, I know it helps to have special emphasis placed on a certain category of grantee, having had experience with the word going out that some of these grants must be given to a tiny college or to blacks; I do not mean to imply any old thing is approved just because there is a quota.

POLGAR: I am in favor of bending backward. I just don't think this is the context in which it has to be spelled out.

UNIDENTIFIED SPEAKER: Woud you clarify, please, what is meant by the training of new investigators?

GARDNER: Scholarships or fellowship training. I was awarded a National Institute of Mental Health grant when it was discovered during the 1950s that there was a great need for mental-health research personnel.

UNIDENTIFIED SPEAKER: Perhaps we should say "interdisciplinary-oriented training." We have plenty of new researchers, but many of them are not qualified because of their lack of interdisciplinary orientation.

REEVES: Isn't it a matter of a new perspective that is not committed to the conventional perspective?

UNIDENTIFIED SPEAKER: Let's not make it too complicated.

GARDNER: May we have a vote on the resolution as read?

[*The resolution was moved, seconded, and passed unanimously.*]

INITIAL PLANNING FOR A CARRYOVER CONFERENCE

KAMM: Our roundtable began with a discussion of the orientation of such a conference, and it was the consensus that it should be action-oriented, a decision derived from the nature of the subject matter. We were to have dealt with this new conference in terms of directions of, and strategies toward, effecting new orientations, new life-styles, and new social structures that would lead to the development of these new life-styles. The presentation of research for its own sake and the concept of a conference as primarily an educational device were both rejected.

Our second decision about the orientation of such a conference was that it should veer away from the biological and should concentrate on social factors. Our third decision was that there should be no presentation of detailed papers or of addresses during the conference, but rather that we should rely, as in this workshop, primarily on previously prepared papers, and that there should be more of them than were available as our bases of discussions. We could then assume certain types of knowledge on the part of the participants, at least with respect to the prepared papers, and concentrate only on discussion during the conference itself.

Next, we considered the nature of the people who should be invited to the conference. We suggest more people and more categories of people than participated in this workshop. The conference should be much larger and more broadly representative of people in the community, of feminist groups, of people who are working with the poor, and of people who are related professionals. With respect to professionals, psychiatrists, architects, and city-planners should be present, because we want to involve them in a new philosophy about the nature of the family and of women and men. We also decided that these professionals should not present their opinions formally or give data on the status of the situation as they see it, but just come as participants. We should also include people who are trying to promote the maintenance of the present situation, that is, people who have not been radicalized as yet. In the mental-health professions, we want people who, when they are presented with a viewpoint and the evidence of needed changes, can go back to their professional societies and their day-to-day professional activities with a new perspective, and can also orient themselves around new sorts of research. In sum, an attempt should be made to contact as participants the people who are working in the community and those who are functioning on a professional level.

Many of the women's groups that are conservative on the issue of changing women's and men's roles should also be invited and brought into the planning for this conference, including women who are concerned with peace and war and consumer problems. It would be a problem to get conservative people to participate in such an action conference, especially since they are conservative precisely because they have not come in contact with the sorts of data and research that we have. But if invitations were sent to all sorts of groups, the people who were receptive would come and thus select themselves. And then taking part in the planning of the conference would help them to develop a new orientation.

We discussed whether we should concentrate on the international scope of the issues or limit the conference only to the United States. On the one hand, it was felt that many other countries, such as Sweden, France, and Poland, have not only developed new institutions, but have also done tremendous amounts of research and developed theories based on this research. Foreign sociologists have developed new perspectives, and we should have information from those sources. But Professor Olesen pointed out, on the other hand, that many of the institutions that have developed in other countries are in some ways irrelevant and inapplicable to the United States, and that if we wanted to have detailed accounts of what is going on in other countries presented by foreign experts in our pre-conference materials, we should select the countries and the cultures very carefully. And we should try to get those people who are going to write about what is going on in their own societies to distinguish clearly between what is actually occurring in their particular society and what they hope, or are trying, to accomplish. Mr. Gill noted at this point that the United States is not quite as parochial as we may think. He said the United States is much farther ahead in terms of social-action groups and in active participation of citizens opposed to their government than are many other countries. And that if we wanted an action-oriented conference, we should concentrate on the types of actions that are going on in the United States, because more action involving people at the lower economic levels is going on here than anyplace in the world.

We went on to talk about the types of topics that should be discussed in the pre-conference papers. These were quite similar to the topics that have been raised during this workshop. Some of them are: child-care time studies, which we noted are occurring in a far greater rate and depth abroad than they are in the United States; the legal framework in various countries; personality types, that is, the nature of the integrated, or androgenous, personalities being produced by other countries; the social philosophies of those countries having different philosophies; educational systems; different patterns of sexuality, that is, what is going on in other cultures and what changes we can and should make in our own.

Some important practical considerations were discussed: What would be the role of the participants of this workshop with respect to developing a task-force for the establishment of a future conference? People in addition to this workshop's participants should be included; the conference would be a direct outgrowth of this workshop, but it would also take in people working in the community, conservative groups, government groups, people representing the various mass media, and professionals. As for financial aid, Professor Olesen listed three types of sources. First of all, the workshop participant may have contacts, and we should all try to follow through on sources known to us. Second, we should approach the established and more conservative women's groups, even the Daughters of the American Revolution; as woman, they may well be interested in this sort of conference. Third, the government seems to be giving out a lot of training grants. Since government agencies seem more interested at this point in training grants and in pure research, we might present the conference as a sensitizing device—that we are sensitizing people to basic social problems and plan to prepare people to go out to change the situation. On this basis, we could consider ourselves as essentially a training agency and apply to the government under this title.

Finally, it was emphasized that the people who come to this conference should feel a certain degree of commitment to organize their professional lives somewhat differently when they return to their home situations. People of the more conservative professional orientations should assume a commitment to go back to their professional organizations and change things. There should also be pressure on the lawyers to change the laws and on the educators to change their syllabi.

TANGRI: I would like to see the whole realm of antifeminism included as a basic focus for action.

UNIDENTIFIED SPEAKER: Will men who resist the male stereotype be represented at this conference?

KAMM: I see no reason why we should not invite men, perhaps from the SEOM, which is the Society for the Elevation of the Oppressed Male in America. One problem we should anticipate is the difficulty communicating with the wide variety of groups we hope will attend. This workshop hasn't had this problem because the participants formed a relatively homogeneous group.

UNDIENTIFIED SPEAKER: Does anybody know people experienced in organizing who can tell us how much such a conference would cost? You would have to pay expenses for many of the participants.

OLESEN: A conference I organized was very small, and the total cost was something like \$2000 or \$2500; we had to raise every penny. We wrote to a number of small foundations in San Francisco and \$500 checks poured in on our heads! I don't mean to make it sound that easy, but if you really go after funding vigorously, it is easier to find than one might surmise.

SASSOWER: The additional point was made as to how this conference could relate itself to the professional-women's organization now in the process of formation; this organization will be one outcome of the professional-women's caucus soon to be held at New York University Law School.

KAMM: There is also a timing element. Dr. Milner made the point that a conference as large as the one we have under consideration would take a tremendous amount of time. We have to take into consideration people's schedules, which are often arranged six months or more in advance. This is long-range planning, but we do not want it to be too long-range, because the action emphasis might become watered-down if too much time elapsed between the planning and the convening of such a conference.

REEVES: A conference of the dimensions you are projecting would have to be "watered-down," at least in terms of size. Dialogue is always impeded in a very large group. It breaks down into smaller groups, and then isolation, not dialogue, develops. I wonder whether, in the interests of ease of financing as well as of creative communication, we ought to consider only a workshop along the philosophy you have outlined, to which people only representative of the various groups you have described would be invited. This approach would be manageable and could serve as an interim step.

MILNER: Was there a decision made during your roundtable discussion to form a permanent carryover task-force as a conference-organizing group?

KAMM: No, there wasn't. I suppose the participants at this workshop should form a task-force, but primarily a task-force to start forming links with the other groups who will be involved in the organization of the conference.

DELL'OLIO: We might ask for volunteers from the workhop, participants willing to stay in contact with one another beyond the workshop and continue the work that it will take to keep this thing going.

CHILMAN: Would you want to have communications sent to everybody who has been involved in this workshop to ask for volunteers? Who would do this, and who would be the people written to? We would need some person to organize.

MILNER: It has just occurred to me that the best way to do this would be via one of those photocopy letters of mine. I could send out a statement to the full list of invitees to this workshop to see who might be willing to serve on a carryover group to make plans for this future conference. I had not intended to continue in the role I assumed for this workshop, but I am willing to finish my job to this extent, to circularize such a request and get such a group working.

CHILMAN: May I urge that such a planning group get in touch with strong organizations and use as consultants some of the people who are old warhorses, with many years of experience in organizational work? In my time I have met people who know how to use power. The League of Women Voters' National Board, for example, is very strong in organizational techniques. There are others. A commitment to action in a conference is fine, but academic women are usually not strong on organizational strategies. One very good strategist is Mary Calderone of SIECUS, who is quite good at getting money and publicity.

GENERAL COMMENTS

MILNER: I think we should note that the resolution we have passed in relation to the Federal Communications Commission must be submitted in our names, as individuals. It would be a violation of the policy of The New York Academy of Sciences to endorse such a resolution.

HEIDE: It might be appropriate to withhold the resolution until additional research could be done on it, and then submit it to the forthcoming professional-women's conference. The resolution would thus carry the impetus of a larger group, and one that is more action-oriented. I suggest, therefore, that we withdraw this resolution.

[*This suggestion was unanimously approved.*]

POSTSCRIPT: ANALYSIS AND EVALUATION

Esther Milner, Ph.D.

Department of Education
Brooklyn College
Brooklyn, N.Y.

Preamble

It was not my original intention to go beyond my roles as workshop-organizer and participant among participants during the workshop. However, it was suggested that some sort of "rounding off" would make a positive contribution to the published proceedings; this suggestion coincided with my post-workshop feeling of a lack of "closure," a feeling that was later reinforced by my protracted exposure to the transcripts of the various plenary sessions. As a result I have assumed, with certain substantial reservations, a third workshop-related role, that of its reactive and evaluative discussant.

I was initially, and remain, reluctant to assume this role for two reasons: First, since I am not conversant with much of the specialized literature related to the workshop's large and complex topic, I do not feel sufficiently qualified to do so; second, it puts me in the position not just of passing judgment on my peers, but of doing so in a unilateral, and therefore unfair, manner, inasmuch as they do not have the opportunity, as they did during the workshop itself, to answer back "for the record." I have divided my postscript into three parts: a miscellaneous collection of supplementary reactive comments, an explicitly evaluative analysis, and a "coda."

Supplementary Reactive Comments

Had I been able to be present at every roundtable discussion group and for the duration of every plenary session—and had had my wits and unlimited time available to me—there are a number of miscellaneous reactive comments I would have liked to make:

1. At least part of the answer to one participant's question concerning the differences in Britain's manner of socializing girls provides another example of Professor Olesen's concept of "reciprocity." As any non-Briton who spends time outside of London quickly discovers, the British people (with the possible exception of the upper class) are even more traditional in their sex-role distinctions and related child-socialization patterns than we are. But Britain's historical role as an imperial and a European power, and the recurrent warfare that has been an integral aspect of that role, has resulted in the development of a cultural pattern that we have not (heretofore, at least) had reason to develop: the generation-to-generation presence at every class level of a population of unmarried and early-widowed women, epitomized by the independent and socially thoroughly useful single women of the upper and upper-middle classes whom George Bernard Shaw, among others, has immortalized for posterity. Women of this sort have, over the centuries, developed a subculture of their own which, in its good-humored competence and sturdy self-respect, reflects the societal regard its members have amply earned. Most British families have within them at least one such woman, and this directly experienced tradition affords every growing girl concrete evidence of a respectable and self-respecting alternate life-style to the more dominant, home-and-child centered pattern. In contrast, our cultural tradition is one of pity for the woman who has not been "spoken for," regardless of her social contributions, and this, too, is directly experienced by American girls as they grow up. This cross-cultural difference directs attention to an important and basic workshop-related area of research and change: the social pressures that impel girls toward marriage and motherhood, and the related inner-psychological pressures that tie girls' sources of self-respect and identity to either marriage or motherhood or to both.

2. To Mimi Keiffer's perspicacious analysis of the reasons Americans continue to want children, I would like to add still another one. The more powerless and threatened and depersonalized Americans come to feel in their public (i.e., occupational, social, and political) life, the more we seek compensatory self-affirmation in our private, "gut-level" life; and the begetting and rearing of children and the attendant projecting of oneself into them are all psychologically self-affirming and self-reassuring activities.

3. In all fairness to modern ethology, which over the past 25 years has been well ahead of animal-experimentation psychologists in its stress on the fundamental importance of evolutionary change in the study of behavior (for example, Nicholas Tinbergen's "The Study of Instinct," 1951), I am obliged to react to one participant's inaccurate picture of contemporary ethology. Such books as "The Naked Ape" and "Men In Groups" represent a way of thinking long discarded by both physical anthropologists and ethologists. The recent publication and best-seller status of these books provide evidence of the mass psychological needs of our time and of the (lack of) ethics of individual writers and publishers, *not* of ethology as a scientific discipline.

4. Some participants played one of our country's most popular contemporary parlor-games: shifting the blame for our *entire* society's sins of both omission and commission with respect to the socialization of each new generation, including our own individual abdication from responsibility therefor, onto the schools. Like most Americans, they preferred not to recognize that when the responsibility for socialization of the next generation, which by its very nature must be shared by every adult and a diversity of social institutions, is piled onto only one such scapegoat-institution, the burden on that institution becomes impossibly heavy—and the schools at every level from kindergarten to college are, quite predictably, falling apart under it.

5. With respect to the existence and the significance of innate differences—physical, physiological, and psychological—between the sexes, the workshop-related aspect of these differences was, unfortunately, missed. The core issue is not what these differences are or are not; our species' mammalian heritage has "programmed" sex-delimited characteristics of at least the first two types into us. Since our species also has a uniquely human genetic potential, biologically, and since that potential has made our species (*a*) primarily and essentially social in basic nature far beyond any other mammal, and (*b*) dependent upon individual experience after birth with other members of our species—i.e., upon individual learning—for the expression of each new generation's built-in potential (only!) for uniquely human behavior, the essential issues are, rather:

a. How does the particular society (including family) into which the individual child is born *interpret* these sex-associated physical and physiological differences (or any other biologically based difference, such as skin color) in its values, practices, and institutions?

b. Do the child-rearing values and practices of that society maximize or minimize these differences?

c. Why does a particular cultural tradition choose to stress or maximize particular sex-associated differences, and why does it do so in the particular ways that it does?

6. The foregoing conceptual groundwork serves an additional purpose: It provides me with most of the analytical tools needed for a dissection of the reasoning in Professor Ruderman's "editorial"—especially of those points that prompted the most discussion among workshop participants.

a. The only valid way that lower-animal data can be used in the analysis of human behavior is in terms of evolutionary trends; we cannot extrapolate directly from lower animals to man. Thus, if a behavioral characteristic is "universal in the animal kingdom," this circumstance provides no guarantee that it also applies to our species—or if that given characteristic is present in our species that the reasons for its presence are unqualifiedly the same as in lower animals. On the contrary, many if not all sex-associated behaviors in our species outside of the sheerly physical-procreative are almost surely due not to simple biological factors but to a complex "mix" of biological, cultural, and individual psychological factors.

By way of example, let me apply this circumstance to one of the sex-associated behaviors referred to by Professor Ruderman. The reasons that women tend voluntarily to defer to men in a wide variety of cultural traditions are developed in the following hypothesis. It is quite possible that an urge to take care of the helpless young of our own (as well as of other mammalian) species has an instinctual basis in the human race and that this instinctual underpinning is somewhat stronger in females than in males because it is biologically adaptive for it to be so. A woman's maternal feeling leads her to appreciate that while she and her daughters or other women are, as biologically female, intrinsically and essentially creative, "external" creativity and achievement are the only ways her sons (and mate) can derive a sense of self and of status—and this feeling was long ago transmuted into an adaptive culture-pattern that has been passed on from generation to generation by both precept and continuing maternal-feeling reinforcement. Even after women's intrinsic creativity has become no longer biologically adaptive nor socially valued, such an ingrained culture-pattern is proving very hard to change. Furthermore, when and where the physical environment is primitive and mere survival is a real accomplishment, it is to a woman's own advantage to foster a female-protective male personality—and "deference" happens to be a highly effective means of manipulation! Such a male personality may not be needed when the physical conditions are no longer primitive and a long life is a virtual certainty for most persons.

The evidence for a basic weakness in the human male psyche is overwhelming, and widely postulated. I was sufficiently intrigued about its possible bases a few years ago to speculate on them at some length in another context, the theoretical monograph on the relationships between human neural and behavioral development which served as one of the sources for my "point-of-departure" paper for this workshop. This analysis,* of the implications for sex differences

* Milner, E. 1967. Human Neural and Behavioral Development: A Relational Inquiry, with Implications for Personality. : 295–307. Charles C Thomas Publ. Springfield, Ill.

in behavior of postulated aspects of this relationship, constitutes another example of the complexity of the mix of contributing factors in a seemingly simple, biologically based characteristic.

b. As for recourse to historical evidence, the only history taught by most of our historians is almost uniformly of one cultural tradition, that of "Western" man. Even when this version of "history" is supplemented by material from other (e.g., Eastern) cultural traditions, the societies involved tend to be at least as complex and "developed" as our own. Cross-cultural data, especially of simple cultures, show no such sex-role uniformities. Thus, to discover why women behave in certain sex-associated ways, one needs to look for factors in the particular cultural tradition involved, not in biology per se. For instance, there is a marked tendency in developed societies toward specialization of function as well as toward interpersonal competition for occupational status. In such societies, and particularly in our own, which does not have a service-class tradition, assigning women the entire caretaking-of-others function has served to free the male to compete and to specialize intensively.

c. The revolutions referred to by Professor Ruderman were not nearly as revolutionary as those who instigated them thought they were. (This is the really fundamental weakness of all "revolutions"!) Only certain aspects of a particular complex cultural tradition were, typically, singled out for change in any particular revolution—and over time these changes became modified because most of the overall cultural matrix had remained untouched. Even when a revolutionary change is fundamental, widespread, and thoroughgoing, no society (or section of a society) lives or has lived in total independence of and isolation from other, unchanged, societies—and this interdependence eventually and unavoidably results in modification of the revolutionary change. Again, one needs to look to a particular complex of social, cultural, and historical factors for an explanation, not to biology per se.

7. By abstracting the nuclear family from the social matrix in which it is embedded and making it the "first-cause" source of all evil, the "polemicists" (to borrow another participant's term) did not merely commit intellectual reductionism, they removed from serious examination an entire workshop-relevant area: the reasons why the middle-class family, formerly the bulwark of our society, is in serious trouble today. I offer the following explanation, only as a "starter."

To the extent that the nuclear family did (and still occasionally does) a good job of child rearing, it was because of the presence of an exceptionally mature parenting-pair. This situation has always been a rare commodity, but in former times in our country the middle- and working-class family received, from both the parents' and the growing child's points of view, a good deal of backup psychological support from either or both extended-family members and the primary-group-relationship networks typical of 19th- and early-20th-century rural and small-town/small-city America. Urbanization, including its secondary phase of suburbanization, has converged with a continuing trend toward specialization of function imposed by advanced industrial development, to impose this chain of events:

a. The extended family structure has virtually disappeared in the United States at the same time that the supportive interest of the nonrelated small-town adult has also evaporated.

b. After World War II, the struggle for consumer status, all-important to the offspring of Depression-era families, intensified to the point that not only was the father virtually removed as a socializing agent from the child, but in a great many economically insecure families the mother was as well, without the interjection of any compensatory primary socializing agents, except, possibly, other children and commercial television.

c. A parallel development in more economically secure family situations was an intensification of the sex-delimited specialization of function described by Alice Rossi, that is, the relegation of the woman to traditional social roles at the very time that such roles required, beyond her children's early years, increasingly less time and creative effort on her part. Two results of this relegation might have been predicted: The more a society refuses women any psychological outlets other than their children, the more likely they are to have large families, and the more endemic becomes the tendency toward over-possessiveness or "momism" among them.

d. More recently, the psychological insecurity of men at virtually all economic levels, occasioned by the convergence of increasingly savage competition and dehumanization in their work-world with early family-experience-induced vulnerabilities, led to a reactive need for a psychological scapegoat; and the "putting-down" not only of women as persons but of women's traditional roles as well became dominant themes in both arts and letters and the mass communications media.

The cumulative result of these various trends is that the individuals forming the parenting-pair have become increasingly less fit psychologically to be parents at the same time that overall social conditions have placed the full load of primary child-socialization on their shoulders. No wonder the "nuclear family" is in trouble and is being attacked by young women who went through adolescence during the past 10 to 15 years!

The cavalier emphasis on complete elimination of the private family, nuclear or otherwise, and the equally cavalier insistence on creation of substitute institutions which place the full responsibility for child rearing on other persons, professionally trained or otherwise, jointly arouse the never-quite-dormant devil's advocate in me and prompt my raising of this question: Are private child-care centers to become the next profitable service-business in the United States, an extension of the already thriving summer-camp industry (especially camps for disturbed children!)? We have already developed, it appears, "child pounds," where, as one such facility (with a delightfully quaint name, of course) advertised during the summer of 1970 over a major New York City radio station, parents who "deserve" to have a carefree, fun-filled weekend, or week, or month, can leave their children—as readily, apparently, as they can drop off their dogs in a similar facility, and both for a substantial fee, naturally. Moni Nag's bewilderment as to why Americans still want children and Urie Bronfenbrenner's recent comment, "American children are disappearing from view and therefore from the social conscience" (*The New York Times,* April 14, 1970), acquire added meaning in light of these recommendations.

I submit that the neofeminists are starting from diametrically the wrong end in their approach to family and social change. Instead of being governed by the "hang-ups" of the current young and older adult generations (which are, in turn, a projection of their parents' frustrations), they—and all of us—need to begin with, and from, these two fundamental questions: (*a*) What are the most species-suited ways of rearing children? (*b*) What sorts of experiences and related institutions are needed for optimal individual development at each successive developmental stage in the post-industrial era we are entering?

8. During the discussion of change-strategies, a particular social-psychological "action principle" related to attitude-change was emphasized:—that

there is no need to wait for a particular "obstructive" attitude to change on an individual basis; if we go ahead and change related laws and institutions, thus forcing external compliance on a mass basis, people's inner feelings will soon come to be in consonance with the legislated behavioral norm. Recent developments in our society are leading me to believe that this cognitive dissonance theory has more limited applicability than its original enunciators realized, and that it is time for social-psychological researchers to take another look at it. It may be that it requires modification somewhat as follows:

This change principle may turn out to apply only to a particular group, those who already have some sort of inner attitudinal ambivalence with respect to the old norm (concerning, for example, school desegregation or abortion).† For such a person, the added social pressure of the law and of respected persons' statements may serve to tip the inner scales in favor of a substantive shift, in inner attitudes as well as outer behavior, to the new norm. But for persons with no sort or degree of ambivalence on the matter, and further, for whom the original attitude is central to the stability of their personality makeup, such externally imposed constraints may have a diametrically opposite effect; it may lead to an even stronger defense of their position and/or to overt flouting of the new law and of duly constituted authority.

It may well be that the increasing social polarizations which are the hallmark of contemporary United States life are at least partially due to imposed changes for which particular groups simply were or are not ready. In so saying, am I recommending, very much like the bigots of both the south and the north, that we should "slow down"? No, but we as change-agents must, rather, follow two "change" tracks at one and the same time—and with at least equal effort and dedication. At the same time that we work on behalf of the external-constraints approach, we must also work, even more vigorously, I believe, in the political arena to create the sorts of economic, social, and psychological conditions that will (*a*) no longer make the old attitude crucial to the stability of the personality makeup of whole population-groups, and (*b*) encourage the development of some sort and degree of ambivalence with respect to the old beliefs and behaviors. It is quite possible that when change-agents, no matter how good their intentions, do not follow both of these tracks at the same time, they are making a major contribution to societal instability.

9. I have sufficient respect for Kate Millett's postulation that the feminist movement is, by its very nature, a humanist movement that I would like to address myself to it. If, as in the instance of Miss Millett herself, "feminism" is, and remains, closely tied to a broad philosophical and psychological orientation concerning the human condition, as well as to a political point of view concerning the kinds of social arrangements most conducive to the amelioration of that condition, then I have no quarrel with the essential aspects of her contention. But this view of the neofeminist ferment is not necessarily the rule among contemporary "angry women;" on the contrary, there are many indications that it is the exception. There was abundant evidence during the workshop, and even more evidence in other feminist-oriented meetings I have attended during the past year or two in an effort to be informed, that "women's liberation" cannot and will not last much longer as a movement distinctively and exclusively committed to the advancement of women in general. Pressures both

† Some sort and degree of inner ambivalence was typical of the groups on which the original research was done or from which the original principle was deduced.

within and without the movement will force it to go in one or both of the following two directions:

a. If its supporters wish to retain its essentially humanist goals and not be obliterated by the gathering reactionary ground swell of our time and country, they will have to join with other socially displaced and/or marginal groups to form a broadly pluralistic, yet cohesive, social and political movement.

b. The professional women whose major aim is to become an integral part of the present establishment represent a potent strain of social-class-bound elitism. If—and as—the polarization of our country into "haves" and "have-nots" continues at its present rapid pace, many of these women will very soon find themselves unable to identify with other have-not women but will, rather, decide that their interest coincides with the male-establishment "haves" on whom they depend for their status and their income.

Indeed, the extent of acceptance of what I have elsewhere termed the "masculine mystique" was sufficiently strong among many workshop participants that I am prompted to go beyond the reference to it in my position paper. To the extent that this attitude represents the wish to broaden the options available to women, I am in favor of it; there will be far fewer unhappy marriages (far fewer marriages!) and miserable children and neurotic females when girls and women can choose their way of life in terms of individual personality and aptitude patterns instead of being bound by a sex-demarcated prescription (just as there will be fewer breakdowns among men if they, too, have a greater variety of life-style options available to them). The point at which the adherents to the "masculine mystique" and I part company is when they make the conversion of all women to their way of valuing and behaving their avowed goal, i.e., when they try to substitute a new rigidity for an old one.‡

We part company for another reason, already referred to in my position-paper. As is the case with any narrowly self-interested group which enters the competition for a bigger slice of the "pie" at a time in a society when the slices are small and getting smaller, proportionately, and many other narrowly self-interested groups are also competing for them, these women will get neither the wider options they seek nor the revolution that a few feminists want. They will, rather, get—indeed, are already getting (as all of us are)—something quite different.

A major reason for the post-World War II regression in the traditionally high status of American women, which had begun to express itself in a trend toward a greater range of life-style options, was this trend's convergence with another, more basic and general societal trend. It came at a time when the traditional male life-style of rugged individualism was being massively challenged by a changing industrial and economic situation. Instead of perceiving this changing situation as the primary source of threat and as necessitating major overall social change, Americans persisted in clinging to the old, now-unadaptive ways of believing and behaving; women's toehold on the higher-

‡ I happen to be partial to this goal in one, reverse-logic, sense, however. There could be no surer way of breaking down the entire present United States "establishment" than to remove from the intensely specialized, hard-driving American male his major emotional safety-valves of dependent wife and family and/or mistresses and subservient female workers! There could also be no more effective way of making "outsiders" aware that the "real meaningfulness" of the male world is an outright myth than by their direct and intensive exposure to every corner of its "insides."

status occupations was perceived as a threatening encroachment on an exclusively male domain (just as a later generation of lower-level male workers have been reacting to groups that had formerly been excluded from occupational competition with them). When a society must make fundamental changes in response to a fundamentally changing situation but instead of doing so continues to adhere to unadaptive reaction-patterns, such a society's treatment of persons who challenge an already fragile status quo serves as a political bellwether. A conspicuous aspect of post-World War I Germany was a reactive putting-down of women after some decades of "enlightenment." Thirty years later, the same sort of thing occurred in our country. Will it turn out to have been a similar political portent for the United States of America?

To return to the pressures currently emerging within the contemporary feminist movement, the split predicted poses a real challenge to those of us who consider women's best interests as coincident with the best interests of all people. How should we conduct ourselves with respect to it? I doubt either the wisdom or the efficacy of my own predilection to take open and direct issue with the self-interested, single-issue dominated approach of the "elitists." An undoubtedly more humane(!)—as well as more effective—approach is expressed in this passage taken from a personal post-workshop communication from a dedicated young academic woman who had participated in it:

> I think it's a mistake to put down those women who at this point, are single-issue oriented. I think they will come to the larger human issues when they realize that the single issues are embedded in a social matrix, the whole of which must be re-examined and changed. People need to be organized "where they're at;" that is, you will find very few individuals willing to discuss alternate life-styles or anything else when their only sense of oppression stems from job discrimination. . . . I see my own involvement with the single-issue group as an effort to raise their level of consciousness, to help them make the transition from individual concerns to human concerns.§

Evaluative Analysis

Participants' Evaluations

Fortunately, I am able to begin this section with an overview of the evaluative reactions of at least a few workshop participants. Within a week or so of the workshop I sent this request to 23 of its participants: "Will you do me the favor of letting me have your evaluative reactions to the workshop? Beyond your general and overall impressions, your comments will be appreciated on such specifics as what was or was not accomplished in light of its intentions, the workshop format and participants, and what remains to be done." The 23 persons contacted were chosen because they represented, in my judgment, the following various "dominant-value" categories of participants that emerged during the course of the workshop:

1. Research-valuing academics/scholars and administrators/practitioners, both

§ A paraphrased version of this eminently sensible statement can perhaps be applied to the workshop itself. Whatever else it may or may not have accomplished, it appears at least to have helped those participants who were narrowly research-oriented *or* action-oriented initially to make the transition from their originally over-specialized concerns to a more broadly conceived understanding of, and approach to, the issue of the workshop.

male and female (with varying degrees of accompanying "feminist" orientation or commitment).

2. Academic and/or research-oriented women with a high(est) priority "feminist" orientation (a few overlap with those in category 1).
3. An older professional-woman generation of committed feminists.
4. A younger generation of college-educated activist neofeminists.

Only eight of these 23 very busy people eventually responded to this request, and of this number, none fell into the fourth category above. The actual distribution of respondents among the other three categories was, again in my judgment: category 1, 5; category 2, 2; category 3, 1. Small as this sample is, their responses seem to be representative of the first three categories of participants—if numerous informal-verbal communications both during and since the workshop may be taken as the criterion. On that presumed basis, a breakdown of their replies, grouped according to key (paraphrased) themes, is hereby presented. The numbers cited indicate not the number of persons giving the response but rather the number of times this reaction was spontaneously provided.

Positive:

1. The heterogeneity of the participants, especially the inclusion of activist-feminists, was a good thing, for especially these reasons: (7)
   a. Dialogue was established among persons of diverse orientations —3.
   b. It exposed me to new ideas and thus has served to broaden my outlook either as a person or as an investigator or both—3.
   c. It contributed to uniformly lively and interesting discussion —1.
2. A particular aspect of the workshop's conception or format was good: (7)
   a. The advance papers were most worthwhile—7.
   b. The agenda was good ("It was the first meeting I had been to in the last two years where we didn't throw out the agenda the first day.")—1.
   c. The prior circulation of papers facilitated interchange during the workshop proper—1.
   d. "The workshop *worked*"—1.
3. The level and the extent of communication was very good in some particular way: (2)
   a. There was real candor—1.
   b. I was given a feeling of emotional support ("you are not alone")—1.

Negative:

1. The participant makeup of the workshop was a handicap: (7)
   a. It tried to be both scholarly and action-oriented, but the latter won out, to my disappointment; or, it proved to be disappointing in the scholarly and scientific sense—4.
   b. "Feminist bias and emotionalism dominated;" and/or "the inviting of the polemicists was detrimental to the scientific and research character of the meeting"—2.
   c. Serious scholars in the field were insufficiently represented —1.
2. A particular aspect of the workshop's conception or format was bad: (7)
   a. There was too much to be discussed in too short a time—1.
   b. The chairpersons were too permissive; they allowed the discussion to wander too far from the topic being discussed —2.
   c. The position papers were not adequately utilized—2.
   d. Firmer structuring was needed (This overlaps with points b & c)—2.
   e. "It was a mistake to link together two such complex and important topics as fertility limitation and women's self-definition; there would have been less vagueness had we focused only on the latter"—1.
   f. An opportunity for evaluation of the workshop should have been provided the last day—1.

This breakdown reveals, among other things, a distinct polarization of the respondents on the role of the activist-feminist subgroup—an interesting pattern in light of the circumstance that the majority of those providing evaluative reactions were themselves not primarily "feminist" in their value-orientation.

Rather than focusing on this polarization per se in my evaluative discussion, my preferred approach is to raise these two fundamental evaluative questions and to give one interested participant's answers to them: To what extent and in what ways were the goals of the workshop realized? To what extent were the goals of the workshop not realized—and *why* were they not (analyzed with a view toward deriving lessons for future similar programs)?

Background Information

Before such an analysis is undertaken, however, certain background information is necessary. Despite the circumstance that the workshop was an invitational event, there were a number of factors beyond the organizer's control which had an important influence upon the particular "mix" of participants who actually attended.

First, the workshop had to be primarily research oriented to be sponsored by the New York Academy of Sciences. Then, too, the funding policy of the Academy is to provide the round-trip fare and a very modest per diem allowance only to those conference/workshop participants who prepare and/or present the basic formal papers. The practical impact on the workshop of this limitation was that beyond those preparing the advance papers, any participants coming from outside the New York City area would either have to be provided for by a supplementary travel-grant from some source other than the Academy or come at her/his own expense. Included in my original list of invitees were a number of research-oriented persons representing a variety of approaches and contributions to the issue who were located in such places as Chicago, Denver, and Seattle. These persons indicated they very much wanted to attend but that subsidization of at least their travel expenses was a basic pre-condition for their doing so. An attempt was made to obtain supplementary grants for this purpose from a governmental agency and a private organization. Neither source "came through;" the reply of the private-organization representative, moreover, happens to provide a truly classic example of what the neofeminists complain about. The impact of this funding situation was that: the majority of those preparing papers were persons living long distances from New York City; all those from outside the New York City area who actually attended either had institutional funding-sources available or had to pay their own way; and those who were willing to pay their own way tended to be those invitees whose commitment to feminist concerns was at least as great or greater than their commitment to research in the area of the workshop topic.

Second, I was fortunate enough to be personally acquainted with a small but highly suitable representation of persons working either as researchers or as related-agency administrators with other-than-middle-class populations. Despite very heavy time-commitments, all of this category who were invited indicated their intention to attend—but last-minute exigencies prevented all but one from doing so, and that one for only one of the two and one-half days of the workshop.

Third, the circumstance of the timing of the Professional Women's Caucus, i.e., that it was held after rather than before the workshop, had a strong influence upon the nature of the participation of a particular subgroup of "workshoppers." This subgroup was composed of professional (including academic) women whose highest-priority personal commitment was and is to feminist concerns per se, and more narrowly, in some instances, to the occupational-advancement interests of women in the professions—an interest which was reflected in the title of their conference: "Breaking Down the Barriers in the Professions." The workshop was utilized by this subgroup as an opportunity to initiate serious planning for this conference at times when the workshop was not in session, reinforced by other interested and supportive workshop participants such as myself. It is my belief that such a prior conference would have drained off at least some of the high emotional charge which the members of this subgroup brought with them to the workshop and that they would have been, as a consequence, more prepared to address themselves to the more delimited, yet more comprehensively feminist issue of the workshop. That these various circumstances had a definite effect on one or more of the workshop's agenda, participant composition, and ongoing deliberations is as obvious as it was, I believe, unavoidable.

"Negatives"

To what extent were the goals of the workshop *not* realized, and *why?*

1. Foremost must come mistakes in the organization of the workshop, errors seen clearly only in retrospect. My purpose in analyzing and presenting these culpabilities is future-positive, since this workshop may turn out to be the first of other open-problem-type programs. Certain categories of participants were under-represented at the workshop. The lack-of-funding exigency was a potent, but not the entire, reason that certain categories of scholarly personnel were either not present at all or present in token numbers, namely, demographers, family sociologists, developmental psychologists, and psychoanalytically oriented researchers. Here, another, quite-realistic factor was operative: such invitees' career-related perception of the invitation itself. Already well-established persons in their field have so many commitments on their time that they are obliged to assign priorities to the many invitations they receive. Those who are not as established as they would like to be are almost invariably motivated by career-advancement concerns. As a result, the frequent initial reaction of persons representative of both these groups is not, "Is the problem at issue important and worthwhile?" but rather, "Who is/are associated with this thing? Is he/she/they at least as big or bigger a name than I am? Will participating in this program enhance my professional visibility?" On the other hand, the relatively few neofeminist activists and professional-women feminists who were invited perceived both the problem and the occasion as highly relevant to their goals and concerns; consequently, nearly all accepted. These respective acceptance-patterns jointly resulted in a proportional over-representation of the dominantly feminist subgroup. Perhaps they also served to minimize the "cult of personality" that too often turns many programs of this type into a ritual status-dance rather than an occasion for really productive communication.

The rationale and the underlying feminist value-orientation of the workshop's issues were both so self-evident to me that I took for granted, in my desire not to over-structure conceptually, that both were at least as obvious to all of the invitees. I should have prepared and sent along with the original invitation a statement making both aspects explicit, rather than presenting these ideas for the first time at the beginning of the workshop, in my introductory remarks.

Despite my carefully thought-out reasons for scheduling the open discussion on alternative feminine life-styles for the evening of the workshop's first day (to serve as a bridge between discussion of the basic background papers and the workshop proper) and for structuring it loosely—I had received, in response to my early requests of invitees for agenda topics, suggestions reflecting subscription to such a wide variety of preferred life-styles that I believed such an "open" structure would provide maximum opportunity for the expression of this diversity—this discussion did not serve its intended role. Obviously, one basic fact of communication and group dynamics is that good *logical* reasons for a particular timing or a particular intellectual structure are often not coincident with *psychological* reality. If I had scheduled this discussion for the evening of the second day and had provided some degree of kickoff structure, the outcome of this session might have been more productive in light of the aims of the workshop.

2. Most of the nonacademic participants and many of the academics as well apparently did not initially grasp the denoted and/or connoted meanings of the workshop issue *or* just how very radical its ramifications were and are for research, for women's advancement and for social change. Perhaps because they themselves had already accepted a fertility-limited life-style to the point of taking it for granted, it was difficult for them to recognize that this issue, when related to women in general, whether here in the United States or in other developed and developing countries, has an explosive potential for initiating an entire new area of developmental and social-psychological, especially personality-formation, research; for initiating a whole series of much-needed, overdue changes in "post-industrial" society; and for tackling the *liberal*—if you please!—male power-establishment on these two separate, but related, scores:

a. Despite the circumstance that top-level national and international social-policy influencers, including ecologically oriented scientists, are agreed upon the urgent need to limit population-growth here in America (finally!) as well as abroad, their control-perspective continues to be bound by the old voluntary technological-gadgetry approach with its continuing limited effectiveness and/or by a more recent advocacy of state-imposed fertility-limitation measures, with all the highly questionable personal and political issues such a course raises.

b. At the very time that the second industrial revolution is making entire categories of workers, both male and female, "excess baggage" in the world of work, overpopulation, rather the need to curb it, is rendering not only an even larger population-category—women—functionally nigh-obsolete in the basic biological sense, but because women's life-style has heretofore been delimited by that basic function, it must also have a major impact upon the secondary structures associated with women's being: social institutions centered around reproduction and child rearing.

If our society continues to ignore the rapidly and steadily growing effects of the convergence of these two social developments, that inertia can result not just in the destruction of representative forms of government but the entire advanced-industrial way of life that is currently in various stages of adoption everywhere on our small planet, its good aspects together with its bad. Perhaps the one truly positive outcome of the workshop from its organizer's point of view is that by its end a few more participants had begun to sense the scope of the workshop issue's potentialities than had done so at its beginning. One can only speculate on how much more might have been accomplished had they *come* to the workshop with such an appreciation!

3. Concerning the contribution to the workshop of various subgroups of participants, I am ambivalent. On the one hand, particular kinds of mind-sets prevented many participants from contributing as much to the workshop as had been hoped. Viewed in retrospect, on the other hand, the various limitations in perspective that were evident *in themselves* provide much information of pertinence to the workshop topic.

By "mind-sets," I mean that the conceptual and analytic perspectives that were brought to bear on workshop-related topics showed a decided tendency to be limited in time (now); place (here, big-city United States); interrelated sociological, historical, and cultural conceptual contexts (very little, single-issue approach dominant); point of judgment/perspective (individual personal situations); and subcultural value-orientation (middle-class individual status-achieving). These entries on the negative side of the participant balance-sheet added up to this circumstance: Far from being the genuinely innovative group the workshop's heuristic aim called for (and the liberal or radical *avant garde* many saw themselves as being), the majority of the participants were a decidedly conservative group, in that either they tended to be bound by the traditionally male life-style and/or the present male-dominated status quo in their change and research projections, *or* the activist subgroup's commitment to a confrontation style of participation as an end in itself was an echo of the young-male protest-establishment, both black and white, who in turn took it over from the activists of a previous generation who justified it then (as they do now) as necessary in power-unequal situations.

There may indeed be justification for utilization of the confrontation approach in actual situations of unequal power, but its application in a problem-focused situation where everyone involved was *equally powerless*—which was very much the case for this workshop—was unfortunate. It not only hindered the workshop deliberations, it was defeating of the activists' own avowed ends. Happily, the relatively few participants concerned came to this realization themselves by the end of the second day, and the final sessions showed the sort of productive commitment I had envisioned their giving it from the beginning.

This belated change on the part of the "activists" was, as noted initially, not the only workshop-positive aspect of the various limiting orientations manifested by participants. When these predispositions themselves are approached from the research perspective referred to by Professor Olesen, i.e., as data bearing on the concerns of the workshop, learnings pertinent to the workshop topic can be derived. This phase of my analysis is in the following section.

"Positives"

What were the positive outcomes of the workshop, viewed in light of its avowed goals?

1. Some of the originally enunciated issues or approaches have been reformulated conceptually and/or heuristically:

a. First and foremost, a post-industrial, fertility-limited way of life must be viewed as affecting boys' and men's self-definitions and life-styles at least as much as it will girls' and women's; it imposes a concomitant need for redefinition of traditionally ascribed male roles and identity. A number of participants expressed this idea in a variety of ways and discussion contexts;

Mrs. Augusta North's comment seems especially noteworthy in that she went yet another step and related both sets of sex-role change to needed changes in the direction of our society. Alice Rossi's "hybrid" model expressed this idea so well prior to the workshop that I decided, despite certain reservations on my part concerning other aspects of her analysis,|| not to add my own formal statement on this issue to the idea-pot of the first evening's discussion. This statement has, however, proven to be so directly germane, in light of various workshop discussions, that I am incorporating it into my analysis at this point; it was originally excerpted from an unpublished address titled "Resolved: That Women's Emerging Freedom of Choice Is a Good Thing for Society—and for Women."

> . . . Many persons, including myself, are convinced that the next 15–20 years will be one of the most—if not *the* most—crucial period(s) in the history of the human race. In order to establish my contention that women's freedom of choice is a good thing as clearly as possible, let me make the following series of far-too-optimistic projections that during this period:
>
> 1. there will not be a nuclear war;
> 2. widespread conception-prevention measures have drastically slowed down the human species' present precipitate dash toward physical and psychological self-suffocation;
> 3. we have learned to use machines to serve us rather than our present trend in the opposite direction;
> 4. women have accustomed themselves in feeling and in behavior to the necessity to allocate only a portion of their long and diverse lives to child bearing and rearing;
> 5. citizens of those countries which are as yet democratic do *not,* as Erich Fromm has put it, "escape from freedom;" that we do not, that is, develop the sort of humanity-denying mass society Orwell pictured in his "1984" and Huxley in "Brave New World;" and finally,
> 6. we have, on the contrary, managed to build new and adaptive and individually satisfying ways of living together.
>
> What *are* the meaningful *cum* adaptive patterns of living and believing that need to become typical in individual lives and in the social life?
>
> Before I am so foolhardy as to offer an answer to this blockbuster of a question, let me first refer to a particular anthropological finding. It is that although the two sexes' differing biological roles in procreation are of course universal, "appropriately" feminine and masculine behavior and personality characteristics vary from culture to culture. Margaret Mead's classic study of sex-roles and personality in three New Guinea tribes [MEAD, M. 1935. Sex and Temperament in Three Simple Societies. Morrow. New York, N.Y.] showed how very differently even geographically adjacent cultures can interpret "proper" male and female behavior. . . . This study clearly demonstrated that "feminine" and "masculine" ways of feeling and behaving are not genetically predetermined among human beings but are the resultant of both obvious and subtle cultural teachings and childhood learnings. The implications of this finding for us is that if we wish to do so, girls and boys can be brought up to be much more alike than different and that the ideal adult personality can be one that reflects an emphasis

|| I cannot agree with the characterization of women's subscription to the preferability of the male world and life-style as a "liberal" position; it is, rather, merely the other side of the conservative (or acceptance of the present situation) coin. To me, "liberal" in this context means retention of the traditional role-divisions as the basic pattern, supplemented by much greater opportunity for, and social acceptance of, the practice of a variety of quite-different life-styles by those men and women who find the traditional sex-roles incompatible with their needs and talents. I also prefer my own term "integrative" to the term "hybrid", partly because it has a more positive connotation.

upon the cultivation of *individual* potentials and aptitudes rather than upon a predetermined and limited sex-demarcated conception.

To return to the question raised earlier: If we forestall "1984" and instead develop a socially humane and individually satisfying style of life a generation hence, what are patterns of living and behaving likely to be?

With machines performing all menial and repetitive physical and mental tasks, occupations centered on concern and caring for others will be upgraded in status; only creative and investigative endeavors are likely to be higher in social and economic regard. Formal education will begin early, cover a much wider variety of activities than it does today, and extend throughout the life-span. The individual family-group will be less isolated than it is in current urban and suburban settings; perhaps the three-generation family-unit will have again become the rule rather than the exception. Personality differentiation—as well as occupational choice—will be determined primarily according to individual disposition and aptitude rather than by sex-identification. Both sexes will be nurturant in their attitudes toward each other and toward not only their own but also others' children. The welfare of the next generation, broadly conceived, will be central in individual value-systems and in the *raison d'etre* of social institutions, with one's own competitive status-drives of secondary importance. The most psychologically mature and competent of both sexes will freely assume the obligation to devote a great deal of their time to community, national, and world political life (defining "political" in its broader sense). That is, the most socially adaptive and personally fulfilling of our present male-associated roles and characteristics will be combined with the most socially adaptive and personally fulfilling of our present female-associated roles and characteristics, and will be held up as ideal-*adult* behavior to *both* boys and girls by their parents and by society.

Supposing that such societal changes as those just pictured actually do come about, how will the individual female life-career be affected by them? For one thing, girls are going to have to be brought up to see marriage, motherhood, and their own family not as their ultimate goals in life but as only one important stage or phase or aspect of a much more varied and broadly responsible adult life-pattern than most women lead today. Women of both greater and lesser education and intelligence will have a far larger range of alternatives concerning the conduct of their individual lives available to them and so will be obliged to make more, and more difficult, choices for and about their own destinies. The issue in this connection is: Will at least those women of greater intelligence and education rise to the challenges and the opportunities which such a humanity-valuing society will not only offer but *require* of them—and not, as many such women are doing today, merely continue to invest their abundant energies in aping the highly competitive, narrowly occupation-centered male life-pattern—a pattern itself on the verge of becoming obsolete, by the way?

I've come a far distance from my original conception of the scope of women's emerging freedom of choice. I began with women's freedom to choose if and when to bear children—and I've arrived at a conception which is at once much broader *and* more fundamental: each woman's freedom to choose whether she is to remain essentially a protected and dependent child all her life, or whether she will accept the obligation to grow up to stand on her own two feet and assume the genuinely adult social responsibilities that will enrich her own and others' lives—whether, that is, she is to aspire to be an individual in her own right, just as we now expect boys and men to do, with all the personal risks and terrors—and ultimate rewards—that struggling to achieve inner autonomy must unavoidably entail. . . .

Perhaps even more basic, such a choice is also crucial for how women handle their most socially important responsibility, motherhood. Many students of human development and behavior, including myself, have come to believe that to the extent to which women are obliged to express themselves vicariously through others, especially their children, rather than through their own direct expressions of aspiration, achievement, and especially feeling, to that extent is each succeeding generation being rendered neurotic. Still worse, it is to that extent that we implant in our children the kinds of overt and latent hostilities and aggressions that have made us protagonists of the so-called "Western enlightenment" [Roszak, T. 1962. The historian as psychiatrist. The Nation. Nov. 24.] the most militaristic and efficient dispensers of death in the history of the human species. . . .

b. The need to incorporate contraceptive technology and information into at least these four broader conceptual or practical frameworks was strongly stressed:

—Our country's practice of power-politics, internationally (developed vs. underdeveloped countries and related ecological impact), domestic-economically (privileged vs. nonprivileged groups) and "sexist;" the first type being termed "demographic imperialism" and the latter two types described as the "internal imperialism of men against women and white against black."

—A two-way relationship with cultural patterns: on the one hand, the impact of contraception on a particular culture; and on the other hand, the impact of a particular culture on the use of contraception. This important point was seriously vitiated, however, by the dearth of data—and subsequent discussion—on the relevance of this point for subcultural patterns in our own complex society (a major research lacuna).

—Comprehensive programs of health care—first, for *all* sectors of the United States population, and by implication, second, for the populations of all countries where population-control programs have been, or need to be, mounted.

—Comprehensive and sustained age-graded educational curricula promoting both physiological and self-understanding.

2. Topic-related ideas of a classically important nature were affirmed and/or highlighted:

a. The differences as well as the necessary relationships between the investigative approach and the activist or application approach were reiterated in this context, to the benefit, hopefully, of both the activists and the investigators.

b. What should have been a major discussion-focus of the workshop, the negative impact of our present ways of socializing girls on their fundamentally important maternal role, was mentioned only in passing—but it *was* at least referred to, for example, in these two passages:

> Unless women's consciousness is expanded, unless she has higher regard for herself as a person, the process of socializing children will not go on in the best possible way for either the children or a just society.

> . . . the psychological uses adults put children to, particularly the use of children as an extension of the self in women. We saw this pattern among women as a substitute for the extension of self through further identity development.

c. It was recognized, at least tacitly, that to confine criticism of television only to its slanted portrayal of women was too self-interestedly limited an approach. Thus, some fundamentally important questions were raised about the role of television in our society: "Should television be educational or merely a reflection of the current state of the community? Who controls television? How should pressure be applied to bring about changes in this medium?" But these questions were not quite fundamental enough. At least one more related question should have been posed: What is the role of advertising in our increasingly mass, power-oriented society?

d. Consistent with her earlier concept of societal "reciprocity," Professor Olesen, using a somewhat exotic example, made the important point that a change imposed in one practice or institution of a society often turns out to have unanticipated effects on other aspects of that society, not all of them positive. This point has important ramifications for change-strategies and strategists in the area of the workshop topic.

e. Professor Nag's concern about United States—not Brazilian or Indian—motivations toward overly large families is both important and well justified, on the score already made in a somewhat-different context: that our country's insistence on a wastefully high physical standard of living is both ecologically and internationally exploitative.

3. A number of references from an external and/or a hostile vantage-point allowed us to see certain of our own cultural (if not subcultural) blind-spots with a greater degree of clarity. Not only was the culture-boundedness of our research approaches highlighted, and to some degree documented (the point should have been more explicitly made that Freud's whole psychosexual development thesis is an excellent, as well as culturally potent, example of just this idea), but also a whole list of ways in which males habitually and quite-unconsciously "put down" females in current United States society. We were also put in our place on another score, tactfully but nevertheless tellingly, by our British visitor, Derek Gill, when he implied that we Americans have a penchant for passing liberal laws on various matters with great fanfare in response to special-group pressures—and then honoring these laws more in the breach than the observance.

4. Many pertinent ideas and approaches were added to the original idea-pool of the workshop. But some of these new approaches were compromised either by failure to consider their broader ramifications or by the manner in which they were presented:

a. Relating the "time-space" concept to parenting responsibilities was a stimulating and potentially a most useful analytic and urban-planning tool. But the issue that should have immediately accompanied this concept was not raised and discussed—that is, what should be our *primary* reference point in applying this tool: the production-needs of our employer, our own personal-status needs in the occupational and social ratrace, or our children's (and our own) needs as growing human beings?

b. Some very germane *goals* of change were enunciated. But insufficient or no attention was given to the manner in which these goals might be realized—a next-step question that can and should be used as an analytical tool for testing the feasibility and even the validity of a particular goal. This omission was especially serious in the instance of the recommendation that child-care centers for all economic levels in our population be provided quickly and widely. Such necessarily concomitant questions as these were not discussed (although they were at least raised by Miss Kamm, to her credit): Who will the child-care-takers be? How will they be trained? What will be taught in these centers?

c. Roxane Dunbar's and Kate Millett's emphasis on relating our society's nuclear-family and child-rearing and "sexism" problems to broader social and political issues and trends was well taken. But I must question whether the directions for their solutions lie, on the one hand, in an old-left (1930s) political ideology, or on the other hand, in the earnest belief that a feminist-oriented society will by its inherent nature *automatically* be a humane society.

d. The importance of including "her story" in the history taught in our public schools was also well taken. But a broader issue than special pleading for yet-another slighted group is at stake here. Homosexuals also, for example, have every right to make the same sort of demand. And "liberated" men could, on the very same premise, argue that it is not a "male" version of history that is taught in our schools at present, but only one very narrow version of masculinity and cultural and political reality; that history is highly biased from a great many males' point of view as well. Of course, all history is, by its very nature, selective in one way or another, and it is *this* understanding that we have to make a basic aspect of the teaching of history in high school (as opposed to the cultural-indoctrination role of elementary-grades history). This understanding is best taught not by adding still more "facts" to those already taught, but to have (small groups of) students undertake to write the history of whatever populations interest her/him/them most, going to the library and original historical materials to do so. This qualification is not intended to minimize the importance of developing broader as well as entirely new conceptual historical frameworks.

e. The closing research-program recommendation was most timely, despite its being more feminist per se than workshop-issue related. The subsumed suggestion most directly related to the workshop-topic, investigation of the relationship between fertility rates and the allocation of roles in the family, is so full of heuristic potential that it bears repetition.

5. The workshop showed that, given the proper conditions, subgroups initially widely disparate in their perspectives and individual life-styles *can* come to communicate with one another, and eventually to be conceptually productive. Thus, by the end of the workshop, even the most confrontation-prone activist had come to recognize that she was "among friends" and that her special presentation techniques might well have been excess baggage. And, from the other direction, there was, also by the end of the workshop, greater understanding and appreciation on the part of most of the research-valuing participants as to why today's feminists believe and behave as they do. Several conditions contributed to these eventual good-communication outcomes: (*a*) the size of not only the roundtable discussion groups but of the entire workshop group was small enough that participants were able readily to meet, and to talk directly to, everyone else; (*b*) even the most skeptical and testing-prone participants found that they really *were* free to say whatever they wished—subject only to rejoinder from other participants; and (*c*) the formal agenda, instead of impeding participative discussion as such preset instruments so often do, turned out to facilitate it, since it progressed clearly and rapidly from what is now known/hypothesized, to what is now wrong, to what should be done differently.

6. Where social phenomena are concerned, social and behavioral scientists are obliged first, to *see* what is going on, second, to describe it as objectively and comprehensively as possible, and, third and most difficult, to try to answer *why* it is occurring, as perspicaciously as present theoretical and other understandings permit. The current feminist ferment has thus far not been "seen" by sociology and psychology as research disciplines. Quite the contrary, there has been a strong tendency to focus on its more extreme manifestations (these too are worthy of serious study) and to use these as justification for dismissing the underlying social and individual substance of that ferment. To shrug off the activists with "they're a bunch of kooks," as I have heard one illustrious sociologist do, is to document precisely what these women are saying.

On the joint premise that women *are* people and that what they do and why they do it must be approached just as seriously as any other psychological and sociological research data (whether one happens to approve of what is being observed or not), this monograph—the proceedings of this workshop—in itself provides a yardstick for evaluation of the workshop in addition to the judgment of the organizer whether the participants were as productive from its outset as they might have been *or* the judgment of The New York Academy of Sciences whether the budget and the staff-time it allocated to this experiment turned out to be commensurate with its outcomes. Those who participated constitute an actual as well as a potential leadership group in the area of the workshop's concern on two scores, research and social action. Hence, the proceedings, by telling us a great deal about the women involved, provides data related to the workshop-issue which are worthy of sociological and/or psychological analysis, and "leads" toward the development of hypotheses for research-formulation and testing.

For example, the circumstance that these women as a group showed, at least initially, certain value and/or perceptually selective orientations, may not have been adaptive for the immediate purposes of the workshop, but the following orientations existed—and therefore call for such questions as: Why? What are their implications for the training of researchers in this cross-subcultural research area?

a. An ethnocentric elitism was both evident and widespread. The term "deviance" was applied to an upper-middle-class elite subgroup of women, and the "ideal life-style" for women both implicitly and explicitly projected was that of this group. Furthermore, this picture was not accompanied by balancing understandings and attitudes that are basically essential among those who wish either to propose and/or do research *or* to influence masses of women to change their life-styles. Thus, they did not manifest awareness of just how limited in applicability their ideal life-style was to the majority of women, both in the United States and the rest of the world. They overlooked the fact that, in Nancy Reeves' words, "[The motivation of most women] for going into the job-market is usually not a form of self-fulfillment but an economic necessity. . . . We make extrapolations of self-fulfillment through work which are not valid for most working women." (And, one might add, for most working men.) Nor were they aware, apparently, that a great many, if not most, women, given the choice, would not voluntarily choose a career-centered way of life.

The demand for child-care facilities was associated with a social-class bias as strong as it was unconscious. Given the continuance of our present societal structure (which most of the group assumed), how can a career-committed woman rear children without the dependable availability of service-personnel, whether they are utilized in her own home or in public or private child-care institutions, or both? As it was, many complaints were voiced about the present home-service crisis; one such coffee-break complaint was followed by this "humorous" comment: "I think it's a good argument for bringing back slavery."

b. Certain topics such as contraception, occupational patterns, child-care centers, male behavior toward women, were approached in a narrowly and immediately self-referrent, self-interested manner—rather than, for example, in the case of contraception, as an instrument of possibly great *general* social good;¶ in the case of occupational patterns, as only one of several possible life-

¶ Having lived through the relatively recent period of jubilation among women that reliable methods under the woman's control had at last been developed, and that women need accordingly no longer be at the mercy of male desires and contraceptive use or non-use, I found the criticism of the "current emphasis" upon woman-use methods to be more than a little nearsighted.

styles available and congenial to women; in the case of child-care centers, with primary concern over what is best for the children and who the child-caretakers should be; and in the case of male behavior toward women, as having causes just as surely as women's behavior does. Some facets of particularly the neofeminist immediate self-interest ideology struck at least two persons attending the workshop in very much the same way. Dr. Goode, who was not present for the first day of the workshop, reacted to these aspects much as I had—as being a variant on the "1984" pattern—and was similarly repelled.

In all fairness, however, one aspect of the evident tendency toward self-reference requires clarification. Women who attend "women's lib" groups are, as a "consciousness-raising" technique, deliberately taught, encouraged, and even forced, to talk freely and frankly about their feelings, their problems, and their lives. A few of the younger women were faithfully practicing their "lessons."

c. There was a tacit acceptance of United States society's present basic patterns as "given" and immutable. Thus, job or career requirements/demands were seen as "prior," and that the individual and family-functioning had to adapt to them; the continuation of our present urban-ecology patterns were taken for granted; commercially subsidized television was considered as inevitable a circumstance of existence as the air one breathes; the belief was endemic that many if not most of women's status-problems would be solved if women only knew how to work as effectively within our present bureaucratic work-world as achieving men have learned to do; there was apparently total unawareness that many more boys and men than girls and women have been and are being destroyed psychologically by the current competitive-achievement male-ascribed life-style. In some instances, there was more than mere tacit acceptance of the status quo; there was an ardent subscription to what I have elsewhere termed the "masculine mystique"—to the belief that the traditional male life-style is unquestioningly the really worthwhile, superior life-style.

d. In the instance of a few participants, one or more of the foregoing mind-sets was associated with a messianic, "true-believer" fervor that led to their deliberate use of well-rehearsed techniques of over-statement and confrontation. The result, at least initially, was not the "necessary shock treatment" that is the stated rationale of activist neofeminists for this style of participation, but poor communication in two directions, to others and from others. Thus, despite the circumstance that many of the ideas thus expressed were decidedly worthwhile, they were overlaid with so much "interfering static," that a real effort was required on the part of the listener to discern the essential point that was being made—an effort other participants were not always willing to make, to judge from a number of the evaluative reactions received. Conversely, their self-picture as bringers of enlightenment to the "unchurched" prevented them, again initially, from recognizing that other participants were at least as committed to the same basic goal as they were but were following somewhat different paths towards it; that other means to the goal, such as the issue of the workshop, might be equally and perhaps even more effective ways of reaching it; and that there might be real merit in points of view and/or a conceptual or structural progression which did not obviously and immediately fit into their preconceived frame of reference.

e. A strong sense of personal grievance was associated with each of the foregoing orientations.

Women such as those who attended the workshop are part of our society's pool of social and behavioral science researchers, from whom will be drawn, presumably, those who will be doing the sort of research the workshop was convened to promote. One qeustion might well be raised in light of this circumstance: What advantage can there be in substituting another set of distorting biases for the current, male-researcher ones, about which there were bitter complaints on the part of many participants? Accordingly, exploration of the etiology of each one of the orientations enumerated *and* of their workshop-issue related implications should be added as another of the workshop's research recommendations.**

ALTERNATIVELY—

In closing, I should like to reiterate the individual character of my analysis by quoting from two other participants' reactions to the workshop, each of which is quite different not only from the other but from mine. In doing so, I am drawing attention to a perceptually based principle popularly known as the "Rashomon effect": the tendency toward individuality of reaction to an ostensibly identical stimulus. Unlike the person quoted second ("B"), the participant quoted first ("A") did not attend the closing sessions, which benefitted from the change in atmosphere previously referred to. The excerpts from a formal report by "B" to her sponsoring organization also provide an illustration of the "plus factor" which may accrue from a particular experience but which is impossible to measure at the time, that is, the occurrence of a *later* major change in individual perspective, a change at least partially influenced by the experience.

Evaluative Reaction of Participant "A"

"It seems to me that the workshop was able to make only limited progress in the direction of analyzing and evaluating research which has been done on 'the impact of fertility limitation on women's life-career and personality,' and of pointing to future research needs. However, most of the advance papers were very good and did accomplish much in the research area. There were excellent behavioral-social scientists at the meeting who produced very good ideas. Unfortunately, the meeting was dominated by the polemicists and propagandists, and relatively little of scientific research value materialized in the discussions, not nearly as much as the scientists could have produced in an environment more favorable to scientific discussion.

"It is ironical to note that the scientists whom the propagandists presumably were trying to convince were already well-acquainted with the position and problems of girls and women in our society. This was not a meeting at which propaganda was needed or could be effective. The propagandists pretty much wasted their energies on a small group of knowledgeable people, and hindered real scientific progress."

** I have addressed myself to the social-context whys underlying the behavior of today's young people on an hypothesizing basis elsewhere (MILNER, E. 1969. Extreme cultural discontinuity and contemporary American adolescent behavior: A relational analysis. Int. J. Soc. Psych. **15**(4): 314–318.)

Evaluative Reaction of Participant "B"

"I found The New York Academy of Sciences workshop to be most rewarding, although not at all what I expected. Instead of a strictly scholarly presentation and debate of theoretical and empirical matters, the meetings acquired, during the course of the three days, an orientation toward action, and therefore sharp political cleavages. . . .

"Both the academic and the political issues discussed stemmed from the recognition that women could no longer make life-time careers out of child bearing and rearing because of the demographic revolution, technological improvements in production of 'home' services and of contraceptives, and higher standards of education for women. The focus was therefore on new life-styles and self-definitions for women and on impediments to the development of these. . . .

"The prospect of full participation by women in all the public spheres of society raised many questions: How should cities be constructed so that women are not imprisoned in private cages by inadequate transportation and impossible distances? Should children be considered the private property of biological or legal parents or should society consider them a shareable social responsibility? Why should 'fathering a child' mean merely planting one's seed, whereas 'mothering' goes on for a lifetime? How many fewer battered children would there be if only wanted children were born and only suitable men and women raised them? What communal and homo- and bisexual arrangements can be tolerated or encouraged which may help to end the sex-dominance patterns that are our unwanted legacy from the past? How can we produce liberated males who may be worthy of sharing a liberated woman's life? How is it that we can send men to the moon but we can not design a place to live in which cleans itself? How many men would opt out of the 'heart-attack/rat-race' syndrome if raising children were defined as being as masculine an activity as raising cash? Whose needs does the 'rat-race' serve anyway?

". . . This broader question, about the nature of the society in which women are to play any of their alternative roles, became the most exciting question of the workshop. The common concern on the part of those raising this question was that the world of jobs and politics be brought closer to the fulfillment of individual human needs for creativity and fellowship, that family, community, and play be valued on a par with politics and work for both sexes, and for all races, social classes, and nations. Such a society would be closer to the values and interests that women have had than it is to the present values and interests of men. . . .

"As a result, the whole tone of the workshop, whose title projects an image of women as 'receptors into which changes are poured and tablets on which changes are writ,' shifted to that of a woman as a *self*-determiner, society-changer, and chooser and controller of devices that she utilizes for her *own* purposes, including, possibly, political ones.

"I therefore anticipate an extremely serious dilemma for researchers in the field of population, which other fields are already experiencing, and which the Women's Liberation Movement will accentuate in this country, namely, the increasing unwillingness of women to be used as objects of study, and for purposes not of their own choosing. The acceptability of male gynecologists experimenting on women's reproductive systems is decreasing, just as is the acceptability of American technocrats experimenting on 'Third World' social systems.

"Researchers, administrators, and others interested in the control of fertility need to come up with creative and bold responses to this dilemma. Providing equal opportunities for women in careers of their choice, and especially in careers in population studies, is thus of critical importance not only for moral reasons but also for the pragmatic need to reduce fertility drastically in the near future. Women will need to be significantly involved in the decision-making process at all levels of professional work in population studies and programs (as, indeed, in other careers) for the fight against population growth to succeed."

RESOURCE BIBLIOGRAPHY

Miriam G. Keiffer, Ph.D., and Patricia A. Warren

Division of Psychological Studies
Educational Testing Service
Princeton, N.J.

Preface

This bibliography is an independent supplement to the proceedings, papers, and discussion sessions of the workshop. It was compiled in two ways. First, participants in the workshop were requested to submit whatever references they thought should be included. About 70% responded. In addition, bibliographies that were collected by other individuals were consulted.

We are particularly indebted to Lucinda Cisler for the use of her bibliography,* which was relied upon not only for references, but also for the beginnings of a cataloging system. And we are especially grateful to Esther Milner for her help in setting up appropriate categories. Kate Millett and Sandra Tangri were kind enough to permit use of the references from their doctoral dissertations. Also, free use was made of the references in Caroline Bird's "Born Female," Betty Friedan's "The Feminine Mystique," Jessie Bernard's "Academic Women," and the publication list of the Women's Bureau of the Department of Labor. There are probably many more bibliographies that were overlooked, but an attempt was made to incorporate materials on hand.

Users of this bibliography will find references categorized alphabetically under general headings. In some cases, references were listed under two headings when they seemed equally pertinent to both. Some titles were extremely difficult to classify because the subjects of the books were not readily identifiable. We therefore apologize if, on closer examination, a book listed under "economics" really deals with "sexuality," although in the light of current events perhaps that is not such inaccurate categorizing. It is our hope that this bibliography will be a useful tool to both researchers and students in the fields concerned with population limitation and women.

References Directly Related to the Issues of the Workshop

The Changing Family

Ackerman, N. 1958. The Psychodynamics of Family Life. New York, N.Y.

*Aries, P. 1962. *Centuries of Childhood. A Social History of Family Life.* Translated by R. Balick. Random House. New York, N.Y.

*Bagdikian, B. H. 1966. Who is sabotaging day care for our children? Ladies Home J. Nov.: 86.

* Cisler's work, "Women: A Bibliography," is constantly updated and contains many references that go beyond the scope of the bibliography prepared for this workshop. Requests for the Cisler bibliography (25¢ each, 10 for $2.00, 30 for $5.00) should be sent directly to Lucinda Cisler, 102 W. 80th St., New York, N.Y. 10024. References from this listing are noted by an asterisk in the left margin.

BELL, N. W. & E. F. VOGEL. 1968. A Modern Introduction to the Family. The Free Press. New York, N.Y.

*BENJAMIN, L. 1966. So You Want to be a Working Mother! McGraw-Hill Book Co. New York, N.Y.

*BETTELHEIM, B. 1969. The Children of the Dream: Communal Child-Rearing and American Education. MacMillan Co. New York, N.Y.

BIRD, C. 1967. What we are finding out about working mothers. Women's Day.

*BLOOD, R. O. & D. WOLFE. 1960. Husbands and Wives, the Dynamics of Married Living. The Free Press. Chicago, Ill.

BRIFFAULT, R. 1927. The Mothers: A Study of the Origins of Sentiments and Institutions. (3 vol.) MacMillan. New York, N.Y.

*BRIFFAULT, R. 1959. The Mothers. Allen & Unwin. London, England.

CAIN, G. G. 1966. Married Women in the Labor Force: An Economic Analysis. University of Chicago Press. Chicago, Ill.

*CALHOUN, A. 1935. The Social History of the Family in America.

*COSER, R. 1964. The Family: Its Structure and Functions. St. Martins.

COTTON, D. W. 1965. The Case for the Working Mother. Stein and Day. New York, N.Y.

*DAHLSTROM, E., Ed. 1967. The Changing Roles of Men and Women. Duckworth. London, England.

*ENGELS, F. 1902. The Origins of the Family, Private Property and the State. Translated by E. Untermann. Charles Kerr. Chicago, Ill.

*FELDMAN, H. 1965. Development of the Husband-Wife Relationship. Cornell University Press. Ithaca, N.Y.

FLETCHER, R. 1962. Britain in the Sixties: The Family and Marriage. Penguin. London, England.

*FOLSOM, J. K. 1943. The Family and Democratic Society. John Wiley & Sons, Inc. New York, N.Y.

GEIGER, H. K. 1968. The Family in Soviet Russia. Harvard University Press. Cambridge, Mass.

*GOODE, W. J. 1956. Women in Divorce.

GOODE, W. J. 1964. The Family. Prentice-Hall. Englewood Cliffs, N.J.

*HARTMAN, S. 1969. Should wives work? McCall's. Feb.: 57.

JEPHCOTT, P., N. SEEAR & J. H. SMITH. 1962. Married Women Working. Allen & Unwin. London, England.

KALISH, R. A., M. MALONEY & A. ARKOFF. 1966. Cross-cultural comparisons of college student marital-role preferences. J. Soc. Psychol. **68:** 41–47.

KINGSBURY, S. H. & M. F. FAIRCHILD. 1935. Factory, Family and Women in the Soviet Union. Putnam. New York, N.Y.

KIRKPATRICK, C. 1938. Nazi Germany. Its Women and Family Life. Bobbs-Merrill. Indianapolis, Ind.

*KOMAROVSKY, M. 1964. Blue-Collar Marriage. Random House. New York, N.Y.

*KOOS, E. 1946. Families in Trouble.

MACE, D. & V. MACE. 1963. The Soviet Family. Doubleday. New York, N.Y.

MAKARENKO, A. S. 1967. The Collective Family. Translated by R. Daglish. Doubleday. New York, N.Y.

MEAD, M. 1953. The impact of cultural changes on the family. *In* The Family in the Urban Community. D. Tyler, Ed. : 3–17. Merrill-Palmer School. Detroit, Mich.

MEAD, M. 1954. Family life is changing. *In* Encyclopedia of Child Care and Guidance. S. M. Gruenberg, Ed. : 675–682. Doubleday & Co. Garden City, N.Y.

MEAD, M. 1954. How fares the American family. *In* Proceedings of the Annual Convention, Atlantic City, N.J., Official Reports and Records. **58:** 58–62. National Congress of Parents and Teachers. Chicago, Ill.

MINCER, J. 1962. Labor force participation of married women. *In* Aspects of Labor Economics. Princeton University Press. Princeton, N.J.

*MOORE, B. M. & W. H. HOLTZMAN. 1967. Tomorrow's Parents. University of Texas Press. Austin, Tex.

MYRDAL, A. & K. VIOLA. 1956. Women's Two Roles: Home and Work. Routledge and Kegan Paul. London, England.

*NATIONAL MANPOWER COUNCIL. 1957. Womanpower and Work in the Lives of Married Women.

*NYE, F. I. & L. W. HOFFMAN, Eds. 1963. The Employed Mother in America. Rand-McNally. New York, N.Y.

O'NEILL, B. P. 1965. Careers for Women After Marriage and Children. MacMillan Co. New York, N.Y.

*O'NEILL, W. 1967. Divorce in the Progressive Era. Yale University Press. New Haven, Conn.

ORDEN, S. & N. BRADBURN. 1969. Working wives and marriage happiness. Amer. J. Sociol. Jan.

PARSONS, T. & R. BALES. 1955. Family, Socialization and Interaction Process. The Free Press. New York, N.Y.

PETERSON, E. T. 1958. The impact of maternal employment on the mother-daughter relationship and on the daughter's role orientation. Unpublished doctoral dissertation. The University of Michigan. Ann Arbor, Mich.

*PLATO. The communal rearing of children. *In* The Republic. Book 5.

*RUDERMAN, F. Child Care and Working Mothers. Child Welfare League of America. New York, N.Y.

*RUSSELL, B. Marriage and Morals. Bantam Press. New York, N.Y.

SCHLESINGER, R. 1949. The Family in the USSR. Routledge. London, England.

*SCHUR, E. M., Ed. 1964. The Family and the Sexual Revolution. University of Indiana. Bloomington, Ind.

SCOFIELD, N. E. 1960. Some changing roles of women in suburbia: A social anthropological case study. Trans. N. Y. Acad. Sci. **22**(6).

SOUTHARD, H. F. 1960. Mothers' dilemma: to work or not? N. Y. Times Mag. July 17.

STOLLENWERK, T. 1968. Back to Work. Ladies: A Career Guide for the Mature Woman. Pilot Books. New York, N.Y.

STOLZ, L. M. 1960. Effects of maternal employment on children: Evidence from research. Child Develop. **31**(4): 749–782.

WOMEN'S BUREAU. 1968. Working mothers and the need for child care services. United States Department of Labor. Wage and Labor Standards Administration. June.

WESTERMARCK, E. 1922. The History of Human Marriage. (5th edit., 3 vol.) MacMillan Co. London, England.

WESTERMARCK, E. 1926. A Short History of Marriage. MacMillan Co. New York, N.Y.

WESTERMARCK, E. 1936. The Future of Marriage in Western Civilization. MacMillan Co. London, England.

WINCH, R. F., R. MCGINNINS & H. R. BARRINGER, Eds. 1962. Selected Studies in Marriage and the Family. Holt, Rinehart & Winston. New York, N.Y.

Social and Psychological Influences on Family Size

ADAMS, J. R. 1963. Psycho-social aspects of family limitation and population control: a selected bibliography of English language sources. (Mimeo available from author, Box 199, Teachers College, Columbia University, New York, N.Y. 10027.)

BETANCUR, J. E. & L. GARCIA DE SOUSA. 1959. Current population changes in Latin America and the implications for religious institutions and behavior. Cath. Sociol. Rev. Spring.

BHANDARI, L. C. 1957. The psychological aspects of family planning. J. Fam. Welfare. **3:** 190–194.

*BLAKE, J. 1961. Family Structure in Jamaica: The Social Context of Reproduction.

BLAKE, J. 1967. Income and reproductive motivation. Pop. Stud. **21**(3): 185–206.

BLAKE, J. 1967. Reproductive ideals and educational attainment among white Americans, 1943–1960. Pop. Stud. Sept.

BLAKE, J. 1968. Are babies consumer durables? Pop. Stud. **22**(1): 5–25.

*BLOOD, R. O. Long-range causes and consequences of the employment of married women. J. Marr. Fam. **27**(1).

BROFENBRENNER, M. & A. BUTTRICK. 1960. Population control in Japan: An economic theory and its application. Law Contemp. Prob. **25**(3): 536–557.

BUMPASS, L. 1967. Stability and change in family size expectations over the first two years of marriage. J. Soc. Issues **23:** 83–98.

CALHOUN, J. B. 1962. Population density and social pathology. Sci. Amer. **206:** 139–148.

CAMPBELL, A. A., P. K. WHELPTON & R. F. TOMASSON. 1961. The reliability of birth expectations of U. S. wives. Int. Pop. Union Conf. Paper No. 70.

CENTERS, R. & G. H. BLUMBERG. 1954. Social and psychological factors in human procreation: A survey approach. J. Soc. Psychol. **40:** 245–257.

CHRISTENSEN, H. T. 1968. Children in the family: Relationship of number and spacing to marital success. J. Marr. Fam. **30:** 283–289.

CICOUREL, A. V. 1967. Fertility, family planning, and the social organization of family life: Some methodological issues. J. Soc. Issues **23:** 57–82.

CLARE, J. E. & C. V. KISER. 1951. Social and psychological factors affecting fertility: XIV. Preference for children of given sex in relation to fertility. Milbank Mem. Fund Quart. **29:** 440–492.

CLARKSON, F. E., S. R. VOGEL, I. K. BROVERMAN & D. M. BROVERMAN. 1970. Family size and sex role stereotypes. Science **167:** 390–392.

CLAUSEN, J. A. 1965. Family size and birth order as influences upon socialization and personality: Bibliography and abstracts. Social Science Research Council. New York, N.Y.

COLLVER, O. A. 1968. Women: Work participation and fertility in metropolitan areas. Demography **5:** 55–60.

CORWIN, A. F. 1963. Contemporary Mexican attitudes toward population, poverty and public opinion. Latin American Monographs, No. 25. University of Florida Press. Gainsville, Fla.

DAVIS, K. 1966. Sociological aspects of genetic control. *In* Genetics and the Future of Man. North-Holland Publishing Co. Amsterdam, The Netherlands.

DAVIS, K. & J. BLAKE. 1956. Social structure and fertility: An analytic framework. Econ. Develop. Cultural Change **4:** 211–235.

DE JONG, G. F. 1965. Religious fundamentalism, socio-economic status, and fertility attitudes in the southern Appalachians. Demography **2:** 540–548.

DE LESTAPIS, S. 1961. Family Planning and Modern Problems: A Catholic Analysis. Herder & Herder. New York, N.Y.

DEVEREUX, G. A. 1960. A Psychoanalytic Study of Contraception. Planned Parenthood Association. New York, N.Y.

DINITZ, S., R. R. DYNES & A. C. CLARKE. 1954. Preferences for male or female children: Traditional or affectional? Marr. Fam. Living **16:** 128–130.

ELLIS, A. 1959. Psychological aspects of discouraging contraception. Realist **1:** 11–13.

FAGLEY, R. M. 1960. The Population Explosion and Christian Responsibility. Oxford University Press. New York, N.Y.

FLANAGAN, J. C. 1942. A study of factors determining family size in a selected professional group. Genet. Psychol. Monogr. **25:** 3–99.

*FLAGEL, J. C. 1947. Population, Psychology, and Peace. C. A. Watts. London, England.

FREEDMAN, D. S., R. FREEDMAN & P. K. WHELPTON. 1960. Size of family and preference for children of each sex. Amer. J. Sociol. **66:** 141–146.

FREEDMAN, R. 1963. The Sociology of Human Fertility: A Trend Report and Bibliography. Basil Blackwell. Oxford, England.

FREEDMAN, R. & L. COOMBS. 1966. Childspacing and family economic position. Amer. Sociol. Rev. **31**(5): 631–648.

FREEDMAN, R. & L. COOMBS. 1966. Economic considerations in family growth decisions. Pop. Stud. **20**(2): 197–222.

FREEDMAN, R., L. C. COOMBS & L. BUMPASS. 1965. Stability and change in expectations about family size: A longitudinal study. Demography **2:** 250–275.

GARAI, J. E. 1964. The effect of information on students' knowledge of population problems and their attitudes toward population control. Psychology **1**(3): 15–20.

GARAI, J. E. & A. SCHEINFELD. 1968. Sex differences in mental and behavioral traits. Genet. Psychol. Monogr. **77:** 199–299.

GIBBONS, W. J. 1956. Fertility control in the light of some recent Catholic statements: I. Eugen. Quart. **3:** 9–15.

GIBBONS, W. J. 1956. Fertility control in the light of some recent Catholic statements: II. Eugen. Quart. **3:** 82–87.

GOLDBERG, D., H. SHARP & R. FREEDMAN. 1959. The stability and reliability of expected family size. Milbank Mem. Fund Quart. **37**(4): 369–385.

GOODE, W. A. 1963. World Revolution and Family Patterns. The Free Press of Glencoe. New York, N.Y.

HAWKES, G. R., L. BURCHINAL & B. GARDNER. 1958. Size of family and adjustment of children. Marr. Fam. Living **20:** 65.

HILL, R., J. M. STYCOS & K. W. BLACK. 1959. The Family and Population Control: A Puerto Rican Experiment in Social Change. University of North Carolina Press. Chapel Hill, N.C.

HOFFMAN, L. 1968. The decision to become a working wife. *In* Family Roles and Interaction: An Anthology. J. Heiss, Ed. Rand-McNally. Chicago, Ill.

HOFFMAN, L. W. & F. WYATT. 1960. Social change and motivations for having larger families: Some theoretical considerations. Merrill-Palmer Quart. **6:** 235–244.

HOFFMEYER, H. 1953. Social and psychological factors limiting the use of anticonceptions. Int. J. Sexol. **7:** 75–76.

HOLLINGWORTH, L. S. 1916. Social devices for compelling women to bear and rear children. Amer. J. Sociol. **22:** 28–29.

HURLEY, J. R. & D. PALONEN. 1967. Marital satisfaction and child density among university student parents. J. Marr. Fam. **29:** 483–484.

JAFFE, F. S. 1964. Family planning and poverty. Marr. Family **27:** 467.

KAHL, J. A. 1967. Modern values and fertility ideals in Brazil and Mexico. J. Soc. Issues **23:** 99–114.

KELMAN, S. R. 1937. Some psychiatric aspects of birth control. Amer. J. Psychiat. **94:** 320.

KISER, C. 1968. Trends in fertility differentials by color and socioeconomic status in the United States. Eugen. Quart. **15**(4): 221–226.

KROGER, W. S. & S. C. FREED. 1951. Psychogynecic aspects of contraception. *In* Psychosomatic Gynecology. W. B. Saunders Co. Philadelphia, Pa. Reprinted, 1963. Wilshire. Hollywood, Calif.

LEWIS-FANING, E. 1949. Report on an enquiry into family limitation and its influence on human fertility during the past fifty years. Papers Roy. Commission Population **I.** Her Majesty's Stationery Office. London, England.

LIEBERMAN, E. J. 1970. Reserving a womb: Case for the small family. Amer. J. Public Health **60**(1): 87–92.

LIEBERMAN, J. E. 1964. Preventive psychiatry and family planning. J. Marr. Fam. Nov.: 471–477.

LORIMER, F. 1954. Culture and Human Fertility. UNESCO. Paris, France.

MENNINGER, K. 1943. Psychiatric aspects of contraception. Bull. Menninger Clin. **7:** 36–40.

MISHLER, E. & C. F. WESTOFF. 1955. A proposal for research on social psychological factors affecting fertility: Concepts and hypotheses. Current Research in Human Fertility. Milbank Memorial Fund. New York, N.Y.

NAG, M. 1962. Factors Affecting Fertility in Non-industrial Societies. Yale University Publications in Anthropology, No. 66. Yale University Press. New Haven, Conn.

NAMBOODIRI, N. K. 1964. The wife's work experience and child spacing. Milbank Mem. Fund Quart. July: 65–77.

NYE, F. I. 1952. Sibling number, broken homes and adjustment. Marr. Fam. Living **14:** 327–330.

POHLMAN, E. 1966. Mobilizing social pressures toward small families. Eugen. Quart. **13**(2)**:** 122–127.

POHLMAN, E. 1967. A psychologist's introduction to the birth planning literature. J. Soc. Issues **23:** 13–38.

POHLMAN, E. W. 1966. Birth control: Independent and dependent variable for psychological research. Amer. Psychol. 21: 967–970.

POHLMAN, E. W. 1967. The Psychology of Birth Planning. Schenkman. Cambridge, Mass.

POHLMAN, E. & K. S. RAO. 1969. Children, teachers and parents view birth planning, II. Children's family size preferences and their reasons. J. Fam. Welfare **15**(3)**:** 54–66.

POLGAR, S. 1966. Sociocultural research in family planning in the United States: review and prospects. Human Organization **25:** 321–329.

POLGAR, S. 1969. Culture and family planning. Paper, Ann. Meet. Soc. Appl. Anthropol. Mexico City, April 10.

RAUF, A. 1958. Psychological aspects of family planning. J. Fam. Welfare **4:** 85–91.

REED, R. B. 1947. Social and psychological factors affecting fertility: The interrelationship of marital adjustment, fertility control, and size of family. Milbank Mem. Fund Quart. **25:** 383–425.

REHWINKEL, A. M. 1959. Planned Parenthood and Birth Control in the Light of Christian Ethics. Concordia. St. Louis, Mo.

REGUENA, M. 1965. Social and economic correlates of induced abortion in Santiago, Chile. Demography **2:** 42.

STYCOS, J. M. 1965. Female employment and fertility in Lima, Peru. Amer. J. Sociol. **70.**

STYCOS, J. M. 1965. Social class and preferred family size in Peru. Amer. J. Sociol. **70:** 651–658.

STYCOS, J. M. 1967. Contraception and Catholicism in Latin America. J. Soc. Issues **23:** 115–134.

SULLOWAY, A. W. 1959. Birth Control and Catholic Doctrine. Beacon Press. Boston, Mass.

WESTOFF, C. F., E. G. MISHLER & L. E. KELLY. 1957. Preferences in size of family and eventual fertility twenty years after. Amer. J. Sociol. **62:** 491–497.

WESTOFF, C. F. & R. H. POTVIN. 1967. College Women and Fertility Values. Princeton University Press. Princeton, N.J.

WHELPTON, P. K. & C. V. KISER, Eds. 1946–1958. Social and Psychological Factors Affecting Fertility. (5 vol.) Milbank Memorial Fund. New York, N.Y.

WYATT, F. 1967. Clinical notes on the motives of reproduction. J. Soc. Issues **23:** 29–56.

ZIMMERMAN, A. 1961. Catholic Viewpoint and Overpopulation. Hanover House. Garden City, N.Y.

Reproduction Control and Limitation Policy

ADAMS, J. R. 1961. Attitudinal ambivalence and choice of contraceptive method. Unpublished doctoral dissertation. Columbia University. New York, N.Y.

AGARWALA, S. N. 1960. Population control in India: Progress and prospects. Law Contemp. Probl. **25**(3): 583.

APTEKAR, H. 1931. Anjea: Infanticide Abortion and Contraception in Savage Society. Goodwin. New York, N.Y.

*BANKS, J. A. & O. BANKS. 1954. Prosperity and Parenthood: A Study of Family Planning among the Victorian Middle Classes. Routledge and Kegan Paul. London, England.

*BANKS, J. A. & O. BANKS. 1964. Feminism and Family Planning in Victorian England. Schoken. New York, N.Y.

*BATES, J. E. & E. S. ZAWADSKI. 1964. Criminal Abortion: A Study in Medical Sociology. Charles C. Thomas Publ. Springfield, Ill.

BERELSON, B. & R. FREEDMAN. 1964. A study in fertility control. Sci. Amer. **210:** 29–37.

BERELSON, B., *et al.*, Eds. 1966. Family Planning and Population Programs. University of Chicago Press. Chicago, Ill.

BLAKE, J. 1965. Demographic science and the redirection of population policy. J. Chron. Dis. **18:** 1181–1200.

BLAKE, J. 1966. Ideal family size among white Americans: A quarter of a century's evidence. Demography **19.**

BLAKE, J. 1967. Family size in the 1960's—a baffling fad? Eugen. Quart. March.

BLAKE, J. 1967. Parental control, delayed marriage, and population policy. Proc. World Population Conf. 1965. **II.** United Nations. New York, N.Y.

BLAKE, J. 1969. Population policy for Americans. Is the government being misled? Science **164:** 522–529.

BOGUE, D. J. 1965. Westside fertility report. (Mimeo available from author, Community and Family Study Center, University of Chicago, Chicago, Ill.)

CALDERONE, M. S., Ed. 1958. Abortion in the United States. (Hoeber) Harper & Row. New York, N.Y.

CALDERONE, M. S., Ed. 1964. Manual of Contraceptive Practice. The Williams & Wilkins, Co. Baltimore, Md.

CARLETON, R. O. 1965. Fertility trends, and differentials in Latin America. Milbank Mem. Fund Quart. **43**(4): Part 2.

CHANDRASEKHAR, S. 1961. Population and Planned Parenthood in India. 2nd edit. Allen & Unwin. London, England.

CISLER, L. 1970. Abortion law repeal: A warning to women. *In* Notes from the Second Year: Radical Feminism. (Reprints available from New Yorkers for Abortion Repeal, P. O. Box 240, Planetarium Station, New York, N.Y. 10024, 15¢ each.)

CISLER, L. 1970. Unfinished business: Birth control and women's liberation. *In* The Hand that Cradles the Rock. R. Morgan, Ed. Random House, New York, N.Y. (Reprints available from author, 102 W. 80th St., New York, N.Y. 10024, 25¢ each.)

COLEMAN, R. W., E. KURTS & S. PROVENCE. 1953. The study of variations of early parental attitudes: A preliminary report. Psychoanal. Stud. Child. **8:** 20–47.

COLLYER, A. O. 1965. Birth Rates in Latin America. Research Series, No. 7. Institute of International Studies. University of California. Berkeley, Calif.

CORNISH, M. J., F. A. RUDERMAN & S. S. SPIVAK. 1963. Doctors and Family Planning. National Committee on Maternal Health. New York, N.Y.

DAVIS, K. 1965. The population impact on children in the world's agrarian countries. Pop. Rev. **9** (1 & 2).

DAY, L. H. & A. T. DAY. 1964. Too Many Americans: Tomorrow's Issue. Houghton-Mifflin. Boston, Mass.

DEVEREUX, C. 1955. A Study of Abortion in Primitive Societies. Julian Press. New York, N.Y.

DICK-READ, G. 1962. Childbirth Without Fear: The Principles and Practices of Natural Childbirth. Dell. New York, N.Y.

DOCTOR X. 1962. Doctor X, the Abortionist. (As told to L. Freeman.) Doubleday. New York, N.Y.

ETZIONI, A. 1968. Sex control, science and society. Science **148:** 1107–1112.
FARBER, S. M. & R. H. L. WILSON, Eds. 1966. The Challenge to Women: The Biological Avalanche. Basic Books, Inc. New York, N.Y.
FIRST INTERNATIONAL CONFERENCE ON FAMILY PLANNING PROGRAMS, PLANNING COMMITTEE. 1966. Family Planning Programs. University of Chicago Press. Chicago, Ill.
FORD, C. S. 1952. Control of conception in cross-cultural perspective. Ann. N. Y. Acad. Sci. **54:** 763–768.
FREEDMAN, R., Ed. 1964. Population: The Vital Revolution. Doubleday. New York, N.Y.
FREEDMAN, R., P. K. WHELPTON & A. A. CAMPBELL. 1959. Family Planning, Sterility, and Population Growth. McGraw-Hill Book Co. New York, N.Y.
*FRYER, P. 1965. The Birth Controllers. Secker and Warburg. London, England.
*GEBHARD, P. H., W. B. POMEROY, C. MARTIN & C. CHRISTENSON. 1958. Pregnancy, Birth and Abortion. (Hoeber) Harper & Row. New York, N.Y.
*GILMORE, C. P. 1969. Something better than the pill? N. Y. Times Mag. July 20: 6.
GLASS, D. V. & D. E. C. EVERSLEY, Eds. 1965. Population in History. Aldine Press. Chicago, Ill.
GOLDBERG, D. & C. H. COOMBS. Some applications of unfolding theory to fertility analysis. Emerging Techniques in Demographic Analysis. Milbank Memorial Fund Round Table.
GRABILL, W. H., C. V. KISER & P. K. WHELPTON. 1958. The Fertility of American Women. John Wiley & Sons, Inc. New York, N.Y.
*GRAHAM, H. 1951. Eternal Eve: The History of Gynecology and Obstetrics. Doubleday. New York, N.Y.
GREEP, R. O., Ed. 1963. Human Fertility and Population Problems. Schenkman. Cambridge, Mass.
*GUTTMACHER, A. F., Ed. 1967. The Case for Legalized Abortion Now. Diablo Press. Berkeley, Calif.
*HAMILTON, V. C. 1940. Some sociologic and psychologic observations on abortion. Amer. J. Obstet. Gynecol. **39**(6): 919–928.
*HAMILTON, V. C. 1941. Some observations on the contraceptive behavior of abortion patients. Human Fert. **5:** 37–41.
HARDIN, G., Ed. 1964. Population, Evolution & Birth Control. W. H. Freeman. San Francisco, Calif.
*HARDIN, G. 1966. The history and future of birth control. Perspect. Biol. Med. **10**(1).
*HARDIN, G. 1967. Semantic aspects of abortion. ETC **24**(3).
*HARDIN, G. 1968. Abortion—or compulsory pregnancy? J. Marr. Fam. **30**(2).
HAUSER, P. M., Ed. 1963. The Population Dilemma. Prentice-Hall. Englewood Cliffs, N.J.
HAUSER, P. M. & O. D. DUNCAN, Eds. 1959. The Study of Population: An Inventory and Appraisal. University of Chicago Press. Chicago, Ill.
*HAVEMANN, E. K. 1967. Birth Control: A Special Time-Life Report. Time-Life. New York, N.Y.
*HIMES, N. A. 1963. A Medical History of Contraception. Gamut Press. New York, N.Y.
*INTERNATIONAL CONFERENCE ON ABORTION. 1968. The Terrible Choice: The Abortion Dilemma. Proceedings, Fall, 1967. Bantam Press. New York, N.Y.
*KARMEL, M. 1959. Thank You, Dr. Lamaze. J. B. Lippincott Co. Philadelphia, Pa.
KISER, C. V., Ed. 1962. Research in Family Planning. Princeton University Press. Princeton, N.J.
KISER, C. V., W. H. GRABILL & A. A. CAMPBELL. 1968. Trends and Variations in Fertility in the United States. Harvard University Press. Cambridge, Mass.

KOYA, Y. 1963. Pioneering in Family Planning. Japan Medical Publishers. Tokyo, Japan.

*LADER, L. 1966. Abortion. Bobs-Merrill. New York, N.Y.

LANDER, L. 1955. The Margaret Sanger Story and the Fight for Birth Control. Doubleday. Garden City, N.Y.

*LASAGNA, L. 1968. Life, Death and the Doctor. Alfred A. Knopf. New York, N.Y.

LEE, N. H. 1969. The Search for an Abortionist. University of Chicago Press, Chicago, Ill.

*LUCAS, R. 1968. Federal constitutional limitations on the enforcement and administration of state abortion statutes. N. C. Law Rev. **46**(4).

MAIR, G. F., Ed. 1949. Studies in Population. Princeton University Press. Princeton, N.J.

MCMAHAN, C. A. 1951. An empirical test of three hypotheses concerning the human sex ratio at birth in the United States, 1915–1948. Milbank Mem. Fund Quart. **29:** 273–293.

*MEAD, M., *et al.* 1967. The Peaceful Revolution: Birth Control and the Changing Status of Women. Planned Parenthood-World Population. New York, N.Y.

MEAD, M., *et al.* 1969. Voluntary population control? Three experts debate possibility. Planned Parenthood News **1**(2): 3.

MEIER, R. L. 1959. Modern Science and the Human Fertility Problem. John Wiley & Sons, Inc. New York, N.Y.

MILBANK MEMORIAL FUND. 1952. Approaches to Problems of High Fertility in Agrarian Societies. Milbank Memorial Fund, New York, N.Y.

MORAN, W. E., Ed. 1965. Population Growth—Threat to Peace? P. J. Kenedy & Sons. New York, N.Y.

*MOSKIN, J. R. 1969. The new contraceptive society. Look. Feb. **4:** 50–53.

MUDD, S., Ed. 1965. The Population Crisis: Implications and Plans for Action. Indiana University Press. Bloomington, Ind.

MYRDAL, A. 1968. Nation and Family: The Swedish Experiment in Democratic Family and Population Policy. Massachusetts Institute of Technology Press. Cambridge, Mass.

*NATIONAL OBSERVER. 1966. The Pill and Its Impact. National Observer Newsbook. New York, N.Y.

*NEUBARDT, S. 1967. A Concept of Contraception. Trident Press. New York, N.Y.

*NEWTON, N. 1955. Maternal Emotions. Harper & Row. New York, N.Y.

*OSOFSKY, H. The Pregnant Teenager. Charles C Thomas Publ. Springfield, Ill.

*PETERSEN, W. 1964. The Politics of Population. Doubleday. New York, N.Y.

PLANNED PARENTHOOD-WORLD POPULATION. A Selected Bibliography for Professionals on Family Planning and Related Subjects. Planned Parenthood, New York, N.Y.

POHLMAN, E. 1968. The timing of first births: A review of effects. Eugen. Quart. **15**(4): 252–263.

POHLMAN, E. W. 1967. Birth Timing and Spacing: Research and Recommendations. Mimeo.

POHLMAN, E. W. 1967. Unwanted conceptions: Research on undesirable consequences. Eugen. Quart. **14:** 143–154.

POLGAR, S. 1965. The impact of new contraceptive methods in impoverished neighborhoods of New York—Rationale and plan of research. Paper, Ann. Meet. Population Ass. Amer.

RAINWATER, L. 1967. Family planning in cross-national perspective: An overview. J. Soc. Issues **23:** 1–12.

RAINWATER, L. & K. WEINSTEIN. 1960. And the Poor Get Children: Sex Contraception and Family Planning in the Working Class. Quadrangle Books. Chicago, Ill.

*RAINWATER, L., *et al.* 1965. Family Design: Marital Sexuality, Family Size, and Contraception. Aldine Press. New York, N.Y.

ROCK, J. 1963. The Time Has Come. Alfred A. Knopf. New York, N.Y.
RODGERS, D. A., F. J. ZIEGLER, J. ALTROCCHI & N. LEVY. 1965. A longitudinal study of the psycho-social effects of vasectomy. J. Marr. Fam. **27:** 59–64.
ROSEN, H., Ed. 1954. Therapeutic Abortion. Julian Press. New York, N.Y.
*ROSSI, A. 1966. Abortion laws and their victims. Trans-action. Sept.–Oct.
*ROSSI, A. 1969. Abortion and social change. Dissent. July-Aug.: 338–346.
*SCHENK, R. U. 1968. Let's think about abortion. Cath. World: 207.
*SCHUR, E. M. 1955. Abortion and the social system. Soc. Prob. Oct.: 94–99.
SHEPS, M. C. & J. C. RIDLEY. 1966. Public Health and Population Changes. Schenkman. Cambridge, Mass.
SHETTLES, L. B. 1961. Conception and birth sex ratios: A review. Obstet. Gynecol. 18: 122–130.
SMITH, D. L. 1967. Abortion and the Law. Western Reserve Press. Cleveland, Ohio.
STEFFEN, T. & R. T. BUSHELL. 1964. The Contraceptive Industry and Its Environment. Carnegie Institute of Technology, Graduate School of Industrial Administration. Pittsburgh, Pa.
*STUART, M. & W. T. LIU. 1969. The Changing Woman: The Impact of Family Planning. Little, Brown & Co. Boston, Mass.
STYCOS, J. M. 1955. Family and Fertility in Puerto Rico. Columbia University Press. New York, N.Y.
STYCOS, J. M. 1963. Obstacles to programs of population control—Facts and fancies. Marr. Fam. Living **25:** 5–13.
STYCOS, J. M. 1964. The Cornell international population program. Milbank Mem. Fund Quart. **28.**
STYCOS, J. M. & K. W. BACK. 1964. The Control of Human Fertility in Jamaica. Cornell University Press. Ithaca, N.Y.
*SWEDISH INSTITUTE FOR CULTURAL RELATIONS WITH FOREIGN COUNTRIES (Box 3306, Stockholm 3, Sweden). 1964. Therapeutic Abortion and the Law in Sweden.
*TANZER, D. 1968. Natural childbirth: Pain or peak experience? Psychol. Today. **2**(5).
THIESSEN, D. D. & D. A. RODGERS. 1961. Population density and endrocrine function. Psychol. Bull. **58:** 441–451.
THOMPSON, W. S. & D. T. LEWIS. 1965. Population Problems. 5th edit. McGraw-Hill Book Co. New York, N.Y.
TIETZE, C. 1960. Selected Bibliography of Contraception: 1940–1960. National Committee on Maternal Health. New York, N.Y.
TIETZE, C. 1962. Surgical Sterilization of Men and Women: A Selected Bibliography. National Committee on Maternal Health. New York, N.Y.
TIETZE, C. 1965. Bibliography of Fertility Control: 1950–1965. National Committee on Maternal Health. New York, N.Y.
TIETZE, C. 1965. History of contraceptive methods. J. Sex. Res. **1:** 69–85.
TIETZE, C. & H. LEHFELDT. 1961. Legal abortion in Eastern Europe. J. Amer. Med. Ass. **175:** 1149–1154.
*VINCENT, C. 1961. Unmarried Mothers. The Free Press. New York, N.Y.
WALDROP, M. F. & R. Q. BELL. 1966. Effects of family size and density on newborn characteristics. Amer. J. Orthopsychiat. **36**(3): 544–550.
WEILER, H. 1959. Sex ratio and birth control. Amer. J. Sociol. **65:** 298–299.
WESTOFF, C. F., R. G. POTTER & P. C. SAGI. 1963. The Third Child. Princeton University Press. Princeton, N.J.
WHELPTON, P. K., A. A. CAMPBELL & J. PATTERSON. 1966. Fertility and Family Planning in the United States. Princeton University Press. Princeton, N.J.
*WHITE, R. B. 1966. Induced abortions: A survey of their psychiatric implications, complications, and indications. Tex. Rep. Biol. Med. **24**(4): 531–558.
WINSTON, S. 1932. Birth control and the sex ratio at birth. Amer. J. Sociol. **38:** 225–231.

*WOODSIDE, M. 1962. Attitudes of women abortionists. Howard J. **11**(2).

Women in Society: Status and Legal Issues

*ANÉR, K. 1966. Swedish Women Today: A Personal Appraisal. Swedish Institute (Box 3306, Stockhold 3, Sweden).

ASTIN, H. S. 1969. The Woman Doctorate in America. Russell Sage. New York, N.Y.

BEBEL, A. 1910. Women and Socialism. Socialist Literature Co. New York, N.Y.

*BEECHER, C. E. 1842. A Treatise on Domestic Economy.

*BERGER, B. 1960. Working-Class Suburb. University of California Press. Berkeley, Calif.

*BERNARD, J. 1964. Academic Women. Pennsylvania State University Press. Philadelphia, Pa.

*BERREMAN, G. 1966. On the role of women. Bull. At. Sci., Nov.

BERRY, J. 1955. Life plans of college women. J. Nat. Ass. Deans Wom. **18:** 76–80.

BERRY, J. & S. EPSTEIN. 1963. Continuing Education of Women: Needs, Aspirations and Plans. The University of Missouri at Kansas City Press. Kansas City, Mo.

BROWN, D. R., Ed. 1968. Women in the Soviet Union. Teachers College. New York, N.Y.

BIRD, C. 1966. Let's draft women, too. Sat. Evening Post. June 18.

*BIRD, C. 1968. Born Female. David McKay Co. New York, N.Y.

*BOORSTIN, D. The Image.

BORCHERS, G. L. 1963. Some investigations concerning the status of faculty women in America. *In* Women in College and University Teaching.

*BORGESE, E. M. 1962. The Ascent of Women. George Braziller, Inc. New York, N.Y.

BRECKENRIDGE, S. P. 1933. Women in the Twentieth Century—A Study of Their Political, Social and Economic Activities. McGraw-Hill Book Co. New York, N.Y.

*CASSARA, B. B., Ed. 1962. American Women: The Changing Image. Beacon Press. New York, N.Y.

CAVAN, S. 1956–1957. The status of women in the professions relative to the status of men. Quart. Amer. Interprofessional Inst. Winter.

COMMITTEE ON EDUCATION AND LABOR. 1948. Equal pay for equal work for women. Repart of the United States House of Representatives, Subcommittee No. 4, of the Committee on Education and Labor. 80th Congress, 2nd Session. Feb. 9, 10, 11 & 13.

THE CONGRESSIONAL RECORD. 1966. Women are being deprived of legal rights by the Equal Employment Opportunity Commission. June 20.

DAEDALUS. 1964. The woman in America. Spring.

*DAHLSTROM, E., Ed. 1967. The Changing Roles of Men and Women. Duckworth. London, England.

DAVID, O. 1957. The Education of Women—Signs for the Future. American Council on Education. Washington, D.C.

DE BEAUVOIR, S. 1953. The Second Sex. Translated by H. M. Parshley. Alfred A. Knopf. New York, N.Y.

DEGLER, C. N. 1964. Revolution without ideology: The changing place of women in America. Daedalus : 653–670.

*DE RHAM, E. 1965. The Love Fraud. Clarkson Potter. New York, N.Y.

*DINGWALL, E. J. 1956. The American Woman.

*DITZION, S. 1953. Marriage, Morals and Sex in America—A History of Ideas. New York, N.Y.

DODGE, N. T. 1966. Women in the Soviet Economy. The John Hopkins Press. Baltimore, Md.

DOLAN, E. F. 1963. Higher education for women: Time for reappraisal. *Higher Educ.* Sept.

EQUAL EMPLOYMENT OPPORTUNITY COMMISSION. First Annual Digest of Legal Interpretations. July, 1965–July, 1967.

ELLMAN, M. 1968. Thinking About Women. Harcourt, Brace & World. New York, N.Y.

EPSTEIN, C. F. 1970. Woman's Place. Options and Limitations in Professional Careers. University of California Press. Berkeley, Calif.

*FANON, F. Studies in a Dying Colonialism.

*FANON, F. The Wretched of the Earth.

FARBER, S. & R. H. L. WILSON, Eds. 1963. The Potential of Women. McGraw-Hill Book Co. New York, N.Y.

*FENBERG, M. 1948. Blame Coke and Blackstone. Wom. Lawyers J. **34**(2): 7.

FIRKEL, E. 1963. Woman in the Modern World. Fides Publ. Notre Dame, Ind.

*FRANCIS, P. 1963. Legal Status of Women.

FRIEDAN, B. 1960. Women are people too! Good Housekeeping. Sept.

FRIEDAN, B. 1961. If one generation can ever tell another. Smith Alumnae Quart. Northampton, Mass. Winter.

*FRIEDAN, B. 1963. The Feminine Mystique. W. W. Norton. New York, N.Y.

*FROST, D. & A. JAY. 1969. Women. *In* The English. Avon Books. New York, N.Y.

GALLEN, R. T. 1965. Wives' Legal Rights. Dell Publ. Co. New York, N.Y.

GINZBERG, E. 1966. Life Styles of Educated Women. Columbia University Press. New York, N.Y.

GINZBERG, E. & A. M. YOHALEM. 1966. Educated American Women: Self-Portraits. Columbia University Press. New York, N.Y.

HALLE, F. 1933. Women in Soviet Russia. Routledge. London, England.

*HERSCHBERGER, R. 1948. Adam's Rib. Pellegrini and Cudahy. New York, N.Y.

JONES, B. & J. BROWN. 1968. Toward a Female Liberation Movement. New England Free Press. Cambridge, Mass.

*KALVESTEN, A. 1966. Social Structure of Sweden. Swedish Institute (Box 3306, Stockholm 3, Sweden).

*KANOWITZ, L. 1967. Law and the married woman. St. Louis U. Law J. **12:** 3.

KANOWITZ, L. 1967. Sex-based discrimination in American law and the single girl. St. Louis U. Law J. **11:** 293–330.

*KANOWITZ, L. 1969. Women and the Law, The Unfinished Revolution. University of New Mexico Press. Albuquerque, N.M.

KIRKPATRICK, C. 1938. Nazi Germany. Its Women and Family Life. Bobbs-Merrill. Indianapolis, Ind.

KOMAROVSKY, M. 1953. Women in the Modern World: Their Education and Their Dilemmas. Little, Brown & Co. Boston, Mass.

*KOMAROVSKY, M. 1964. Blue-Collar Marriage. Random House. New York, N.Y.

LAMSON, P. L. 1968. Few are Chosen. American Women in Political Life Today. Houghton-Mifflin Co. Boston, Mass.

*LEIJON, A. Swedish Women—Swedish Men. Swedish Institute for Cultural Relations with Foreign Countries (Box 3306, Stockholm 3, Sweden).

LEONARD, M. C., Ed. 1963. Equal Rights Amendment: Questions and Answers Prepared by the Research Department of the National Woman's Party. Document No. 164. Government Printing Office.

*LESSING, D. 1960. In Pursuit of the English.

LEWIS, E. E. 1968. Developing Woman's Potential. Iowa State University Press. Ames, Iowa.

*LEWIS, O. 1961. The Children of Sanchez. Vintage Books. New York, N.Y.

*LEWIS, O. 1965. LaVida. Vintage Books. New York, N.Y.

LIFTON, R. J., Ed. 1964. The Woman in America. Beacon Press. Boston, Mass.

*LINNÉR, B. Sex and Society in Sweden. Pantheon Books. New York, N.Y.

LUCE, C. B. 1967. Is it now or never for women? McCall's. April.

*MCVEETY, J. 1967. Law and the single woman. Wom. Lawyers J. **53**(1): 10.

*MICHAEL, D. 1965. Cybernation. Center for the Study of Democratic Institutions. Santa Barbara, Calif.

MILLETT, K. 1970. Sexual Politics. Doubleday. New York, N.Y.
MINNEAPOLIS TRIBUNE. 1967. Women claim job laws "protect" them too much. Jan. 15.
MONK, D. 1970. Defining the new feminists. Los Angeles Times. Jan. 4.
*MORRIS, R. B. 1958. Studies in the History of American Law : 126–201.
*MURRAY, P. & M. EASTWOOD. 1965. Jane Crow and the law: Sex discrimination and Title VII. George Washington Law Rev. **34**(2): 232.
*NEWCOMER, M. 1959. A Century of Higher Education for American Women. New York, N.Y.
NEW YORK TIMES MAGAZINE. 1960. The woman with brains. Jan. 17.
*PATAI, R., Ed. 1967. Women in the Modern World. The Free Press. New York, N.Y.
*PILPEL, H. & T. ZAVIN. 1962. Your Marriage and the Law. P. F. Collier, Inc. New York, N.Y.
POLLACK, J. H. 1965. Girl dropouts: a neglected national tragedy. Parade. Sept. 26.
*POLLAK, O. 1950. The Criminality of Women. University of Pennsylvania Press. Philadelphia, Pa.
*POLSTER, E. 1967. Conscription: The war on women and children. (Speech available from Women's International League for Peace and Freedom, 2006 Walnut St., Philadelphia, Pa. 19103.)
*POTTER, D. 1962. American Women and American Character. Stetson University Press. De Land, Fla.
*PRUETTE, L. 1924. Women and Leisure. A Study of Waste. E. P. Dutton & Co. New York, N.Y.
*RAINWATER, L., R. P. COLEMAN & G. HANDEL. 1959. Workingman's Wife: Her Personality, World, and Life Style. Oceana Publ. New York, N.Y.
*REICH, W. 1945. The Sexual Revolution. Farrar, Straus & Giroux. New York, N.Y.
*RIEGEL, R. E. 1968. American Feminists. University of Kansas Press. Lawrence, Kan.
RIESMAN, D. 1965. Some dilemmas of women's education. Educ. Rec. Fall.
*RÖSSEL, J. 1965. Women in Sweden. Swedish Institute (Box 3306, Stockholm 3, Sweden).
ROSSI, A. S. 1964. Equality between the sexes: An immodest proposal. Daedalus. Spring : 607–652.
ROSSI, A. S. 1969. Sex equality: The beginnings of ideology. The Humanist. Sept./Oct.
SCOFIELD, N. E. 1960. Some changing roles of women in suburbia: A social anthropological case study. Trans. N. Y. Acad. Sci. **22**(6).
*SCOTT, A. F. 1962. The "new women" in the new South. S. Atlantic Quart. **61.**
*SIMON, R. J., S. M. CLARK & K. GALWAY. 1967. The woman Ph.D.: A recent profile. Soc. Prob. **15**(2).
*SIMON, R. J., S. CLARK & L. L. TIFFT. 1966. Of nepotism, marriage, and the pursuit of an academic career. Sociol. Educ. **39**(4).
*SNOW, H. 1968. Women in Modern China. Humanities Press. New York, N.Y.
*SPIRO, M. Kibbutz.
STERN, E. M. 1949. Women are household slaves. Amer. Mercury. Jan.
STRACHEY, R., Ed. 1936. Our Freedom and its Results. Hogarth Press. London, England.
*SWEDISH INSTITUTE FOR CULTURAL RELATIONS WITH FOREIGN COUNTRIES. 1965. Swedish Divorce Laws. (Box 3306, Stockholm 3, Sweden.)
*SWEDISH INSTITUTE FOR CULTURAL RELATIONS WITH FOREIGN COUNTRIES. 1968. The Status of Women in Sweden: Report to the United Nations. (Box 3306, Stockholm 3, Sweden.)
*TARBELL, I. 1912. The Business of Being a Woman. MacMillan Co. New York, N.Y. THIS WEEK. 1967. Sex and civil rights. March 19.

UNITED NATIONS. 1963. Political rights of women in member nations of the United Nations. *In* Women in the World Today. Int. Rep. 2, United Nations Rept. A/5456. Reprinted by Women's Bureau. Washington, D.C.

UNITED STATES DEPARTMENT OF LABOR, BUREAU OF EMPLOYMENT SECURITY. 1942. Occupations suitable for women. Washington, D.C.

*UNITED STATES DEPARTMENT OF LABOR, WOMEN'S BUREAU. Know Your Rights. Washington, D.C.

*UNITED STATES DEPARTMENT OF LABOR, WOMEN'S BUREAU. Leaflet No. 10. Washington, D.C.

WALL STREET JOURNAL. 1967. Women's groups fight last vestiges of bias on job, before the law. May 23.

WARE, C. 1970. Woman Power: The Movement for Women's Liberation. Tower Publications, Inc. New York, N.Y.

*WEST, A. 1968. Who takes advantage of American women? Men. Vogue. May : 198.

*WHITE, L. 1950. Educating Our Daughters. Harpers. New York, N.Y.

WOERISHOFFER, C. 1945. Women during the war and after. Graduate Department of Social Economy and Social Research. Bryn Mawr College. Bryn Mawr, Pa.

*WOLFF, J. 1958. What Makes Women Buy. McGraw-Hill Book Co. New York, N.Y.

WOMEN'S BUREAU. 1966. College Women Seven Years After Graduation. Bulletin 292. Washington, D.C.

Women and the World of Work

*ABBOTT, E. 1910. Women in Industry: A Study in American Economic History.

ASTIN, H. S. 1969. The Woman Doctorate in America. Russell Sage. New York, N.Y.

*BAGDIKIAN, B. H. 1966. Who is sabotaging day care for our children? Ladies Home J. Nov. : 86.

*BAKER, E. F. 1964. Technology and Women's Work. Columbia University Press. New York, N.Y.

*BAKER, M. 1962. Women who work. Int. Soc. Rev. Summer.

*BEECHER, C. E. 1842. A Treatise on Domestic Economy.

*BENJAMIN, L. 1966. So You Want to be a Working Mother! McGraw-Hill Book Co. New York, N.Y.

BERRY, J. 1955. Life plans of college women. J. Nat. Ass. Deans Wom. **18:** 76–80.

BIRD, C. 1967. What we are finding out about working mothers. Woman's Day. Sept.

*BIRD, C. 1968. Born Female. David McKay Co. New York, N.Y.

*BLOOD, R. O. Long-range causes and consequences of the employment of married women. J. Marr. Fam. **27**(1).

BLOUSTEIN, E. J. 1968. Man's work goes from sun to sun but woman's work is never done. Psychol. Today **1**(10): 38.

*BOONE, G. 1942. The Woman's Trade Union League.

BORCHERS, G. L. 1963. Some investigations concerning the status of faculty women in America. *In* Women in College and University Teaching.

BORING, E. G. 1951. The woman problem. Amer. Psychol. **6:** 679.

BOYNTON, P. L. & R. D. WOOLWINE. 1942. The relationship between the economic status of high school girls and their vocational wishes and expectations. J. Appl. Psychol. **26:** 399–415.

*BROWNLEE, J. 1967. Where is the professional woman? Wom. Lawyers J. **53**(1): 14.

BRYAN, A. I. & E. G. BORING. 1947. Women in American psychology: Factors affecting their professional careers. Amer. Psychol. **2:** 3–20.

CAIN, G. G. 1966. Married Women in the Labor Force: An Economic Analysis. University of Chicago Press. Chicago, Ill.

CAVAN, S. 1956–1957. The status of women in the professions relative to the status of men. Quart. Amer. Interprofessional Inst. Winter.

COCKBURN, P. 1967. Women university graduates in continuing education and employment. An exploratory study initiated by the Canadian Federation of University Women, 1966. Toronto, Canada.

COLLINS, J. 1969. Women in the universities. The Radical Teacher. Dec. 30 : 13–14.

COMMITTEE ON EDUCATION AND LABOR. 1948. Equal pay for equal work for women. Report of the United States House of Representatives, Subcommittee No. 4, of the Committee on Education and Labor. 80th Congress, 2nd Session. Feb. 9, 10, 11 & 13.

THE CONGRESSIONAL RECORD. 1966. Women are being deprived of legal rights by the Equal Employment Opportunity Commission. June 20.

COOPER, J. D. 1964. A Woman's Guide to Part-Time Jobs. Dolphin Books. New York, N.Y.

COTTON, D. W. 1965. The Case for the Working Mothers. Stein & Day. New York, N.Y.

*CUSSLER, M. 1958. The Woman Executive. Harcourt, Brace & World. New York, N.Y.

*DEXTER, E. A. 1950. Career Woman of America, 1776–1840. Marshall Jones Co. Francetown, N.H.

*DICHTER, E. The Strategy of Desire.

DUN'S REVIEW. 1966. Women—Industry's newest challenge. August.

EQUAL EMPLOYMENT OPPORTUNITY COMMISSION. 1966. The First Annual Report. House Document No. 86.

EPSTEIN, C. F. 1970. Woman's Place: Options and Limits in Professional Careers. University of California Press. Berkeley, Calif.

*FAVA, S. 1960. The status of women in professional sociology. Amer. Sociol. Rev. **25:** 271–276.

FEDERAL WOMAN'S AWARD STUDY GROUP ON CAREER FOR WOMEN PROGRESS REPORT TO THE PRESIDENT. 1967. March 3.

FLEXNER, E. Woman's Work in America.

HARBESON, G. E. 1967. Choice and Challenge for the American Woman. Schenkman. Cambridge, Mass.

*HARTMAN, S. 1969. Should wives work? McCall's. Feb. : 57.

*HATTERER, L. J. 1966. The woman artist. *In* The Artist in Society: Problems and Treatment of the Creative Personality. Grove Press. New York, N.Y.

*HENRY, A. 1923. Women and the Labor Movement.

HEYWOOD, A. 1951. There is a Right Job for Every Woman. Doubleday & Co. Garden City, N.Y.

INDUSTRIAL RELATIONS. 1968. Women in the labor force. **7**(3).

JEPHCOTT, P., N. SEEAR & J. H. SMITH. 1962. Married Women Working. Allen & Unwin. London, England.

KENISTON, E. & K. KENISTON. 1964. An American anchronism: The image of women and work. Amer. Scholar. **33:** 355–375.

KINGSBURY, S. H. & M. FAIRCHILD. 1935. Factory, Family and Women in the Soviet Union. G. P. Putnam. New York, N.Y.

KUNDSIN, R. B. 1965. Where are our women in science? Howard Med. Alumni Bull. Winter.

KYRK, H. 1946. Who works and why. Ann. Amer. Acad. Pol. Soc. Sci. May.

LAMBECK, R. 1968. 380 Part-Time Jobs for Women. Bell Publishing Co. New York, N.Y.

*MARMOR, J. 1968. Women in medicine: importance of the formative years. J. Amer. Med. Wom. Ass. **23**(7).

*Mattfeld, J. A. & C. G. Van Aken, Eds. 1965. Women and the Scientific Professions. Massachusetts Institute of Technology Press. Cambridge, Mass.

Miller, M. M. 1961. Women in university teaching. J. Amer. Ass. Univ. Women **54.**

Mincer, J. 1962. Labor force participation of married women. *In* Aspects of Labor Economics. Princeton University Press. Princeton, N.J.

Minneapolis Tribune. 1967. Women claim job laws "protect" them too much. Jan. 15.

*Morse, N. S. & R. S. Weiss. 1955. The function and meaning of work and the job. Amer. Sociol. Rev. **20:** 191–198.

*Murray, P. & M. Eastwood. 1965. Jane Crow and the law: Sex discrimination and Title VII. George Washington Law Rev. **34**(2)**:** 232.

Myrdal, A. & K. Viola. 1956. Women's Two Roles: Home and Work. Routledge and Kegan Paul. London, England.

*National Manpower Council. 1957. Womanpower and Work in the Lives of Married Women.

National Science Foundation. 1961. Women in Scientific Careers. Govt. Printing Office. Washington, D.C.

Neff, W. F. 1929. Victorian Working Women. Columbia University Press. New York, N.Y.

New York Post. 1967. Now jobs for women: a survey. Aug. 21.

New York Times. 1965. De-sexing the job market (Editorial). Aug. 21.

*Nye, F. I. & L. W. Hoffman, Eds. 1963. The Employed Mother in America. Rand-McNally. New York, N.Y.

O'Neill, B. P. 1965. Careers for Women after Marriage and Children. MacMillan Co. New York, N.Y.

Orden, S. & N. Bradburn. 1969. Working wives and marriage happiness. Amer. J. Sociol. Jan.

Parrish, J. 1962. Women in top level teaching and research. J. Amer. Ass. U. Women **55:** 102.

Peterson, E. T. 1958. The impact of maternal employment on the mother-daughter relationship and on the daughter's role orientation. Unpublished doctoral dissertation. The University of Michigan. Ann Arbor, Mich.

Peterson, E. T. 1964. Working women. Daedalus **93:** 671–699.

*Pinch-Beck, I. Women Workers in the Industrial Revolution.

*Pressman, S. 1968. Sex discrimination in employment and what you can do about it. Wom. Lawyers J. **54**(4)**:** 6.

Rosenfeld, C. & V. C. Perrella. 1965. Why women start and stop working: A study in mobility. Monthly Labor Rev. Sept.

Rossi, A. 1967. Working wives: How well is business talking their language? Management Rev. April.

Royster, V. 1964. The work mystique. Wall St. J. June 24.

*Ruderman, F. Child Care and Working Mothers. Child Welfare League of America. New York, N.Y.

Russo, Jr., S. A. & W. Laas. 1968. Women! Business Needs You! A Back-to-Business Guide for Modern Women. Popular Library. New York, N.Y.

*Schreiner, O. 1911. Woman and Labour. Fisher Unwin. London, England.

Scobey, J. & L. P. McGrath. 1968. Creative Careers for Women. A Handbook of Sources and Ideas for Part-Time Jobs. Essandess Special Editions (Simon & Schuster). New York, N.Y.

Scofield, N. E. & B. Klarman. 1968. So You Want to Go Back to Work! Random House. New York, N.Y.

*Simon, R. J., S. M. Clark & K. Galway. 1967. The woman Ph.D.: A recent profile. Soc. Probl. **15**(2).

*Simon, R. J., S. Clark & L. L. Tifft. 1966. Of nepotism, marriage and the pursuit of an academic career. Sociol. Educ. **39**(4).

SLOCUM, W. L. & L. T. EMPEY. 1957. Occupational planning by high school and college girls. J. Home Econ. **49:** 125–126.

*SMITH, G. 1964. Help Wanted: Female, A study of Demand and Supply in a Local Job Market for Women. Rutgers Institute of Management and Labor Relations. New Brunswick, N.J.

*SMUTS, R. W. 1959. Women and Work in America. Columbia University Press. New York, N.Y.

SOCIAL RESEARCH, INC. Bringing women back to work: A study of the woman at home and the manpower white glove girl. Social Research, Inc. Chicago, Ill.

SOUTHARD, H. F. 1960. Mothers' dilemma: To work or not? N.Y. Times Mag. July 17.

*SPRUILL, J. C. Women's Life and Work in the Southern Colonies. University of North Carolina Press. Chapel Hill, N.C.

STERN, M. B. 1963. We the Women: Career Firsts of Nineteenth Century America. Schulte Publishing Co. New York, N.Y.

STOLLENWERK, T. 1968. Back to Work, Ladies: A Career Guide for the Mature Woman. Pilot Books. New York, N.Y.

STOLZ, L. M. 1960. Effects of maternal employment on children: Evidence from research. Child Develop. **31**(4): 749–782.

SYSIHARJU, A. 1960. Equality, Home and Work: A Socio-psychological Study on Finnish Student Women's Attitudes Toward the Woman's Role in Society. Mikkelissa. Helsinki, Finland.

TANGRI, S. S. 1969. Role-innovation in occupational choice. Doctoral dissertation. University of Michigan. Ann Arbor, Mich.

UNITED STATES DEPARTMENT OF LABOR, BUREAU OF EMPLOYMENT SECURITY. 1942. Occupations suitable for women. Washington, D.C.

UNITED STATES DEPARTMENT OF LABOR. 1969. Handbook on Women Workers. Bulletin 294. Women's Bureau. Washington, D.C.

UNITED STATES DEPARTMENT OF LABOR, WAGE AND LABOR STANDARDS ADMINISTRATION, WOMEN'S BUREAU. 1968. Working Mothers and the Need for Child Care Services. June. Washington, D.C.

*UNITED STATES DEPARTMENT OF LABOR, WOMEN'S BUREAU. 1968. The Fuller Utilization of the Woman Physician. Washington, D.C.

*UNITED STATES DEPARTMENT OF LABOR, WOMEN'S BUREAU. Know Your Rights. Washington, D.C.

*UNITED STATES DEPARTMENT OF LABOR, WOMEN'S BUREAU. Leaflet no. 10. Washington, D.C.

U. S. NEWS & WORLD REPORT. 1967. Where job changes will be best in the years just ahead. Jan. 2.

WALL STREET JOURNAL. 1967. Women's groups fight last vestiges of bias on job, before the law. May 23.

*WEIL, M. W. 1961. An analysis of the factors influencing married women's actual or planned work participation. Amer. Sociol. Rev. **26:** 91–96.

*WHITE, J. J. 1967. Women in the law. Mich. Law Rev. **65:** 1051.

WINTER, E. L. 1967. Women at Work: Every Woman's Guide to Successful Employment. Simon & Schuster. New York, N.Y.

WOERISHOFFER, C. 1945. Women during the war and after. Graduate Department of Social Economy and Social Research, Bryn Mawr College. Bryn Mawr, Pa.

*WOLFLE, D. 1954. America's Resources of Specialized Talent.

*WOMEN IN THE (SERVICE) INDUSTRY: A MINORITY REPORT. 1969. Inst. Mag. **64** (3): 87–110.

WOMEN'S BUREAU. 1966. College Women Seven Years after Graduation. Bulletin 292.

ZISSUS, C. 1964. A study of the life planning of 550 freshman women at Purdue University. J. Nat. Ass. Wom. Deans Couns. **27**(4): 143–159.

Psychological Issues and Problems

ABRAHAM, K. 1922. Manifestations of the female castration complex. Int. J. Psychoanal. **3.**

AGRIST, S. S. 1969. The study of sex roles. J. Soc. Issues **25:** 215.

BAILYN, L. 1964. Notes on the role of choice in the psychology of professional women. Daedalus. Spring : 700–710.

*BALINT, A. 1937. Psychology of menstruation. Psychoanal. Quart. May.

BARUCH, R. 1967. The achievement motive in women: Implications for career development. J. Personality Soc. Psychol. **5**(3): 260–267.

*BENEDEK, T. 1952. Psychosexual Function in Women. Ronald Press. New York, N.Y.

*BERNARD, J. 1968. The Sex Game. Prentice-Hall. Englewood Cliffs, N.J.

BIBRING, G. L. 1959. Some considerations of the psychological processes in pregnancy. Psychoanal. Stud. Child. **14:** 113–121.

BIBRING, G. L., T. F. DWYER, D. S. HUNTINGTON & A. F. VALENSTINE. 1961. A study of the psychosocial processes in pregnancy and of the earliest mother-child relationship. Psycholanal. Stud. Child **16:** 9–72.

*BONAPARTE, M. 1965. Female Sexuality. Grove Press. New York, N.Y.

BOYNTON, P. L. & R. D. WOOLWINE. 1942. The relationship between the economic status of high school girls and their vocational wishes and expectations. J. Appl. Psychol. **26:** 399–415.

*BRENTON, M. 1967. The American Male: A Penetrating Look at the Masculinity Crisis. Coward-McCann. New York, N.Y.

BROWN, N. O. 1959. Life Against Death. Random House. New York, N.Y.

*CHADWICK, M. 1932. The Psychological Effects of Menstruation. Nervous and Mental Disease Publ. Co. New York, N.Y.

CHAPMAN, J. D. 1968. The Feminine Mind and Body. Citadel Press. New York, N.Y.

COHN, D. L. 1943. Love in America, An Informal Study of Manners and Morals in American Marriage. Simon & Schuster. New York, N.Y.

*DE MARTINO, M. F., Ed. 1966. Sexual Behavior and Personality Characteristics. Grove Press. New York, N.Y.

DEPREE, S. 1962. The influence of parental achievement expectations and role definitions on achievement motive development in girls. Unpublished honors thesis. University of Michigan. Ann Arbor, Mich.

*DEUTSCHE, H. 1945. The Psychology of Women, A Psychoanalytic Interpretation. (2 vol.) Grune & Stratton. New York, N.Y.

*DEXTER, L. A. 1964. The Tyranny of Schooling. Basic Books. New York, N.Y.

DHULEY, N. B. 1965. Masculine complex in adolescent girls. Psychol. Stud. **10**(1): 51–53.

ELLIS, A. 1955. The Folklore of Sex. New York, N.Y.

*ELLIS, A. 1962. The American Sexual Tragedy.

*ELLIS, H. Man and Woman.

ERIKSON, E. 1950. Childhood and Society. W. W. Norton. New York, N.Y.

ERIKSON, E. 1959. Identity and the life cycle, selected papers. Psychol. Issues **1**(1).

ERIKSON, E. 1964. Insight and Responsibility. W. W. Norton. New York, N.Y.

ERIKSON, E. 1968. Identity Youth and Crisis. W. W. Norton. New York, N.Y.

ERIKSON, E. H. 1964. Inner and outer space: Reflections on womanhood. Daedalus. Spring : 582–606.

*FLUGEL, J. C. 1934. Men and Their Motives. London, England.

FORD, C. S. & F. A. BEACH. 1951. Patterns of Sexual Behavior. Harper Bros. New York, N.Y.

FRENCH, E. G. & G. S. LESSER. 1964. Some characteristics of achievement motives in women. J. Abnorm. Soc. Psychol. **68:** 119–128.

FREUD, S. 1962. Three Contributions to the Theory of Sex. Translated by J. Strachey. W. W. Norton. New York, N.Y.

FREUD, S. 1965. Feminity, lecture XXXIII. *In* New Introductory Lectures on Psychoanalysis. W. W. Norton. New York, N.Y.

FROMM, E. Sex and character: The Kinsey report viewed from the standpoint of psychoanalysis. *In* Sexual Behavior in American Society.

*GAGNON, J. H. 1965. Sexuality and sexual learning in the child. Psychiatry **8:** 212–228.

GHEI, S. N. 1966. Needs of Indian and American college females. J. Soc. Psychol. **69:** 3–12.

*GOLDBERG, P. 1968. Are women prejudiced against women? Trans-action. April.

GOODE, W. J. 1960. Norm commitment and conformity to role-status obligations. Amer. J. Sociol. **66:** 246–248.

*GORDON, R. E. & K. K. GORDON. 1960. The Split Level Trap.

*GRAY, M. 1967. The Normal Woman. Scribner's. New York, N.Y.

*HALL, M. H. 1969. A conversation with Masters and Johnson. Psychol. Today **3**(2): 50–58.

*HART, H. & E. HART. 1935. Personalities and the Family. New York, N.Y.

HARTLEY, R. E. 1960. Children's concepts of male and female roles. Merrill-Palmer Quart. **6:** 83–91.

HARTLEY, R. E. 1964. A developmental view of female sex-role definition and identification. Merrill-Palmer Quart. **10:** 3–16.

HEIST, P. 1962. The motivation of college women today: A closer look. J. Amer. Ass. Univ. Women **55.**

HELSON, R. M. 1961. Creativity, sex, and mathematics. Proc. Conf. Creative Person, Oct. 13–17. Institute for Personality Assessment and Research and University Extension. University of California, Liberal Arts Department. Berkeley, Calif.

*HILLIARD, M. 1960. Women and Fatigue. Doubleday & Co. New York, N.Y.

*HIMELHOCH, J. & S. F. FAVA, Eds. 1955. Sexual Behavior in American Society. W. W. Norton. New York, N.Y.

HORNER, M. 1969. Fail: Bright women. Psychol. Today. Nov.

HORNER, M. S. 1968. Sex differences in achievement motive and performance in competitive and non-competitive situations. Unpublished doctoral dissertation. The University of Michigan. Ann Arbor, Mich.

*HORNEY, K. Female Psychology. W. W. Norton. New York, N.Y.

*HORNEY, K. Feminine psychology. *In* New Ways in Psychoanalysis. W. W. Norton. New York, N.Y.

JAHODA, M. & J. HAVEL. 1955. Psychological problems of women in different social roles—A case history of problem formulation in research. Educ. Rec. **36:** 325–333.

KAGIN, J. 1964. The acquisition and significance of sex-typing. *In* Rev. Child Develop. Res. M. Hoffman, Ed. Russell Sage. New York, N.Y.

KALISH, R. A., M. MALONEY & A. ARKOFF. 1966. Cross-cultural comparisons of college student marital-role preferences. J. Soc. Psychol. **68:** 41–47.

KESTENBERG, J. 1956. On the development of maternal feelings in early childhood. Psychoanal. Stud. Child. **11.**

KESTENBERG, J. 1956. Vicissitudes of female sexuality. J. Amer. Psychoanal. Ass. **4:** 453–476.

*KINSEY, A. C. 1953. Sexual Behavior in the Human Female. W. B. Saunders Co. Philadelphia, Pa.

*KLEIN, V. 1946. The Feminine Character, History of an Ideology. Kegan Paul. London, England.

KOMAROVSKY, M. 1946. Cultural contradictions and sex roles. Amer. J. Sociol. **52:** 184–189.

KOMAROVSKY, M. 1950. Functional analysis of sex roles. Sociol. Rev. August.

*KRONHAUSEN, D. & E. KRONHAUSEN. The Sexually Responsive Female.

KRICH, A., Ed. 1965. The Sexual Revolution, Pioneer Writings on Sex. (2 vol.) Dell Publ. Co. New York, N.Y.

*KURTZ, R. M. 1968. Body image—Male and female. Trans-action. Dec. : 25–27.
*LAING, R. D. 1960. The Divided Self: An Existential Study in Sanity and Madness. Tavistock-Barnes and Noble. New York, N.Y.
*LEGMAN, G. 1968. The Rationale of the Dirty Joke: An Analysis of Sexual Humor. Grove Press. New York, N.Y.
LIPINSKY, B. G. 1965. Sex-role conflict and achievement motivation in college women. Dissertation. University of Cincinnati. Cincinnati, Ohio.
LUNDBERG, F. & M. FARNHAM. 1947. Modern Women: The Lost Sex. Grossett & Dunlap. New York, N.Y.
*MACCOBY, E., Ed. 1966. The Development of Sex Differences. Stanford, Calif.
MALINOWSKI, B. 1927. Sex and Repression in Savage Society. The Humanities Press. New York, N.Y.
MASLOW, A. H. 1939. Dominance, personality and social behavior in women. J. Soc. Psychol. **10:** 3–39.
*MASLOW, A. H. 1942. Self-esteem (dominance feeling) and sexuality in women. J. Soc. Psychol. **16:** 259–294.
*MASLOW, A. H. 1954. Motivation and Personality. Harper & Row. New York, N.Y.
*MASLOW, A. H. 1956. Self-actualizing people: A study of psychological health. *In* Self: Explorations in Personal Growth. C. E. Moustakas, Ed. Harper & Row. New York, N.Y.
*MASTERS, W. H. & V. E. JOHNSON. 1966. Human Sexual Response. Little, Brown & Co. Boston, Mass.
MATHEWS, E. & D. V. TIEDEMAN. 1964. Attitudes toward career and marriage and the development of life style in young women. J. Counsel. Psychol. **11**(4): 375–384.
MCKEE, J. P. & A. C. SHERRIFFS. 1959. Men's and women's belief, ideals and self-concepts. Amer. J. Sociol. **64:** 356–363.
MEAD, M. 1947. Age patterning in personality development. Amer. J. Orthopsychiatry **17**(2): 231–240.
*MEAD, M. 1949. Male and Female. William Morrow & Co. New York, N.Y.
MEAD, M. 1951. Cultural contexts of aging. *In* No Time To Grow Old. New York State Joint Legislative Committee on Problems of the Aging. Legislative Document No. 12: 49–51.
MEAD, M. 1967. The life cycle and its variation: The division of roles. Daedalus. Summer.
*MEYERS, T. 1966. The clitorid woman. Psychiat. Quart. **40**(2): 248–257.
MILNER, E. 1949. Effects of sex roles and social status on the early adolescent personality. Genet. Psychol. Monogr. **40:** 235–325.
*MONEY, J., Ed. 1965. Sex Research. New Developments. Rinehart & Winston. New York, N.Y.
*NEISSER, E. 1967. Mothers and Daughters. Harper & Row. New York, N.Y.
POLLAK, O. & A. S. FRIEDMAN, Eds. Family Dynamics and Female Sexual Delinquency. Science and Behavior Books, Inc. Palo Alto, Calif.
*RAINWATER, L., R. P. COLEMAN & G. HANDEL. 1959. Workingman's Wife: Her Personality, World and Life Style. Oceana Publ. New York, N.Y.
*REICH, W. 1942. The Function of the Orgasm. Orgone Institute Press. New York, N.Y.
REICH, W. 1945. The Sexual Revolution. Toward a Self-Governing Character Structure. Translated by T. P. Wolfe. Farrar, Straus & Giroux. New York, N.Y.
*REICH, W. 1961. Listen Little Man! Noonday Press. New York, N.Y.
REIK, T. 1949. Of Love and Lust. Farrar, Straus & Cudahy. New York, N.Y.
REIK, T. 1960. The Creation of Women. George Braziller. New York, N.Y.
*RHEINGOLD, J. C. 1964. The Fear of Being a Woman: A Theory of Maternal Destructiveness. Grune & Stratton. New York, N.Y.
*ROBINSON, M. 1959. The Power of Sexual Surrender. Doubleday & Co. New York, N.Y.

RODGERS, D. A., F. J. ZIEGLER, J. ALTROCCHI & N. LEVY. 1965. A longitudinal study of the psycho-social effects of vasectomy. J. Marr. Fam. **27:** 59–64.

ROHEIM, G. 1932. Psychoanalysis of primitive cultural types. Int. J. Psychoanal. **18.**

ROSE, A. M. 1951. The adequacy of women's expectations for adult roles. Soc. Forces **30**(1): 69–77.

*ROSENFELS, P. 1966. Love and Power: The Psychology of Interpersonal Creativity. Libra.

*RUITENBEEK, H. M. 1962. The Male Myth. Dell Publ. Co. New York, N.Y.

*SALZMAN, L. 1967. Psychology of the female: A new look. Arch. Gen. Psychiat. **17:** 195–203.

*SAMPSON, R. V. 1965. The Psychology of Power. Pantheon Press. New York, N.Y.

*SANFORD, N., Ed. 1962. The American College. John Wiley & Sons, Inc. New York, N.Y.

*SANFORD, N. 1967. Self and Society: Social Change and Individual Development. Atherton Press. New York, N.Y.

SARLIN, C. N. 1963. Feminine identity. J. Amer. Psychoanal. Ass. **9:** 790–816.

*SCHEINFELD, A. 1944. Women and Men. Harcourt, Brace. New York, N.Y.

*SEWARD, G. H. 1946. Sex and the Social Order. McGraw-Hill Book Co. New York, N.Y.

SHERFEY, M. J. 1966. The evolution and nature of female sexuality in relation to psychoanalytic theory. J. Amer. Psychoanal. Ass. **14**(1).

SHERMAN, J. A. 1967. Problem of sex differences in space perception and aspects of intellectual functioning. Psychol. Rev. **74**(4): 290–299.

*SKARD, A. G. 1967. Maternal deprivation: the research and its implications. J. Marr. Fam. **27**(3).

SMITH, M. A. 1961. Compliance and defiance as it relates to role conflict in women. Diss. Abstr. **22**(2): 646.

*SOUBIRAN, A. 1968. Open Letter to a Woman of Today. James H. Heineman, Inc. New York, N.Y.

*STERN, K. 1965. The Flight from Woman. Noonday Press. New York, N.Y.

*STOLLER, R. J. 1968. Sex and Gender: On the Development of Masculinity and Femininity. Science House. New York, N.Y.

*STRECKER, E. 1946. Their Mother's Sons. Philadelphia, Pa.

SYSIHARJU, A. 1960. Equality, Home and Work: A Socio-Psychological Study on Finnish Student Women's Attitudes Toward the Woman's Role in Society. Mikkelissa. Helsinki, Finland.

TANGRI, S. S. 1969. Role-innovation in occupational choice. Doctoral dissertation. University of Michigan. Ann Arbor, Mich.

*TARBELL, I. The Ways of Woman. MacMillan & Co. New York, N.Y.

*TERMAN, L. & C. C. MILES. 1936. Sex and Personality: Studies in Masculinity and Femininity. McGraw-Hill Book Co. New York, N.Y.

THOMAS, W. I. 1967. The Unadjusted Girl (1923). Harper & Row. New York, N.Y.

*THOMPSON, H. B. 1903. The Mental Traits of Sex. University of Chicago Press. Chicago, Ill.

TORRANCE, E. P. 1960. Changing reactions of preadolescent girls to tasks requiring creative scientific thinking during a thirteen month period. *In* New Educational Ideas. Proc. Third Minnesota Conf. Gifted Children.

TURNER, R. H. 1964. Some aspects of women's ambition. Amer. J. Sociol. **70**(3): 271–285.

*UESUGI, T. C. & W. E. VINACKE. 1963. Strategy in a feminine game. Sociometry **26:** 75–88.

VAERTUNG, M. & M. VAERTUNG. 1932. The Dominant Sex. A Study in the Sociology of Sex Differentiation. Allen & Unwin. London, England.

VANDEN BERG, J. H. 1961. The Changing Nature of Man. W. W. Norton. New York, N.Y.

VEROFF, J., S. WILCOX & J. W. ATKINSON. 1953. The achievement motive in high school and college age women. J. Abnorm. Soc. Psychol. **48:** 108–119.

WALLIN, P. 1950. Cultural contradictions and sex roles: A repeat study. Amer. Sociol. Rev. **15:** 288–293.

*WATTS, A. Nature, Man and Woman.

*WEININGER, O. 1966. Sex and Character. James H. Heineman, Inc. London, England.

WEISSTEIN, N. 1969. Woman as nigger. Psychol. Today. Oct.

ZISSUS, C. 1964. A study of the life planning of 550 freshman women at Purdue University. J. Nat. Ass. Wom. Deans Couns. **27**(4)**4:** 153–159.

REFERENCES INDIRECTLY RELATED TO THE ISSUES OF THE WORKSHOP

Female Physiology and Sexuality

*BALINT, A. 1937. Psychology of menstruation. Psychoanal. Quart. May.

BENEDEK, T. 1960. The organization of the reproductive drive. Int. J. Psychoanal. **41:** 1–15.

*BERGLER, E. & W. S. KROGER. 1954. Kinsey's Myth of Female Sexuality: The Medical Facts. Grune & Stratton. New York, N.Y.

*BLOCH, I. 1908. The Sexual Life of Our Time in Its Relation to Modern Civilization. London, England.

*BRECHER, R. & E. BRECHER. 1966. An Analysis of Human Sexual Response. New American Library. New York, N.Y.

*BULLOUGH, V. L. 1964. The History of Prostitution.

CALVERTON, V. F. & S. D. SCHMALHAUSEN. 1929. Sex in Civilization. MacCauley. New York, N.Y.

*CHADWICK, M. 1932. The Psychological Effects of Menstruation. Nervous and Mental Disease Pub. Co. New York, N.Y.

*COHN, D. L. 1943. Love in America, An Informal Study of Manners and Morals in American Marriage. Simon & Schuster. New York, N.Y.

*COWAN, J. 1869. The Science of a New Life. New York, N.Y.

*DITZION, S. 1953. Marriage, Morals and Sex in America—A History of Ideas. New York, N.Y.

ELLIS, A. 1955. The Folklore of Sex. New York, N.Y.

*ETZIONI, A. 1968. Sex control, science and society. Science. Sept. **13:** 1107–1112.

FORD, C. S. & F. A. BEACH. 1951. Patterns of Sexual Behavior. Harper Bros. New York, N.Y.

*GAGNON, J. H. 1965. Sexuality and sexual learning in the child. Psychiatry **8:** 212–228.

*GRAY, M. 1967. The Normal Woman. Scribner's. New York, N.Y.

*GREENWALD, H. The Call Girl.

*HALL, M. H. 1969. A conversation with Masters and Johnson. Psychol. Today **3**(2)**:** 50–58.

*HEGELER, I. & S. HEGELER. 1963. An ABZ of Love. Translated by D. Hobner. Medical Press of New York. New York, N.Y.

*HENRIQUES, F. 1960. Love in Action: The Sociology of Sex. E. P. Dutton & Co. New York, N.Y.

*HENRIQUES, F. 1961. Stew and Strumpets: A Survey of Prostitution. MacGibbon & Kee. London, England.

*HENRIQUES, F. 1962. Prostitution in Europe and the Americas.

*HIRSCH, A. H. 1963. The Love Elite. (The Story of Woman's Emancipation and Her Drive for Sexual Fulfillment). Julian Press. New York, N.Y.

*HUNT, M. 1962. Her Infinite Variety: The American Woman as Lover, Rival, and Mate.

*KINSEY, A. C. 1963. Sexual Behavior in the Human Female. W. B. Saunders Co. Philadelphia, Pa.

*KRONHAUSEN, P. & E. KRONHAUSEN. The Sexually Responsive Female.

MALINOWSKI, B. 1927. Sex and Repression in Savage Society. The Humanities Press, New York, N.Y.
MALINOWSKI, B. 1962. Sex, Culture and Myth. Harcourt, Brace & World, New York, N.Y.
*MARCUSE, H. 1955. Eros and Civilization. Beacon Press. New York, N.Y.
*MASTERS, W. H. & V. E. JOHNSON. 1966. Human Sexual Response. Little, Brown & Co. Boston, Mass.
MASTERS, W. H. & V. E. JOHNSON. 1970. Human Sexual Inadequacy. Little, Brown & Co. Boston, Mass.
*MEAD, M. 1935. Sex and Temperament in Three Primitive Societies. William Morrow & Co. New York, N.Y.
*MEAD, M. 1949. Male and Female. William Morrow & Co. New York, N.Y.
MEAD, M. 1961. Cultural determinants of sexual behavior. *In* Sex and Internal Secretions. W. C. Young, Ed. 3rd edit. **2:** 1433–1479. The Williams & Wilkins Co. Baltimore, Md.
*MONTAGUE, A. The Natural Superiority of Women.
*MONEY, J., Ed. 1965. Sex Research. New Developments. Rinehart & Winston. New York, N.Y.
*REICH, W. 1965. The Sexual Revolution. Farrar, Straus & Girony. New York, N.Y.
RODGERS, D. A., F. J. ZIEGLER, J. ALTROCCHI & N. LEVY. 1965. A longitudinal study of the psycho-social effects of vasectomy. J. Marr. Fam. **27:** 59–64.
*SCHEINFELD, A. 1944. Women and Men. Harcourt, Brace. New York, N.Y.
*STOLLER, R. J. 1968. Sex and Gender: On the Development of Masculinity and Femininity. Science House. New York, N.Y.
*TARBELL, I. The Ways of Woman. MacMillan & Co. New York, N.Y.
*TAYLOR, G. R. 1953. Sex in History. Thames & Hudson. London, England.
THIESSEN, D. D. & D. A. RODGERS. 1961. Population density and endocrine function. Psychol. Bull. **58:** 441–451.
TIETZE, C. 1962. Surgical Sterilization of Men and Women: A Selected Bibliography. National Committee on Maternal Health. New York, N.Y.
*WATTS, A. Nature, Man, and Woman.
*WEININGER, O. 1966. Sex and Character. James H. Heineman, Inc. London, England.
*WULFFEN, E. 1935. Woman as a Sexual Criminal. Falstaff Press. New York, N.Y.
*YOUNG, W. Eros Denied: Sex in Western Society. Grove Press. New York, N.Y.

Related Social Commentary

*BELL, D., Ed. 1968. Toward the Year 2,000: Work in Progress. Houghton-Mifflin. Boston, Mass.
*BELLAMY, E. Looking Backward.
*DE RHAM, E. 1969. How Could She Do That? Clarkson Potter. New York, N.Y.
FISHMAN, K. D. 1966. Children at stake. N.Y. Times Mag. Dec. 11.
*HAWES, E. 1939. Men Can Take It. Random House. New York, N.Y.
*HAWES, E. 1943. Why Women Cry, or, Wenches with Wrenches. Reynal & Hitchcock. New York, N.Y.
*LYNES, R. 1963. The Domesticated Americans. Harper & Row. New York, N.Y.
*MANNES, M. More in Anger.
*MARCUSE, H. 1964. One-Dimensional Man. Beacon Press. New York, N.Y.
*MAY, E. 1964. The Wasted Americans. New York, N.Y.
*MCLUHAN, H. M. 1951. The Mechanical Bride.
*MCLUHAN, H. M. 1964. Understanding Media.
MEAD, M. 1962. Introduction. *In* American Women: The Changing Image. B. B. CASSARA, Ed. : ix–xv. Beacon Press. Boston, Mass.
MEAD, M. & F. B. KAPLAN, Eds. 1965. Epilogue. *In* American Women. : 181–204. Scribner & Sons. New York, N.Y.

MEAD, M. 1969. The American Woman today. *In* The 1969 World Book Year Book. : 78–95. Field Enterprises Educational Corporation. Chicago, Ill.
MEZERIK, A. C. 1945. Getting rid of the women. Atlantic Monthly. June.
*MONTAGUE, A. The Natural Superiority of Women.
*SMITH, L. Killers of the Dream.
STERN, E. M. 1949. Women are household slaves. Amer. Mercury. Jan.
THURBER, J. & E. B. WHITE. 1964. Is Sex Necessary? Dell Publ. Co. New York, N.Y.
*WINICK, C. 1968. The New People.
*WYLIE, P. Generation of Vipers.

General Works: Historical, Philosophical, Religious, Anthropological, and Sociological

*ADAMS, M. 1967. The Right to be People. J. B. Lippincott Co. Philadelphia, Pa.
*ANTHONY, S. B., E. C. STANTON & I. H. HARPER. History of Women's Suffrage.
BACHOFEN, J. J. 1967. Myth, Religion and Mother Right. Bollinger Series. Princeton, N.J.
*BARDECHE, M. 1969. History of Women.
*BEARD, M. 1931. On Understanding Women. Longmans, Green & Co. London, England.
*BEARD, M. 1946. Women as Force in History.
*BELFORT BAX, E. 1913. The Fraud of Feminism. Grant Richards. London, England.
*"MARGARET BENNETT" (pseud.). The Feminine Mistake, or, Alice in Womanland.
*BETTELHEIM, B. 1962. Symbolic Wounds: Puberty Rites and the Envious Male. P. F. Collier, Inc. New York, N.Y.
*BRITTAIN, V. 1953. Lady into Women: A History of Women from Victoria to Elizabeth II. MacMillan & Co. New York, N. Y.
*BROWN, M. M. 1962. The Secret Life of Jeanne D'Arc. Vantage Press. New York, N.Y.
*CALLAHAN, S. 1965. The Illusion of Eve. Sheed & Ward. New York, N.Y.
*CARROL, M. Prolegomena to the Study of Greek Religions.
*CASH, W. J. 1941. The Mind of the South. New York, N.Y.
CHERNYSHEVDKY, N. G. 1863. What is to be Done? Russia.
*COX, H. 1965. The Secular City. MacMillan & Co. New York, N.Y.
CRAWLEY, E. 1927. The Mystic Rose. Methuen. London, England.
*DALY, M. 1968. The Church and the Second Sex. Harper & Row. New York, N.Y.
*DANGERFIELD, G. 1961. The Strange Death of Liberal England, 1910–1914. Capricorn Books. New York, N.Y.
*DEGLER, C. N. 1958. Out of Our Past.
*DE ROUGEMONT, D. 1956. Love in the Western World. Pantheon Press. New York, N.Y.
*DINER, H. 1965. Mothers and Amazons: The First Feminine History of Culture. Julian Press. New York, N.Y.
*DOLLARD, J. 1937. The sexual gain. *In* Caste and Class in a Southern Town.
*DRINKER, S. Music and Women.
*DUNN, N. 1965. Talking to Women.
*DURKHEIM, E. Suicide.
*EATON, C. Freedom of Thought in the South.
*FAWCETT, M. G. 1912. Women's Suffrage. The People's Books. London, England.
*FLEXNER, E. 1966. Century of Struggle: The Woman's Rights Movement in the United States. Belknap Press, Harvard University. Cambridge, Mass.
FULFORD. 1957. Votes for Women. Farber & Farber. London, England.
FURNESS, C. F. 1931. The Genteel Female, An Anthology. Alfred A. Knopf. New York, N.Y.
GANS, H. 1962. The Urban Villagers. The Free Press. New York, N.Y.

GANS, H. 1967. The Levittowners.
GAVRON, H. 1966. The Captive Wife. Routledge & Kegan Paul. London, England.
*GILMAN, C. P. 1898. Women and Economics. Charlton Co., New York, N.Y.
*GILMAN, C. P. 1914. The Man-Made World: Our Androcentric Culture. Charlton Co. New York, N.Y.
GOLDBERG, D. 1963. The Creative Woman. David McKay Co. New York, N.Y.
*GOODMAN, P. & P. GOODMAN. 1944. Communitas.
*GOODWIN, M., Ed. 1951. Nineteenth Century Opinion. Pelican Books. New York, N.Y.
GRAHAM, A. 1934. Ladies in Revolt. The Woman's Press. New York, N.Y.
GRIMES, A. P. 1967. The Puritan Ethic and Woman Suffrage. Oxford University Press. New York, N.Y.
*GRIMKÉ, A. Appeal to the Christian Women of the South
*GRIMKÉ, S. Letters on Equality of the Sexes.
*HACKER, H. 1951. Women as a minority group. Soc. Forces **30:** 60–69.
*HAGOOD, M. 1939. Mothers of the South. University of North Carolina Press. Chapel Hill, N.C.
*HALL, E. T. 1963. The Silent Language. Premier Books. New York, N.Y.
*HARDING, E. 1955. Woman's Mysteries. Pantheon Press. New York, N.Y.
*HAWES, E. 1948. Anything but Love. Rinehart Publ. Co. New York, N.Y.
*HAYS, H. R. 1964. The Dangerous Sex, The Myth of Feminine Evil. G. P. Putnam. New York, N.Y.
*HENRY, J. Culture Against Man.
*HERNTON, C. C. 1965. Sex and Racism in America. Grove Press. New York, N.Y.
*HIMMELFARB, G. 1968. Victorian Minds. Weidenfeld-Nicholson. London, England.
*HINDS, W. A. 1961. American Communities. Corinth. Books. New York, N.Y.
*HINTON, W. 1966. Fan-Shen. Random House. New York, N.Y.
*IRWIN, I. H. 1934. Angels and Amazons: 100 Years of American Women.
*IRWIN, I. H. 1934. The Story of the Woman's Party. New York, N.Y.
*JACOBS, J. 1961. The Death and Life of Great American Cities. New York, N.Y.
*KENNEDY, R. W. 1953. The House and the Art of Its Design. Reinhold Publ. Co. New York, N.Y.
*KIRA, A. 1966. The Bathroom: Criteria for Design. Cornell University Press. Ithaca, N.Y.
*KLEIN, V. 1946. The Feminine Character, History of an Ideology. Kegan Paul. London, England.
*KRADITOR, A. 1965. The Ideas of the Woman Suffrage Movement, 1890–1920. Columbia University Press. New York, N.Y.
*KRADITOR, A. 1968. Up From the Pedestal, Landmark Writings in the American Woman's Struggle for Equality. Quadrangle Books. Chicago, Ill.
*LAMB, F. & H. PICKTHORN. 1968. Locked-Up Daughters. Hodder-Stoughton. London, England.
*LASCH, C. The New Radicalism in America, 1889–1963.
*LEONARD, E. A. 1965. The Dear-Bought Heritage. University of Pennsylvania Press. Philadelphia, Pa.
LEONARD, E. A., S. H. DRINKER & M. Y. HOLDEN. 1962. The American Woman in Colonial and Revolutionary Times, 1565–1800. University of Pennsylvania Press. Philadelphia, Pa.
LERNER, G. 1966. Changes in the status of women: 1800–1840. Paper, read at the American Historical Association Meeting, Dec.
LEWIS, F. 1967. The femininity thing. N.Y. Post. April 17.
*LUDOVICI, L. J. 1965. The Final Inequality. W. W. Norton. New York, N.Y.
*LUTZ, A. 1968. Crusade for Freedom: Women in the Antislavery Movement. Beacon Press. New York, N.Y.
*MARCUS, S. 1966. The Other Victorians: A Study of Sexuality and Pornography in Mid-Nineteenth Century England. Basic Books. New York, N.Y.

*MARTINEAU, H. 1837. Society in America. (2 vols.) Saunders & Otley. New York, N.Y.

MCGREGOR, O. 1955. The social position of women in England 1850–1914: A bibliography. Brit. J. Sociol. March.

MCLENNON, J. 1885. The Patriarchal Theory. MacMillan & Co. London, England.

MEAD, M. 1940. The arts in Bali. Yale Rev. **30**(2): 335–347.

*MEAD, M. 1943. And Keep Your Powder Dry. William Morrow & Co. New York, N.Y.

MEAD, M. 1966. The case for drafting all boys—and girls. Redbook. Sept.

*MENCKEN, H. L. 1922. In Defense of Women. Alfred A. Knopf. New York, N.Y.

*MERRIAM, E. After Nora Slammed the Door.

MILL, J. S. 1966. The Subjection of Women (1869). Oxford University Press. London, England.

*MYRDAL, G. 1944. An American Dilemma. (2 vols.) Harper Bros. New York, N.Y.

*NEVINSON, M. 1911. Ancient Suffragettes.

*O'MEARA, W. 1968. Daughters of the Country: The Women of the Furtraders and Mountain Men. Harcourt, Brace & World. New York, N.Y.

*O'NEILL, W. L. 1968. Feminism as a radical ideology. *In* Dissent: Explorations in the History of American Radicalism. A. E. Young, Ed. : 273–300. Northern Illinois University Press. De Kalb, Ill.

O'NEILL, W. L. 1969. Everyone was Brave, the Rise and Fall of Feminism in America. Quadrangle Books. Chicago, Ill.

*PACKARD, V. The Hidden Persuaders.

*PACKARD, V. 1968. The Sexual Wilderness: The Contemporary Upheaval in Male-Female Relationships. David McKay Co. New York, N.Y.

PANKHURST, E. 1914. My Own Story. Everleigh Nash. London, England.

*PANKHURST, S. 1931. The Suffragette Movement. Longmans, Green & Co. New York, N.Y.

PARSONS, T. 1954. Age and sex in the social structure of the United States. *In* Essays in Sociological Theory. The Free Press. Glencoe, Ill.

PUTNAM, E. J. 1970. The Lady: Studies of Certain Significant Phases of Her History (1910). The University of Chicago Press. Chicago, Ill.

*RAINWATER, L. & W. L. YANCEY. 1967. The Moynihan Report and the Politics of Controversy. Massachusetts Institute of Technology Press. Cambridge, Mass.

*RAMELSON, M. The Petticoat Rebellion.

*REID, M. 1848. Woman, Her Education and Influence. New York, N.Y.

REYNOLDS, M. 1920. The Learned Lady in England, 1650–1760. Houghton-Mifflin. Boston, Mass.

ROESCH, R. 1967. Women in Action—Their Questions and Their Answers. John Day Co. New York, N.Y.

*ROGERS, K. M. 1966. The Troublesome Helpmate. A History of Misogyny in Literature. University of Washington Press. Seattle, Wash.

RUBIN, T. I. 1961. In the Life. MacMillan & Co. New York, N.Y.

RUSKIN, J. 1902. Of queens gardens. *In* Sesame and Lilies. Homewood. Chicago, Ill.

*RUSSELL, D. 1925. Hypatia, or, Woman and Knowledge. E. P. Dutton & Co. New York, N.Y.

SCOTT, A. F. 1964. After suffrage: Southern women in the 1920's. J. Soc. Hist. **30**: 298–318.

*SILLEN, S. 1955. Women Against Slavery. Masses & Mainstream. New York, N.Y.

*SINCLAIR, A. 1965. The Emancipation of the American Woman. Harper & Row. New York, N.Y.

*SPRAGUE, W. 1940. Women and the West. Boston, Mass.

*STAMPP, K. The Peculiar Institution.

*STEVENS, D. Jailed for Freedom.

STRACHEY, R. 1928. The Cause: A Short History of the Woman's Movement in Great Britain. G. Bell & Sons. London, England.
*TAVES, I. 1968. Women Alone. Funk & Wagnalls. New York, N.Y.
TEMPERLEY, H. W. V. 1925. The sale of wives in England in 1823. The History Teacher's Miscellany **3:** 66.
*THEOBALD, R. *et al.* 1967. Dialogue on Women. Bobbs-Merrill. Indianapolis, Ind.
THOMAS, C. 1943. Women in Nazi Germany. Gollancz. London, England.
THOMAS, E. 1966. The Women Incendiaries. George Braziller. New York, N.Y.
*THOMAS, W. I. 1907. Sex and Society. Richard G. Badger. Boston, Mass.
*THOMPSON, W. 1825. Appeal of One Half of the Human Race, Women, Against the Pretensions of the Other Half, Men. London, England.
TIGER, L. 1969. Men in Groups. Random House. New York, N.Y.
*TURNER, E. S. 1955. A History of Courting. E. P. Dutton & Co. New York, N.Y.
*WAKEFIELD, D. 1968. Supernation at Peace and War. (Atlantic) Little, Brown & Co.
WALSH, C. M. 1917. Feminism. Sturgis & Watton. New York, N.Y.
*WIETH-KNUDSEN, K. A. 1928. Feminism, a Sociological Study of the Woman Question from Ancient Times to Present Day. Constable. London, England.
*WOLLSTONECRAFT, M. 1792. A Vindication of the Rights of Women.
*WOODWARD, H. 1960. The Lady Persuaders. New York, N.Y.
*WOODY, T. H. 1929. A History of Women's Education in the United States. (2 vol.)
*WOOLF, V. 1929. A Room of One's Own. Harcourt, Brace & World. New York, N.Y.
*WOOLF, V. 1938. Three Guineas. Harcourt, Brace & World. New York, N.Y.

Printed in the United States of America